Bereavement Care for Families

D1553692

Grief is a family affair. When a loved one dies, the distress reverberates throughout the immediate family, and even into the extended family. Family therapy has long attended to issues of loss and grief, yet not as the dominant therapeutic paradigm. *Bereavement Care for Families* changes that: it is a practical resource for the clinician interested in better understanding the universal issue of bereavement. This book draws upon the evidence supporting family approaches to bereavement care and also provides clinically oriented, strategic guidance on how to incorporate family approaches into other models. Chapters set forth a detailed, research-based, therapeutic model that clinicians can use to facilitate therapy, engage the ambivalent, deal with uncertainty, manage family conflict, develop realistic goals, and more. Any clinician sensitive to the roles family members play in bereavement care need look no further than this groundbreaking text.

David W. Kissane, MD, is an academic psychiatrist, psycho-oncology researcher, author, professor, and head of psychiatry for Monash University, Melbourne, Australia. From 2003 to 2012 he was chairman of the Department of Psychiatry and Behavioral Sciences at Memorial Sloan-Kettering Cancer Center and is currently an adjunct professor of psychiatry at the Weill Medical College of Cornell University in New York. His books include *Family-Focused Grief Therapy*, *Handbook of Communication in Oncology and Palliative Care*, and *Handbook of Psychotherapy in Cancer Care*.

Francine Parnes, MA, MA, JD, is an award-winning journalist who has written extensively for *The New York Times*, The Associated Press, and other leading news organizations. Formerly a reporter and editor at *The Denver Post* for 10 years, she was a member of the staff that won a Pulitzer Prize for its coverage of the Columbine High School shootings. Previously, she was an attorney in New York and Los Angeles.

THE SERIES IN DEATH, DYING, AND BEREAVEMENT
ROBERT A. NEIMEYER, CONSULTING EDITOR

FORMERLY THE SERIES IN DEATH EDUCATION, AGING, AND HEALTH CARE
HANNELORE WASS, CONSULTING EDITOR

Brammer—*How to Cope with Life Transitions: The Challenge of Personal Change*

Cleiren—*Bereavement and Adaptation: A Comparative Study of the Aftermath of Death*

Corless & Pittman-Lindeman—*AIDS: Principles, Practices, and Politics, Abridged Edition*

Corless & Pittman-Lindeman—*AIDS: Principles, Practices, and Politics, Reference Edition*

Curran—*Adolescent Suicidal Behavior*

Davidson—*The Hospice: Development and Administration, Second Edition*

Davidson & Linnolla—*Risk Factors in Youth Suicide*

Degner & Beaton—*Life-Death Decisions in Health Care*

Doka—*AIDS, Fear, and Society: Challenging the Dreaded Disease*

Doty—*Communication and Assertion Skills for Older Persons*

Epting & Neimeyer—*Personal Meanings of Death: Applications for Personal Construct Theory to Clinical Practice*

Haber—*Health Care for an Aging Society: Cost-Conscious Community Care and Self-Care Approaches*

Hughes—*Bereavement and Support: Healing in a Group Environment*

Irish, Lundquist, & Nelsen—*Ethnic Variations in Dying, Death, and Grief: Diversity in Universality*

Klass, Silverman, & Nickman—*Continuing Bonds: New Understanding of Grief*

Lair—*Counseling the Terminally Ill: Sharing the Journey*

Leenaars, Maltsberger, & Neimeyer—*Treatment of Suicidal People*

Leenaars & Wenckstern—*Suicide Prevention in Schools*

Leng—*Psychological Care in Old Age*

Leviton—*Horrendous Death and Health: Toward Action*

Leviton—*Horrendous Death, Health, and Well-Being*

Lindeman, Corby, Downing, & Sanborn—*Alzheimer's Day Care: A Basic Guide*

Lund—*Older Bereaved Spouses: Research with Practical Applications*

Neimeyer—*Death Anxiety Handbook: Research, Instrumentation, and Application*

Papadatou & Papadatos—*Children and Death*

Prunkl & Berry—*Death Week: Exploring the Dying Process*

Ricker & Myers—*Retirement Counseling: A Practical Guide for Action*

Samarel—*Caring for Life and Death*

Sherron & Lumsden—*Introduction to Educational Gerontology, Third Edition*

Stillion—*Death and Sexes: An Examination of Differential Longevity Attitudes, Behaviors, and Coping Skills*

Stillion, McDowell, & May—*Suicide Across the Life Span: Premature Exits*

Vachon—*Occupational Stress in the Care of the Critically Ill, the Dying, and the Bereaved*

Wass & Corr—*Childhood and Death*

Wass & Corr—*Helping Children Cope with Death: Guidelines and Resource, Second Edition*

Wass, Corr, Pacholski, & Forfar—*Death Education II: An Annotated Resource Guide*

Wass & Neimeyer—*Dying: Facing the Facts, Third Edition*

Weenolsen—*Transcendence of Loss over the Life Span*

Werth—*Rational Suicide? Implications for Mental Health Professionals*

Bereavement Care for Families

Edited by
David W. Kissane and Francine Parnes

Routledge
Taylor & Francis Group

NEW YORK AND LONDON

First published 2014
by Routledge
711 Third Avenue, New York, NY 10017

and by Routledge
27 Church Road, Hove, East Sussex BN3 2FA

© 2014 Taylor & Francis

Routledge is an imprint of the Taylor & Francis Group, an informa business

The right of the editors to be identified as the author of the editorial material, and of the authors for their individual chapters, has been asserted in accordance with sections 77 and 78 of the Copyright, Designs and Patents Act 1988.

All rights reserved. No part of this book may be reprinted or reproduced or utilized in any form or by any electronic, mechanical, or other means, now known or hereafter invented, including photocopying and recording, or in any information storage or retrieval system, without permission in writing from the publishers.

Trademark Notice: Product or corporate names may be trademarks or registered trademarks, and are used only for identification and explanation without intent to infringe.

Library of Congress Cataloging-in-Publication Data

Bereavement care for families / Editors, David W. Kissane & Francine
 Parnes.— 1 Edition.
    pages cm. — (Series in death, dying, and bereavement)
  1. Bereavement. 2. Grief therapy. 3. Family psychotherapy. I. Kissane,
David W. (David William) editor of compilation.
  BF575.G7B457 2014
  155.9'37—dc23
  2013024088

ISBN: 978-0-415-63737-4 (hbk)
ISBN: 978-0-415-63738-1 (pbk)
ISBN: 978-0-203-08461-8 (ebk)

Typeset in Minion
by Apex CoVantage, LLC

MIX
Paper from
responsible sources
FSC
www.fsc.org   FSC® C014174

Printed and bound in the United States of America by Sheridan Books, Inc. (a Sheridan Group Company).

ACC LIBRARY SERVICES AUSTIN, TX

For Jimmie C. Holland, who has tirelessly nurtured the development of psycho-oncology as a discipline and given so much to us all

Contents

About the Editors

David W. Kissane, MD, MPM, FRANZCP, FAChPM, is an academic psychiatrist, psycho-oncology researcher, and author. He is Professor and Head of the Department of Psychiatry at Monash University in his hometown Melbourne, Australia. Until 2012 he was the Chairman of the Department of Psychiatry and Behavioral Sciences at Memorial Sloan-Kettering Cancer Center in New York. He is also an Adjunct Professor of Psychiatry at the Weill Cornell Medical College of Cornell University in New York. Previously, Dr. Kissane was the Foundation Chair of Palliative Medicine at the University of Melbourne.

Dr. Kissane's academic interests include group, couples, and family psychotherapy trials, communication skills training, studies of existential distress, and the ethics of end-of-life care. He is best known for his model of family therapy delivered to "at risk" families during palliative care and continued into bereavement, which seeks to prevent complicated grief and depression during mourning. His work on demoralization as a variation of depression in the medically ill has preceded interventions to promote meaning-based coping. For patients with early stage breast cancer, Dr. Kissane developed a cognitive-existential model of group therapy, which decreased fear of recurrence. For patients with advanced breast cancer, his trial of supportive-expressive group therapy showed the prevention of depression alongside improved quality of life. More recently, his psychotherapy research has explored the benefits of intimacy-enhancing couples therapy in prostate cancer.

At Memorial Sloan-Kettering, David Kissane established the *"Comskil"* Communication Skills Training and Research Laboratory, which developed an applied curriculum for oncology and trained more than 1,000 clinicians. His books include the *Handbook of Psychotherapy in Cancer Care* (2011), *Cancer and Depression* (2011), *Handbook of Communication in Oncology and Palliative Care* (2010), and *Family Focused Grief Therapy* (2002). He was awarded the Jimmie C. Holland Chair in Psycho-Oncology at Memorial Sloan-Kettering and was honored by the International Psycho-Oncology Society in 2008 with their Arthur Sutherland Award for lifetime achievement. Dr. Kissane lives with his wife, Nicola, in Melbourne, Australia, where they enjoy time spent with their four children.

Francine Parnes, MA, MA, JD, is an award-winning freelance journalist who has written feature articles on a wide variety of topics for news outlets including *The New York Times*, The Associated Press, and *The Denver Post*.

Ms. Parnes received her master's degrees in comparative literature and German at the University of Michigan–Ann Arbor, where she was a teaching fellow. Subsequently, she earned her law degree at Loyola Law School in Los Angeles, where she was an Articles Editor of the *Loyola Law Review*. She is admitted to practice law in California, New York, and Washington, D.C.

Ms. Parnes began her journalism career as the Fashion Editor at the now-defunct *Los Angeles Herald Examiner* and then contributed frequently to the *Los Angeles Times*. Subsequently, she reported on fashion and other features for more than 10 years for The Associated Press. During her 10 years at *The Denver Post*, she built a style section and was also a member of the staff that won a Pulitzer Prize for *The Denver Post's* coverage of the Columbine High School shootings. Thereafter, for *The New York Times*, her reporting covered a spectrum of subjects including religion, business travel, style, home design, and book reviews.

As a newspaper reporter, Ms. Parnes has had an abiding interest in serving the readership by covering useful topics concerning health and relationships. As a cancer survivor, she has served on an advisory board in psychiatry at Memorial Sloan-Kettering Cancer Center in New York. As a primary caregiver, she attends to her family in Westchester County, New York.

Contributors

Nicole Alston, MSW
Recruitment Coordinator & Community Liaison,
Complicated Grief Treatment Research Program,
Columbia University School of Social Work;
Bereavement Coordinator,
Pediatric Palliative & End-of-Life Care,
Circle of Life Children's Center,
Newark, NJ, USA.

Pauline Boss, PhD
Professor Emeritus,
Department of Family Social Science,
University of Minnesota,
St. Paul, MN, USA.

Bridgette Boucher, MS, LMSW
Family Therapist,
Department of Psychiatry & Behavioral Sciences,
Memorial Sloan-Kettering Cancer Center, New York;
Teacher of Learning Disorders,
Department of Education,
New York, NY, USA.

Carla M. Dahl, PhD, CFLE
Founding Partner,
The Mobius Group,
St. Paul, MN, USA.

Francesca Del Gaudio, MPsych
Research Coordinator,
Department of Psychiatry & Behavioral Sciences,
Memorial Sloan-Kettering Cancer Center, New York;
Doctoral Candidate,
Department of Psychiatry,

University of California San Francisco,
San Francisco, CA, USA.

Isabelle Dumont, PhD
Adjunct Professor,
Department of Oncology, McGill University;
Clinical Instructor and Supervisor,
Clinique de Médecine Familiale Notre-Dame,
Montréal, QC, Canada.

Sarah Gehlert, PhD
E. Desmond Lee Professor of Racial and Ethnic Diversity,
The George Warren Brown School of Social Work & Department of Surgery,
School of Medicine,
Washington University in St. Louis,
St. Louis, MO, USA.

Cynthia A. Gerhardt, PhD
Associate Professor of Pediatrics and Psychology,
College of Medicine,
The Ohio State University;
Center for Biobehavioral Health,
The Research Institute at Nationwide Children's Hospital,
Columbus, OH, USA.

Darcy Harris, PhD, FT
Associate Professor and Thanatology Coordinator,
Department of Interdisciplinary Programs,
King's University College at Western University,
London, ON, Canada.

J. Shep Jeffreys, EdD, FT
Assistant Professor of Psychiatry,
Department of Psychiatry & Behavioral Sciences,
The Johns Hopkins School of Medicine;
Affiliate Assistant Professor, Pastoral Counseling,
Loyola University Maryland;
Department of Psychiatry,
Howard County General Hospital,
Columbia, MD, USA.

Su Jin Kim, LCSW
Clinical Social Worker, Family Therapist & Research Affiliate,
Department of Psychiatry & Behavioral Sciences,
Memorial Sloan-Kettering Cancer Center,
New York, NY, USA.

David W. Kissane, MD, MPM, FRANZCP, FAChPM
Professor and Head—Discipline of Psychiatry,
Department of Psychiatry,
Faculty of Medicine, Nursing & Health Sciences,
Monash University;
Monash Medical Centre,
Clayton, Victoria, Australia;
Adjunct Professor of Psychiatry, Weill Medical College of Cornell University and
Memorial Sloan-Kettering Cancer Center,
New York, NY, USA.

Marguerite S. Lederberg, MD
Emeritus Attending Psychiatrist,
Department of Psychiatry & Behavioral Sciences,
Memorial Sloan-Kettering Cancer Center;
Professor Emerita of Clinical Psychiatry,
Weill Medical College of Cornell University;
Adjunct Associate Professor of Psychiatry at Mount Sinai School of Medicine,
New York, NY, USA.

Tomer T. Levin, MBBS, FAPM, ACT
Associate Attending Psychiatrist,
Department of Psychiatry & Behavioral Sciences,
Memorial Sloan-Kettering Cancer Center,
New York, NY, USA.

Wendy G. Lichtenthal, PhD
Assistant Attending Psychologist,
Department of Psychiatry & Behavioral Sciences,
Memorial Sloan-Kettering Cancer Center;
Assistant Professor of Psychology in Psychiatry,
Weill Medical College of Cornell University,
New York, NY, USA.

Teresa T. Moro, AM, LSW
Doctoral Candidate,
School of Social Service Administration,
The University of Chicago,
Chicago, IL, USA.

Anna C. Muriel, MD, MPH
Division Chief and Assistant Attending Child Psychiatrist,
Pediatric Psychosocial Oncology,
Dana Farber Cancer Institute;
Assistant Professor of Psychiatry,
Harvard University,
Boston, MA, USA.

Lailea Noel, MA
Doctoral Candidate,
The George Warren Brown School of Social Work,
Washington University in St. Louis,
St. Louis, MO, USA.

Julian L. North, BA (Psychology Hons)
Lecturer,
School of Social Sciences and Psychology,
University of Western Sydney,
Sydney, NSW, Australia.

Stephanie Rabenstein, MSc, RMFT
Child and Family Therapist,
Child and Adolescent Mental Health Care Program-Outpatients,
Children's Hospital, London Health Sciences Centre,
London, ON, Canada.

John S. Rolland, MD, MPH
Professor of Psychiatry & Co-Director,
Chicago Center for Family Health,
Pritzker School of Medicine, University of Chicago,
Chicago, IL, USA.

Valerie R. Samuels, MA
Educator & Author,
"Be Not Afraid" Network;
The Compassionate Friends,
Charlotte, NC, USA.

Diana C. Sands, PhD
Director,
Bereaved by Suicide Centre for Intense Grief,
Sydney, NSW, Australia.

Tammy Schuler, PhD
Postdoctoral Clinical Research Fellow,
Department of Psychiatry & Behavioral Sciences,
Memorial Sloan-Kettering Cancer Center,
New York, NY, USA.

Peter Steinglass, MD
President Emeritus,
Director, Ackerman Center for Substance Abuse and the Family,
Ackerman Institute for the Family;
Clinical Professor of Psychiatry,

Weill Medical College of Cornell University,
New York, NY, USA.

Corinne Sweeney, MA
Department of Psychology,
Fairleigh Dickinson University;
Research Study Assistant,
Department of Psychiatry & Behavioral Sciences,
Memorial Sloan-Kettering Cancer Center,
New York, NY, USA.

Froma Walsh, MSW, PhD
Co-Director, Chicago Center for Family Health,
Mose & Sylvia Firestone Professor Emerita, School of Social Service Administration,
Department of Psychiatry, Pritzker School of Medicine,
University of Chicago,
Chicago, IL, USA.

Lori Wiener, PhD
Director, Psychosocial Support and Research Program,
Staff Scientist, Pediatric Oncology Branch,
Center for Cancer Research,
National Cancer Institute,
Bethesda, MD, USA.

Talia I. Zaider, PhD
Assistant Attending Psychologist,
Department of Psychiatry & Behavioral Sciences,
Memorial Sloan-Kettering Cancer Center,
New York, NY, USA.

Series Editor's Foreword

Grief, as the contributors to this volume recognize, is inherently a family affair. Indeed, it is the culture, customs, and context of family life that both constrain expressions of mutual mourning and support individuals attempting to reorganize their lives together in the aftermath of a common loss. It is curious, then, that most contemporary bereavement theories and research studies espouse an individualistic perspective that all but "erases" the subtle processes by which families negotiate loss, blurring them into generic concepts like "support" that disguise as much as they reveal. Missing in such accounts—as well as in the equally individualistic practices they support in grief therapy—is an appreciation of the interactional, interpersonal, and often intergenerational factors that shape adaptation following the death of a family member. This book takes a long stride in the direction of rectifying this imbalance.

In their felicitous selection of topics and authors, Kissane and Parnes have assembled a veritable handbook on *Bereavement Care for Families*. In chapter after chapter, the book considers losses unfolding gradually in the context of palliative care; traumatically as a result of suicide or violence; tragically in cases of the unborn, infants, and children; and inexorably in the lives of elders. Viewing all such challenges through the twin lenses of family systems theory and the accumulating research literature, the authors of each chapter scrupulously harvest "news you can use" in treating real clients, conveyed in the form of flexible principles of practice easily adapted to a range of settings. Predicated on sensitive assessment of "at risk" individuals and families, several chapters help readers discern what grieving families need from professionals and from one another. Similarly, contributors bring these principles to life in vivid accounts of numerous actual treatments, whether these include participation of the ill family member in end-of-life settings or commence on referral after a sudden, unexpected death. The range of approaches illustrated in these case studies fairly captures the scope of contemporary clinical practice, informed by expressive arts interventions, cognitive behavioral procedures, linear and circular questioning of family members, and structural therapies that mitigate family conflict and instead foster communication and conciliation.

Ultimately, what emerged for me in a week of pleasurable perusing of these pages was a sharpened sense of how the very family context that is stressed and challenged by loss can be mobilized as a matrix of meaning making, mutual soothing, and eventual resilience. I trust that your own exploration of this intelligent, well-organized, and immensely practical volume will pay similar dividends for you as a reader and ultimately help hone the systemic sophistication required for all of us to work well with grieving families.

Robert A. Neimeyer, PhD
Series Editor
University of Memphis
July 2013

Preface

And Abraham came to mourn for Sarah and to cry for her.

—Genesis 23:2

As far back as biblical times and through to the present day, it is the rare person who passes through life without experiencing the distress of grieving for a beloved family member. If love endures, ultimately it leads inevitably and irrevocably to loss. Death is the destination; such is the reality of life's limits. The Old Testament relates that when the matriarch Sarah died, her spouse, Abraham, proceeded to grieve and bewail the loss. Indeed, not only is there "a time to be born, and a time to die," but there is also "a time to mourn" (Ecclesiastes 3:2–4).

If a loved one's demise leads us to anguish, traditionally it is the family that offers us support. The family is expected to gather and to provide consolation and the comfort of familiarity, even as death imposes radical, unwelcome change. Accordingly, for psychotherapy to be effective, it is clear that much of the clinician's focus needs to be on the family as a whole.

Yet strikingly, within the disciplines of psychology, psychiatry, and allied health, bereavement care for families as a whole remains a relatively new approach. Individuals all too often continue to be treated solely on their own. With this text, we hope to help change this status quo.

Considering the critical need for patient support during a time of distress, it may seem surprising that family-centered care has been slow to develop. Yet the reality is that within medicine, the prevailing paradigm is individual care. As we have pursued our studies, we have become convinced of the benefits that can flow from the family model. Although we recognize that some of the bereaved will always need individual therapy and others will be helped by groups, the family model is a third, broad approach that bridges both modalities.

It is an age-old question: what do you say to someone who has suffered the loss of a beloved family member? And, more recently, how do therapists ideally harness the resources of the family as a whole to best help grieving individuals? These questions rise to the forefront when treating the bereaved in the context of the family.

The formal clinical beginnings of viewing bereavement within a family framework date to 1965, when pioneering therapists Norman Paul and George Grosser described the role of family therapy in an intervention called operational mourning. In the 1970s, additional clinicians such as psychiatrist Murray Bowen and social worker Lily Pincus championed the cause. In the 1990s, the Melbourne-based Family Focused Grief Therapy Trial demonstrated how a preventive approach could be offered to families that were considered "at risk" for complicated grief. This approach brought promising new benefits, including reduced rates of clinical depression during bereavement.

More recently, the U.S.-based Family Grief Therapy Trial has highlighted the advantages of starting therapy during palliative care and continuing it into bereavement. As this book goes to press, the results from this dose intensity of therapy trial will become available in 2014. Accordingly, today the door has been further opened for groundbreaking psychosocial care; this volume seeks to elucidate this approach.

In editing this book, David W. Kissane has taken responsibility for overseeing the science, striving to see an evidence base for management principles and ensuring that authors present substantively what is novel and clinically relevant. As co-editor, Francine Parnes has overseen the many voices of contributors throughout these 19 chapters. This book was conceptualized as a guide for clinicians, and the editors hope that it will prove useful to any therapist seeking insight into bereavement within the family.

We have many people to thank: first and foremost, our authors, who have given so generously of their time, experience, and knowledge. We are deeply grateful for their willingness to share their perspectives on family-centered bereavement care and thus help shape this volume. Many of the contributors are active clinicians whose wisdom and insight enrich all that they have written.

Several of our chapters have been written by therapists associated with the Family Grief Therapy Trial at Memorial Sloan-Kettering Cancer Center in New York. The National Cancer Institute within the National Institutes of Health funded this work (R01 CA 115329). We thank Ann O'Mara, Head of Palliative Care Research in the Community Oncology and Prevention Trials Research Group of the Division of Cancer Prevention for her gracious and untiring support of this project.

Many staff members at Memorial Sloan-Kettering contributed to this project over the past decade. Maria Farberov, Rachel Bell, Jacqueline Simpronio, and Shira Hichenberg provided superb study management, while Erica Kerr, Megan Eisenberg, Moriah Brier, Francesca Del Gaudio, Mary Gray, Melissa Masterson, and Stephanie Napolitano both recruited and stayed in touch with many family members throughout this large trial. Therapists came from the Ackerman Institute for Families in New York and from Memorial Sloan-Kettering Cancer Center. Another contribution came from postdoctoral fellows Talia I. Zaider, Isabelle Dumont, Wendy G. Lichtenthal, and Tammy Schuler, all of whom have gone on to become stellar scholars in their own right. Their writing in this book is a fine testament to that.

Our peer-group supervision for therapists has been an especially rich and wonderful experience of trust, mutual support, creativity, and sensitivity. Together, therapists reviewed their work with families, developed hypotheses about what was happening, and strengthened their plans for where to next take the therapeutic work. This process was capably facilitated by Marguerite S. Lederberg, Margery Elson, Richard Glassman, Nessa Coyle, Matthew Dean, Susie Kim, and Bridgette Boucher, to name but a few. Indeed, innumerable clinical colleagues with whom we have worked over the past decade have contributed so much to patient care and collegial support. They have been one enormous family.

Manuscripts mature through the consistent efforts of a very willing team. Laurie Schulman at Memorial Sloan-Kettering and Heather Thiessens at Monash University coordinated behind the scenes, while our commissioning editor, Anna Moore, from Routledge was ever encouraging and patient. Clinical psychologist Robert A. Neimeyer proved to be a stalwart colleague, who first encouraged us during an Association for Death Education and Counseling conference to write this book. He gave generously of his time in writing the foreword. Our families also exhibited remarkable tolerance and understanding as we dedicated ourselves to this text. Deep gratitude goes from Francine Parnes to Brent Bowers, a very talented wordsmith and her former editor at *The New York Times*. He is a treasured role model, esteemed friend, and everything one could hope for in an editor.

Now we turn this volume over to clinicians and trust that it will inspire and guide the care of patients and their families—and even help them to flourish. We also hope that readers will use this book to glean insights and pathways into the family bereavement process that affects us all. For all concerned, there is more to learn about family-centered care and much still to tackle and accomplish in establishing the model of care.

David W. Kissane and Francine Parnes
May 2013

Part I
Overview of the Clinical Development of Bereavement Care for Families

This section presents the theoretical underpinnings of family-centered care in bereavement. We examine the nature of family grief, family systems theory, and models of family therapy, whether delivered in bereavement or for loss experienced by families when a member has a physical or mental illness. We conclude with the ethics of family bereavement care, which are central to every clinical approach.

1 Family Grief

David W. Kissane

Sophie was just 15 in 1877 as she lay listlessly on her bed, dying from consumption, the archaic term for tuberculosis. Beside her were her brothers, Edvard, 14, and Andreas (known within the family as Peter), 12; and sisters, Laura, 10, and Inger Marie, 9. Befitting the mournfulness, the children's father, Christian, and their aunt, Karen, led them in prayer. Early death was not unfamiliar to this family: tuberculosis had laid claim to their mother the very year when Inger Marie was born. Although Christian was a physician, he could not thwart the ravages of nature such as the "white plague" of tuberculosis that afflicted his wife and children. Times were harsh. The Norwegian capital where they lived, Kristiania, later called Oslo, suffered extremely bleak winters. And it would be some years before the discovery of the bacterium Mycobacterium tuberculosis, by Robert Koch in 1882, and another half century before effective treatment became available to prevent a death scene such as this.

Grief in the Family of Edvard Munch

This was the family of the expressionist artist and lithographer Edvard Munch (1863–1944). He himself was sick for much of his childhood, undoubtedly also afflicted with consumption. To occupy long days spent at home, he learned to draw, sketching medicinal bottles, room interiors, and even Sophie, unwell in her bed. This love of art was bred in the family (see Figure 1.1). His paternal grandfather's first cousin, Jacob, had been a respected artist, and Edvard's mother and older sister encouraged his childhood drawing. By age 13, Edvard, who had viewed works by the Norwegian landscape school, was already practicing by copying their paintings.

Edvard's mother, who had seen one of her sisters die from consumption during childhood, was likewise unwell for much of her married life. Readily fatigued and rendered breathless by short moments of exertion, she sat for extended periods in an armchair by the window. With the birth of each of her four children, her health became more fragile. Expecting that her days were numbered, she wrote her children a letter (now held in the Munch Museum), expressing her love and exhorting them to sustain their faith and trust in God. Munch's papers include an account of his memory of his dying mother, which one biographer, Sue Prideaux, described as revealing through this period his inner "emotional chaos" (Prideaux, 2005, p. 330, note 318). Edvard's account, however, was necessarily limited: in accordance with the custom of that era, the children were dispatched to a neighbor's house while their mother was buried.

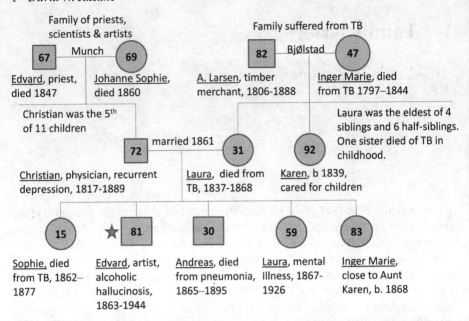

Figure 1.1 Genogram of the family of the expressionist artist Edvard Munch * (1863–1944) showing the extent of physical and mental illness, with Munch's resultant cumulative exposure to death and grief. Edvard's mother died when he was 5, Sophie when Edvard was 14, Christian when he was 26, and Andreas when he was 32, while his sister Laura was mentally ill for many years.

Munch's father, Christian, was the son of a priest. Christian's family had lived in poor parts of rural Norway, where education, particularly the study of history, was highly regarded. So was religion, and the family—which included Christian's uncle, a bishop and poet—was devout. Christian considered his bouts of unhappiness to be sins of ingratitude for all that God had given him. The death of his wife after just seven years of marriage brought deep grief and worry about how he would care for their five children. Christian became more fervent in his piety and often told the youngsters that their mother was watching over them from heaven. Fortunately, Aunt Karen, his wife's 29-year-old single sister, was able to move into the family home to help raise the boys and girls.

Always addressed by the Norwegian title Tante Karen, she was devoted to the children and brought joy and nurturing into an otherwise sad household. The younger siblings thought of her as their mother, but Sophie and Edvard turned to each other for security and companionship. Because both were ill, they spent extended periods home from school together. Sophie encouraged Edvard's drawings; their bond became deep and strong.

Sophie's death was therefore life-impacting for Edvard, who lost in his big sister, his soul mate and maternal imago. At age 14, he understood her decline and witnessed his father's distress and impotence at her wasting away into death with a hacking cough, fevers, profound weakness, and eventual delirium. This time, Edvard attended the funeral. Even so, his diary remains silent about his feelings, which were repressed for many years. Eventually, his grief was expressed through his painting.

Tuberculosis was not the only affliction that was prominent in the family; so was mental illness. Christian suffered from recurrent bouts of depression, while Edvard's younger sister, Laura, was hospitalized for an extended sickness involving periods of catatonia, hallucinations, and chronic insanity. Eventually, she died from cancer. In 1895, Edvard's brother, Peter, succumbed to pneumonia at the young age of 30. The only one of the siblings to marry, Peter left behind a pregnant wife. Munch himself, during his middle age, deteriorated into periods of heavy drinking, necessitating an eight-month hospitalization for alcoholic hallucinosis.

At age 16, Edvard studied engineering at a technical college, learning to draw to scale and in perspective. But by the time Edvard was 18, art won through as his career choice, and he enrolled at the Royal School of Art and Design of Kristiania. Although his morbidly pious father continued to provide a small allowance, he harshly condemned Edvard's drinking binges. More significantly, his father, who deplored the influence of the bohemians upon his son, even destroyed Edvard's early nude paintings. It was Edvard's art teacher, Christian Krohg, who nurtured his confidence and affirmed his talent to portray the deep emotional tone of whatever he painted. At age 23, Edvard described in his diary his image of his favorite sister, Sophie, *The Sick Child* (1886), as his first "soul painting" (Prideaux, 2005, p. 83). His efforts finally paid off when a state scholarship to study art led him, then 26, to move to Paris in 1889. However, his father's death later that year forced Edvard's return to Oslo, and thereafter he supported his family. Grief with its deep suffering had returned to his family of origin.

Edvard's art similarly captured in poignant color the devastating emotions he both witnessed around him and felt personally. Melancholy, sickness, existential angst, and soul pain! Each face and bodily pose on his canvasses depicted the state of mind of those about him. His great 1895 canvas, *Death in the Sickroom*, portrayed the varied, yet heart-felt responses of his family struggling with loss as death fell, yet again, upon another family member. Their mournfulness was an intensely felt family sorrow.

Munch's grief was undoubtedly pathological, given its chronicity and impact on his life. Preferring to withdraw from others, he retreated for extended periods. He assuaged his wretchedness with bouts of heavy drinking, whether absinthe, whiskey, or wine. Choosing not to follow the impressionist art of that era, he turned to paint from the soul, reworking for many years his mental images of the death room. Aunt Karen became a loyal and supportive presence, sitting for many hours as the model for his grieving mother figure. His records show that he reworked the painting of *The Sick Child* numerous times, a pieta of a "dying child and anguished mother" (Prideaux, 2005, p. 86). Munch's relationship with Tante Karen deepened, and, in later years, he would write to her regularly, share all his concerns, and come to trust her deeply. They exchanged sums of money to help each other through phases of poverty. As Munch eventually became successful, he loyally supported his family.

But family was not Munch's only source of love. Munch had two romantic loves, Millie and Tulla. Millie was the passionate belle of his early adulthood, appearing in many paintings of love, dancing, jealousy, and the femme fatale. This first relationship broke up consensually. He later fell in love with Tulla and traveled with her to Italy. She sought marriage, but his memories of sickness and the pain of loss from his childhood led him to fear this commitment. Eventually, Tulla tired of his avoidance and chose instead to marry another friend. Humiliated by her decision, Munch turned again to drinking.

Fighting with Tulla was sometimes dramatic: during one skirmish, a gun misfired, causing Munch to lose a finger. As he drank more heavily, he became paranoid with auditory hallucinations, necessitating hospitalization for six months in 1908.

Upon recovery, Munch chose a more solitary life. In 1909, he bought an 11-acre property at Ekely, outside of Oslo, where he spent much of his remaining life. He kept many of his paintings, woodcuts, and lithographs. A cherished, sentimental possession was the wicker chair that his sister Sophie had sat in beside her bed. It served as a linking object that he long treasured.

Clearly, Munch experienced much grief throughout his life, which he portrayed so poignantly on his canvases. Today, as we view these works in art galleries and museums, we recognize that he knew the nature of family grief.

The Theory of Family Grief

Loss, death, and mourning afflict not only each bereaved person, but the pain reverberates among the clan. Too often the clinician focuses on the individual—the patient who presents on that particular day. The bereaved spouse seeks solace; the mother laments the death of her child. It is easy to respond to whoever appeals for help. Yet invariably, the family constitutes the fundamental context in which bereavement occurs (Kissane, 1994). Most importantly, the family influences the pattern of mourning that unfolds through its traditions and pursuit of religious, cultural, and ethnic norms. Family leaders may dictate what to do, when to be stoic, when to shed tears, and how to comfort one another. Curiously, the script that the family follows can be recognized from generation to generation, fostering either compassionate support or avoidant silence, depending on their custom.

In Munch's family, their Christian religion provided a schema that deemed death to be God's will, circumstances to be accepted in faith, with hope for a heavenly reunion. The related piety required stoic acceptance and moderated any emotional expression. Moreover, children were to be protected from overt emotional display. They were sent away to save them from witnessing adult distress. The family rallied with loving intent, and a devoted sister like Tante Karen sacrificed her personal future for the sake of her deceased sister's children. Practicality prevailed! But the empathic support that might permit ready expression and sharing of feelings was replaced by a more rigid oppression and fundamental religious stance that had been accepted across several generations.

The face of the artist, Edvard Munch, is blank across many works of his family gathered around the deathbed. His father prays fervently; his aunt nurses the sick. His younger sisters are disconnected—one saddened with lowered head, the other staring off into the distance. Edvard's brother awkwardly holds the door, seemingly anxious to escape. Here we see the differential responses within the group, the dominant sense appearing centrifugal, allowing bewilderment and suffering to be privately contained despite the presence of each other. No perception of mutual support can be found in these paintings. Albeit an unconscious process, a pattern of family response style is nonetheless apparent—and the historical data suggest that it is maladaptive.

Edvard's early grief is complicated with avoidance, chronicity, inertia, and melancholy. He sits alone by the shore, sometimes gazes out the window from a darkened room, and paints self-images accompanied by a skeleton arm. Instead of his family uniting supportively, the outward force drives them into isolation. Edvard suffered ridicule by fellow artists whose canvasses were awash with the color and the beauty of nature. His world was a stark, threatening commentary on the harshness of life, replicating the silence of his family of origin. His realism confronted, frightened, and was unwelcome by non-comprehending critics in his social milieu. His only retreat was to pursue another escape—the carefree attitudes of the bohemians, albeit without healing.

Range of Family Responses

Families are greatly influenced in their response to loss by (1) their culture, its customs and taboos; (2) their immediate experience of the loss (whether anticipated, traumatic, stigmatized, or unexpected); (3) familial traditions that have encoded a pattern of response across the generations (either comforting or avoidant; distorting via blame, idealization, fear, or fatalism; or prolonging via memorialization and "stuck-ness"); and (4) their support network, which either connects or alienates (Kissane, 1994). Although individuals within a family will differ in their emotionality—for instance, mothers may be more expressive than fathers—the family as a whole guides the gestalt of the members' response style.

It is up to the clinician to interpret how a response style is adaptive, drawing upon the strengths of the family, or how it proves restrictive, hindering healing and resumption of a creative life. The adaptive response promotes mutual support and comfort, with open sharing of thoughts and feelings, and trust in one another's willingness to listen and help. It is built on a deep level of commitment found in the bonds of the family. The cohesiveness of the family and its ease of communication prevail. In contrast are families that block communication, blame one another, and, in the process, become conflictual, fractured, and distant. These families reveal a dysfunctionality that potentially harms a natural mourning process. Clinicians need to guide the development of management plans and support needs of families deemed "at risk."

Empirical studies of family grief in the Melbourne Family Grief Study pinpointed five patterns of functioning that predicted bereavement outcomes for the members of these families (Kissane, Bloch, Dowe et al., 1996). Two response styles were adaptive and termed *supportive* and *conflict-resolving*. Supportive styles show strong teamwork, genuine readiness for mutual support, and openness to sharing thoughts and feelings with one another. Conflict-resolving styles also demonstrate good communication, with tolerance for a difference of opinions. Family members could fight but sustained respect for each other.

Two patterns of family functioning were clearly dysfunctional. The most fractured families become help rejecters, fairly set in their use of distance to survive their mutual antagonism. Relationship breakdown reverberates through each generation as hostility drives members apart, hence the name *hostile* families. The resultant alienation places members at risk for psychiatric disorders, which proved prominent in observational studies (Kissane, Bloch, Onghena et al., 1996). The second type of dysfunctional family is defined as *help-accepting*: these families carried high rates of mental illness among their family members, yet they welcomed assistance. This is empowered by a greater muting of their disagreements, hence the name *sullen* families, in which their anger is turned inward and their members often develop clinical depression. Sullen families are greatly aided by family therapy, which, if provided prophylactically during palliative care, can contain their distress and ameliorate psychiatric morbidity during bereavement (Kissane et al., 2006).

Finally, in between the adaptive and dysfunctional types of families is an *intermediate* group, with mid-range levels of communication, cohesion, and conflict. These families deteriorate under the strain of bereavement but can also be helped preventively by family therapy commencing during palliative care and continuing into bereavement. The Melbourne study showed the benefit of a family-centered model of care during terminal illness whenever family functioning poses a risk of more morbid outcomes.

Recognition of Families "at Risk" of Complicated Grief

Across nearly 20 years of scholarship, with trials of family therapy conducted both in Australia and the United States, a simple screening approach has proven helpful to identify families at risk according to their relational functioning (Kissane & Bloch, 2002). Well-validated as a screening tool, the Family Relationships Index (Moos & Moos, 1981) uses 12 items through which family members present their perception of levels of (a) cohesion, (b) communication, and (c) conflict. Clinicians can also appraise these "three C's" of relational life through direct questions about each family's teamwork, openness in sharing feelings, and tolerance of differences of opinion. Deficit in any of these fundamental relational modes can place a family at risk. When harnessed together, these three processes foster adaptation; yet when absent, the developmental pathway to healing grief is hindered. Because these processes are central in the functional life of a family, therapists benefit from optimizing them. Lichtenthal and Sweeney elaborate further on families with complicated grief in Chapter 17.

Family Life Cycle

Another framework, which likewise offers significant insight into a family's adaptation to loss, considers where the family is at within its life cycle. Walsh and McGoldrick (1991) focused on this in their seminal tome, *Living beyond Loss*. Death can occur in childhood, adolescence, young adulthood, the middle years, or most frequently, in old age. Families can also be *young* with babies and broad hopes for their future, more *established* with tasks of active rearing and educating their children, *launching* as adolescents prepare to separate and move to independence, *renegotiating* their direction and agenda in the middle years, and *celebrating* as the next generation emerges with grandchildren and old age descends on the original parents. Each phase of the family life cycle brings new challenges, with potential for mishaps and grief along the way. Froma Walsh expands on the family life cycle in Chapter 2. The adaptability of the family can be significantly influenced by its stage along this life cycle, what hurdles are present, and what other support from the wider community is available.

This life cycle perspective also brings up people's common assumptions about what to expect, how their world ought to be, and their different levels of preparedness for what might lie ahead. Parkes (1972) spoke of this as the assumptive world (i.e., that set of beliefs, ideas, and expectations that people and families carry). The assumptive world naturally changes throughout the life cycle, and more is said about it in this chapter when Colin Murray Parkes's contribution to bereavement research is further considered. A highly informative examination delves into where each family is at, what it expects, and what assumptions it carries as a group.

Family Rituals

Humankind turns to metaphors, symbols, and even prescribed behaviors to assist its adaptation to change and passage through the life cycle. Whether contextualized by religion or by culture, our use of ritual invariably embraces the family. We celebrate birthdays, gather to witness the union of marriage, sometimes vacation together and, when death intervenes, mourn together. The family is central to the process of ritual, and these traditions, in turn, assist each family in negotiating its challenges and stresses throughout the years. Ritual enriches life and helps bind relatives together in their respective family units. Such customs provide families with a paradoxical capacity to acknowledge differences of opinion, share difficult feelings, and move toward healing (Imber-Black, 2003). In this more secular world that steadily changes its use of ritual, recognizing the contribution of rituals to family life is crucial. Rituals comfort families coping with death because they impart a structure through which feelings can be shared to allow healing.

The Contribution of Culture

Societies usually evolve toward the betterment of their community. They cultivate distinct ways that people live together, develop norms, create an identity, and forge coherence. We talk of this as the culture of the society. Spirit and enthusiasm emerges; a national unity builds; it feels good to belong! Any sense of togetherness is deepened through the use of a local dialect, an idiom that fosters greater shared understanding and confidence in a common destiny. Education reinforces further development and enrichment, as respect grows for creativity. Art, music, theater, literature, and storytelling further consolidates the customs of the community. Symbols develop, along with metaphors, fairy tales for the young, songs to accompany the phases of life, recipes and special dishes to feed the clan, and celebrations that repeat with the seasons of the year. These patterns of behavior adopted by groups become the way to do it, their tradition, and the way of life. Families are pivotal to the transmission of culture which, in turn, shapes the manner in which families mourn.

Thus, in the Munch family, we can identify a number of cultural influences. They were private about their grief, discouraging openness, and they sent the children away to protect them from any distress seen at a funeral. They were very religious, and their religion told them to accept God's will. This was intended to comfort them in their grief. Family loyalty was strong and fostered some mutual support. Alcohol consumption, even in excess for men, was acceptable to ease the pain of loss.

As the ethos of any family develops, an ethical stance is generally adopted because it serves the common good. Such goals are fundamental to survival, and successful values become identified and maintained for the benefits they bring. Both the family and the larger social group define what is good and nurture its development. It is commonly encoded in a family's rules and socially adopted as laws. And as the collective process further matures, definitive roles are pursued in a collaborative manner that progressively advantages the majority. Families grow and mature through the complementarity that different roles bring together for the greater good of the whole group.

Roles within the Family

Gender traditionally defines many of these roles; age defines others. The resultant diversity is enriching; the mutual support fosters interdependency while respecting individuality. Families inevitably need their members to complement one another; roles become embedded and a core feature of family life. Mothers and fathers nurture their young; elders model how it is best done; the young imitate and repeat the cycles of life. Hunters and gatherers, providers and homemakers, artists and educators: families need leaders and followers, decision makers, and caregivers; every type of activity can be welcome and necessary for the benefit of all.

When illness interferes with the accomplishment of key tasks, another person is commissioned to take up that role. Such adaptiveness and flexibility is crucial to sustain the work of the family as it goes about rearing its young and optimizing its life. Goodwill, teamwork, grace and diligence, respect, and harmony are needed to be successful—and at the heart of this, love and generosity must win over rivalry, jealousy, and envy for the family to achieve its creative goals and provide security for its clan.

Functionality

And so we return to recognition of how a competent family achieves its desired goals of raising its young to adulthood and independence. It needs teamwork, commitment, and loyalty; it needs processes that are smooth, coordinated, and directed; its constituents may make varied contributions to build the overall gestalt; rules and traditions can guide members toward some sense of the shared agenda; celebration and joy are vital to mark its progress; and caregiving and support for its vulnerable and ill are as critical as feeding, nurturance, and education are to its young. From time to time, the family will know hardship and struggle, meet unfairness or wrong, need to fight against evil, and want to find strength and courage from within. The family's capacity to adapt and tolerate differences of opinion is crucial to its survival. Awareness of talent, resilience, and sources of creativity will increase its joy and harmony.

What is obvious from all of this is that a family is a system with reciprocal influences and experiences. Its relationships shape it and determine its well-being. Its values, ethos, and ease of communication advance its problem solving and adaptiveness. Its legacy and history are hugely determinative of how it approaches fresh challenges in life.

The Munch family provides a clear example of the sometimes random events that befall families. Illness, burden, and loss can alter the family's direction. Temperament and genetics impact the family's robustness. Patterns of behavior that seem scripted through its beliefs, customs, and culture affect its functionality. Relationships are key, so that the journey is thereby shared.

In the Munch family, love and generosity empower the family's survival through the devotion and encouragement of an older sister, the sacrifice and loyalty of an aunt, steady income generation by the father, and the willingness of the extended family to lend support. Ultimately, Edvard took over the role of provider, his creativity became the source of financial security, and his constancy held the more vulnerable together.

Mourning, Resolution, and Creativity

Long ago, psychoanalysis recognized that mourning is an adaptive coping response through which we grieve and lament a loss, adjust to the resultant change, and then move forward with renewed vitality and effort (Deutsch, 1937). Let us consider now some of the key historical theorists and their contributions to understanding the mourning process.

Noteworthy among psychoanalysts, Melanie Klein described pining loss in infants when the breast, mother, or parent is unavailable, and also how they mature and develop regard for, concern for, and eventually love of the other person whom they need in life (Klein, 1940). This pattern of pining loss—from the very first year of an infant's life—is repeated throughout adulthood.

Freud contrasted adaptive mourning with the development of depression after loss. In *Mourning and Melancholia*, he showed how relationships that had been dominated by ambivalent feelings were difficult to mourn, risking any residual anger becoming channeled by the bereaved into guilt to cause a depressive illness (Freud, 1917). Although Freud spoke of using grief work to sever relational bonds to the deceased, bereavement researchers have rejected this hypothesis about breaking bonds: clearly the relationship is refashioned, with lifelong memories of the deceased that persist (Stroebe & Schut, 2001).

The first empirical study of grief occurred during World War II, when observations of people bereaved by the war were combined with those of survivors of the Cocoanut Grove nightclub fire in Boston (Lindemann, 1944). Among the clinical phenomena were distress, numbness, preoccupation with sad memories of the deceased, guilt or anger, disorganized behavior, and even identification with the symptoms of prior illnesses of the deceased.

Attachment Theory

A huge leap forward in understanding came with the scholarship of the British psychiatrist John Bowlby. In 1961, within a theory of attachment that built a clear model of the nature of human relationships, he described four patterns of relational bonds— secure, anxiously insecure, avoidant, and overly dependent (Bowlby, 1961, 1969). Attachment was understood as a process that advanced survival of the species through the infant's development of a trusting relationship with the mother. From this secure base, the toddler could then begin to explore its environment, while also retaining confidence in the dependability of its parents. Any lapse in such availability might cause frustration and insecurity in a more anxious child, who feared separation and potential abandonment. By contrast, some children cultivate an air of self-sufficiency with a more avoidant response that appears to feign, "I'm OK." Other children become agitated, disorganized, and even hostile when they sense abandonment (Ainsworth, Blehar, Waters, & Wall, 1978).

Attachment theory was consolidated as an interpersonal process that defined the quality of early patterns of relationship, only for these patterns to be subsequently repeated in adulthood and throughout life (Fonagy, 2001). These relational patterns assist clinicians to understand bereavement responses, wherein insecure attachment styles predict difficulties mourning any loss.

Families can contain similar models of attachment as a group: some being secure and mutually supportive, others avoidant, some anxious with unmet needs, and others fractured, in which cutoffs and distance between relatives prevail (Kissane, 1994). Hence, the typology of family functioning in bereavement, as described in the Melbourne Family Grief Study, is consistent with Bowlby's model of attachment theory (Kissane, Bloch, Dowe et al., 1996; Kissane, Bloch, Onghena et al., 1996).

Psychosocial Transition—The Assumptive World

Colin Murray Parkes was a close colleague of John Bolwby. Parkes worked at St. Christopher's Hospice in London and cared for the bereaved relatives of dying cancer patients. He described the manner in which loss altered the bereaved's assumptive world (Parkes, 1972)—that set of notions, beliefs, and ideas about life that are carried by social and cultural groups of people in a taken-for-granted manner (Janoff-Bulman, 1989). Within the assumptive world lies a series of core expectations: life is fair, good health is deserved, we are worthy, the world is benevolent, the elderly die before the young, and what happens makes sense (Janoff-Bulman, 1992). These assumptions could be shattered dramatically by sudden death, whereas a long illness permits gradual accommodation of new or revised views. The mourning process requires some rebuilding of the inner world and refashioning old assumptions until new meaning and purpose are discerned that allow life to proceed constructively. Families also need to do this and gradually alter the collective beliefs they hold as a group. Discussion of each individual's ideas with others helps shape and rework assumptions until they facilitate resolution of grief so the family can reengage in its creative future.

The Dual-Process Model of Coping with Bereavement

Stroebe and Schut (2001) described a very helpful model of coping with bereavement whereby periods of time focused on loss-oriented grief work oscillate with periods spent on restoration-oriented living. During the former, waves of distress and tearfulness may accompany reminiscences about the deceased; during the latter, new activities, roles, and interests take time out from the pain of grief. The dynamic movement back and forth serves as an adaptive regulatory process that confronts the loss and then takes time out from this.

Families also alternate between a focus on the loss and attention to ongoing living. One family member may recognize the depth of emotional pain being expressed by a relative and, once the distress is acknowledged, choose to distract their attention to another activity. The adaptive family as a whole has its wisdom in recognizing when such movement is needed to sustain the balance between looking back and moving forward. But when a family gets stuck in its sorrow, an attending clinician may need to tactfully redirect the family's efforts externally toward socialization, mutual support, and reorientation toward community engagement and activities.

Resolution of Mourning and New Creativity

The length of time needed for mourning is broadly proportional to the strength of the bonds of attachment. Implicit in this observation is that the pain of grief gradually wanes, mood improves, and a different kind of sadness emerges (Lazare, 1989). Memories of the lost person become generally positive, and relative equanimity develops when talking about the deceased. Activities clearly become enjoyable again; new interests are taken up. This process for the individual is mirrored by the family, whose group conversations provide models for one another of this process as it unfolds.

New creativity is possible once grief has healed. George Polloch (1989) described the mourning-liberation process as fresh inspiration and ingenuity arising from—and shaped by—the healing from grief. Polloch perceived Gustav Mahler's greatest symphonies in this light. Munch also exemplifies this process, whereby his artistic genius took shape from his experience of loss and mourning, influencing some of his most expressive works.

This type of fresh engagement is an important goal of any therapeutic support. Remarkably, this goal sits in sharp contrast to some of the bereavement literature that, while emphasizing the maintenance of bonds with the deceased, has suggested that mourning might last indefinitely. Such thinking is flawed. The construct of "prolonged grief disorder" highlights the pathological nature of chronic grief (Prigerson et al., 2009), where the bereaved become stuck in their sadness, with narrowing of their life. Fostering creativity is part of the restoration-oriented path to recovery.

Grief as a Family Affair

The earliest studies of family grief interventions showed how individual models of bereavement care can fail to heal grief when perpetuating factors exist in the family (Lieberman, 1978; Rosenthal, 1980). Murray Bowen recognized how emotional unavailability limited family harmony, whereas effective communication and mutual support empowered healing (Bowen, 1976). Froma Walsh will expand upon this systemic perspective and its importance in making sense of the family's contribution to grief and mourning (see Chapter 2). The family constitutes the natural support network of the bereaved as well as the social environment most affected by the loss. It would therefore appear to be a natural focus of clinical activity in bereavement (Paul & Grosser, 1965; Pincus, 1974).

Despite these early observations, a family-centric approach to bereavement care has long been neglected (Kissane et al., 1994). The dominant model of therapy has been individually oriented, whether within psychodynamic, cognitive-behavioral, self-psychology, or other therapeutic schools. The failure to focus on the family as a resource has been a missed opportunity for potential support. On the other hand, intervention with the family can be challenging if its homeostatic force (tendency to maintain the status quo) seems intent upon remaining dysfunctional in nature.

When a bereaved individual seeks psychological counseling, the therapist can suggest that relatives come along to provide support (Kissane & Hooghe, 2011). Through their help, one goal here is to introduce multiple perspectives into the therapy room (Seikkula, Arnkil, & Hoffman, 2006). The resultant dialogue is enriched by their stories that generate varied levels of meaning and fresh comprehension in the interpersonal space in which grief is shared. Points of tension become a worthwhile focus so that dissonance is shaped into respect for different views and coping styles.

As the family searches to find meaning in both the deceased's life and the resultant loss, collective meaning making develops that is distinct from any individual's (Nadeau, 2008). Families construct meaning together as their shared understanding of what occurred. This develops by characterizing the person and comparing her with others, by making sense of random events in a manner meaningful to the family, and through the choice of words, phrases, or metaphors specific to the ethos of each family—what Nadeau terms "family speak" (Nadeau, 1998). Thus, a lost child might be prayed to as the family's new guardian angel. Both positive and negative conclusions can be reached by families—some constructive and others constraining. Responding to both, therapists restate and reframe their observations, guiding the family in its search for meaning as a pathway to adaptation and growth.

Conclusion

The family of Edvard Munch illustrates the salient contribution that relational life makes to coping and adaptation to loss. Having lost his mother at a young age, Edvard bonded to his sister, Sophie, and they strove together as a subsystem in their family to help others to cope and manage. But the subsequent loss of Sophie taxed Edvard to the limit, causing complicated grief for both him and the family as a whole. Many years were needed to heal their pain.

Munch and his family were inextricably woven together in a world shaped by their social poverty, religious hope, and cultural richness. They were stricken by cumulative loss. They struggled for some time until remarkable resilience and creativity helped them emerge and recover from their grief. Munch's painting became an artistic triumph, his expressionism a living testimony to his family's journey.

In considering bereavement care for families, the relational network is paramount. It offers context, culture, continuity, and resource; it has formed the stage of loss but is also the theater of the future. The family as a whole presents an ally for therapists to recognize and harness. It is the crucible of emotional life, containing both legacy and dreams. Undoubtedly, grief is a family affair and an invitation for family-centered care.

References

Ainsworth, M., Blehar, M., Waters, E., & Wall, S. (1978). *Patterns of attachment: A psychological study of the strange situation.* Hillsdale, NJ: Erlbaum.
Bowen, M. (1976). Family reaction to death. In P. J. Guerin (Ed.), *Family therapy: Theory and practice* (pp. 335–348). New York: Gardner.
Bowlby, J. (1961). Processes of mourning. *International Journal of Psychoanalysis, 17,* 317–340.
Bowlby, J. (1969). *Attachment and loss: Vol. 1. Attachment* (2nd ed.). New York: Basic Books.
Deutsch, H. (1937). Absence of grief. *Psychoanalytical Quarterly, 6,* 12–22.
Fonagy, P. (2001). *Attachment theory and psychoanalysis.* New York: Other Press.

Freud, S. (1917). *Mourning and melancholia* (J. Strachey, A. Freud, A. Strachey, & A. Tyson, Trans., Vol. 14). London: Hogarth.

Imber-Black, E. (2003). Ritual themes in families and family therapy. In E. Imber-Black, J. Roberts, & R. A. Whiting (Eds.), *Rituals in families and family therapy* (pp. 47–83). New York: W. W. Norton.

Janoff-Bulman, R. (1989). Assumptive worlds and the stress of traumatic events: Applications of the schema construct. *Social Cognition, 7*(2), 113–136.

Janoff-Bulman, R. (1992). *Shattered assumptions: Towards a new psychology of trauma.* New York: Free Press.

Kissane, D. (1994). Grief and the family. In S. Bloch, J. Hafner, E. Harari, & G. Szmukler (Eds.), *The family in clinical psychiatry* (pp. 71–91). Oxford: Oxford University Press.

Kissane, D., & Bloch, S. (2002). *Family focused grief therapy: A model of family-centred care during palliative care and bereavement.* Buckingham: Open University Press.

Kissane, D., Bloch, S., Burns, W. I., Patrick, J. D., Wallace, C. S., & McKenzie, D. P. (1994). Perceptions of family functioning and cancer. *Psycho-Oncology, 3,* 259–269.

Kissane, D., & Hooghe, A. (2011). Family therapy for the bereaved. In R. A. Neimeyer, D. L. Harris, H. R. Winokuer, & G. F. Thornton (Eds.), *Grief and bereavement in contemporary society: Bridging research and practice* (pp. 287-302). New York: Routledge.

Kissane, D., McKenzie, M., Bloch, S., O'Neill, I., Chan, E., Moskowitz, C., & McKenzie, D. (2006). Family focused grief therapy: A randomized controlled trial in palliative care and bereavement. *American Journal of Psychiatry, 163,* 1208–1218.

Kissane, D. W., Bloch, S., Dowe, D. L., Snyder, R. D., Onghena, P., McKenzie, D. P., & Wallace, C. S. (1996). The Melbourne Family Grief Study, I: Perceptions of family functioning in bereavement. *American Journal of Psychiatry, 153,* 650–658.

Kissane, D. W., Bloch, S., Onghena, P., McKenzie, D. P., Snyder, R. D., & Dowe, D. L. (1996). The Melbourne Family Grief Study, II: Psychosocial morbidity and grief in bereaved families. *American Journal of Psychiatry, 153,* 659–666.

Klein, M. (1940). Mourning and its relation to manic-depressive states. *International Journal of Psychoanalysis, 21,* 125–153.

Lazare, A. (1989). Bereavement and unresolved grief. In A. Lazare (Ed.), *Outpatient psychiatry: Diagnosis and treatment* (2nd ed., pp. 381–397). Baltimore: Williams and Wilkins.

Lieberman, S. (1978). Nineteen cases of morbid grief. *British Journal of Psychiatry, 132,* 159–163.

Lindemann, E. (1944). Symptomatology and management of acute grief. *American Journal of Psychiatry, 101,* 141–148.

Moos, R. H., & Moos, B. S. (1981). *Family environment scale manual.* Stanford, CA: Consulting Psychologists Press.

Nadeau, J. W. (1998). *Families making sense of death.* Thousand Oaks, CA: Sage.

Nadeau, J. W. (2008). Meaning-making in bereaved families: Assessment, intervention and future research. In M. S. Stroebe, R. O. Hansson, H. Schut, & W. Stroebe (Eds.), *Handbook of bereavement research and practice: Advances in theory and intervention* (pp. 511–530). Washington, DC: American Psychological Association.

Parkes, C. (1972). *Bereavement: Studies of grief in adult life.* New York: International Universities Press.

Paul, N. L., & Grosser, G. H. (1965). Operational mourning and its role in conjoint family therapy. *Community Mental Health Journal, 1,* 339–345.

Pincus, L. (1974). *Death and the family.* New York: Pantheon.

Polloch, G. H. (1989). *The mourning-liberation process* (Vol. 1). New Haven, CT: International University Press.

Prideaux, S. (2005). *Edvard Munch—Behind the scream.* New Haven, CT: Yale University Press.

Prigerson, H. G., Horowitz, M. J., Jacobs, S. C., Parkes, C. M., Aslan, M., Goodkin, K., . . . Maciejewski, P. K. (2009). Prolonged grief disorder: Psychometric validation of criteria proposed for *DSM-V* and *ICD-11*. *PLoS Med, 6*(8), e1000121. doi:10.1371/journal.pmed.1000121

Rosenthal, P. A. (1980). Short term family therapy and pathological grief resolution with children and adolescents. *Family Process, 19,* 151–159.

Seikkula, J., Arnkil, T. E., & Hoffman, L. (2006). *Dialogical meetings in social networks.* London: Karnac Books.

Stroebe, M., & Schut, H. (2001). Model of coping with bereavement: A review. In M. Stroebe, R. Hansson, W. Strobe, & H. Schut (Eds.), *Handbook of bereavement research: Consequences, coping, and care* (pp. 375–403). Washington, DC: American Psychological Association.

Walsh, F., & McGoldrick, M. (Eds.). (1991). *Living beyond loss: Death in the family.* New York: W. W. Norton.

2 Conceptual Framework for Family Bereavement Care

Strengthening Resilience

Froma Walsh

The death of a family member is often a profound loss for the entire family. This chapter presents a family systems conceptual framework for clinical assessment and intervention to facilitate adaptation in the wake of loss. Drawing together developments in theory, research, and practice, I consider the impact of death on the family as a functional unit, with far-reaching implications for all members and their relationships. I describe family challenges and risk factors for maladaptation and highlight transactional processes that foster family resilience.

From an Individual Focus to a Systemic Lens

Clinical approaches to death and loss throughout the mental health and bereavement fields, influenced strongly by the medical model, have focused on grief by an individual. From early psychoanalytic and child development literature to more recent cognitive-behavioral and constructivist approaches, the preponderance of theory, research, and practice has focused on the loss of a significant dyadic relationship for an individual—a child, parent, spouse, or sibling. Developmental approaches have examined the impact of loss on individuals at various phases over the life course.

Attachment theory has offered a well-researched basis for understanding the roots of grief in early childhood bonds with parents or other caregivers (Bowlby, 1980). According to this theory, insecure early attachments influence bereavement difficulties with both loss of the primary bond and with loss in adult relationships, leading to reactions including prolonged grief, inhibited grief, and postbereavement anxiety and depression (Mikulincer & Shaver, 2008; Rubin, Malkinson, & Witzum, 2012).

Family systems theory expanded our view of human functioning and dysfunction to include the transactional processes in the broad network of relationships. Murray Bowen (1978) described the loss experience as profoundly influenced by and, in turn, influencing family processes. In his clinical research, he observed how death or a threatened loss disrupts a family's functional equilibrium. Beyond the usual grief reactions of close relatives, emotional shockwaves can reverberate throughout an entire family system immediately or long after a death, operating through the underlying interdependence of family members. Norman Paul (Paul & Grosser, 1965) observed that unattended grief at the loss of a parent, spouse, child, sibling, or other important family member may precipitate strong and harmful reactions in other relationships, from marital distancing and divorce to precipitous replacement, extramarital affairs, and even sexual abuse. John

Byng-Hall (2004) expanded Bowlby's theories on attachment and loss through a systemic lens to demonstrate how complex dynamics affect families across the generations. In our early research and clinical practice, Monica McGoldrick and I noted serious complications of traumatic and unattended losses throughout the family system and across the generations (McGoldrick & Walsh, 2004, 2011; Walsh & McGoldrick, 1991, 2004). To advance a family systems approach in the assessment and treatment of bereavement, we articulated the following developmental framework.

A Developmental Systemic Framework

From a family systems orientation, bereavement is viewed in terms of transactional processes involving those who die and their survivors in a shared multigenerational family life cycle (McGoldrick & Walsh, 2004, 2011; Walsh & McGoldrick, 2004). A systemic approach attends to the chain of influences throughout the family relational network. Legacies of loss find expression in continuing patterns of interaction and mutual influence among the survivors over their life course and across the generations. The pain of death touches relatives' relationships with others outside the family who may never have even known the person who died.

A death in the family creates multiple losses, including the loss of unique relationships for every member, loss of functional roles, loss of the intact family unit, and loss of hopes and dreams for all that might have been. Death can disrupt a family's assumptive world (see Chapter 1) and its overall equilibrium. Distress may stem not only from grief, but also from changes in the realignment of the family emotional field (Kuhn, 1977). As Bowen (1978) observed, the intensity of the emotional reaction is influenced by the family integration at the time of the loss and by the importance of the lost member in family life. A significant loss can shake the foundation of the family, modifying its structure and requiring reorganization of the household and role functions. The impact of loss is greater if the deceased had a more central role, such as primary breadwinner, caregiver, or matriarch. The loss of an only child or one with special needs leaves a particular void. A death in highly conflicted or estranged relationships may be unexpectedly traumatic because it is too late to repair bonds.

When significant losses have been unattended or disconnected, symptoms are more likely to appear in a child or other vulnerable family member, or interpersonal conflict may erupt, without the family connecting such reactions to the loss. The family may even vigorously deny the suggestion of a possible linkage. Therefore, to better understand the meaning of symptoms and facilitate healing, it is important that the therapist assess the total family configuration, the place occupied by the dying or deceased member, and the family's overall level of functioning. The genogram and timeline are essential tools to guide family inquiry and schematize complex family patterns (McGoldrick, Gerson, & Petry, 2008).

Family Bereavement in Its Socio-Cultural Context

A systemic approach focuses on the social context of loss and how a family adapts. Multiple, recursive influences connect individuals, families, communities, larger social systems, and cultural variables. Socio-cultural factors such as poverty, discrimination, and inadequate health care render some families at higher risk for life-threatening conditions, traumatic losses, and complications in recovery with less support on which to rely (Walsh, 2006, 2007).

We explore ways that a family's community and cultural connections can support their adaptation to loss (Falicov, 2007; McGoldrick et al., 2004). Likewise, we inquire about the significance of a family's spiritual beliefs and practices, which often surface with death and loss, whether based in religious or existential concerns (Walsh, 2009b). Families that believe in an afterlife commonly find comfort in contemplating the passage of their relative to a heavenly realm and reunion with deceased loved ones and ancestors. Some faith concerns, however, can exacerbate family grief, such as religious condemnation for unrepented sins, or for suicide, sexual orientation, or failure to follow prescribed rites at death.

Nature of the Death

The impact of a death in the family is also influenced by risk factors in the loss situation and surrounding family processes (Walsh & McGoldrick, 2004), particularly in the nature and circumstances of the death.

Sudden or Prolonged Dying Process

With sudden death, family members lack time to prepare for the loss, deal with unfinished business, or even say good-bye. At the other extreme, chronic conditions and prolonged dying can deplete family caregiving and financial resources and sideline the needs of other members. Relief at the end of patient suffering can ease the pain of loss, yet provoke feelings of guilt. Moreover, families increasingly grapple with agonizing end-of-life decisions regarding treatment and life support efforts. These dilemmas can raise profound ethical and religious concerns and generate intense, long-lasting conflict within the family, making their consultations and advance planning crucial.

Ambiguous, Unacknowledged, and Stigmatized Losses

Family mourning can be impeded by ambiguity surrounding a loss, as when a loved one is missing but his or her fate is uncertain, or when the individual is in cognitive decline with dementia, which can bring gradual losses of personhood, relationships, and even recognition of loved ones (Boss, 1999). Deaths that are disenfranchised—unacknowledged or minimized by others—leave the bereaved unsupported in their grief, as commonly occurs with miscarriages, or the death of a former spouse, the very elderly, or a cherished companion animal (Doka, 2002; Walsh, 2009a). Losses for same-sex couples and families can be complicated by family or religious disapproval and by legal disenfranchisement. Stigma, common with suicide, post-traumatic stress disorder, or HIV/AIDS, can foster secrecy, misinformation, and estrangement, thus impairing family and social support, critical care, and prevention efforts.

Violent Death and Traumatic Loss

Complicated family grief is, of course, common with violent and traumatic deaths (Walsh, 2007). Most killings in community violence are sparked by personal grievances and are

targeted, not random. Family members, struggling to comprehend these acts, often rumi-
nate over whether they might have made a difference. Sensitive inquiry about recent or
past traumatic loss is important, particularly in war, refugee experiences, major disasters,
or chronic, complex trauma and violence. Post-traumatic stress symptoms affect many
family members and their ongoing relationships (Figley, 1998). Mass trauma, with loss
of hope or the impetus for retaliation—the latter often to seek justice or restore family or
collective group honor—can perpetuate suffering and mutually destructive cycles across
the generations. Strengthening the resilience of affected families and communities helps
them to rebuild their lives (Walsh, 2007).

A Family Life Cycle Perspective

A family life cycle perspective considers the reciprocal influences of several generations
as they move forward over time and as they approach and respond to loss (McGoldrick & Walsh, 2004; Walsh & McGoldrick, 2013). A death in the family is not simply a
short-term event; it may involve a complex set of changing conditions with a history and
a future course. Well-functioning families tend to have an evolutionary sense of time
and acceptance of a continual process of growth, change, and loss over the generations
(Beavers & Hampson, 2003). This perspective helps members to see disruptive losses
and transitions as milestones on their shared passage through life. In contrast, very dysfunctional families show maladaptive patterns in dealing with losses, often becoming
stuck in the past or rushing ahead and cutting themselves off from painful memories
and contacts.

Throughout their life cycle, surviving family members seek to make sense of each
death, as they integrate this with their other life experiences, especially losses. Their construction of the death may change over time, and it may influence present and future
approaches to other losses. Each loss ties in with all other losses, yet is unique in its
meaning.

Timing of Loss in the Family Life Cycle

The particular timing of a loss influences family adaptation (McGoldrick & Walsh,
2011). Construction of a family timeline by a therapist can facilitate the tracking of
significant losses and other critical events in the multigenerational system (McGoldrick
et al., 2008).

Untimely Losses

Complicated mourning in the immediate and extended family is common when deaths
shatter chronological or social expectations, particularly early spousal, parent, or child
loss (Rando, 1986; Worden, 2001). Families often experience untimely losses as unjust, ending a life and relationships before their prime and dashing shared hopes and dreams for
the future. For survivors, these losses can be shocking and isolating, without emotional
preparation or social support by peers. In families raising children, combined financial,
homemaking, and child-rearing demands can deplete energy and complicate mourning

for the bereaved. Certainly, the death of a child is especially hard to bear and produces long-lasting grief. Survivor guilt can block parents and siblings from achieving success or satisfaction in life. When a sibling is expected to fulfill parents' hopes and dreams, conflicting family injunctions to replace—but not surpass—the lost child can derail the sibling's life pursuits (Legg & Sherick, 1979; Walsh & McGoldrick, 1991).

Pile Up of Multiple Losses and Other Stressors

When a death coincides with other stress or loss, incompatible demands and cumulative strains are likely to overload family functioning and interfere with grief (McGoldrick & Walsh,2011;Walsh&McGoldrick,1991,2004).Complications are more likely when bereavement coincides with other stressful family transitions that require redefinition of roles and relationships—such as marriage, birth of a child, launching of young adult children, divorce, or remarriage and stepfamily formation. At such times, extended kin and social support are crucial to facilitate attention to grief and to other relationships and transitional challenges. This situation ushers in heightened vulnerability and risk for subsequent problems, particularly in under-resourced families and communities (Walsh, 2006).

Past Losses and Intergenerational Legacies

The convergence of developmental and multigenerational strains increases distress and the risk for dysfunction (McGoldrick & Walsh, 2011). If past losses have been shattering or mourning was unattended, problematic legacies can fuel catastrophic fears of death and loss. When painful memories and emotions are reactivated, family members may lose perspective, conflate immediate situations with past events, and become overwhelmed by or cut off from unbearable feelings and contacts. It is important for a therapist to note anniversary patterns, such as a child's symptoms upon reaching the age of an older sibling's death. Some families function well until they reach a developmental milestone that was traumatic a generation earlier. In several striking clinical cases, an adolescent's violent act or suicide attempt occurred at the same age that a parent had experienced a violent death (Byng-Hall, 2004; Walsh & McGoldrick, 1991, 2004). Byng-Hall theorized that such unresolved traumatic loss scenarios are transmitted through covert family scripts and replicated in the next generation.

The New Normal Family: Many Varied Pathways through Life

Today, with a broader societal definition of what comprises family and varied life trajectories, an expanded view of the family life cycle is required. Most lives do not fit into the sequential developmental stages described as normative in past decades (Walsh, 2012). For example, during one's lifetime, it is now increasingly common to marry two or more times and to rear children at different developmental phases, often across households, and to have periods of cohabitation or single parenting. Children and parents are likely to transition in and out of household and kinship arrangements over a more fluid life course. In today's more complex arrangements, families can find themselves buffering transitions entailing multiple losses, thus restabilizing and reconfiguring their lives.

With many such varied relational pathways through life, the family may overlook significant losses, which often entail more complicated grief. For example, when couples lack the legal protection of marriage and parental rights, surviving partners may be denied death benefits and continuing relationships with children they have raised. In divorced families, the death of the custodial parent may spark conflicts between the grandparents and the non-custodial parent over the custody and future rearing of children. Further, the death of an uninvolved non-custodial parent may be complicated by residual feelings from the divorce, including the children's sense of abandonment. In another situation, the death of a former spouse or once-close relative may bring surprisingly strong and complex grief reactions. Children's losses of kin or step relations who have been important to them at some phase in their development may also be significant. With the death of a remarried parent where loyalty conflicts persist, children from the prior marriage may vehemently contest a will that favors a stepparent and stepchildren. Fraught decisions about burial or comingling of ashes with the first spouse can rekindle their old reunion fantasies to unite their parents for all time.

From Family Dysfunction to Family Resilience Orientation

Attention to family processes in clinical theory, research, and practice has tended to focus on identifying and reducing dysfunctional patterns and risks for maladaptation to loss. A growing body of research on non-clinical families reveals a broad range of family functioning in dealing with life challenges (Walsh, 2012), although few studies as of the date of this publication focus on systemic processes in bereavement (Traylor, Hayslip, Kaminski, & York, 2003).

In my own work, I was impressed by the strengths, supportive bonds, and potential for positive growth forged by so many families from tragic loss and other devastating experiences. I redirected my attention from how families falter in response to serious life challenges to how families can recover and regain the ability to thrive. This is family resilience.

Theory and research on individual resilience (Bonanno, 2004; Luthar, 2006), post-traumatic growth (Tedeschi & Calhoun, 2004), and family stress, adaptation, and robustness (Patterson, 2002) have informed my development of a family resilience framework to guide clinical practice (Walsh, 1996, 2003). Synthesizing findings in the literature on resilience and well-functioning families, nine key processes appear in three domains of family functioning, which clinicians can facilitate: family belief systems, organizational resources, and communication/problem-solving processes (Walsh, 2003, 2006). This framework has been applied in intervention and prevention services with families facing a range of adverse situations and, in particular, in family bereavement and traumatic loss (Walsh, 2006, 2007, 2012). Other researchers have also applied a resilience orientation in work with traumatic losses (e.g., Boss, 2007; Landau & Saul, 2004).

Beyond coping and adaptation, family development of resilience can yield personal and relational transformation and positive growth. For instance, whereas the death of a child often heightens risk for marital distancing and divorce, other couples report that their bond was strengthened through the tragedy (Oliver, 1999). Through their collaboration and mutual support, struggling couples and families often emerge from painful losses stronger and more resourceful in meeting challenges (Greeff & Human, 2004). Families may develop new insights and abilities, reappraising life priorities and committing to a new purpose in memory of their loved one, such as compassionate help for others who are suffering or social action to benefit the community (Walsh, 2006). A death or threatened loss can heighten appreciation of loved ones and spur efforts to repair grievances. Legacies of resilience can be found in adaptive response to past events, inspiring current efforts. Family histories, stories, and role models of courage, tenacity, and ingenuity in dealing with painful losses can offer inspiration to face new challenges (Walsh, 2007).

Family Adaptation to Loss

Death poses shared adaptational challenges for families, with immediate and long-term ramifications for all members, their relationships, and their shared identity and future vision (Shapiro, 1994). Family adaptation to loss does not mean a quick resolution, in the sense of some complete, "once-and-for-all" getting over it. Mourning processes have no orderly sequence or fixed timetable, and significant losses may not be fully resolved. Mourning and recovery are gradual processes over time, usually lessening in intensity; yet various facets of grief may reemerge with unexpected intensity, particularly with anniversaries and other nodal events. For family members, a dynamic oscillation occurs in adaptive coping over time, alternating between loss and restoration, attending at times to grief and at other times to ongoing and new challenges (Stroebe & Schut, 2010). Adaptive mourning involves transforming the relationship with the deceased from physical presence to continuing bonds through spiritual connection, memories, deeds that honor the dead, and stories that are passed through kinship networks and across the generations (Klass, 2009; Walsh & McGoldrick, 2004).

Facilitating Family Adaptational Tasks

Families have their own coping styles, influenced by their socio-cultural context, values, and resources. Although mindful of the wide variation in individual responses to loss (Wortman & Silver, 1989), as well as diverse cultural and religious influences (Rosenblatt, 2013; Walsh, 2009b), our research and clinical experience suggest that certain crucial family challenges, if not addressed, can increase members' vulnerability to dysfunction and the risk of family conflict and dissolution. Family adaptation and resilience involve four transactional processes that assist in coping with the loss and moving forward with life. They entail how a family (1) approaches a threatened or impending loss; (2) facilitates emotional sharing, mutual support, and meaning making; (3) buffers disruptions and reorganizes to meet new demands; and (4) fosters reinvestment in life (Walsh, 2006). We conceptualize these four challenges as tasks (as does Worden, 2008, for individual bereavement), which families actively engage in and which clinicians can facilitate. These four major family tasks promote immediate and long-term adaptation for family members and strengthen them as a functional unit (Walsh & McGoldrick, 1991, 2004).

Shared Acknowledgment of the Death and Loss

Family members, each in their own way, need to confront the reality of a death and grapple with its meaning for themselves, each other, and the family as a whole. In most cultures, adaptation is facilitated by direct contact with the dying person and allowing children the opportunity to express their love and say good-bye (Bowen, 1978). Those unable to accept the reality of death may avoid contact or become angry with others who are grieving, often sparking long-term conflict and cutoffs.

With sudden, unexpected death, mourning starts abruptly, and families may need help managing chaotic, overwhelming feelings and practical matters. By contrast, with threatened or expected loss, there is more time for emotional preparation and crucial decision making. The anticipation of loss can heighten appreciation of loved ones, especially when relationships have been taken for granted or blocked by petty grievances. Where relationships have been wounded in the past, therapists may find an opportunity to help members repair grievances and make amends (Walsh, 2006). We encourage families to shift priorities and draw on resources so that they can make the most of their time. They often report that despite the sorrow of loss, this was their most precious time together.

A *family life review* can be valuable for many families, including the dying person. A conjoint format expands the benefits of individual life-review sessions that are found to facilitate the integration and acceptance of one's life and approaching death (Walsh, 2011). Sharing reminiscences can be helpful for couples and family members, incorporating multiple perspectives and subjective experiences of their life over time. When families share their varied perceptions on hopes and dreams, satisfactions and disappointments, this process enlarges the family story, builds mutual empathy, and can heal old wounds. Earlier conflicts or hurts that led to cutoffs or frozen images and expectations can be reconsidered from new vantage points. Misunderstandings and faulty assumptions can be clarified, and relationships can be brought up to date. Individuals facing death can often become more open and forthright about earlier transgressions or shame-laden secrets. Past mistakes and hurts can be more readily acknowledged, opening possibilities for forgiveness. At life's end, the simple words, "I'm truly sorry" and "I love you" mean more than ever. Precious end-of-life conversations can be recorded. Family photos, scrapbooks, genealogies, and other stories of family history can be preserved and passed onto future generations.

Shared Experience of the Loss

Family and community rituals marking the end of a life and passage to the hereafter have been central in possibly every culture and religion over the millennia (Walsh, 2009b). I actively encourage family members' participation in funeral and burial or cremation rites, as well as later visits together to the grave or memorial site, which provide opportunities to pay respects, share grief, and comfort one another (Imber-Black, 2012). Whether through religious or secular memorial tributes, I encourage family members to find meaningful ways to celebrate and honor the life of their loved one and their time together. It is never too late to hold a memorial service, lay a headstone at a grave, hold a ceremony to scatter ashes, or plant a tree in memory of a loved one. Still, not all occasions will necessarily be embraced. After a death, family holidays, birthdays, and special events, for example, are often painful for survivors, who may avoid them altogether. I encourage survivors instead to find ways to remember the deceased on these occasions as they move on with life.

It is important for clinicians to foster a family climate of trust, empathic support, and respect for varied responses to loss. Open communication is vital, given the turmoil in the immediate aftermath of loss and the complexity of family mourning processes over time. Tolerance is needed for the wide range and fluctuation of feelings of family members, depending on their developmental phase; unique relationships with the deceased and implications of the loss; individual coping styles; different pacing in recovery; and the role functioning and demands of other life challenges. At different moments, strong emotions may surface, including complicated and mixed feelings of anger, disappointment, helplessness, relief, guilt, and abandonment, which are present to some extent in most family relationships. Fears of intense feelings or conflict can lead members to avoid ongoing contact and communication about the loss experience. Blocked grief may explode in family conflict or cutoff. A family may scapegoat or extrude a member who directly expresses unacceptable feelings, such as anger toward the deceased. The shock and pain of a traumatic loss can shatter family cohesion, leaving members isolated and unsupported in their grief. Fragmented aspects of this complicated grief may be expressed by various family members: one may carry all the sadness, while another expresses only anger; another may show relief.

The mourning process also involves family members' active efforts to make meaning of the loss situation. The meaning of a loss and responses to it are shaped by the family belief system, which, in turn, may be modified by these loss experiences. Members' stories, explanations, and expectations are influenced by multigenerational, cultural, and spiritual belief systems, as well as the family's position in their social world. Clinicians can support family efforts to comprehend the loss—including its ongoing and future implications—and to place it in some meaningful perspective that fits coherently with their life experience and aspirations. Gaining a shared sense of coherence fosters resilience in mastering their challenges, often yielding new purpose and stronger bonds (Antonovsky & Sourani, 1988; Nadeau, 2008; Walsh, 2003, 2006). Coming to terms with loss involves finding ways to weave the experience into the fabric of both individual and relational life passage.

Reorganization of the Family System

The death of a family member often leaves a hole in the fabric of the family, disrupting established patterns of functioning. For adaptive flexibility and cohesion/connectedness, families may need to realign relationships and redistribute role functions to compensate for the loss and restabilize family life.

Yet family roles and responsibilities may interfere with grieving. For instance, a parent's imperative as financial provider may block emotional expression to maintain control for job functioning. This can reverberate in lack of support to a grieving spouse and distancing or conflict in the couple's relationship. In single-parent families, children may collude to keep a bereaved parent strong because everyone depends on him or her (Fulmer, 1983). It is important for the therapist to help overburdened family members structure the time and space needed for their own grieving and to rally the contributions of others to provide essential respite.

With the death of a member vital to family functioning, family reorganization often requires attention before members can deal with their own grief. It is important for families to buffer disruptions in daily life and to pace their reorganization. Rigid adherence to old patterns of family life may no longer fit emerging priorities. Some families take flight from losses by quickly disposing of all of the deceased's clothes and other possessions or by moving precipitously out of their homes or communities. These dislocations generate more disruptions in family life and social supports; uprooted children may also need to adjust to new schools and the loss of friends.

Reinvestment in Other Relationships and Life Pursuits

As time passes, survivors need to reconfigure their lives and relationships to move forward, reenvisioning life aspirations. Some who have experienced lengthy anticipatory loss during the decedent's protracted illness may be ready to move on emotionally much sooner than others (Rolland, 1990). In some cases, the formation of other attachments may be blocked by overidealization of the deceased, a sense of disloyalty, or fear of another loss. Well-intentioned relatives may urge precipitous remarriage to fill the deceased parent's former role with children. Yet if the loss has not been integrated, children may resist acceptance of a new stepparent, deeming it disloyal. Likewise, unmourned losses can create complications in new relationships, such as when the bereaved seek immediate replacement through affairs, precipitous marriages, pregnancies, or overattachment with another child. Therapists can encourage families to navigate and pace their journey ahead.

Family Assessment and Intervention

Taking a broadly inclusive view of the family, a systemic assessment attends to the multiple influences in bereavement throughout the relational network, including important roles and relationships within and beyond households, biological and step relations, and informal kinship bonds. The genogram and timeline, noting family dynamics, structural patterns, relational resources, and past loss experiences, guide family inquiry and intervention planning (McGoldrick, Gerson, & Petry, 2008). The therapist should evaluate the general level of family functioning, state of relationships, and changes with the loss, including potential resources in the extended family network. The therapist should explore (1) the impact of the death and loss on the family system, its members, and their relationships; and (2) the family approach to the loss situation, including its preparedness, immediate coping responses, and long-term adaptive strategies. Both the factual circumstances of a death and the matrix of meanings it holds for the family need careful exploration.

Clinicians do well to focus all family assessments not only on problematic family patterns but also on positive influences that can contribute to resilience, whether past, present, and potential. Therapists should ask about the ways in which a family has dealt with adversity, examining models and stories of resilience in the multigenerational family network that might inspire efforts to master current bereavement challenges. The search for relational resources is worthwhile to garner practical and emotional support through extended kinship and social networks. How might aunts, uncles, godparents, or nonresidential parents contribute, each in their own ways, to shore up resources, or rally as a collaborative team to prepare for the loss and provide mutual support once death occurs? Many sources of support are needed for the bereaved to revision their future and rebuild their lives. Families are encouraged to draw on their cultural and spiritual foundations, such as healing rituals, contemplative practices, and involvement in their faith community. Where spiritual distress impedes recovery processes, consultations with chaplains or other pastoral care professionals prove invaluable, as befits the family's spiritual orientation.

Contemporary family therapy approaches are collaborative and strengths-oriented, and they draw from various models—from intergenerational, Bowen, and attachment models to structural/strategic and postmodern narrative approaches (Walsh, 2011). Family contact may range from consultation and brief intervention to more intensive therapy, flexibly combining individual, couple, and family sessions (e.g., Kissane, Lichtenthal, & Zaider, 2007) to work with various members and subsystems (e.g., spousal, siblings, or extended kin) as their issues surface. Decisions at various points are guided by a systemic view of loss and recovery processes. Psychoeducational and resilience-oriented multi-family groups (e.g., Rolland & Walsh, 2006; Walsh, 2012) are finding increasing application with couples or families facing similar adaptive challenges with loss (e.g., perinatal losses, refugee settlement, and disaster recovery) for sharing useful information, mutual support, and strategies for coping and resilience. Therapists offer compassionate listening to family members' shared and unique experiences of loss, affirm their strengths alongside their suffering and struggle, and encourage their mutual support and active collaboration for adaptation and resilience.

Conclusion

Death and loss pose painful and far-reaching adaptational challenges for families. A family systems framework for clinical practice addresses the reverberations of a death for all members, their relationships, and their role as a functional unit, attuned to each family's life passage and socio-cultural context. This approach to loss is guided by an appraisal of the family's adaptational challenges, variables that heighten vulnerability and risk, and processes that foster recovery and resilience. In helping families deal with their losses, we enable them to live and love fully beyond loss.

References

Antonovsky, A., & Sourani, T. (1988). Family sense of coherence and family adaptation. *Journal of Marriage and the Family, 50,* 79–92.

Beavers, W. R., & Hampson, R. B. (2003). Measuring family competence: The Beavers systems model. In F. Walsh (Ed.), *Normal family processes* (3rd ed., pp. 549–580). New York: Guilford Press.

Bonanno, G. A. (2004). Loss, trauma, and human resilience. *American Psychologist, 59,* 20–28.

Boss, P. (1999). *Ambiguous loss.* Cambridge, MA: Harvard University Press.

Boss, P. (2007). *Traumatic loss, recovery, & resilience.* New York: W. W. Norton.

Bowen, M. (1978). *Family therapy in clinical practice.* New York: Jason Aronson.

Bowlby, J. (1980). *Attachment and loss: Vol. 3. Loss, sadness, and depression.* London: Hogarth Press.

Byng-Hall, J. (2004). Loss and family scripts. In F. Walsh & M. McGoldrick (Eds.), *Living beyond loss: Death in the family.* New York: W. W. Norton.

Doka, K. (2002). *Disenfranchised grief.* Champaign, IL: Research Press.

Falicov, C. J. (2007). Working with transnational immigrants: Expanding meanings of family, community and culture. *Family Process, 46,* 157–172.

Figley, C. (1998). *The traumatology of grieving.* San Francisco, CA: Jossey-Bass.

Fulmer, R. (1983). A structural approach to unresolved mourning in single parent family systems. *Journal of Marital and Family Therapy, 9*(3), 259–270.

Greeff, A., & Human, B. (2004). Resilience in families in which a parent has died. *American Journal of Family Therapy, 32,* 27–42.

Imber-Black, E. (2012). The value of rituals in family life. In F. Walsh (Ed.), *Normal family processes* (4th ed., pp. 483–497). New York: Guilford Press.

Kissane, D., Lichtenthal, W. G., & Zaider, T. (2007). Family care before and after bereavement. *OMEGA—Journal of Death and Dying, 56,* 21–32.

Klass, D. (2009). Bereavement narratives: Continuing bonds in the twenty-first century. *Mortality, 14,* 305–306.

Kuhn, J. S. (1977). Realignment of emotional forces following loss. *Family, 5,* 19–20.

Landau, J., & Saul, J. (2004). Facilitating family and community resilience in response to major disasters. In F. Walsh & M. McGoldrick (Eds.), *Living beyond loss: Death in the family* (2nd ed., pp. 285–309). New York: W. W. Norton.

Legg, C., & Sherick, I. (1979). The replacement child: A developmental tragedy. *Child Psychiatry & Human Development, 7,* 113–126.

Luthar, S. (2006). Resilience in development: A synthesis of research across 5 decades. In D. Cicchetti & D. J. Cohen (Eds.), *Developmental psychopathology* (2nd ed., Vol. 3, pp. 739–795). Hoboken, NJ: Wiley.

McGoldrick, M., Gerson, R., & Petry, S. (2008). *Genograms: Assessment and intervention* (3rd ed.). New York: W. W. Norton.

McGoldrick, M., Schlesinger, J. M., Hines, P. M., Lee, E., Chan, J., Almeida, R., . . . Petry, S. (2004). Mourning in different cultures. In F. Walsh & M. McGoldrick (Eds.), *Living beyond loss: Death in the family* (2nd ed., pp. 119–160). New York: W. W. Norton.

McGoldrick, M., & Walsh, F. (2004). A time to mourn: Death and the family life cycle. In F. Walsh & M. McGoldrick (Eds.), *Living beyond loss: Death in the family* (2nd ed., pp. 27–46). New York: W. W. Norton.

McGoldrick, M., & Walsh, F. (2011). Death, loss, and the family life cycle. In M. McGoldrick, B. Carter, & N. Garcia Preto (Eds.), *The expanding family life cycle* (4th ed., pp. 278–291). Boston: Allyn & Bacon.

Mikulincer, M., & Shaver, P. (2008). An attachment perspective on bereavement. In M. Stroebe, R. Hansson, H. Schut, & W. Stroebe (Eds.), *Handbook of bereavement research: 21st century perspectives* (pp. 87–112). Washington, DC: American Psychological Association.

Nadeau, J. W. (2008). Meaning-making in bereaved families: Assessment, intervention, and future research. In M. Stroebe, R. Hansson, H. Schut, & W. Stroebe (Eds.), *Handbook of bereavement research: 21st century perspectives* (pp. 511–530). Washington, DC: American Psychological Association.

Oliver, L. E. (1999). Effects of a child's death on the marital relationship: A review. *OMEGA—Journal of Death and Dying, 39*(3), 197–227.

Paterson, J.M. (2002). Integrating family resilience and family stress theory. *Journal of Marriage and the Family, 64,* 349-360.

Paul, N., & Grosser, G. (1965). Operational mourning and its role in conjoint family therapy. *Community Mental Health, 1,* 339–345.

Rando, T. (Ed.). (1986). *The parental loss of a child.* Champaign, IL: Research Press.

Rolland, J. (1990). Anticipatory loss: A family systems developmental framework. *Family Process, 29,* 229–244.

Rolland, J. S., & Walsh, F. (2006). Facilitating family resilience with childhood illness and disability. [Special issue on the family.] *Pediatric Opinion, 18,* 1–11.

Rosenblatt, P. C. (2013). Family grief in cross-cultural perspective. [Special issue. Bereavement: Family perspectives.] *Family Science, 4*(1), 12–19.

Rubin, S. S., Malikson, R., & Witzum, E. (2012). *Working with the bereaved: Multiple lenses on loss and mourning.* New York: Routledge.

Shapiro, E. (1994). *Grief as a family process: A developmental approach to clinical practice.* New York: Guilford Press.

Stroebe, M., & Schut, H. (2010). The dual process model of coping and bereavement: A decade on. *OMEGA—Journal of Death and Dying, 61,* 273–289.

Tedeschi, R. G., & Calhoun, L. G. (2004). Posttraumatic growth: Conceptual foundations and empirical evidence. *Psychological Inquiry, 15,* 1–18.

Traylor, E., Hayslip, B., Kaminski, P., & York, C. (2003). Relationships between grief and family system characteristics: A cross-lagged longitudinal analysis. *Death Studies, 27,* 575–601.

Walsh, F. (1996). The concept of family resilience: Crisis and challenge. *Family Process, 35,* 261–281.

Walsh, F. (2003). Family resilience: A framework for clinical practice. *Family Process, 42*(1), 1–18.

Walsh, F. (2006). *Strengthening family resilience* (2nd ed.). New York: Guilford Press.

Walsh, F. (2007). Traumatic loss and major disasters: Strengthening family and community resilience. *Family Process, 46,* 207–227.

Walsh, F. (2009a). Human–animal bonds: The role of pets in family systems and family therapy. *Family Process, 48*(4), 481–499.

Walsh, F. (2009b). Spiritual resources in adaptation to death and loss. In F. Walsh (Ed.), *Spiritual resources in family therapy* (2nd ed., pp. 81–102). New York: Guilford Press.

Walsh, F. (2011). Family therapy: Systemic approaches to practice. In J. Brandell (Ed.), *Theory and practice in clinical social work* (2nd ed., pp. 153–178). Thousand Oaks, CA: Sage.

Walsh, F. (Ed.). (2012). *Normal family processes: Growing diversity and complexity* (4th ed.). New York: Guilford Press.

Walsh, F., & McGoldrick, M. (1991). *Living beyond loss: Death in the family.* New York: W. W. Norton.

Walsh, F., & McGoldrick, M. (2004). Loss and the family: A systemic perspective. In F. Walsh & M. McGoldrick (Eds.), *Living beyond loss: Death in the family* (2nd ed., pp. 3–26). New York: W. W. Norton.

Walsh, F., & McGoldrick, M. (2013). Bereavement: A family life cycle perspective. [Special issue. Bereavement: Family perspectives.] *Family Science, 4*(1), 20–27.

Worden, J. W. (2001). *Children and grief: When a parent dies.* New York: Guilford Press.

Worden, J. W. (2008). *Grief counseling and grief therapy* (4th ed.). New York: Springer.

Wortman, C., & Silver, R. (1989). The myths of coping with loss. *Journal of Counseling and Clinical Psychology, 57,* 349–357.

3 The Family with Chronic Physical Disorders
An Integrative Model

John S. Rolland

Illness, disability and death are universal experiences in families. The real question is not if we will face serious health issues in our families, but when in our lives they will occur, under what conditions, how serious they will be, and for how long. With major advances in medical technology, ever-growing numbers of families are living with chronic disorders for longer periods and coping with multiple conditions simultaneously. This chapter provides a normative, preventive model for psychoeducation, assessment, and intervention with families facing chronic and life-threatening conditions. This model offers a systemic view of healthy family adaptation to serious illness as a developmental process over time amid the complexities of contemporary family life.

Over the past 30 years, family-centered, collaborative, biopsychosocial models of health care have grown and evolved (Doherty & Baird, 1983; Engel, 1977; McDaniel, Campbell, Hepworth, & Lorenz, 2005; McDaniel, Hepworth, & Doherty, 2013; Miller, McDaniel, Rolland, & Feetham, 2006; Rolland, 1994a, in press; Seaburn, Gunn, Mauksch, Gawinski, & Lorenz, 1996; Wood et al., 2008). There is substantial evidence for the mutual influence of family functioning, health, and physical illness (Carr & Springer, 2010; D'Onofrio & Lahey, 2010; Weihs, Fisher, & Baird, 2001) and the usefulness of family-centered interventions with chronic health conditions (Campbell, 2003; Hartmann, Bazner, Wild, Eisler, & Herzog, 2010; Kazak, 2005; Law & Crane, 2007; Martire, Lustig, Schulz, Miller, & Helgeson, 2004; Martire, Schulz, Helgeson, Small, & Saghafi, 2010; Shields, Finley, Chawla, & Meadors, 2012). Weihs and colleagues (2001) summarized the increasing body of research regarding the impact of serious illness on families across the life span and the relationship of family dynamics to illness behavior, treatment adherence, and disease course.

There is a clear need for a conceptual model that guides both clinical practice and research, which comprehensively organizes our thinking about all the complex interactions among biological disease, the patient, family members/caregivers, and involved health care providers. This model should accommodate the changing landscape of interactions between these parts of the system over time.

Most families enter the world of illness and disability without a psychosocial map. Appropriate clinical interventions, family education, and national policies to support these families are lacking. To create a normative context for their illness experience, families need the following foundation:

1. They need a systems-based psychosocial understanding of the condition. This means learning the expected pattern of practical and affective demands arising

from the illness over the course of the condition. Families need a time frame for disease-related developmental tasks associated with different phases of the unfolding disorder.

2. Families need to understand themselves as a systemic functional unit able to deliver care and support.

3. Families need an appreciation of individual and family life cycle patterns and transitions to facilitate their incorporation of changing developmental priorities in relation to evolving challenges of a chronic disorder.

4. Finally, families need to understand the cultural, ethnic, spiritual, and gender-based beliefs that guide the type of caregiving system and meanings they construct. Family understanding in these areas facilitates a more holistic integration of the disorder and the family as a functional family-health/illness system evolving over time.

Overview of Family Systems Illness Model

How can we organize this large and complex landscape in a manner useful to clinicians and families dealing with chronic illness? The Family Systems Illness (FSI) model (Rolland, 1990, 1994a, 2005, 2010, 2013, in press) can provide a useful framework for evaluation, formulation, and intervention with families. This model was developed primarily through clinical experience with more than 1,500 families at the Chicago Center for Family Health, affiliated with the University of Chicago. The model is grounded in a strengths-oriented perspective, viewing family relationships as a potential resource, and emphasizing possibilities for resilience and growth, not just their liabilities and risks (Walsh, 2006). Positioning the family as the interactive focal point, this model is based on a systemic interaction between an illness and family that evolves over time. The goodness of "fit" between the psychosocial demands of the disorder chronologically and the family style of functioning and resources is a prime determinant of successful versus dysfunctional coping and adaptation.

The FSI model distinguishes three dimensions: (1) "psychosocial types" of physical disorders, (2) major phases in their evolution, and (3) key family system variables. Family variables given particular emphasis include the following: the family and individual life cycles, particularly in relation to the time phases of a disorder; multigenerational legacies related to illness and loss; and belief systems (including influences of culture, ethnicity, spirituality, and gender) (see Figure 3.1).

Psychosocial Types of Illness

The standard disease classification is based on purely biological criteria clustered to establish a medical diagnosis and treatment plan, rather than on the psychosocial demands on patients and their families. I have proposed a different classification scheme that provides a better link between the biological and psychosocial worlds—thereby clarifying the relationship between chronic illness and the family (Rolland, 1984, 1994a). This typology seeks to define meaningful and useful categories with similar psychosocial demands for a wide array of chronic illnesses affecting individuals across the life span. Illness patterning can vary in terms of *onset, course, outcome,*

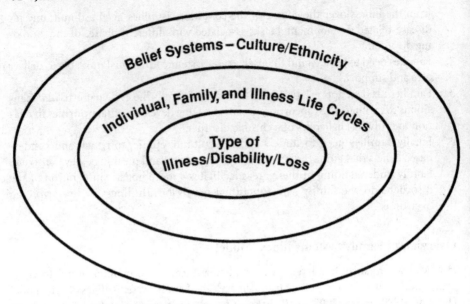

Figure 3.1 The Family Systems Illness model integrates dimensions of the illness with the life cycle of the person and family and their culturally determined belief systems. Adapted from J. S. Rolland, *Families, Illness, & Disability: An Integrative Treatment Model* (New York: Basic Books, 1994). Adapted with permission.

incapacitation, and the *level of uncertainty* about its trajectory. Let us examine each of these variables.

Onset. Illnesses can be divided into those that have either an acute clinical onset, such as a stroke, or gradual onset, such as dementia. For acute onset illnesses, affective and practical changes are compressed into a short time, requiring more rapid family mobilization and crisis management skills. In such situations, families need to be helped to tolerate highly charged emotional situations, exchange roles flexibly, problem-solve efficiently, and utilize outside resources.

Course. The course of chronic diseases can take three general forms: progressive, constant, or relapsing/episodic. With a *progressive* disease, such as metastatic cancer, disability worsens in a stepwise or gradual way. As the disease progresses, the family typically lives with perpetual symptoms and the prospect of continual changes in relationships and roles. Family caregivers may experience exhaustion with few periods of relief from the demands of the illness, and there may be new caretaking and financial challenges over time.

With a *constant*-course illness, the occurrence of an initial event, such as a single heart attack or spinal-cord injury, is followed by a stable biological course. Typically, after an initial period of recovery, the illness is characterized by some clear-cut deficit or limitation. The family is faced with a semi-permanent change that is stable and predictable over time. For example, a young woman's successful treatment for uterine cancer may include a hysterectomy, whereby she (and her spouse or partner) must absorb the loss of her childbearing ability. The potential for family exhaustion exists without the strain of new role demands over time.

A *relapsing* or *episodic* course illness, such as back problems or some forms of treatment-responsive chronic leukemia, is distinguished by stable low-symptom periods that alternate with periods of flare-up or exacerbation. Families are strained by both the frequency of transitions between crisis and non-crisis, and the ongoing uncertainty of *when* a recurrence will occur. This requires family flexibility to alternate between two patterns of family organization. The wide psychological discrepancy between low-symptom periods versus flare-up is particularly taxing.

Outcome. The extent to which a chronic illness leads to death or shortens one's life span clearly has profound psychosocial impact. The continuum ranges from illnesses that do not typically affect the life span to those that are progressive and usually fatal, such as some metastatic cancers. An intermediate, more unpredictable category includes both illnesses that can shorten the life span, such as heart disease, and those that can cause sudden death, such as hemophilia. A major difference between these kinds of outcomes is the degree to which the family experiences anticipatory loss and its pervasive effects on family life (Rolland, 1990, 2004, 2006b).

Incapacitation. Disability can involve impairment of cognition (e.g., dementia), impaired sensation (e.g., blindness), impaired movement (e.g., stroke with paralysis), decreased stamina (e.g., heart disease), and disfigurement (e.g., mastectomy), as well as social stigma (e.g., HIV/AIDS). The extent, kind, and timing of disability typically affect the degree of family stress. For instance, combined cognitive and motor deficits caused by a major stroke generally necessitate greater family reorganization than a condition without cognitive impairment. For progressive diseases, like Alzheimer's disease, cognitive disability looms as an increasing problem in later phases of the illness, allowing a family more time to prepare for anticipated changes; likewise, the ill member may participate in disease-related family planning while still cognitively able (Boss, 2005).

Level of Uncertainty. The *predictability* of the specific way in which a disease unfolds, and at what rate, overlie all other variables. For illnesses with highly unpredictable courses, such as non-Hodgkin's lymphoma or multiple sclerosis, family coping and future planning can be hindered by anticipatory anxiety and ambiguity about what family members will actually encounter. Families that can put long-term uncertainty into perspective are best prepared to avoid the risks of exhaustion and dysfunction. For conditions with long-range risks, including genomic disorders, families can manage uncertainty by enhancing the following capacities: acknowledge the possibility of loss, sustain hope, and build flexibility into both the family's and each member's life cycle planning that conserves and adjusts major goals and helps circumvent the forces of uncertainty (Rolland, 1990, 2004).

By combining the kinds of onset, course, outcome, incapacitation, and predictability into a grid, we generate a typology that clusters illnesses according to similarities and differences in patterns that pose differing psychosocial demands.

Time Phases of Illness

Too often, discussions of "coping with cancer" or "dealing with life-threatening or terminal disease" approach illness as a static state, thus failing to appreciate the evolution of illness processes over time. The concept of time phase allows clinicians to think longitudinally and to understand chronic illness as an ongoing process with landmarks,

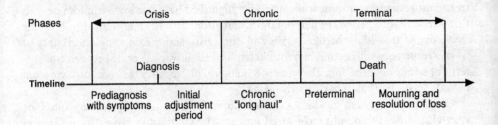

Timeline and Phases of Illness

Figure 3.2 The timelines and time phases of illness. Adapted from J. S. Rolland, *Families, Illness, & Disability: An Integrative Treatment Model* (New York: Basic Books, 1994). Adapted with permission.

transitions, and changing demands. Each phase poses its own psychosocial challenges and developmental tasks that may require different strengths, attitudes, or changes for family adaptation. Core psychosocial themes in the natural history of chronic disease can be described as three major phases: *crisis*, *chronic*, and *terminal* (see Figure 3.2 and Table 3.1). Let us discuss each phase.

Crisis. The *crisis phase* includes any symptomatic period before diagnosis through the initial readjustment period after a diagnosis and initial treatment planning. This phase presents various tasks for the ill member and family: (1) learning to cope with any symptoms or disability, (2) adapting to health care settings and treatment procedures, and (3) establishing and maintaining workable relationships with the health care team. Families optimize well-being when they can do the following: (1) view the challenge of illness as a shared challenge; (2) create illness meanings that promote family mastery and competence; (3) grieve for the loss of health; (4) gradually accept the illness as long term while maintaining a sense of continuity between their past and future; (5) pull together to cope with the immediate crisis; and (6) in the face of uncertainty, develop flexibility toward future goals.

During this initial adjustment period, health care professionals can influence a family's sense of competence and strategies used to accomplish these developmental tasks. Initial meetings and advice given at the time of diagnosis can be considered a "framing event." Because families are so vulnerable at this point, clinicians need to be extremely sensitive in their interactions with them. Who is included or excluded, such as the patient, from a discussion can be interpreted by the family as a message of how they should plan future communication. For instance, if a clinician meets with parents separately from an adolescent to give them information about a cancer diagnosis and prognosis, they may assume they were being instructed implicitly to protect their child from any discussion of the illness. Clinicians should ask both patients and family members whom they wish to include in important discussions.

With life-threatening conditions that can cause sudden death, there is a higher premium on early frank conversation. Knowing an ill member's wishes concerning heroic

Table 3.1 Time Phases of Illness Developmental Challenges

CRISIS PHASE

1. The family understands itself in systems terms
2. Gains psychosocial understanding of illness
   a) in practical and emotional terms
   b) in longitudinal and developmental terms
3. Gains appreciation of developmental perspective (individual, family, illness development)
4. Crisis reorganization
5. Creates meaning that promotes family mastery and competence
6. Views challenge of illness as a shared one in "we" terms
7. Accepts permanence of illness or disability
8. Grieves loss of family identity before chronic disorder
9. Acknowledges possibilities of further loss while sustaining hope
10. Develops flexibility to ongoing psychosocial demands of illness
11. Learns to live with symptoms
12. Adapts to treatments and health care settings
13. Establishes functional collaborative relationship with health care providers

CHRONIC PHASE

1. Maximizes autonomy for all family members given constraints of illness
2. Balances connectedness and separateness
3. Minimizes relationship skews
4. Mindfulness to possible impact on current and future phases of family and individual life cycles
5. Lives with anticipatory loss and uncertainty
6. Balances open communication (vs. avoidance, denial) and proactive planning with need to live a "normal" life, while keeping threatened loss in perspective

TERMINAL PHASE

1. Completing process of anticipatory grief and unresolved family issues
2. Supports the terminally ill member
3. Helps survivors and dying member live as fully as possible with time remaining
4. Begins the family reorganization process

Source: Adapted from J. S. Rolland, *Families, Illness, & Disability: An Integrative Treatment Model* (New York: Basic Books, 1994). Adapted with permission.

medical efforts and life support can benefit everyone. For example, in one family in which the father had serious heart disease, he and everyone else became emotionally paralyzed by fear because he and the family had avoided end-of-life decision making. Fortunately, family consultations facilitated communication whereby the father expressed his wishes regarding the limits on lifesaving efforts. This relieved his family members because they knew his feelings if they had to make life-and-death decisions. For the father, this gave him a sense of personal control over the end of his life and freed his energy to focus on living well and maximizing his physical well-being. Despite the short-run challenge of having end-of-life discussions, clinicians should keep in mind that many of the most wrenching end-of-life experiences for families occur when the wishes of a dying member are unknown or have been disregarded.

Chronic. The *chronic phase* can be marked by constancy, progression, or episodic change. It is the long haul or "day-to-day living with chronic illness" phase. Salient goals include the following: (1) pacing and avoiding burnout, (2) minimizing relationship skews between the patient and other family members, (3) maximizing autonomy and preserving or redefining individual and family developmental goals within the constraints of the illness, and (4) sustaining intimacy in the face of threatened loss. It is important for the family to try to maintain the semblance of a normal life during this period. If the illness is potentially fatal, this is a time of "living in limbo." For certain highly debilitating but not clearly fatal illnesses, such as a massive stroke or dementia, the family can feel saddled with an exhausting problem "without end." The therapist should encourage maximal autonomy for *all* family members in the face of prolonged adversity, which helps to offset feelings of being trapped and helpless.

For long-term disorders, customary patterns of intimacy for couples become skewed by discrepancies between the ill spouse and well spouse/caregiver (Rolland, 1994b). As one young husband lamented about his wife's cancer, "It was hard enough two years ago to absorb that, even if she was cured, her radiation treatment would make pregnancy impossible. Now I find it unbearable that her continued uncertain battle with cancer makes it impossible to go for our dreams like other couples our age." Normative ambivalence and escape fantasies often remain underground and contribute to survivor guilt and prolonged grief. Psychoeducational family interventions that normalize such emotions related to threatened loss can help prevent destructive cycles of blame, shame, and guilt.

When clinicians inquire about and validate the psychosocial burden of caregivers, especially well spouses, they help prevent the burden of care from becoming the only currency in family relationships. This helps families to see life-threatening illness as a challenge that is shared. In contrast, when families see the illness as solely within the domain of the patient, this misperception can be a major contributor to dysfunctional family dynamics.

Terminal. In the *terminal phase,* the inevitability of death becomes apparent and dominates family life. The family must cope with issues of separation, death, mourning, and beginning the reorganization process needed to resume family life beyond the loss (Walsh & McGoldrick, 2004). Families adapt best when they can shift their view of mastery from controlling the illness to a successful process of "letting go." Optimal coping involves emotional openness and dealing with numerous practical tasks, such as using this opportunity to share precious time together, acknowledge the impending loss, deal with unfinished business, and say their good-byes. The patient and key family members may still need to decide about such matters as a living will; the extent of medical heroics desired; preferences about dying at home, in the hospital, or at hospice; and wishes about a funeral or memorial service and burial or cremation.

Transitions between Phases. Critical transition periods link the three time phases. These are times when families reevaluate the appropriateness of their previous life structure in the face of new illness-related developmental challenges. Therapists can help families resolve unfinished business from the previous phase and thus facilitate movement through the transitions. Families can become permanently frozen in an adaptive structure that has outlived its utility (Penn, 1983). For example, the usefulness of pulling together in the crisis phase can become stifling for some family members through the chronic phase.

The New Genetics and an Extended Illness Timeline

With the mapping of the human genome comes burgeoning scientific knowledge that is rapidly increasing our understanding of the mechanisms, treatment, and prevention of disease. New genetic technologies allow physicians to test for increased risk of developing a serious and life-threatening illness before it actually occurs. This means that individuals and families can now be living with information about illness risk long before loved ones have developed symptoms (Miller et al., 2006). This significantly increases the amount of time and energy that families spend considering an illness and lengthens the timeline to include non-symptomatic phases (Rolland & Williams, 2005). These phases are awareness, pretesting, test/posttesting, and long-term adaptation once the risk is known. These time periods are distinguished by questions of uncertainty and include fundamental issues such as the potential amount of genetic knowledge medically available, decisions about how much of that information various family members choose to access, and living with the psychosocial impact of those choices.

For some, the emotional strain begins when predictive testing becomes available, continuing through the decision to pursue testing and the initial post-testing adaptation. For others, this phase begins as individuals reach significant developmental milestones at which testing is recommended. Still others become interested in testing to determine if having children may mean passing on a mutation. Other women receive recommendations to be tested for hereditary breast and ovarian cancer genes 10 years earlier than the age when a first-degree relative—a mother, sister, or daughter—received their diagnosis. Still others in high-risk families may want to know once they turn 18, as consideration of what age to start a family and whether hormonal contraception should be used (Maloney et al., 2012).

During the post-testing phases, families need to accept the permanence of the genetic information and develop meanings that preserve their sense of competency in the face of future uncertainty or loss (Rolland, 2006b; Werner-Lin, 2008). Some individuals, however, will have negative test results for dominant genes, yet still carry elevated familial risk, with uncertainty continuing about yet-to-be-identified genes.

The involvement of the health care system is very different with predictive testing as opposed to a diagnosed illness. Despite the enormous psychosocial impact when testing results are positive, families usually have limited contact with genetic counselors after initial testing. This highlights the need for ongoing, family-centered, collaborative approaches to prevent isolation, anxiety, and depression.

As clinicians, we can orient families to the value of prevention-oriented consultations at key future life cycle transitions, when the experience of genetic risk will likely be heightened. Family members' concerns about loss may surface, which they had postponed or thought were "worked through." Clinicians should prepare families that concerns about genetic risk and decisions about whether to pursue genetic testing will be more activated with upcoming transitions, such as launching young adults, marriage or partner commitments, and starting a family. Also, such feelings can be reactivated by critical events, such as the genetic testing of another family member, diagnosis of a serious illness in relatives or friends, and the death of a loved one. Clinicians can help family members decide when further family discussion would be helpful, who would be appropriate to include, and how to discuss genetic risk with children or adolescents.

As the new genetics unfolds, families and clinicians are facing unprecedented and complex clinical and ethical challenges. Families will increasingly be able to choose to receive genetic information about their future health risks or fate. Some key research questions include the following: Which individuals and families will benefit by genetic risk screening and knowledge of their health risks or fate? How can we as clinicians best help family members reach decisions about whether to pursue predictive testing? Who are the relevant individuals to include in these decisions? Spouses or partners? Extended family?

Clinical Applications of Family Therapy with Physical Illness

This integrative model provides a framework for clinical practice by facilitating a family's understanding of chronic illness and disability in psychosocial terms. Attention to features of onset, course, outcome, and incapacitation provides markers that focus clinical assessment and intervention with a family. An illness timeline delineates the psychosocial developmental phases of an illness, including each phase with its own salient developmental challenges. The family's mastering of initial crisis phase–related tasks provides a foundation for its successful adaptation over the long haul. Attention to time allows the clinician to assess family strengths and vulnerabilities in relation to the present and future phases of the illness. The psychosocial demands of any condition can be thought about in relation to each illness phase and to different components of family functioning (e.g., communication, problem solving, and role flexibility).

The model clarifies treatment planning. Goal setting is guided by awareness of the aspects of family functioning most relevant to the particular type or phase of an illness. Sharing this information with the family and deciding on specific goals offers a better sense of control and realistic hope. This process empowers families in their journey of living with a chronic disorder. Also, it educates them to look for warning signs to seek help at appropriate times for brief, goal-oriented treatment. This framework is useful for timing family consultations or "psychosocial checkups" to coincide with key illness transition points.

There is value to prevention-oriented, multi-family, psychoeducational or support groups and workshops for patients and their families (Gonzalez & Steinglass, 2002; Steinglass, 2011), which provide cost-effective preventive services that decrease family isolation, increase networking, and can identify high-risk families (see Chapter 4). Multi-family groups can be designed to deal with different types of conditions (e.g., progressive, life-threatening, and relapsing). Brief psychoeducational "modules," timed for critical phases of particular types of diseases, enable families to digest manageable portions of a long-term coping process. In time-limited (e.g., four sessions) or one-day formats, couples and families can increase coping skills and discuss common disease-related relationship challenges with others in similar situations. For instance, through the Chicago Center for Family Health, we have developed programs in partnership with local medical centers to help families dealing with diabetes and cystic fibrosis, and, in collaboration with the Multiple Sclerosis Society, there is the Resilient Partners Program for couples living with multiple sclerosis.

Family Assessment in the Setting of Physical Illness

As chronic conditions become incorporated into the family system and all of its dynamics, family coping is influenced by illness-oriented processes that include the family's understanding of how the illness will develop over time and any related family belief systems.

Multigenerational Legacies of Illness, Loss, and Crisis

A family's current behavior, and therefore its response to illness, cannot be adequately understood apart from its history (Bowen, 1993; Byng-Hall, 2004; McGoldrick, Garcia-Preto, & Carter, 2010; Walsh & McGoldrick, 2004). Clinicians can use historical questioning and construct a basic genogram and timeline (McGoldrick, Gerson, & Petry, 2007) to track nodal events and transitions and thereby understand a family's organizational shifts and coping strategies as a system in response to past stressors and, more specifically, to past illnesses. This inquiry helps explain and predict the family's current style of coping, adaptation, and meaning making. A multigenerational assessment helps to clarify areas of strength and vulnerability. It also identifies high-risk families burdened by past unresolved issues and dysfunctional patterns that cannot absorb the challenges presented by a serious condition.

In this assessment, a central goal is to identify areas of consensus and "learned differences" (Penn, 1983) that are sources of cohesion, resilience, or potential conflict. Patterns of coping, replications, shifts in relationships (e.g., alliances, triangles, and cutoffs), and sense of competence are noted. These patterns can be transmitted across generations as family pride, myths, taboos, catastrophic expectations, and belief systems (Walsh & McGoldrick, 2004).

For example, a couple came for a consultation regarding marital discord when the wife believed her husband's basal cell carcinoma was fatal, despite the oncologist's favorable prognosis. In the consultation interview, when asked about prior experiences with illness and loss, the wife revealed that her own father had died tragically of a misdiagnosed malignant melanoma. She had a catastrophic fear based on both sensitization to cancer—particularly any related to the skin—and the possibility of human error by health professionals. Had the oncologist inquired about prior experiences at the time of diagnosis, earlier intervention would have been facilitated.

It is also useful when the clinician inquires about other forms of loss (e.g., divorce or migration), crisis (e.g., job loss or a traumatic event), and protracted adversity (e.g., poverty, racism, war, or political oppression). These experiences can provide transferable sources of resilience and effective coping skills in the face of a serious health problem (Walsh, 2006). Clinicians should ask specifically about positive family-of-origin experiences with illness and loss that can serve as models to adapt to the current situation.

Interweaving of Individual, Family, and Illness Development

A developmental lens provides a powerful way to construct a normative framework for serious illness. It is vital for clinicians doing this to understand the intertwining of three evolutionary threads: illness, individual, and family development.

Concepts of human and family development have evolved from models that centered on a basic, somewhat invariant, sequence and unfolding of phases to ones that are more varied, fluid, and multidimensional, consistent with contemporary individual and family life course trajectories (McGoldrick et al., 2010). Serious health conditions are one example of major, often unexpected, life challenges that can significantly alter the sequence and character of a family's life course and that of its members. For purposes of this discussion, "life structure" is a useful central concept for both family and individual development. Life structure refers to core elements (e.g., work, child rearing, and caregiving) of an individual's or family's life at any phase of the life cycle. Individual and family development have in common the notion of phases (each with its own developmental priorities) and are marked by the alternation of life structure–building/maintaining (stable) and life structure–changing (transitional) phases (Levinson, 1986). The primary goal of a building/maintaining phase is to form a life structure and enrich life within it, based on the key choices an individual/family made during the preceding transition. Transition phases are somewhat more fluid because previous individual, family, and illness life structures are reappraised in the face of new developmental challenges that may involve major changes rather than minor alterations.

At a macro level, the family life cycle can be viewed as oscillating between phases where family developmental tasks require intense bonding or relatively higher cohesion, as in early child rearing, and phases such as families with adolescents, when the external family boundary is loosened, with increasing personal identity and autonomy (Combrinck-Graham, 1985). Ethnic and racial differences influence the specific cultural expression of these phases.

These unifying concepts also provide a foundation for understanding the experience of chronic disorders. The life cycle again contains alternating transition and life structure–building/maintaining phases. And particular phases can be characterized as requiring relatively greater or lesser degrees of family cohesion. Illness, individual, and family development each pose priorities and challenges that move through phases of being more or less in sync with each other.

Generally, serious disorders exert an inward cohesive pull on the family system. Analogous to the addition of a new family member, illness onset sets in motion an inside-the-family focused process of socialization to illness. Symptoms, loss of function, the demands of shifting or acquiring new illness-related roles, and the fears of further disability and/or death all push a family to focus inward.

The need for family cohesion varies enormously with different illness types and phases. Progressive diseases over time inherently require greater cohesion than, for instance, constant-course illnesses. The ongoing addition of new demands with illness progression keeps a family's energy focused inward, often impeding the development of other members. After an initial period of adaptation, a constant-course disease (without severe disability) permits a family to get back on track developmentally. Relapsing illnesses alternate between periods of drawing a family inward and times of release from immediate disease demands. But, the on-call nature of many such illnesses keeps part of the family focus inward despite asymptomatic periods, hindering the natural flow between phases of development.

In clinical assessment, a basic question is: What is the fit between the psychosocial demands of a condition and family and individual life structures and developmental tasks at a particular point in the life cycle? Also, how will this fit change as the course of the illness unfolds in relation to the family's and each member's development?

Any transition in individual or family life cycle development will tend to magnify issues related to existing and anticipated loss. Transition periods are often characterized by upheaval, rethinking of prior commitments, and openness to change. Such times often hold a greater risk for the illness to become either embedded or ignored in planning for the next life phase. During a transition period, the process of thinking through future commitments can bring to the forefront family norms regarding loyalty through sacrifice and caregiving. The following example highlights this point.

Case Example

In one Latino family, the father named Miguel, a factory worker and the primary financial provider, had a heart attack. His rehabilitation was uneventful, including appropriate life-style modifications and a return to work. The family, including the oldest son, then 15, seemed relatively unaffected. Two years later, Miguel experienced a second, more life-threatening heart attack and became totally disabled. His son had dreams of going away to college. The specter of financial hardship and the perceived need for a "man in the family" created a serious dilemma for the family and this son, which surfaced with his precipitously declining academic performance and alcohol abuse. A fundamental clash arose between the son's developmental issues of individuation and the ongoing demands of a progressive heart disease, with the family's related fears of loss. The son feared that if he were to move away, he might never see his father alive again. Thus, there was a clash between three transition periods: (1) the illness transition to a more disabling, progressive, and life-threatening course; (2) the son's individual transition to early adulthood with individuation, leaving home, and educational pursuits; and (3) the family's developmental transition from the "living with teenagers" to "launching young adults" phase. It also illustrates the significance of the type of illness: one that was less incapacitating and less life-threatening might have interfered less with individual and family developmental priorities. At the time of initial diagnosis, a clinician's inquiry about anticipated major transitions over the next three to five years and discussing them in relation to the specific kind of heart disease and its related uncertainties would help avert a future crisis.

It is essential to situate these developmental issues in the context of cultural values, socioeconomic considerations, availability of family or community resources, and access to health care. In many cultures, as in this Latino family, a strong emphasis on loyalty to family needs might normatively take priority over individual goals, especially with a major illness or disability.

If the particular illness is progressive, relapsing, increasingly incapacitating, and/ or life-threatening, then the unfolding phases of the disease will be punctuated by numerous transitions. A family will need to alter its life structure more frequently to accommodate the shifting and increasing demands of the disease. This keeps the illness in the forefront of a family's consciousness, constantly impinging on its attempts to get back "in phase" developmentally.

The transition from the crisis to the chronic phase is the key juncture at which the intensity of the family's socialization to living with chronic disease is lessened. In this sense, it offers a window of opportunity for the family to reestablish or sometimes chart a "new normal" developmental course.

An overarching goal is to deal with the developmental demands of the illness without family members sacrificing their own or the family's development as a system over time. It is important for clinicians to determine whose life plans were or might be cancelled, postponed, or altered, as well as when plans put on hold and future developmental issues will be addressed. Using this framework, clinicians can anticipate developmental nodal points and offer prevention-oriented consultations. Therapists can help family members to strike a healthier balance, with life plans that resolve feelings of guilt, avoid any sense of excessive responsibility or hopelessness, and find family and external resources that support pursuing personal goals while also providing care for the ill member.

Health Beliefs

When illness strikes, a primary developmental challenge for families is to create meaning for the illness experience that promotes a sense of competency and mastery (Kleinman, 1988; Rolland, 1994a, 1998, in press; Wright & Bell, 2009). Because serious illness is often experienced as a betrayal of our fundamental trust in our bodies and belief in our invulnerability (Kleinman, 1988), creating an empowering narrative can be a formidable task. Health beliefs help us grapple with the existential dilemmas of our fear of death, our tendency to want to sustain our denial of death, and our attempts to reassert control when suffering and loss occur. They serve as a cognitive and interpersonal map that guides decisions and action, and they provide a way to approach new and ambiguous situations to sustain coherence in family life, facilitating continuity between past, present, and future (Antonovsky & Sourani, 1988; Reiss, 1981). A therapist's inquiry into and curiosity about family beliefs is perhaps the most powerful foundation stone of collaboration between families and health professionals (Rolland, 1998; Wright & Bell, 2009). Growing research evidence shows that family members' distress about illness and genetic risk is more closely associated with perceived risk or appraisals of seriousness than with any objective characteristics of the disease (Franks & Roesch, 2006; Hurley, Miller, Rubin, & Weinberg, 2006).

In the initial crisis phase, clinicians can inquire about key family beliefs that shape the family's narrative and coping strategies, including beliefs about (1) normality; (2) mind-body relationship, control, and mastery; (3) assumptions about what caused an illness and what will influence it's course and outcome; (4) meanings attached by a family, ethnic group, religion, or the wider culture to symptoms (e.g., chronic pain) (Griffith & Griffith, 1994; McGoldrick et al., 2005) or specific diseases (e.g., HIV/AIDS) (Sontag, 2001); (5) multigenerational factors that have shaped a family's health beliefs and response to illness; and (6) anticipated nodal points in illness, individual, and family development when health beliefs will likely be strained or may need to shift. Clinicians should also assess the fit of health beliefs among family members as well as between the family and health care system and wider culture.

BELIEFS ABOUT NORMALITY

Family beliefs about what is normal or abnormal, and the importance members place on conformity and excellence in relation to the average family, have far-reaching implications for adaptation to serious illness. When family values allow having a "problem" without self-denigration, it enables them to seek outside help and yet maintain a positive identity. When families define seeking help as weak and shameful, any kind of resilience is undercut. Essentially, with chronic disorders, in which problems are to be expected and the use of professionals and outside resources are necessary, a belief that pathologizes this normative process adds insult to injury.

Two excellent questions to elicit these beliefs are, "How do you think other *average* families would deal with a similar situation to yours?" and "How would a family *ideally* cope with your situation?" Families with strong beliefs in high achievement and perfectionism are prone to apply standards that are impossible to achieve in situations of illness. Particularly with untimely conditions that occur early in the life cycle, additional pressures arise to keep up with socially expected developmental milestones of age peers. If life cycle goals take longer or need revision, the family requires a flexible belief about what is normal and healthy. This kind of flexibility helps sustain hope.

THE FAMILY'S SENSE OF MASTERY FACING ILLNESS

It is vital that a therapist determine how a family defines mastery or control in general and in situations of illness (Taylor, Kemeny, Reed, Bowers, & Gruenwald, 2000; Thompson & Kyle, 2000). A family may adhere to a different set of beliefs about control when dealing with biological as opposed to typical day-to-day issues. Therefore, it is important that the clinician inquire about (1) each family's core values, (2) their beliefs about control of illness, and (3) the seriousness of the specific disease. For instance, regardless of the actual prognosis in a particular case, cancer may be equated with "death" or "no control" because of medical statistics, cultural myth, or prior family history. On the other hand, families may have enabling stories about a member or friend, who, in spite of cancer and a shortened life span, lived a "full" life centered on effectively prioritizing the quality of relationships and goals. Clinicians can highlight these positive narratives as a means to help families counteract cultural beliefs that focus exclusively on control of biology as defining success.

A family's beliefs about mastery strongly affect its relationship to an illness and to the health care system. Beliefs about control can affect treatment adherence and a family's preferences about participation in their family member's treatment and healing process. When families view disease course/outcome as a matter of chance, they tend to establish marginal relationships with health professionals, especially in the United States, and they may not adhere to treatment recommendations. Also, poor minority families too often receive inadequate care or lack access, which may lead to a fatalistic attitude and lack of engagement with health care providers, whom they may not trust to help. Because any therapeutic relationship depends on a shared belief system about what is therapeutic, a compatible mind-set among the patient, family, and health care team is essential. Families that feel misunderstood by health professionals are often reacting to a lack of joining at this basic value level.

The goodness of fit between the family's and therapist's beliefs about mastery can vary, depending on the illness phase. For some disorders, the crisis phase involves protracted care outside the family's direct control. This may be stressful for a family that prefers to tackle its own problems without outside control and "interference." The patient's return home may increase the family's workload but allows members to reassert more fully their competence and leadership. In contrast, a family guided more by a preference for external control by experts can expect greater difficulty when the ill member returns home. Recognition by therapists of such normative differences in beliefs about control can guide an effective psychosocial treatment plan tailored to each family's needs and affirming rather than disrespecting its core values.

In the terminal phase, a family may certainly feel least in control of the biological course of the disease and the decision making regarding the overall care of the dying member. Families that strongly believe they should be involved in a member's health care may need to assert themselves more vigorously with health providers. More specifically, effective decision making about the extent of heroic medical efforts requires that the provider respects the family's basic beliefs (Lynn, Schuster, Wilkinson, & Simon, 2007).

Clinicians should carefully judge the relative usefulness of minimization versus direct confrontation with and acceptance of painful realities. Often both are needed. The healthy use of minimization, or selective focus on the positive, and timely uses of humor should be distinguished from denial. The skilled clinician can support both the usefulness of hope and the need for treatment to control the illness or a new complication. Families can be helped to confront denial and illness severity when there is hope that preventive action or medical treatment can affect the outcome, or when an illness is entering its terminal phase. Yet, to cope with an arduous, uncertain course, families often need simultaneously to acknowledge the condition while minimizing treatment risks or the likelihood of a poor outcome.

FAMILY BELIEFS ABOUT THE CAUSE OF AN ILLNESS

When a significant health problem arises, most of us wonder, "Why me (or us)?" and "Why now?" (Roesch & Weiner, 2001). We attempt to construct an explanation or story that helps organize our experience. With the limits of current medical knowledge, tremendous uncertainties persist about the relative importance of myriad factors, leaving individuals and families to make idiosyncratic attributions about what caused an illness. A family's causal beliefs need to be assessed by the clinician separately from its beliefs about what can influence the outcome. In my clinical experience, it is important that the therapist elicit *each* family member's explanation. Responses will generally reflect a combination of medical information and family mythology. Beliefs might include the following: punishment for prior misdeeds (e.g., an affair); blame of a particular family member ("Your drinking made me sick!"); a sense of injustice ("Why am I being punished?"); genetics (e.g., cancer runs on one side of the family); unhealthy habits by the patient (e.g., smoking); neglect by parents (e.g., sudden infant death syndrome); religious beliefs (God's will); or simply bad luck.

Optimally, family narratives respect the limits of scientific knowledge, affirm the family's basic competency, and promote the flexible use of multiple biological, psychosocial, and spiritual healing strategies. In contrast, causal attributions by the family that invoke blame, shame, or guilt are particularly important for the clinician to uncover, as they can derail family coping and adaptation. Even worse, with a life-threatening illness, a blamed family member may be held accountable if the patient dies. Decisions about treatment often become confounded and filled with tension. The following case vignette illustrates how self-blame may remain hidden and the importance of early inquiry.

Case Example

Lucy and Tom G., a young couple, had a five-year-old child, Susan, who was terminally ill with leukemia. The pediatric oncologist offered the parents the choice between an experimental treatment with a low probability of success or halting treatment. Tom's position was, "Let's stop; enough is enough." Lucy, on the other hand, felt, "We must continue; we can't let her die." The couple could not reach an agreement, and the physician was immobilized. He requested a consultation for the couple.

When the consultant asked, "What is your explanation of how your daughter got leukemia?" the critical story emerged. Tom considered it bad luck. Lucy, however, had a very different belief. During her pregnancy with Susan, Lucy's father had a heart attack and died several months later from a second episode. Lucy felt that her period of great stress and grief had adversely affected Susan's intrauterine life. After Susan's birth by normal delivery, Lucy continued to mourn the loss of her father. She came to believe that this affected the quality of her bonding with Susan and led to a hidden depression in her infant. Further, Lucy had read research linking depression with lowered effectiveness of the immune system, which could, in turn, decrease normal surveillance and clearing of cancer cells from the body. She believed this combination of factors caused her child's cancer, which would have been avoided if she had been a more competent mother. Lucy said she had never shared this story with anyone—including her husband—because no one had ever asked, and she felt very ashamed. She had hoped for a cure, so that the whole issue could be resolved. She could not accept stopping treatment if it meant that Susan's death would then be her fault.

BELIEF SYSTEM ADAPTABILITY

Because illnesses vary enormously in their responsiveness to psychosocial factors, *both families and providers need to distinguish* beliefs about a family's overall participation in a long-term disease process, beliefs about their ability to control the biological progression of an illness, and their flexibility in applying these beliefs. A family's sense of competence or mastery depends on their grasp of these distinctions. Optimal family and provider narratives respect the limits of scientific knowledge, affirm basic patient and family competency, and promote the flexible use of multiple biological and psychosocial healing strategies.

A family's belief in their participation in the total illness process can be considered independent of whether a disease is stable, improving, or in a terminal phase. Sometimes, mastery and the attempt to control biological processes coincide, as when a family tailors its behavior to help maintain the health of a member with cancer in remission. This might include changes in family roles, communication, diet, exercise, and balance between work and recreation. Optimally, if an ill family member then enters the terminal phase of the illness, expressions of mastery need to be transformed to the process of letting go, which eases suffering and allows the provision of palliative care (Lynn et al., 2007).

Thus, flexibility, within both the family and the health care team, is a key variable in optimal family functioning. Rather than linking mastery in a rigid way with biological outcome (survival or recovery) as the sole determinant of success, families can define control in a more "holistic" sense, with their involvement and participation in the overall process as the main criteria defining success. This is analogous to the distinction between "curing the disease" and "healing the system." Psycho-social-spiritual healing may influence the course and outcome, but a positive disease outcome is not necessary for a family to feel successful. This flexible view of mastery can facilitate the quality of relations within the family, or between the family and health care professional, to become more central to criteria of success. The health care provider's competence becomes valued from both a technical and caregiving perspective, not solely linked to the biological course.

ETHNIC, SPIRITUAL, AND CULTURAL BELIEFS

Ethnic, racial, and spiritual beliefs and dominant cultural norms can strongly influence the family values concerning health and illness (McGoldrick et al., 2005; Rolland, 2006a; Walsh, 2009). Significant ethnic differences regarding health beliefs often emerge during a major health crisis. Although families can represent a continuum that frequently reflects a blend of different ethnic, racial, and spiritual beliefs, health professionals need to be mindful of the diversity of belief systems of various subpopulations in their community, particularly as these are expressed in different behavioral patterns. Cultural norms vary in such areas as the definition of the appropriate "sick role" for the patient; the kind and degree of open communication about the disease; who should be included in the illness caregiving system (e.g., extended family, friends, and professionals); who is the primary caretaker and do gender norms apply (most often wife/mother/daughter/daughter-in-law); and what kind of rituals are viewed as normative at different illness phases (e.g., hospital bedside vigils, healing, and funeral rituals). This is especially true for racial minority groups (e.g., African American, Asian, and Hispanic) who may experience discrimination or marginalization from the prevailing Euro-American culture.

In order to forge a workable alliance that can endure long-term illness, clinicians need to be mindful of these cultural differences among themselves, the patient, and the family (Seaburn et al., 1996). Effective collaboration occurs when professionals explore and understand families' cultural and spiritual beliefs about illness and healing. Otherwise, families may distance themselves from health care providers and community resources, which represents a major source of non-adherence issues and treatment failure. Sometimes, professionals need flexibility to suspend their need to be in charge. This requires their acceptance that patients, not physicians, retain final responsibility for decisions about their bodies.

FIT AMONG HEALTH CARE PROVIDER, HEALTH SYSTEM, AND FAMILY BELIEFS

During any major life cycle or illness transition, family members may not all share the same beliefs. For instance, with severe disability or terminal illness, one member may want the patient to return home, whereas another prefers long-term hospitalization or transfer to an extended-care facility. Because the primary caregiver is typically the wife/

mother, she is apt to bear most of the burdens and overwhelming demands of care. But families that anticipate this can modify their rules and avert the risk of family caretaker overload, resentment, and deteriorating family relationships.

The murky boundary between the chronic and terminal phase highlights the risk that a professional's beliefs collide with the family's. Physicians can feel bound to a technological imperative that requires them to exhaust all possibilities at their disposal, regardless of the odds of success. Families may not know how to interpret continued lifesaving efforts, assuming real hope where virtually none exists. Health care professionals and institutions can collude in a pervasive societal wish to deny death as a natural process truly beyond technological control (Becker, 1973). Endless treatment can represent the medical team's inability to separate a general value placed on controlling diseases from their beliefs about participating in a patient's total care, which includes bio-psycho-social-spiritual well-being.

Conclusion

Facing the risks and burdens of chronic or life-threatening illness, the most resilient families are able to harness that experience to improve the quality of life. Families can achieve a healthy balance between accepting limits and promoting autonomy and connectedness.

A serious illness or brush with death provides an opportunity for family members to confront catastrophic fears about loss. This can lead to a better appreciation of life, with new perspectives, clearer priorities, and closer relationships (Walsh, 2006). Seizing opportunities can replace procrastinating until the "right moment" comes around or passively waiting for the "dreaded moment." Serious illness, by exposing life's fragility and preciousness, provides families with an opportunity to heal unresolved issues. For advanced stage illnesses, clinicians should help families focus on more immediately attainable goals that enrich their everyday lives.

Living well despite the strains and uncertainties of illness can be a monumental challenge. The FSI model addresses this challenge and makes the inevitable strains more manageable. Attending to the psychosocial demands of different conditions over time within a multigenerational, developmental, and belief system context can provide a strengths-based framework—a common language that facilitates collaborative, creative problem solving and quality of life for families facing illness, disability, and loss.

References

Antonovsky, A., & Sourani, T. (1988). Family sense of coherence and family adaptation. *Journal of Marriage and the Family, 50,* 79–92.

Becker, E. (1973). *The denial of death.* New York: Free Press.

Boss, P. (2005). *Loss, trauma, and resilience: Therapeutic work with ambiguous loss.* New York: W. W. Norton.

Bowen, M. (1993). *Family therapy in clinical practice.* New York: Jason Aronson.

Byng-Hall, J. (2004). Loss and family scripts. In F. Walsh & M. McGoldrick (Eds.), *Living beyond loss: Death in the family* (pp. 85–98). New York: W. W. Norton.

Campbell, T. (2003). The effectiveness of family interventions for physical disorders. *Journal of Marital and Family Therapy, 29,* 263–281.

Carr, D., & Springer, K. W. (2010). Advances in families and health research in the 21st century. *Journal of Marriage and the Family, 72,* 743–761.

Combrinck-Graham, L. (1985). A developmental model for family systems. *Family Process, 24,* 139–150.

Doherty, W., & Baird, M. (1983). *Family therapy and family medicine: Towards the primary care of families.* New York: Guilford Press.

D'Onofrio, B. M., & Lahey, B. B. (2010). Biosocial influences on the family: A decade review. *Journal of Marriage and the Family, 72,* 762–782.

Engel, G. L. (1977). The need for a new medical model: A challenge for biomedicine. *Science, 196,* 129–136.

Franks, H. M., & Roesch, S. C. (2006). Appraisals and coping in people living with cancer: A meta-analysis. *Psycho-Oncology, 15,* 1027–1037.

Gonzalez, S., & Steinglass, P. (2002). Application of multifamily discussion groups in chronic medical disorders. In W. R. McFarlane (Ed.), *Multifamily groups in the treatment of severe psychiatric disorders* (pp. 315–340). New York: Guilford Press.

Griffith, J., & Griffith, M. (1994). *The body speaks.* New York: Basic Books.

Hartmann, M., Bazner, E., Wild, B., Eisler, I., & Herzog, W. (2010). Effects of interventions involving the family in the treatment of adult patients with chronic physical diseases: A meta-analysis. *Psychotherapeutics and Psychosomatics, 79,* 136–148.

Hurley, K., Miller, S. M., Rubin, L., & Weinberg, D. S. (2006). The individual facing genetic issues: Information processing, decision making, perception, and health-protective behaviors. In S. M. Miller, S. H. McDaniel, J. S. Rolland, & S. L. Feetham (Eds.), *Individuals, families, and the new era of genetics: Biopsychosocial perspectives.* New York: W. W. Norton.

Kazak, A. (2005). Evidence-based interventions for survivors of childhood cancer and their families. *Journal of Pediatric Psychology, 30*(1), 47–49.

Kleinman, A. (1988). *The illness narratives: Suffering, healing, and the human condition.* New York: Basic Books.

Law, D., & Crane, R. (2007). The influence of individual, marital, and family treatment on high utilizers of health care. *Journal of Marital and Family Therapy, 29,* 353–363.

Levinson, D. J. (1986). A conception of adult development. *American Psychologist, 41,* 3–13.

Lynn, J., Schuster, J. L., Wilkinson, A., & Simon, L. N. (2007). *Improving care for the end of life: A sourcebook for health care managers and clinicians* (2nd ed.). New York: Oxford University Press.

Maloney, E., Edgerson, S., Robson, M., Brown, R., Offit, K., Bylund, C., & Kissane, D. (2012). What women with breast cancer discuss with clinicians about risk for their adolescent daughters. *Journal of Psychosocial Oncology, 30*(4), 484–502.

Martire, L., Lustig, A., Schulz, R., Miller, G., & Helgeson, V. (2004). Is it beneficial to involve a family member? A meta-analysis of psychosocial interventions in chronic illness. *Health Psychology, 23,* 599–611.

Martire, L., Schulz, R., Helgeson, V., Small, B., & Saghafi, E. (2010). Review and meta-analysis of couple-oriented interventions for chronic disease. *Annals of Behavioral Medicine, 40,* 325–342.

McDaniel, S., Campbell, T., Hepworth, J., & Lorenz, A. (2005). *Family-oriented primary care* (2nd ed.). New York: Springer.

McDaniel, S., Hepworth, J., & Doherty, W. (Eds.). (2013). *Medical family therapy: A biopsychosocial approach to families with health problems* (2nd ed.). New York: Basic Books.

McGoldrick, M., Garcia-Preto, N., & Carter, B. (2010). *The expanded family life cycle: Individual, family and social perspectives* (4th ed.). New York: Allyn & Bacon.

McGoldrick, M., Gerson, R., & Petry, S. (2007). *Genograms in family assessment* (3rd ed.). New York: W. W. Norton.

McGoldrick, M., Pearce, J. K., & Garcia-Preto, N. (2005). *Ethnicity and family therapy* (3rd ed.). New York: Guilford Press.

Miller, S., McDaniel, S., Rolland, J., & Feetham, S. (Eds.). (2006). *Individuals, families, and the new era of genetics: Biopsychosocial perspectives.* New York: W. W. Norton.

Penn, P. (1983). Coalitions and binding interactions in families with chronic illness. *Family Systems Medicine, 1,* 16–25.

Reiss, D. (1981). *The family's construction of reality.* Cambridge, MA: Harvard University Press.

Roesch, S., & Weiner, B. (2001). A meta-analytic review of coping with illness: Do causal attributions matter. *Journal of Psychosomatic Research, 50,* 205–219.

Rolland, J. S. (1984). Toward a psychosocial typology of chronic and life-threatening illness. *Family Systems Medicine, 2,* 245–263.

Rolland, J. S. (1990). Anticipatory loss: A family systems developmental framework. *Family Process, 29,* 229–244.

Rolland, J. S. (1994a). *Families, illness, & disability: An integrative treatment model.* New York: Basic Books.

Rolland, J. S. (1994b). In sickness and in health: The impact of illness on couples' relationships. *Journal of Marital and Family Therapy, 20,* 327–349.

Rolland, J. S. (1998). Beliefs and collaboration in illness: Evolution over time. *Families, Systems and Health, 16,* 7–27.

Rolland, J. S. (2004). Helping families with anticipatory loss and terminal illness. In F. Walsh & M. McGoldrick (Eds.), *Living beyond loss: Death in the family* (2nd ed.). New York: W. W. Norton.

Rolland, J. S. (2005). Cancer and the family: An integrative model. *Cancer, 104*(S111), 2584–2595.

Rolland, J. S. (2006a). Genetics, family systems, and multicultural influences. *Families, Systems, & Health, 24,* 425–442.

Rolland, J. S. (2006b). Living with anticipatory loss in the new era of genetics: A life cycle perspective. In S. M. Miller, S. H. McDaniel, J. S. Rolland, & S. L. Feetham (Eds.), *Individuals, families, and the new era of genetics: Biopsychosocial perspectives.* New York: W. W. Norton.

Rolland, J. S. (2010). Chronic illness and the family life cycle. In M. McGoldrick, N. Garcia-Preto, & E. Carter (Eds.), *The expanded family life cycle: Family and social perspectives* (4th ed.). Boston: Allyn & Bacon.

Rolland, J. S. (2013). Family adaptation to chronic medical illness. In A. Heru (Ed.), *Working with families in medical settings: A multidisciplinary guide for psychiatrists and other mental health professionals.* New York: Routledge.

Rolland, J.S. (in press). *Treating illness and disability in families: An integrative model.* New York: Guilford Press.

Rolland, J. S., & Williams, J. K. (2005). Toward a biopsychosocial model for 21st century genetics. *Family Process, 44,* 3–24.

Seaburn, D., Gunn, W., Mauksch, L., Gawinski, A., & Lorenz, A. (Eds.). (1996). *Models of collaboration: A guide for mental health professionals working with physicians and health care providers.* New York: Basic Books.

Shields, C., Finley, M., Chawla, N., & Meadors, P. (2012). Couple and family interventions in health problems. *Journal of Marital & Family Therapy, 38,* 265–281.

Sontag, S. (2001). *Illness as metaphor and AIDS and its metaphors.* New York: Picador.

Steinglass, P. (2011). Multiple family groups for adult cancer survivors and their families. *Family Process, 50,* 393–410.

Taylor, S., Kemeny, M., Reed, G., Bowers, J., & Gruenwald, T. (2000). Psychological resources, positive illusions, and health. *American Psychologist, 55,* 99–109.

Thompson, S., & Kyle, D. (2000). The role of perceived control in coping with the losses associated with chronic illness. In J. Harvey & E. Miller (Eds.), *Loss and trauma: General and close relationship perspectives.* Philadelphia, PA: Brunner-Routledge.

Walsh, F. (2006). *Strengthening family resilience* (2nd ed.). New York: Guilford Press.

Walsh, F. (Ed.). (2009). *Spiritual resources in family therapy* (2nd ed.). New York: Guilford Press.

50   *John S. Rolland*

Walsh, F., & McGoldrick, M. (Eds.). (2004). *Living beyond loss: Death in the family.* New York: W. W. Norton.

Weihs, K., Fisher, L., & Baird, M. (2001). *Families, health, and behavior.* Commissioned report: Institute of Medicine, National Academy of Sciences. Washington, DC: National Academy Press.

Werner-Lin, A. (2008). Beating the biological clock: The compressed family life cycle of young women with BRCA gene alterations. *Social Work in Health Care, 47,* 416–437.

Wood, B. L., Lim, J., Miller, B., Cheah, P., Zwetsch, T., Ramesh, S., & Simmens, S. (2008). Testing the biobehavioral model in pediatric asthma: Pathways of effect. *Family Process, 47,* 21–40.

Wright, L. M., & Bell, J. (2009). *Beliefs and illness: A model for healing.* Calgary, Alberta, Canada: 4th Floor Press.

4   The Family with Mental Illness

Peter Steinglass and Tammy Schuler

We start with a widely endorsed assertion: no matter how competent a family may be in dealing with life challenges, a major mental illness in a close relative invariably has a profound and potentially devastating impact on family life. As a psychiatric condition like schizophrenia spectrum disorder, bipolar disorder, or chronic substance abuse takes hold in a family member, close relatives encounter many new challenges. They are witness to highly distressing behavioral and cognitive changes in the patient; their routines and living arrangements are disrupted; and new financial burdens arise, generated by the patient's behavior (Awad & Voruganti, 2008; van der Voort, Goossens, & van der Bijl, 2007).

These illnesses create experiences akin to loss events—whether loss of health, dreams, career, or sense of certainty in life. Accordingly, they bring grief and the need to cope. At the same time, families are typically called upon to play a central caregiving role, which often includes learning how to administer components of highly complex, long-term treatment plans (Lefley, 1996).

Beyond these challenges, many families have little familiarity or experience with delusions, paranoia, or thought disorders associated with major mental illness. Likewise, relatives may be unaware of resources for education, symptom management, or support. Moreover, relatives may be coping with mental illness of a family member when, due to biological and/or environmental factors, they themselves are at increased risk of symptoms of mental illness during their lifetimes (Jang, 2005).

Given these challenges, one would have expected that many years back, clinicians, sensitive to the stress of coping with mental illnesses, would have routinely implemented effective family-focused therapy programs. Alas, this was not the case. Only recently have clinicians acknowledged the importance of providing support for families in the long-term management of chronic mental illness. Further, family-interaction researchers had several false starts when proposing that parents had an etiological role in the onset of their chidlren's major mental illnesses. This led to a growing schism between families and mental health professionals. Instead of viewing family therapists as allies, many families felt blamed for creating and/or perpetuating the mental illness.

Beginning in the 1980s, however, a reconceptualization of the relationship between mental illness and family functioning led to major advances not only in conceptual models, but also in family-focused interventions—with positive results in both formal and informal clinical trials (e.g., Fals-Stewart, O'Farrell, Birchler, Córdova, & Kelley, 2005; McFarlane, Link, Dushay, Marchal, & Crilly, 2004; Miklowitz, 2006). Further, over the past two decades, family therapy evolved as mental health professionals partnered more effectively with families during the chronic phase of major mental illness; after all, families are often the de facto "treatment team" for patients with persistent mental illnesses (Gurman, 2008; Madsen, 1999; Nichols & Schwartz, 2005).

A Brief History of Evolving Ideas about Families and Mental Illness

Although obviously somewhat simplified, the field of family therapy has approached major mental illness by encompassing four distinct approaches. Two of these approaches were in direct opposition to each other, whereas the others complemented and reinforced the overall picture of the intersection between the onset and course of major mental illnesses and family life. These four approaches are as follows:

1. An approach that focused on family pathology/dysfunction as a major etiological factor in the development of mental illnesses like schizophrenia. We will call this view the *deficit approach*.
2. A countervailing approach that emerged partly as a reaction to widespread criticism that the deficit approach inadvertently pathologized families. This view, which we will call the *family as resource* approach, focuses on a family's potentially positive role for an individual struggling with psychiatric illness.
3. An approach that has attempted to identify specific family characteristics correlated with the pattern of relapse/recovery of cyclical disorders like schizophrenia, bipolar disease, or chronic alcoholism. This approach pays particular attention to the influence of family factors on *clinical course*.
4. An approach that has focused on how family functioning is influenced by multiple stresses due to the behavior and needs of the mentally ill family member. This is a *family impact* approach.

The Deficit Approach

Beginning in the 1960s and 1970s, a series of studies on families with schizophrenic members purported to identify aspects of communication that resembled the types of thought disorders characteristic of schizophrenia spectrum disorders. These findings prompted family interaction researchers to speculate whether disordered family communication plays an etiological role in the development of schizophrenia. In other words, a purportedly pathological aspect of family behavior might cause a major mental disorder. Although the specific identified aspects of communication varied from one investigator to another—called either "double-bind" or "transactional deviance" or "pseudomutuality"—in each instance, the inference was that pathology within the family could cause major mental illness (Dixon & Lehman, 1995).

The "deficit" family model is primarily of interest at this point because of its historical significance and concomitant influence on the family therapy field. Although this model held sway, clinical efforts focused on identifying problematic families and offering them family therapy. The working assumption seemed to be that families were to blame for the development of mental illness. Further, correcting dysfunctional (pathological) family behavior problems would be a necessary step in reversing psychotic symptomatology, especially certain types of thought disorders.

These hypotheses, as intriguing as they seemed at the time, had at least two major unintended consequences. First, as evidence grew that possible genetic factors predisposed people to develop schizophrenia (and later comparable evidence for bipolar disorders), the view that family behavior, as opposed to genes, might cause major mental illness seemed far off base. Second, those family therapy approaches that invariably pathologized families understandably left them angry, confused, and misunderstood.

The Family as Resource Approach

As criticism of these "pathology-based" family treatment approaches grew—along with mounting evidence that communication patterns like the "double-bind" were not unique to families with psychotic members—family therapists increasingly challenged earlier assumptions about relationships between family behavior and major mental illness. What emerged was a new focus that sought to identify aspects of family behavior that might enhance coping with challenges associated with conditions like schizophrenia.

The basic argument here is that families have the potential to serve a protective or preventive role in strengthening an individual's resistance to illness and can also play a determinant role in successful adherence to treatment regimens in the presence of illness. In both roles, it is the family to a large extent that teaches and reinforces behaviors that may diminish risk of illness, along with reducing symptomatology and detrimental behavior once a condition has manifested itself.

This switch—from seeing the family as a potential agent (cause) of major mental illness to family as an ally (resource) in implementing short- and long-term treatment plans—has been profound. In turn, relationships between family and therapist have emphasized partnership and collaboration, rather than an inadvertent adversarial stance among patient, family, and therapist (Nichols, 2012).

Simply put, the therapist now views the family as attempting to cope with a distressing and challenging psychiatric condition and assumes that, until proved otherwise, the family is trying its best to help its psychiatrically disordered member. If the family's efforts prove to be counter-productive, the initial assumption is that the family's behavior results from misguided beliefs about what would be most helpful, not dysfunctionality or malicious intent at any stage. Clearly, this shift from an emphasis on deficits to family strengths has led to the therapist becoming a collaborator/consultant to the family (Wynne, McDaniel, & Weber, 1986). This has also been a major rationale for the development of family-focused psycho-educational interventions, which have been among the most successful innovations in treating major mental illnesses (Falloon, Held, Coverdale, Roncone, & Laidlaw, 1999; Steinglass, Bennett, Wolin, & Reiss, 1987).

Further, this view is consistent with a biopsychosocial approach whereby interactions among genetic predispositions, personality, and environment (in this case, family environment) combine to either exacerbate or attenuate the development of major mental disorders (McFarlane, Dixon, Lukens, & Lucksted, 2007). Particularly intriguing is a series of studies that has combined family interaction and behavioral genetics perspectives, with initial focus on the differential expression of major depressive disorder in at-risk individuals (e.g., Pike, McGuire, Hetherington, Reiss, & Plomin, 1996; Reiss et al., 1995; Reiss, Neiderhiser, Hetherington, & Plomin, 2003).

The Clinical Course Approach

Overlapping with the "resource approach" is a third line of inquiry, focusing primarily on how (if at all) the family influences the differential *course* of major mental illnesses. Seminal data emerging in the 1970s and 1980s identified an attribute of family interaction: a family member's degree of critical or disparaging comments during a structured research interview, which were highly correlated with recidivism/rehospitalization rates of schizophrenic patients. This attribute, labeled expressed emotion (EE) by Vaughan and Leff (1976), proved so robust a predictor of relapse rates of schizophrenia (and later bipolar illness) that researchers subsequently sought to tease out which specific components of EE seemed to be the culprits (Hooley, 1998; Hooley, Rosen, & Richters, 1995).

From this research emerged a hypothesis proposing that the level of EE (high vs. low) related to family members' beliefs about the reasons behind the patient's behavior, especially the negative symptoms associated with persistent psychiatric disorders (Barrowclough & Hooley, 2003). In high-EE families, a patient's loss of motivation was attributed not to the illness but rather to obstinacy or laziness and thus was subject to criticism. Such beliefs then impacted the illness course and treatment (including the all-important issue of treatment adherence). In this sense, the research examined how family and illness variables mutually reinforce one another as the illness moves into its chronic phase. This is critically important for conditions like schizophrenia or bipolar disorder. The research question being asked was what aspects of family behavior serve to maintain the chronicity of mental illnesses, and vice versa.

Research into EE remains the most fully developed explication of the relationships between a family environmental characteristic and the clinical course of major mental illnesses. Yet the more researchers have examined this reciprocal relationship, the more complex the story has become. As with most chronic conditions, whether medical or psychiatric, the impact of major mental illness on the family may vary with patient characteristics such as diagnosis, demographic factors such as age, and developmental stage (van der Voort et al., 2007). The challenge for families is clearly heightened when the illness is accompanied by suicidal gestures, physical threats, coexisting substance abuse, or homelessness (Mueser & Jeste, 2008). Further, the degree to which a family member is affected may also relate to his or her age, developmental stage, relationship, and degree of contact with the patient.

Thus, one would be hard-pressed to argue there is a clearly definable response pattern characteristic of families coping with a mentally ill member, any more than we have been able to identify typologies of families associated with different psychiatric disorders. Further compounding this problem is determining how much a family's specific response style emanates from factors within the family versus its reaction to perceived stigmatization, particularly in light of societal views toward mental illness. And once this stigmatizing process runs its course, views of both patient and family become subject to negative stereotyping, and the family more likely assumes that help will be difficult to obtain.

The Family Impact Approach

Today, a vast body of literature shows that living with a family member with persistent mental illness is associated with significant psychiatric symptomatology on the part of parents, spouses, and children. Perhaps the most important aspect of the story concerns "caretaker burden." Caring for a psychiatrically impaired person can leave a caretaker feeling worn down and overwhelmed by a combination of factors including financial strain, social isolation, management of negative symptomatology, and more.

Although the magnitude of this impact varies with the availability of external resources, in the case of severe mental illness such as dementia, psychotic disorders, and disabling mood disorders, caregiving by family members may be necessary rather than elective. The data demonstrate that caregiving for someone with mental illness is associated with increased stress (van Wijngaarden, Schene, & Koeter, 2004), heightened emotional distress (Perlick et al., 2007), decreased life satisfaction (Brodaty, Thompson, Thompson, & Fine, 2005), poorer quality of life (Zauszniewski, Bekhet, & Suresky, 2008), lowered immunity (Kiecolt-Glaser, Marucha, Malarkey, Mercado, & Glaser, 1995), and poorer physical health—in addition to a substantially increased financial burden that is sometimes even crippling (Awad & Voruganti, 2008). As just one dramatic example, Kiecolt-Glaser and her colleagues (2011) reported that the combination of caregiving for a relative with dementia, when the caregiver has a personal history of childhood adversity, such as abuse, is associated with shorter telomeres, a measure of aging, with a 7- to 15-year shorter life span compared to caregivers without a history of childhood adversity.

In summary, the journey from fault finding to strength recognition and from high EE to caregiver education and support has been fruitful in bringing the field to an enriched understanding of pathways that optimally harness families as strategic resources for their ill relatives.

Family Therapy Approaches for Treatment of Severe Mental Illness

Family-focused interventions aim at both helping families cope with mental disorder and addressing behaviors identified as risk factors for recidivism or poor treatment adherence. These interventions have been most fully developed for families coping with major psychotic disorders—schizophrenia spectrum and bipolar disorders. Additional progress has also been made in the development of family interventions to treat childhood and adolescent behavioral disorders (Alexander, Robbins, & Sexton, 2000) and chronic substance abuse (O'Farrell & Fals-Stewart, 2003). Although a full discussion of all advances exceeds the scope of this chapter, we will focus on major psychotic disorders and substance abuse disorders to elucidate some exciting developments.

Schizophrenia and Bipolar Disorders

As data have accumulated from family interaction and behavioral genetics studies over the past 20 years, both genetic diatheses and family environment have been incorporated as risk/protective factors in the timing of the onset and episodic course of disorders like schizophrenia and bipolar disease. With EE as the most thoroughly studied family environmental risk factor, family therapy researchers have been energetically designing and testing intervention programs focused on (1) assessing the extent to which EE is present in a particular family and (2) developing methods for converting "high-EE" into "low-EE" behavior. For example, therapy might target potentially aversive communication patterns and teach family members alternative communication styles. These intervention programs have suggested pathways for including families in the treatment of severely mentally ill patients and have also demonstrated in randomized clinical trials how powerful these treatment approaches can be (McFarlane et al., 2004).

Although intervention protocols have varied in content and format, by and large they have been viewed by the field as a "family psycho-educational" approach. Virtually all these treatment models include both informational and experiential components, addressing communication patterns and family interactional behavior. Generally paired with pharmacotherapy, the approach recognizes that psychotic disorders are usually only partly remediable by medication—and that families have a significant effect on their relative's clinical course.

The family psycho-educational approach has come to include methods for facilitating changes in communication as well as providing information about the illness and coping strategies to offset the family's sense of caregiving burden. Families are taught that their behavior toward the patient can facilitate or impede recovery by compensating for deficits. For example, a family might interfere with recuperation during an acute psychotic episode if, in their natural enthusiasm to promote and support progress, they create unreasonable demands and expectations. In turn, the same family could have a dramatically positive effect on recovery by *gradually* increasing expectations and *gently* supporting an incremental return of functioning (McFarlane et al., 2004).

Researchers have developed empirically supported practice guidelines to address family needs for information and to provide clinical guidance and ongoing family support. Overall, research has demonstrated that family psycho-education during a posthospitalization period, when combined with neuroleptic regimens, was related to delayed relapse among schizophrenic patients. Research has also shown that this education dramatically improves family understanding, well-being, and patient outcomes in a reciprocal relationship (Penn & Mueser, 1996). To further underscore these points, Goldstein and Miklowitz (1995) have concluded that the effect size of family psycho-education in reducing recidivism is equal to or greater than the treatment effectiveness of pharmacotherapy alone.

The descriptor "psycho-education" can be somewhat misleading as its name does not necessarily confer its vital therapeutic elements. In addition to didactic techniques, the psycho-education approach includes a broad array of cognitive, behavioral, and supportive therapeutic strategies. It often utilizes a consultative framework and shares key characteristics with other family-based interventions. Also critical to success is an emphasis on establishing a non-judgmental, non-pathologizing patient-family-therapist partnership to address the challenges associated with major mental illness.

Several family-based treatment formats with roots in family psycho-education have emerged, with varying degrees of current empirical support. Components that vary across these formats include the following:

1.   Number of families treated simultaneously and by whom, for example, individual family consultation; professionally led family psycho-education (Anderson, Hogarty, & Reiss, 1980; Falloon, Boyd, & McGill, 1984); single-family and multi-family group formats (McFarlane et al., 2004); family-led information and support classes, such as those offered by the National Alliance for Mental Illness (NAMI; Pickett-Schenk, Cook, & Laris, 2000); and family groups for other relatives;

2. Duration and frequency of treatment;
3. Setting, such as hospital or home-based;
4. The degree to which cognitive, behavioral, emotional, rehabilitative, and systemic techniques are utilized.

In support of multi-family group formats, McFarlane and colleagues (2004) underscore that families benefit from access to each other, to learn of other families' successes and failures. Finally, all modalities share a focus on family resiliency and strengths, in keeping with the non-judgmental, non-pathologizing therapist stance deemed so essential to the success of these treatment models. A set of examples will be described subsequently, in the context of treatments for other forms of psychopathology such as bipolar disorder and substance use disorders.

In an attempt to specify the critical elements of family-based treatment for schizophrenia, the World Schizophrenia Fellowship (1998) wrote a set of consensus guidelines encompassing goals, principles, and methods. Goals included ensuring the best possible outcomes for patients and alleviating suffering in families by supporting them in their family member's recovery. The highlighted principles included building a collaborative relationship; addressing social and clinical needs, including medication management; utilizing family strengths; addressing feelings of loss; improving communication and problem solving; resolving conflict; and providing information, crisis planning, flexibility, and continuity of care.

In patients diagnosed with bipolar disorder, high rates of relapse and/or worse symptomatology have been associated with family members' high levels of critical, hostile, or emotionally overinvolved behaviors (e.g., Miklowitz, 2006). Here, too, similar family-focused psycho-educational treatments are effective.

When patients are treated with pharmacotherapy and family psycho-education, these data convincingly show that patients experience fewer relapses or longer delays before relapsing, as compared to families treated with other modalities, such as the pairing of crisis management and pharmacotherapy. These effects are moderated by the degree of EE reported by families, such that findings are particularly robust in "high EE" families compared to "low EE." Further, differences in outcomes for families treated with family psycho-education/pharmacotherapy relative to crisis management/pharmacotherapy remained unexplained by medication differences or treatment compliance (Miklowitz et al., 2000).

Substance Abuse

Our second example of the emerging family-oriented treatment approaches for major mental illness pertains to alcoholism and drug abuse. Although not as fully developed as the work on schizophrenia and bipolar disorder, three decades of research and clinical experience with substance abusers and their families present a strong case that understanding substance abuse within a family context adds a powerful perspective.

Here is another example where a psychiatric disorder can produce havoc for the family. Substance abuse creates a myriad of emotional responses in families, including grief, despair, angst, helplessness, hopelessness, and uncertainty about the future. To corroborate this point, one need only mention incidence rates of physical violence, sexual abuse, financial crises, divorce, effects on children, and the like (Rotunda & O'Farrell, 1997). Hence, it is encouraging that support for the value of including families as components of substance abuse treatment programs now comes from multiple directions.

Recent literature reviews have consistently pointed to three main findings: (1) involvement of family members during the pretreatment phase significantly improves engagement of substance abusers in treatment, (2) involvement of the family also improves retention in treatment, and (3) long-term outcomes are more positive when families and/or social networks are components of the treatment approach (Edwards & Steinglass, 1995; Miller, Meyers, & Tonigan, 1999; O'Farrell & Fals-Stewart, 2003; Rowe & Liddle, 2003; Stanton & Heath, 2005; Thomas & Corcoran, 2001).

The evidence is indisputable—and impressive—that when family members are included in the initial stages of contact, the substance user is much more likely to ultimately become engaged in active treatment. For example, a review by Stanton (2004) of 11 separate family-oriented programs designed to increase engagement of a substance-abusing family member reported a powerful impact—upward of 65% engagement rates—as compared to wait-list control groups, which averaged 6% engagement rates. Findings have likewise emerged regarding the efficacy of marital and family treatment approaches in reducing the negative effect of substance misuse disorders and of sustaining those positive outcomes (Copello, Velleman, & Templeton, 2005; Miller & Wilbourne, 2002).

Further, here is a positive example of how family-oriented approaches to treatment have expanded our ideas about appropriate criteria for assessing beneficial results, in that both non-patient and patient posttreatment functioning counts in assessing overall success of a treatment program. Nowhere is this more evident than in the addictions field. Instead of a sole focus on cessation of alcohol or drug use as the criterion of success, family therapy researchers have expanded the outcomes to include the substance user's interpersonal relationships and social functioning, a more multi-dimensional definition of harm reduction (McCrady, Stout, Noel, Abrams, & Nelson, 1991; O'Farrell & Fals-Stewart, 2006). Separate assessments of relationship functioning of spouses or partners (or parental functioning, if the study concerns adolescent drug users) have provided a far richer picture of the impact of treatment programs on family life.

Unfortunately, this evidence of benefit has been slow to translate into comprehensive treatment programs. Although many researchers advocate involving family members in treatment and recovery, the welfare and psychosocial functioning of these family members are not necessarily given equal weight in assessing the effectiveness of the treatment approach. That is, in the vast majority of programs, families continue to be seen as adjunctive to the abusers' treatment, with rehabilitation taking primacy. Consequently, families are typically included only after individual treatment targeted at detoxification and restabilization of the abuser has been achieved.

Thus, once again, despite growing evidence of the effectiveness of family-oriented treatment approaches, they remain underutilized. This includes behavioral treatment models such as O'Farrell and Fals-Stewart's Behavioral Marital Therapy (BMT) model (2006), which has received extensive testing in randomized clinical trials (Fals-Stewart et al., 2005). At the same time, these studies, although yielding powerful evidence in support of BMT, are limited to therapy with the marital dyad. They do not directly address the impact of adolescent substance abuse or the effect of parental alcoholism/

drug abuse on children. Thus far, attempts to test the effectiveness of systemically based family therapy approaches have proved far more difficult to operationalize (Rohrbaugh, Shoham, Spungen, & Steinglass, 1995) but still deserve closer attention.

An example is the Systemic Motivational Therapy model described by Steinglass and colleagues (Steinglass, 2008, 2009). This is particularly interesting because not only is it solidly rooted in family systems theory, but it also draws heavily on core concepts of motivational interviewing (Miller & Rollnick, 2013), a highly successful individual treatment model for substance abuse. Further, it is a good example of how a systemically oriented family therapist might approach a substance abuse problem within a family, in that (1) the assessment phase of treatment includes all family members, (2) treatment goals are developed with input from all family members, and (3) alteration of alcohol or drug use is conceptualized as detoxification of both the family system and the individual abuser.

Future Directions for Family Care during Mental Illness

Today, compelling data support using a family-oriented perspective in treatment programs for the long-term care of patients with chronic psychiatric disorders—and also in early intervention programs identifying at-risk individuals during the prodromal stages. Yet the prevalent anti-family bias of many clinicians needs to be challenged before the real value of family-focused support and treatment programs is fully realized. Even though some clinicians remain hard-pressed to identify typologies of families associated with different psychiatric disorders, families often feel blamed and criticized—justly or unjustly—rather than supported by mental health professionals.

Note, for example, the studies by Corrigan and colleagues utilizing a nationally representative sample that demonstrated that family role co-varies with public perceptions of stigma (Corrigan, Watson, & Miller, 2006, 2007). Blame for onset of mental illness and when the mentally ill relative exhibited low treatment adherence was attributed to the family. When public attitudes leaned this way, support for families decreased.

Countering these negative stereotypes about mentally ill patients are several innovations from both lay and professional communities. Strong examples from families themselves include National Alliance on Mental Illness (NAMI), a grassroots organization that has made major strides in transforming public attitudes toward mental illnesses, and the Al-Anon/Alateen movements in the substance abuse arena. In parallel, as the family therapy professional community has moved away from the pathologizing "deficit" view toward a non-blaming "resource" view of families, the therapy field now overlaps quite comfortably with an advocacy group like NAMI.

Interestingly, the caregiving literature has been particularly salient in elucidating interrelationships among family functioning, family stress, and clinical course of psychiatric illness. Although not labeled a "family systems" approach, caregiving is one area where families are included in the evaluation of the success of treatment. At the same time, most support programs for caregivers do not directly include patients. In this respect, they differ substantially from family therapy models like McFarlane's (2002) multifamily group (MFG) model, Anderson and colleagues' (1980) family therapy approach for schizophrenia, or Steinglass and colleagues' (1987) therapy model for substance abuse.

In a fusion between the caregiving literature in which patients are generally not included as intervention participants, and the mental health literature in which they are included, Kissane, Bloch, McKenzie, McDowall, and Nitzan (1998) described an intervention targeting the entire family unit, comprising patients plus their relatives, to improve bereavement-related outcomes in families facing a relative's terminal cancer. In the preliminary line of research of Kissane, Bloch, Dowe et al. (1996) and Kissane, Bloch, Onghena et al. (1996), well-functioning families that showed high cohesion and mutual support, and in which difference of opinion was well tolerated, evidenced substantially better psychosocial outcomes compared to those families exhibiting more dysfunctional interaction patterns such as lower cohesiveness, lower expression, and greater interpersonal conflict.

Clear parallels exist between worsened outcomes for dysfunctional families coping with bereavement and dysfunctional families coping with mental illnesses. In the crises of both bereavement and mental illness, a dysfunctional family can unwittingly handicap clinical course, care provision, and healing. Moreover, the principles and goals that guide family-based treatments for bereavement and mental illness share key characteristics: a collaborative family-therapist relationship; prophylactic intervention across domains of communication, conflict, and emotional distress; dissemination of information and continuing care as appropriate; and importantly, always capitalization on the family's resiliency.

Conclusion

Clearly, mental illness brings great grief, stress, and challenge to families. Two main lines of systemic thinking substantially increase the potential usefulness of family-oriented approaches for treatment of major mental illness. The first approach stresses how to better understand and utilize specific positive/adaptive aspects of family behavior to protect at-risk individuals from developing clinical illness. The second approach focuses on supporting families in their efforts to manage destabilizing symptomatology, improving treatment adherence, and decreasing recidivism. Much work remains to be done before the potential of these ideas and clinical innovations can be fully utilized as standard components of "best practice" for the treatment of major mental illness.

References

Alexander, J., Robbins, M., & Sexton, T. (2000). Family-based interventions with older, at risk youth: From promise to proof to practice. *Journal of Primary Prevention, 21,* 185–205.

Anderson, C., Hogarty, G., & Reiss, D. (1980). Family treatment of adult schizophrenic patients: A psychoeducational approach. *Schizophrenia Bulletin, 6,* 490–505.

Awad, A. G., & Voruganti, L. N. P. (2008). The burden of schizophrenia on caregivers: A review. *Pharmacoeconomics, 26,* 149–162.

Barrowclough, C., & Hooley, J. M. (2003). Attributions and expressed emotion: A review. *Clinical Psychology Review, 23,* 849–880.

Brodaty, H., Thompson, C., Thompson, C., & Fine, M. (2005). Why caregivers of people with dementia and memory loss don't use services. *International Journal of Geriatric Psychiatry, 20,* 537–546.

Copello, A., Velleman, R., & Templeton, L. (2005). Family interventions in the treatment of alcohol and drug problems. *Drug and Alcohol Review, 24,* 369–385.

Corrigan, P. W., Watson, A. C., & Miller, F. E. (2006). Blame, shame, and contamination: The impact of mental illness and drug dependence stigma of family members. *Journal of Family Psychology, 20,* 239–246.

Dixon, L., & Lehman, A. (1995). Family interventions for schizophrenia. *Schizophrenia Bulletin, 21,* 631–643.

Edwards, M. E., & Steinglass, P. (1995). Family therapy treatment outcomes for alcoholism. *Journal of Marital and Family Therapy, 21,* 475–509.

Falloon, I., Boyd, J., & McGill, C. (1984). *Family care of schizophrenia.* New York: Guilford Press.

Falloon, I., Held, T., Coverdale, J., Roncone, R., & Laidlaw, T. M. (1999). Psychosocial intervention for schizophrenia: A review of long-term benefits of international studies. *Psychiatric Rehabilitation Skills, 3,* 268–290.

Fals-Stewart, W., O'Farrell, T., Birchler, G., Córdova, J., & Kelley, M. (2005). Behavioral couples therapy for alcoholism and drug abuse: Where we've been, where we are, and where we're going. *Journal of Cognitive Psychotherapy, 196,* 229–246.

Goldstein, M., & Miklowitz, D. (1995). The effectiveness of psychoeducational family therapy in the treatment of schizophrenic disorders. *Journal of Marital and Family Therapy, 21,* 361–376.

Gurman, A. S. (2008). A framework for the comparative study of couple therapy: History, models, and applications. In A. Gurman (Ed.), *Clinical handbook of couple therapy* (pp. 1–26). New York: Guilford Press.

Hooley, J. (1998). Expressed emotion and psychiatric illness: From empirical data to clinical practice. *Behavior Therapy, 29,* 631–646.

Hooley, J., Rosen, L., & Richters, J. (1995). Expressed emotion: Toward clarification of a critical construct. In G. Miller (Ed.), *Experimental psychopathology* (pp. 88–120). New York: Academic Press.

Jang, K. L. (2005). *The behavioral genetics of psychopathology.* Mahwah, NJ: Lawrence Erlbaum Associates.

Kiecolt-Glaser, J. K., Gouin, J.-P., Weng, N.-P., Malarkey, W. B., Beversdorf, D. Q., & Glaser, R. (2011). Childhood adversity heightens the impact of later-life caregiving stress on telomere length and inflammation. *Psychosomatic Medicine, 73,* 16–22.

Kiecolt-Glaser, J. K., Marucha, P. T., Malarkey, W. B., Mercado, A. M., & Glaser, R. (1995). Slowing of wound healing by psychological stress. *The Lancet, 346,* 1–3.

Kissane, D. W., Bloch, S., Dowe, D. L., Snyder, R. D., Onghena, P., MacKenzie, D.P., & Wallace, C. S. (1996). The Melbourne Family Grief Study, I: Perceptions of family functioning in bereavement. *American Journal of Psychiatry, 153,* 650–658.

Kissane, D. W., Bloch, S., McKenzie, M., McDowall, A. C., & Nitzan, R. (1998). Family grief therapy: A preliminary account of a new model to promote family functioning during palliative care and bereavement. *Psycho-Oncology, 7,* 14–25.

Kissane, D. W., Bloch, S., Onghena, P., MacKenzie, D. P., Snyder, R. D., & Dowe, D. L. (1996). The Melbourne Family Grief Study, II: Psychosocial morbidity and grief in bereaved families. *American Journal of Psychiatry, 153,* 659–666.

Lefley, H. P. (1996). *Family caregiving in mental illness.* Thousand Oaks, CA: Sage.

Madsen, W. C. (1999). *Collaborative therapy with multi-stressed families: From old problems to new futures.* New York: Guilford Press.

McCrady, B. S., Stout, R. L., Noel, N. E., Abrams, D. B., & Nelson, H. F. (1991). Effectiveness of three types of spouse-involved behavioral alcoholism treatment. *British Journal of Addictions, 86,* 1415–1424.

McFarlane, W. (2002). *Multifamily groups in the treatment of severe psychiatric disorders.* New York: Guilford Press.

McFarlane, W., Dixon, L., Lukens, E., & Lucksted, A. (2007). Family psychoeducation and schizophrenia: A review of the literature. *Journal of Marital and Family Therapy, 29,* 223–245.

McFarlane, W., Link, B., Dushay, R., Marchal, J., & Crilly, J. (2004). Psychoeducational multiple family groups: Four-year relapse outcome in schizophrenia. *Family Process, 34,* 127–144.

Miklowitz, D. (2006). A review of evidence-based psychosocial interventions for bipolar disorder. *Journal of Clinical Psychiatry, 67*(Suppl. 11), 28–33.

Miklowitz, D. J., Simoneau, T. L., George, E. L., Richards, J. A., Kalbag, A., Sachs-Ericsson, N., & Suddath, R. (2000). Family-focused treatment of bipolar disorder: 1-Year effects of a psycho-educational program in conjunction with pharmacotherapy. *Biological Psychiatry, 48,* 582–592.

Miller, W., & Wilbourne, P. (2002). Mesa Grande: A methodological analysis of clinical trials of treatments for alcohol use disorders. *Addiction, 97,* 265–277.

Miller, W. R., Meyers, R. J., & Tonigan, J. S. (1999). Engaging the unmotivated in treatment for alcohol problems: A comparison of three strategies for intervention through family members. *Journal of Consulting and Clinical Psychology, 67,* 688.

Miller, W. R., & Rollnick, S. (2013). *Motivational interviewing: Helping people change.* (3rd ed). New York: Guilford Press.

Mueser, K. T., & Jeste, D. V. (Eds.). (2008). *Clinical handbook of schizophrenia.* New York: Guilford Press.

Nichols, M. (2012). *Family therapy: Concepts and methods* (10th ed.). Boston: Allyn & Bacon.

Nichols, M. P., & Schwartz, R. C. (2005). *The essentials of family therapy* (2nd ed.). Boston: Pearson Education.

O'Farrell, T., & Fals-Stewart, W. (2003). Alcohol abuse. *Journal of Marital and Family Therapy, 29,* 121–146.

O'Farrell, T., & Fals-Stewart, W. (2006). *Behavioral couples therapy for alcoholism and drug abuse.* New York: Guilford Press.

Penn, P. I., & Mueser, K. T. (1996). Research update on the psychosocial treatment of schizophrenia. *American Journal of Psychiatry, 153,* 607–617.

Perlick, D. A., Rosenheck, R. A., Miklowitz, D. J., Chessick, C., Wolff, N., Kaczynski, R., . . . STEP-BD Family Experience Collaborative Study Group. (2007). Prevalence and correlates of burden among caregivers of patients with bipolar disorder enrolled in the Systematic Treatment Enhancement Program for Bipolar Disorder. *Bipolar Disorder, 9,* 262–273.

Pickett-Schenk, S., Cook, J., & Laris, A. (2000). Journey of Hope program outcomes. *Community Mental Health Journal, 36,* 413–424.

Pike, A., McGuire, S., Hetherington, E. M., Reiss, D., & Plomin, R. (1996). Family environment and adolescent depressive symptoms and antisocial behavior: A multivariate genetic analysis. *Developmental Psychology, 32,* 590–604.

Reiss, D., Heatherington, E. M., Plomin, R., Howe, G. W., Simmens, S. J., Henderson, S. H., . . . Law, T. (1995). Genetic questions for environmental studies: Differential parental behavior and psychopathology in adolescence. *Archives of General Psychiatry, 52,* 925–936.

Reiss, D., Neiderhiser, J., Hetherington, E., & Plomin, R. (2003). *The relationship code: Deciphering genetic and social influences on adolescent development.* Cambridge, MA: Harvard University Press.

Rohrbaugh, M., Shoham, V., Spungen, C., & Steinglass, P. (1995). Family systems therapy in practice: A systemic couples therapy for problem drinking. In B. Bongar & L. Beutler (Eds.), *Comprehensive textbook of psychotherapy: Theory and practice* (pp. 228–253). New York: Oxford University Press.

Rotunda, R., & O'Farrell, T. (1997). Marital and family therapy of alcohol use disorders: Bridging the gap between research and practice. *Professional Psychology: Research and Practice, 28,* 246–252.

Rowe, C., & Liddle, H. (2003). Substance abuse treatment: Families and family life. *Journal of Marital and Family Therapy, 29,* 97–120.

Stanton, M. D. (2004). Family treatment approaches to drug abuse problems: A review. *Family Process, 18,* 251–280.

Stanton, M. D., & Heath, A. W. (2005). Family-based treatment: Stages and outcomes. In R. J. Frances, S. I. Miller, & A. H. Mack (Eds.), *Clinical textbook of addictive disorders* (3rd ed., pp. 528–558). New York: Guilford Press.

Steinglass, P. (2008). Family systems and motivational interviewing: A systemic-motivational model for treatment of alcohol and other drug problems. *Alcoholism Treatment Quarterly, 26*(1/2), 9–29.

Steinglass, P. (2009). Systemic-motivational therapy for substance abuse disorders: An integrative model. *Journal of Family Therapy, 31,* 155–174.

Steinglass, P., Bennett, L. A., Wolin, S. J., & Reiss, D. (1987). *The alcoholic family.* New York: Basic Books.

Thomas, C., & Corcoran, J. (2001). Empirically based marital and family interventions for alcohol abuse: A review. *Research on Social Work Practice, 11,* 549–575.

van der Voort, T. Y. G., Goossens, P. J. J., & van der Bijl, J. J. (2007). Burden, coping and needs for support of caregivers of patients with a bipolar disorder: A systematic review. *Journal of Psychiatric and Mental Health Nursing, 14,* 679–687.

van Wijngaarden, B., Schene, A. H., & Koeter, M. W. J. (2004). Family caregiving in depression: Impact on caregivers' daily life, distress, and help seeking. *Journal of Affective Disorders, 81,* 211–222.

Vaughan, C. E., & Leff, J. P. (1976). The influence of family and social factors on the course of psychiatric illness. *British Journal of Psychiatry, 129,* 125–137.

World Schizophrenia Fellowship. (1998). *Families as partners in care: A document developed to launch a strategy for the implementation of programs of family education, training, and support.* Toronto: World Schizophrenia Fellowship.

Wynne, L., McDaniel, S., & Weber, T. (1986). *Systems consultation: A new perspective for family therapy.* New York: Guilford Press.

Zauszniewski, J. A., Bekhet, A. K., & Suresky, M. J. (2008). Factors associated with perceived burden, resourcefulness, and quality of life in female family members of adults with serious mental illness. *Journal of the American Psychiatric Nurses Association, 14,* 125–135.

5 Ethical Dimensions of Family Bereavement Care

Tomer T. Levin and Marguerite S. Lederberg

To choose a pathway to healing that is morally sound when conducting family therapy with the bereaved, it is essential that therapists appreciate the complexity of ethical dilemmas. This chapter details the often unique ethical challenges encountered in such therapy, including screening while avoiding labeling families, informed consent, competing needs, boundaries, confidentiality and truth telling, duration of therapy, competency, the quandaries of modern technology, and countertransference.

Before delving into these ethical issues, we review the philosophical and clinical frameworks that are used to identify and analyze moral issues. Learning how to unpack ethical dilemmas will give the reader the necessary tools to appreciate the subsequent ethical challenges.

Guiding Ethical Frameworks for Family Therapy

Principlism

Principlism is the most widely used framework today, although it is not technically a theory. It employs mid-level ethical principles, thus avoiding the polarity of more absolutist approaches that are based on one superseding value. The four main principles, or values, used in this framework are as follows:

1. *Beneficence:* In the family therapy setting, this means that the family's welfare is a central aim and that psychological interventions are intended to be for the good of the family.
2. *Nonmaleficence:* This means doing no harm; psychological interventions should not cause damaging side effects. It is sometimes subsumed in the full spectrum of beneficent behaviors.
3. *Autonomy, or Respect for Persons:* This is a core principle that affirms that each person's own values must be respected throughout the course of any treatment—hence the importance accorded to the process of informed consent, which demands that patients understand the advantages, disadvantages, and alternatives to proposed psychological treatments so that they can make the choice that best serves their needs, values, and risk tolerance.
4. *Justice:* In family therapy, personal justice requires that caregivers treat each family member with equal care, honesty, and commitment. For example, each member of the fictive family must be given a voice so that the loudest voice does not steal the

stage. Social justice refers to the fair allocation of medical resources and is discussed later in the chapter.

Principlism leads to the right exploratory questions. These questions in turn address important ethical issues, but these issues can conflict head-on with each other. A family demanding more care for its loved one than the patient desires is imposing its view of beneficence over the patient's autonomy. Balancing these views requires a stance of compromise, which speaks to the work of family therapy. Similarly, justice can be easily compromised by overworked clinicians and overextended health systems in which a decrease in the quality of care is almost unavoidable.

Despite these problems, principlism is widely used in everyday health care ethics because each principle has its own validity. Exploring the role of each one in a given case reliably identifies the most severe disjunctions in the system. These principles lead to the right questions, even if they do not produce clear answers. The following section reviews theories that purport to help find the answers.

Utilitarianism (Consequentialism)

Utilitarianism is an ethical theory that focuses on outcome: it posits that one should maximize benefit and minimize harmful consequences. However, when the motivating principles are less important than the outcome, there is not much guidance about the selections of actions taken and the cost to the individuals involved. For example, for some cancer patients, life can be prolonged, and this can be considered a positive outcome. However, the expense of this outcome might be prolonged suffering and decreased benefit from full palliative care. Families often differ with the patient or among themselves regarding the course to follow, causing disagreements and profound pain.

Deontology

Based on Kantian writings, deontology focuses on absolute values of right and wrong, emphasizing our universal obligations to carry out certain duties and avoid other intrinsically wrong actions that would be unacceptable in all societies. One example is our obligation to tell the truth, which is a widely accepted, universal obligation. This informs the truth-telling movement in cancer and palliative care, which sees the moral correctness of telling patients and families of their diagnosis and prognosis. However, universality is hard to come by, and beliefs routinely conflict in human groups, especially families. Furthermore, invoking absolutes can too easily lead to abuse of authority and neglect of individual needs.

Case Example

Consider the case of a 65-year-old lymphoma patient who wanted to shield his nonagenarian parents from his diagnosis and chemotherapy. His perceived duty to protect his parents overrode his obligation to tell the truth, even if it meant fabricating explanations about why he had lost hair and weight. His parents died peacefully, never knowing that he had cancer, and the dutiful son went on to make a full recovery.

Deontological thinking might question whether parents of any age would *not* notice that their son was ill and whether this "white lie" was indeed effective. Could it have induced his parents to lie in return by pretending that everything was fine to protect their son's fragile self-image and perceived duty? Consider the implications of his parents discovering his fabrication if he had been hospitalized or, worse still, had died. They could have been devastated by his mistruth and attempt to shield them.

By deontological logic, open communication is probably a more reliable approach and may have been equally helpful in this situation; indeed, always telling the cancer truth is how most therapists would approach this case. Truth telling is discussed in further detail subsequently.

Virtue Theory

Virtue theory dates back to the Greek philosophers, who greatly valued the development of character. They outlined what they deemed the basic virtues that constitute a "good" human being. Virtue theory has been used more formally by religious institutions and discussed by many philosophers right up to the present. Good values are essential for care providers, but there is no such requirement for patients. They must be ethically treated even if they are criminals (although justice requires that it be done with adequate regard for caregiver safety).

Ethics of Care

Ethics of care first came to the fore in 1982, with Carol Gilligan's book *In a Different Voice,* which commented that moral theories that invoked right or wrong answers for dilemmas reflected a typically masculine viewpoint and ignored the importance of relationships—something that came more naturally to women. The book received an expected amount of criticism. It was followed in 1984 by *Caring: A Feminine Approach to Ethics and Moral Education,* by Nel Noddings, the first of many books in which she elaborated her belief that "natural caring" as manifested more clearly but not exclusively in mothers, could, and did, grow into a more generalized "ethical caring." Noddings also reviewed how these feelings extended to men as well. She has been criticized by some for being a feminist and by feminists for relegating women to feminine roles. Nevertheless, her constructs have now been respected widely and adopted as the ethics of care by other commentators who agree on the importance of relationships in providing moral care.

This ethical model is manifested in concepts such as the physician-patient-family dynamic, compassionate care, charity, friendship, love, and altruism. It critiques the previous theoretical approaches as being too detached from the real world and instead focuses on the here and now. The ethics of care acknowledges the vulnerability of some family members compared to others and the need to care and shield them. It can be criticized, however, for its lack of moral rules that deal with subjectivity and risk, which can impede useful ethical debate. But the perfect theory has yet to be described.

Importantly, care ethics in a variety of forms can complement principlism, and these two frameworks are often evoked together. Principlism invokes common moral principles, whereas the ethics of care captures the realities of being human. A human is an unfinished piece of work, struggling daily with the emotions caused by fate and the connections with others around him or her. The combination of these two approaches tries to address both areas, leading to a fuller, cooperative endeavor.

Case Example

When she needed assistance with bathing, dressing, and ambulating, a frail 70-year-old widow dying of metastatic lung cancer had a stubborn independence and rigidity. This made it difficult for her devoted daughter to care for her. The final crisis came when the patient drove away her nursing aides. Clearly, the mother might receive better care in a 24/7 nursing facility, but she adamantly refused to leave her familiar apartment. The patient's trusted oncologist recommended transfer to a hospice for end-of-life medical and nursing care. This could only be achieved by declaring her to lack the capacity to make medical decisions, activating her daughter as her health care agent. It would be a huge moral blow to a woman who valued her autonomy—the same autonomy that had fueled her navigation of life's earlier adversities.

The daughter advocated that her mother's wishes be respected, and the oncologist accepted this plan. Gaining a new and understanding palliative care nurse, the daughter cared for her dying mother at home. She died peacefully a few days later in her own bed, her daughter at her side.

This case reflects how an ethics of care can be integrated smoothly into a case where autonomy could have been challenged painfully but was saved by the love of a daughter and the understanding of a physician.

Integrative Clinically Based Frameworks

The next section discusses three integrative methods, including case-centered ethics, the situational diagnosis, and ethical codes, that are more directly embedded in the clinical situation. These reflect patient-centered ethics in the everyday work of clinics and medical centers.

Case-Centered Ethics

This is not so much a moral theory as a sensible acceptance that one should learn from experience. The culture of medical training values learning from experience, as reflected in practices such as case conferences, mortality and morbidity meetings, and autopsies.

Hospital ethics committees routinely review clinical cases on a case-by-case basis, where they attempt to learn from prior experience and use this knowledge to inform future ethical dilemmas. For example, the case of a dying patient languishing on a ventilator might lead to introducing palliative care earlier in subsequent cases. Case-centered ethics can still be criticized because one precedent may not be generalizable and the method is easily skewed by personal opinions. It can easily conflict with pluralistic societal values. Stopping intravenous hydration, for example, may be acceptable to one patient, yet violate the sensitivities of another, who perceives it as abandoning a thirsty, dying person. But case-centered ethics does open the door to flexibility and to changes that may be based on human emotions, such as the feelings aroused in staff as they watch a patient through long days on the ventilator.

The Situational Diagnosis

Ethical principles need to be applied to real people facing difficult personal decisions. Here, an integrative framework is helpful.

Marguerite Lederberg, a psychiatrist-ethicist at Memorial Sloan-Kettering Cancer Center, noted that complicated ethics consultations often evoke intense feelings among patients and families that usually flow onto staff members, with resultant confusion (Lederberg, 1997). Close entanglements exist between psychiatric and ethical issues, sometimes resulting in pseudo-psychiatry consultations that should have gone to an ethics committee, or pseudo-ethics cases that belonged in psychiatry. Lederberg referred to the following analysis as making a "situational diagnosis" to help identify and understand the ethical issues at hand. It is important to identify five contextual areas:

1. The patient and family's psychological needs and possible responses to them.
2. The role of their family dynamics and possible interventions.
3. The involvement of relevant medical caregivers or individuals with a defined involvement and possible responses.
4. The relationship between the family/patient and these staff members, how it could be affecting the process, and what can be done about it.
5. The presence of legal or institutional constraints that must be accepted.

The outlining of these issues and the recommended solutions do not reveal anything about the process to follow, but they indicate that qualified clinicians see a reasonable way to begin, and insure that they have a reliable, detailed oversight of the situation and were not entrapped by their own or other participants' strong emotions.

This analysis also points out that problems and disagreements for which the clinician has no prescriptions are ethical issues, needing a different approach. This is the time to use the four principles (principlism) to ask questions, explore as many theories as seem to apply without being didactic, and, as the situation develops, hear and respect every voice, and let the ethics of care guide the process to a solution that is both moral and humane.

Where the resources exist, a multidisciplinary approach—calling upon ethics, psychiatry, palliative care, social work, legal, chaplaincy, case management/discharge planning, and patient advocacy—is often required to support the integrative conceptualization and address the component issues. The private practitioner is encouraged to have some established colleagues and familiar resources for both types of problems.

J. J. Fins, an ethicist-physician at Weill Cornell Medical College in New York, also takes a pragmatic approach, viewing ethical principles as hypothetical guides that generate a range of reasonable moral options, which in turn require debate and reflection in order to reach consensus (Fins, Bacchetta, & Miller, 1997). He calls this method of ethical problem solving "clinical pragmatism." For Fins, the essential element is the *interpersonal process* of garnering consensus that can withstand ethical scrutiny. Democracy is present. There may be more than one ethically acceptable solution; all parties are entitled to be heard and collaboratively reach a consensus guided, if need be, by ethics consultants.

Codes of Ethics

Ethical codes have been developed to guide moral conduct, but they could benefit from being more detailed and focused on the need to anticipate and respond to specific ethical challenges that arise in clinical settings. The Association for Death Education and Counseling (ADEC), one of the oldest interdisciplinary thanatology organizations, outlines detailed ethical guidelines that cover general conduct; competence; responsibilities to patients, other professionals, employers, and society at large; confidentiality and privacy; education; and research (ADEC, 2004).

Specific Ethical Challenges in Family Grief Therapy

Role of the Therapist

The duties of an individual therapist are well defined. The focus is on the patient, boundaries are carefully observed, and privacy is preserved under all but a few very specific conditions.

But problems increase exponentially with the number of individuals in the family group. Conflicts of opinion are common, and disagreements that unevenly affect the welfare of different family members also arise, especially during times of crisis concerning major issues. The seasoned family therapist learns how to remain neutral and nurture a spirit of benign curiosity that allows the members to communicate with each other in new ways.

Complex situations require many medical resources, whose distribution falls under the ethical principle of social justice. For example, families in geographically isolated areas should not be denied family grief therapy because they live too far from tertiary care centers where resources may be concentrated. Telemedicine may be helpful to equalize such geographical limitations to care, but this too may not be readily available. Similarly, when hospitals and governments negotiate contracts with health insurance companies, provision should be made for affordable access to family therapy that is free from deductibles or co-pays, which both may be prohibitive for low-income groups. Although not all therapists can impact health policy or hospital administration, the therapist is frequently advocating for resources on behalf of the family and using professional knowledge of the health system to achieve social justice goals.

The gap between needs and resources may be great, and the therapist must work through his or her own responses to inequality in deciding how to engage these issues with limited or difficult options.

Screening and Measuring Outcomes versus Labeling

In family therapy, assessments of family function, depression and anxiety, and similar issues are helpful to objectively screen families' suitability for therapy. These assessments are equally helpful to measure response to treatment, an important aspect of the current environment of data-driven outcomes.

For example, the Family Relationships Index measures communication, cohesion, and conflict and predicts the risk of members developing pathological grief in the Family Focused Grief Therapy model (Kissane et al., 2006). Although such a screening tool offers the hope of an intervention, it could also pathologize if a label were applied to a family. The family might easily experience it as checking if they are "sick" or "bad." In crisis, they already feel bad enough! Great care is needed to avoid inadvertent labeling.

Consider the case of one family member, told by his psychiatrist that he had a mental illness, major depression, characterized by "abnormal brain chemicals." For many years, this reinforced the notion that he "had to take medications" and accorded him a special sick role in the family. Such labeling negates the possibility that depression offers a chance to rethink life strategies within the context of family therapy and thus may ultimately be an adaptive opportunity.

In family grief therapy, it is always helpful to phrase screening in positive terms as a tool to see who might benefit from interventions that bridge severe stresses and vulnerability, using a team approach. In communicating this to patients, "we" statements emphasize the clinical team's supportive and collaborative approach to screening, whereas "you" statements suggest labeling.

Informed Consent

Who constitutes the family? This is an important question concerning informed consent for family therapy in light of the potential diversity of the modern family. For example, in blended families, stepparents may play a role that is either pivotal or peripheral. One aunt may be a second parent, while another might be a distant relative. A person who has deliberately avoided the family for many years may wisely be excluded from family therapy—or invited in, depending on the circumstances. Fiancés, ex-spouses, friends, neighbors, in-laws, and grandparents may all be considered fictive kin. Including the appropriate family members in a process of informed consent speaks to the principles of autonomy, beneficence, and nonmaleficence. It also invokes an ethics of care. For example, there are advantages to including a 12-year-old child in the informed consent process as a way of respecting his or her autonomy and giving room to that child's voice in the family, even though it may not necessarily be a legal requirement. It shows caring. Although children under 12 are probably too young, this boundary is fluid, as some younger children may be more mature and older children less so.

What of the person who refuses to participate in family therapy, be it a dying patient or another key family member? Should that person be persuaded or coerced into participating? An overly paternalistic approach compromises a person's autonomy; on the other hand, an ethics of care might suggest that a guiding therapist's voice is helpful to draw outlying family members into therapy, overcoming their initial resistance.

Competing Needs

Although a systems approach advocates for all the participants in a system equally—and certainly this is possible in family therapy—two other dynamics are also possible.

First, the urgency of the patient's medical and psychological needs usurps that of family members who receive less psychological "airtime." This is not uncommon in unstable and life-threatening medical situations.

The second dynamic is where another family member's needs are so great that they distract from the overall family therapy. This should be considered if during family therapy it becomes apparent that one member has a major psychiatric problem such as substance abuse, generalized anxiety, or bipolar depression that has never been treated. Should the focus of the therapy now segue to this person's addiction or disorder? One danger is that the family therapy gets diverted to serve the needs of that member, raising the ethical issue of distributive justice. Another danger is scapegoating: labeling this member may adversely impact the family's cohesion, so vital in the grief therapy process. On the other hand, therapists have a unique set of skills that allow them to diagnose and help treat such problems; to ignore a festering issue such as substance abuse may be disadvantageous in the long term.

Thus, it is crucial that the therapist be aware of competing needs—and here, even the therapist is not immune to his or her competing needs, as in the example of "caseness." This refers to the need of therapists and researchers to define what is pathological and what is normal. Yet in many psychological syndromes, the phenomena being identified as pathological criteria are evolving. Furthermore, grief, whether pathological or not, can have a large component of cultural heterogeneity. Finally, time heals for some, but predictive models for those in need of timely help versus those who will be healed in time are not absolute. With the ethical dictum of *primum non noncereum* (i.e., first do no harm), therapists must ensure that their well-intentioned therapeutic efforts do not upset a delicate but functional equilibrium.

Boundaries of Therapy

Conventional family therapy is based on firm boundaries of regular, time-limited sessions in a professional office, with no inappropriate touching of the patient and no inter-session contact. Dying and grief changes this formula, forcing the therapist to adapt, thereby creating ethical challenges.

Dying patients are physically vulnerable. They are often dressed in pajamas; medical devices and tubes may intrude. Not uncommonly, a nightgown may fall open, an ostomy bag may gurgle feces, or a urinary catheter bag may be carried around with the patient. Therapists may be expected to and should, if appropriate, help patients become more physically comfortable. If a therapist shows revulsion when witnessing deteriorating bodily function, trust and the therapeutic relationship are compromised. The therapist should help the patient be as autonomous as possible by covering up exposed body parts, if appropriate, and by assisting the patient to sit comfortably. Accepting a timely hug in family grief therapy may be therapeutic, whereas rejecting it could adversely impact the therapy. In conventional therapy, hugs would usually be frowned upon as a boundary violation.

Conducting therapy in the family home creates additional boundary issues. Should the therapist accept an offer of refreshments or use the family bathroom to relieve him or herself? Consideration of seating is an issue. Placing the therapist in the armchair traditionally assigned to the head of the household may impinge on the boundaries of usual family dynamics. Sitting in chairs and sofas of different heights, or sitting on a rug, can create power disparities and compromise the therapist's neutrality. Intrusions from well-intentioned neighbors can create privacy issues. Telephone calls, for instance from a doctor's office, may have to be answered, thus disrupting the conventionally acceptable therapeutic parameters.

Whether the therapist should attend the funeral or remembrance ceremony and whether cards should be sent on anniversaries of the death cannot be governed by overly rigid protocols; here the ethical principles of nonmalfeasance, care, and autonomy are important. A therapist might, in one extreme example, intrude on a family funeral by accepting a central role among the front rows ahead of other mourners, thereby displacing some family members. Ultimately, this may harm the family and certainly would compromise the autonomy of the functioning family unit, which the therapy tries so hard to promote. On the other hand, a therapist's humble, nonintrusive attendance at a funeral might be remembered as a moving gesture of care, aiding the family's healing process and furthering the therapy goals. From the countertransference perspective, participation in a commemorative ceremony may help the therapist, who also has a need to grieve the loss of the patient.

The family in crisis at a time of death is often paralyzed, and the therapist may be tempted to offer a paternalistic approach in governing the family. Alternatively, the family may inadvertently propel the therapist into an advisory capacity. For example, if the family insists that the therapist play a leading role in the remembrance ceremony, the therapeutic goal of helping to affirm family strengths might be compromised. Here the therapist can guide the family to assume autonomous responsibilities and simultaneously maintain a respectful distance, which is helpful yet not intrusive.

Maintaining Confidences and Truth Telling

Secrets are ubiquitous in family therapy and present an ethical quandary, which can be premised on open communication and respect.

Often a secret is revealed by a member as an aside to the therapist, before or after a meeting. Here, it is useful for the therapist to suggest that the issue be raised at the next meeting. In general, colluding by promising to keep the secret is, as most family therapists know, a recipe for strife. Nevertheless, rigid rules can conflict with pragmatics.

One common family secret is news of a terminal prognosis, for fear that the bad news will shatter the recipient emotionally or destroy their hope. If the therapist explores the evidence supporting such beliefs and offers help in case of emotional distress, it can go a long way toward helping family members communicate optimally. It is also helpful to clarify the prognosis, which is often misunderstood or underappreciated.

To illustrate, one psychiatry consultation, in keeping with Lederberg's approach, offered support to a distressed family in conflict, while simultaneously suggesting that truth telling, albeit potentially difficult, would be a more productive way forward.

Case Example

A dying woman's husband met an untimely death. Her brother was her health care agent and decided that she should be spared the cruel agony of mourning her husband's death while also preparing for her own death. This created an enormous conflict for the patient's teenage son who, sitting at his mother's bedside, was forced to pretend that his father was away on a prolonged overseas business trip, while at the same time hiding his own terrible grief. Worse perhaps, his mother could not comfort him in his grief, and he could not comfort her. The therapist, called in to consult on the case, refused to collude with the secret keeping. He told the patient the difficult truth about her husband's death.

With the truth out in the open, the patient and her son were able to grieve the loss of the husband together. The mother was able to guide her son beyond his grief and discuss his future life, which would now unfold with his uncle as his guardian. Together with this, they had the opportunity to discuss her impending death, and she was able to comfort him in his anticipatory mourning. It was a profound and unforgettable last act of mothering.

Culture can also impact truth telling. This is especially salient where hierarchical roles are important to the family structure. Here there is an expectation that one family member will assume responsibility for the truth in the role of a patriarch or a dutiful child; family grief therapy should attempt to understand and explore these issues.

Avoidant coping (which is often called denial, or burying your head in the ground) is a common response, especially when people are overwhelmed. When patients say that they do not want to hear about death or dying, is it ethical for the therapist or family to refrain from truth telling, even if death is inevitable? Or should the patient be confronted with the truth? In the interest of nonmaleficence, most therapists would agree that encumbering a patient with the truth is ultimately not helpful. Gently exploring thoughts and perceptions of end-of-life goals of care is, however, therapeutic. Indeed, when avoidant coping is eventually supplanted by problem-focused coping, it signals a meaningful turning point in the therapy.

Where the secret is perceived to be shameful, such as incest, rape, infidelity, crime, or abortion, the question of "privacy versus truth telling" needs to be carefully balanced with the goals of the family therapy and the family system.

Case Example

Maria, age 65, received a diagnosis of a high-grade colon cancer four years previously and underwent bowel surgery. Two years later, secondaries developed in her liver and lung, necessitating chemotherapy. Eventually, her disease worsened and second-line chemotherapy was introduced. Nausea, fatigue, and loss of appetite gradually developed, suggesting the development of imminent liver failure. Maria's oncologist wanted to discuss the goals of care with her and her family because it seemed that she had entered the dying phase. On one occasion, she had told him, "I am ready, doctor!"

However, before the oncologist could speak to Maria, her physician-son cornered him in the corridor, demanding that she now receive single-agent Capecitabine. He asked the oncologist not to tell his mother that she was dying to preserve her hope.

Family communication was conflict-laden, with the son acting as a physician–decision maker and marginalizing the father. The daughter, who had despised her brother's bullying, therefore avoided visiting her mother and instead called her father every day. The oncologist did not want to start Capecitabine but worried about being sued if he declined. Somewhat demoralized, he considered the options of an ethics consultation, bringing in a family therapist, or a beach vacation.

Analyzing this case from the ethical perspective, truth telling is a central issue: if the oncologist cannot communicate effectively with the patient and make collaborative decisions, the patient's autonomy is severely compromised. If futile treatment is started, this constitutes malfeasance. The oncologist, with beneficence and an ethics of care at heart, feels coerced by the son's demand for silence. The result is moral distress. Poor family communication, complicated dynamics, and festering anger are hard to unpack from the ethical issues. Yet all of these issues must be addressed in order to implement an ethically tenable solution that is acceptable to all.

Duration of Grief Therapy

Grieving families can appear so abjectly helpless that they frequently desire to continue therapy for longer than may be needed. The question arises whether a model of brief intervention should be morphed into longer-term therapy. Fostering undue dependency is an autonomy concern, as is deviating from the agreement made during the informed consent process.

Pragmatics and flexibility may rule the day: relevant family members in need can be referred to individual therapy, while the therapist promotes and validates the autonomy of the family unit by ending the focused intervention as planned. Another option is completing a time-limited intervention as planned and reevaluating adaptation (or lack thereof) in three and then six months, with a view to further time-limited booster therapy if necessary.

Competency

To maximize beneficence and minimize the potential for harm, family grief therapy should be carried out by practitioners who have demonstrable competence in carrying out their duties. Evidence-based approaches are preferable to interventions that rely on good attention alone, reflecting advances in the fields of thanatology and psychology.

Technology Challenges

Technological advances, especially in telemedicine, bring the promise of offering family therapy to more bereaved people spread over a greater geographical area, possibly bypassing international borders and continents, and at a lower unit cost. With technology, new ethical challenges emerge and old principles remain, such as competency, informed consent, documentation, representation to the public, fees, termination, and nonmalfeasance (Barnett, 2011).

The most promising types of platforms are video chat programs such as Skype, which allow multiple parties to videoconference simultaneously at low or no cost. This could potentially allow a hospice patient and his wife in New Jersey, a daughter in Arizona, a son stuck in traffic with a cell phone, and the therapist in New York to all participate in family grief therapy.

Informed consent should address the potential for privacy violation by unauthorized users accessing private health information. Other parties listening in on the videoconference also represent a potential challenge to privacy. Technology failure in the middle of therapy is a possibility; it is appropriate for the therapist to discuss using the telephone as a fallback measure.

Out-of-session use of technology, such as e-mailing, texting, or "Skyping" the therapist between meetings creates complex boundary issues but does potentially improve communication. It certainly avoids the more primitive default: leaving a message with a personal assistant, who transcribes a note to be left on the therapist's chair, which he or she will discover upon returning.

It is worthwhile specifying in advance if the therapist is accessible via e-mail, texting, telephone, or video chat and the reasonable response time to such messages. Charges for incidental communication should be clarified and insurance coverage for telemedicine, if any, verified. More complex is how the therapist can be certain that the person e-mailing or texting is in fact the patient and not someone else who has accessed the patient's computer. The approach to termination should also be specified in advance.

With discounted, online grief counseling proposed by some funeral parlors, experienced therapists have expressed concern. Nevertheless, it is likely that the field will have to deal with the ethics of such grief counseling just as Las Vegas and Disney weddings, once unthinkable, are now common. There is already a firm trend toward moving cancer support services online, and it is likely that grief services will follow. Licensing of Internet therapists across state and international borders, with related medico-legal insurance, has still not been worked out. If online therapy in thanatology is to prosper, attention to the inherent ethical challenges will be essential.

Countertransference

It is important that the therapist be aware of countertransferential responses activated by family grief therapy. For example, a therapist's overidentification with a patient or family can impact neutrality and may lead to boundary distortions such as a desire to physically comfort a patient. A therapist's own world, religious, or cultural views could be inadvertently imposed upon the therapy. One less common yet important example of this is when a therapist colludes with a patient's request for physician-assisted suicide, without appreciating his or her own unconscious countertransferential support for "the right to die." A therapist's own personal crisis, such as family illness or divorce, can impair him or her and result in emotional unavailability. Burnout or therapy fatigue is a well-documented danger; therapists should guard their work/life balance carefully.

Self-disclosure can sometimes be helpful to illustrate a particular point, but all too often, statements such as "I also lost my mother to cancer" detract from the goals of therapy by turning the therapist into a quasi-patient. Gamino and Ritter (2009), authors of *Ethical Practice in Grief Counseling*, acknowledge and examine their countertransference, writing that their ethical life values are rooted in a personal Christian value system. Such an open approach allows their background attitudes to be understood and analyzed productively, although this sort of personal information would not be typically shared in therapy. Personal therapy, direct and peer-group supervision, and accessing mentorship can increase awareness of countertransference blind spots.

Conclusion

Lederberg (1997) pointed out that ethical conflicts unfold in a multidimensional context that includes psychosocial, legal, and institutional domains. In reaching an ethically tenable outcome, unpacking these contextual issues is often just as important as the moral issues themselves. Gamino and Ritter (2009) similarly emphasized the significance of understanding the person, the problem, the place, the principles, and the decision-making process in reaching an ethical decision.

Recognizing this complexity and the utility of healthy debate in addressing ethical dilemmas, all hospitals in the United States are mandated to have a clinical ethics committee. These forums provide a platform for reconciling ethics with the personal context and provide support for implementing ethically acceptable solutions. In sum, when faced with ethical dilemmas, our strong recommendation is to analyze them within a collegial and supportive setting that gives room for all voices.

References

Association for Death Education and Counseling (ADEC). (2004). *Code of ethics.* Revised July 28, 2010. Retrieved from http://www.adec.org/Code_of_Ethics.htm

Barnett, J. E. (2011). Utilizing technological innovations to enhance psychotherapy supervision, training, and outcomes. *Psychotherapy, 48,* 103–108.

Fins, J. J., Bacchetta, M. D., & Miller, F. G. (1997). Clinical pragmatism: A method of moral problem solving. *Kennedy Institute of Ethics, 7,* 129–145.

Gamino, L., & Ritter, R. (2009). *Ethical practice in grief counseling.* New York: Springer.

Gilligan, C. (1982). *In a different voice.* Boston: Harvard University Press.

Kissane, D. W., McKenzie, M., Bloch, S., Moskowitz, C., McKenzie, D. P., & O'Neill, I. (2006). Family focused grief therapy: A randomized, controlled trial in palliative care and bereavement. *American Journal of Psychiatry, 163,* 1208–1218.

Lederberg, M. S. (1997). Making a situational diagnosis: Psychiatrists at the interface of psychiatry and ethics in the consultation-liaison setting. *Psychosomatics, 38,* 327–338.

Noddings, N. (1984). *Caring: A feminine approach to ethics and moral education.* Los Angeles: University of California Press.

Part II

Grief Therapy with Families— A Practical Approach to Care Delivery

Here we discuss how to deliver family therapy in palliative care and bereavement. Whether assessing families or applying strategies to optimally assist them, the clinician needs to approach family bereavement in a manner that is culturally sensitive. We provide a narrative account exemplifying therapy from the Family Focused Grief Therapy Trial to convey the experience of both the family and the therapist.

6   Assessing Bereaved Families

Talia I. Zaider

The family is often the primary context in which grief is acknowledged and shared. In his classic essay, *Family's Reaction to Death*, Murray Bowen argues that loss in the family can precipitate powerful "emotional shock waves" that ripple through a family system, both within and across generations (Bowen, 1978). As our aging population grows and medical advances extend survival even for the terminally ill, families are increasingly living with multiple, mounting losses, well before a death occurs (Okun & Nowinski, 2011). Family grief is therefore not necessarily a discrete event with a clear beginning and end (Rosenblatt, 1996).With illness or death come shifts in family roles, responsibilities, routines, and rituals. In addition to these changes, loss in the family inevitably reactivates prior losses, and the family's response can further solidify or transform attitudes toward death and grief for future generations.

In the aftermath of a death, the family faces the task of reconstituting over time its basic functions, such as parenting and keeping traditions. It is only through a developmental and contextually sensitive assessment that we can make sense of the impact of loss on family life, recognize areas of fragility, and identify the sources of resilience that can be harnessed to empower healing. This chapter presents a road map for therapists to assess the bereaved family, determine the need for more intensive psychosocial care, and formulate a focus for continued support. As in any therapeutic encounter, we recognize that the assessment process itself is meant to be interventive. By inquiring into the functioning of a bereaved family, we are both gathering data and inviting expressiveness and reflection among family members themselves, thus forging a path toward increased mutual support. Table 6.1 outlines the broad sequence of strategies used in the assessment process that follows.

The Narrative of the Loss

Every family holds multiple, sometimes contradictory, stories about the person who died, the experience of the loss itself, and the emotional and pragmatic needs following a death. By eliciting each family member's perspective and avoiding a focus on those who present with the most overt distress, the clinician is better able to sustain engagement with the group as a whole and allow diverse perspectives to emerge safely. As an assessment tool, the ensuing storytelling illuminates both negative and positive family meanings, such as: Why did the death occur? How preventable or unfair was it considered? What larger purpose may it have held? This allows the family to co-create new, adaptive family meanings around the loss (Nadeau, 2008). In this chapter, I suggest several key areas of inquiry to guide discussion and help "thicken" the narrative that unfolds about a death in the family.

Table 6.1 Key Strategies Used to Assess Bereaved Families

1. Story of the person and the loss

   a. Who was this person? His/her multiple roles and contributions to family life?

   b. How did he/she die? How was the death experienced by the family?

   c. Review the funeral ritual and burial

2. Story of family coping and relationships

   a. Assess family tasks: acknowledging death, sharing grief, and reorganizing family

   b. Understand relational patterns, past and present

   c. Make explicit style of communication, cohesion, and conflict resolution

3. The family genogram

   a. Basic structure and timelines

   b. Coping responses to critical events

   c. Patterns of relating across generations

   d. Strengths and vulnerabilities

4. Summarize key concerns and strengths

   a. Affirm strengths alongside issues of concern

   b. Achieve consensus about goals

   c. Plan future therapy as needed

The Person

The therapist begins by helping the family share their memories of the lost member, in his or her various roles and relationships, both inside and outside the family. Here the therapist hears about those qualities most cherished by the family and learns about aspects of the relative's legacy that continue to influence family life, including his or her values, passions, and contributions to family and community. Taking time to engage in a kind of "joining" with the deceased member, through the family's eyes, enables the therapist and family to include him or her in their growing relationship. If the therapist knew the deceased family member, an empty chair could be placed in the room to mark his or her presence symbolically. Circular questions that invite the family to respond on behalf of the lost member (e.g., "How would Roberta describe her role in this family? What did she most appreciate about being in this family?") also help bring the loved one's voice into the room. As noted by Michael White, the paradigm of "saying hello"—rather than saying good-bye to the person who has died—helps to counter the common perception that a complete closure or detachment is the optimal outcome (White, 1989).

A family that struggles to discuss and openly acknowledge a loss is served well by a therapist who can comfortably facilitate an open discussion about death and dying, while speaking in direct language. Bowen explains this principle well when he writes:

In my work with families, I carefully use direct words, such as death, die, and bury, and I carefully avoid the use of less direct words, such as passed on, deceased, and expired. A direct word signals to the other that I am comfortable with the subject, and it enables others to also be comfortable. A tangential word may appear to soften the fact of death; but it invites the family to respond with tangential words, and the conversation soon reaches the point that one wonders if we are talking about death at all. The use of direct words helps to open a closed emotional system. I believe it provides a different dimension in helping the family to be comfortable within themselves. (Bowen, 1978, p. 343)

The Death

Factual information about the death itself is crucial to understanding the family's response to loss. Was this a "good death" or a disappointing one? Evidence suggests that difficult circumstances surrounding a loss, such as sudden, violent, or accidental deaths, can confer added risk for psychosocial morbidity in bereavement (Burke & Neimeyer, 2012). A disappointing death can result from poor symptom management, unanticipated timing, a perception of abandonment or alienation from the medical team or close friends, and/or feelings of guilt and inadequacy in caregiving. An elderly woman who lost her sister unexpectedly during a hospital admission for cancer treatment described immense guilt because she could not keep a promise that her sister would die at home. When the family in a conjoint session contributed alternative perspectives, it helped unburden this woman from feeling she had failed to protect her sister's wishes. In other instances, intense residual anger is expressed in the story of the death, as family members give voice to the fundamental unfairness of the loss and/or criticize certain professional helpers, such as the hospice nurse, home aide, physician, or other family members who were perceived as uncaring or uncommitted at the end of life.

A therapist should ask how news of the death was shared, who was present at the death, and whether there was an opportunity to say good-bye, confide in loved ones, and/or exchange wishes. The degree to which the family experienced a sense of solidarity at the end of life, as opposed to conflict or misunderstanding, can signal the potential for further growth in mutual support through bereavement.

Research suggests that caregivers, patients, and health care practitioners alike consider certain experiences especially valuable at the end of life. These include the opportunity to feel prepared for death and dying, to make clear end-of-life care plans, and to ensure adequate pain control and symptom management for the patient (Hebert, Prigerson, Schulz, & Arnold, 2006; Steinhauser et al., 2000). In a prospective study of bereaved family caregivers of dementia patients, those who felt they were not "prepared" for the death of their loved one—for example, if they had limited communication with their physicians about the prospect of death, dying, or bereavement—experienced significantly higher levels of depression, anxiety, and complicated grief symptoms in bereavement, compared to those who reported feeling "prepared" for the loss (Hebert et al., 2006). Thus, the stories that emerge about the final days of a family member's life can potentially explain or foretell a complicated or maladaptive grieving process.

The Funeral

The therapist should elicit an account of how the family honored and memorialized the lost family member. The way in which these ceremonies are organized can illuminate areas of strength and vulnerability across various aspects of family functioning, such as decision making, negotiation of differences in interfaith or blended families, and coordination of roles. The therapist will often hear about customs that are steeped in a family's culture or religion and should inquire about the meaning of the family's adherence to these practices. Rituals and customs at a time of death connect the family to a larger community and invite an open sharing of grief. The therapist should ask how much this broader support has been subsequently sustained and to what degree family members can find sources of support outside the family when needed. The family's capacity for teamwork and mutual support can be revealed via their answers to the therapist's questions about all that happened, what reactions family members had to any rituals performed, and *how* the family prepared for, and participated in, these practices (Imber-Black & Roberts, 1998).

Prior "stress fractures" in family relationships can become magnified during this time, generating considerable frustration and alienation. In the case of one couple grieving the loss of their teenage son, the father immersed himself passionately in planning a memorial service. Much to his dismay, the mother preferred to remain uninvolved, doubtful that she would attend. Further inquiry revealed differences in the meaning that this service held for each parent: the father was eager to shore up solidarity with others and witness the broad impact of his son's life, whereas the mother lamented having to "share" her son's memory with a larger, less intimate public, preferring instead to honor the parental bond privately.

As the therapist elicits the family's narrative about the loss and all that has subsequently transpired, he or she should make note of the family's implicit and explicit assumptions about grief itself, its expected duration, and what they feel will help or hinder its resolution. Does the family consider talking about grief helpful, necessary, or likely to make things worse? When a family member is *not* expressing acute distress, is he or she perceived as "in denial" or "not dealing with the loss"? Or does the family worry that an intensely grieving family member is "not functioning"?

One woman who lost her husband to advanced prostate cancer discussed how socially active she remained following his death, accepting invitations to various engagements and resuming volunteer work that had been deferred during his illness. She worried that she was "running away" from her grief but also believed that she could only keep friends by being a "good widow" who was active and emotionally intact. Some family members may present a mandate to "move on," whereas others go to great efforts to sustain "continuing bonds" with their loved one (Klass, Silverman, & Nickman, 1996). As will be discussed later, beliefs about what constitutes a "good" grieving process are often informed by models of grief from generations past.

Impact at a Family Level—Coping

Like most major life transitions, loss is fundamentally a relational experience. The most relevant and available support network for most bereaved individuals is the family, and its capacity to provide a safe, empathic, and supportive climate is paramount. Research literature shows considerable evidence that when family relationships are fraught with conflict, constrained communication, and/or poor teamwork, members of the family are at significant risk for psychiatric morbidity in bereavement (Kissane, Bloch, Dowe et al., 1996; Kissane, Bloch, Onghena et al., 1996). Any focused assessment therefore needs to include a systemic examination of relationship patterns, both current and long-standing, that are likely to help or hinder the family's journey with loss.

McGoldrick and Walsh (2004) put forth a model of adaptation to loss that guides the assessment of family coping across several key tasks:

1. *Shared Acknowledgment of the Reality of Death.* This is made possible when there is clarity and open communication about the cause and circumstances of death. The authors note the importance of including children in this process, warning that the urge to shield them from a dying family member may further inflame rather than reduce their anxiety and confusion.

2. *Shared Experience of the Loss Itself.* Three areas of inquiry are most relevant:

   a. Did all family members actively and jointly participate in efforts to memorialize the deceased family member, such as planning events, speeches, and tributes, or have some members been excluded from this process?

   b. To what degree do families enable versus constrain the sharing of grief, particularly when emotional responses do not conform to expectation? What is the level of tolerance for the full range of emotional responses experienced in the family, or are certain reactions, such as anger and relief, excluded or blocked?

   c. To what extent do family members' roles and responsibilities shape differential grieving responses? For example, if one family member is seen as psychologically fragile, do others collude to protect him or her by minimizing their own grief? Who becomes protective and caregiving, and who is most cared for? What role does gender play? For example, is there solidarity and mutual support among the women of the family, to the exclusion of the men, or vice versa?

3. *Reorganization of the Family System.* Adaptation is optimized when the family can maintain stability for its members, such as by holding onto familiar rules, roles, and routines, but is also sufficiently flexible to modify patterns of relating, delegate new roles, and allow for the growth of new relationships, when necessary. The difficulty of reassigning the role of the lost family member depends on how vital a role was played: Was he or she a breadwinner? The emotional "barometer" of the family? The conflict mediator? Achieving the balance between continuity of roles and change is often difficult for families. The therapist can raise awareness of this balance and empower the family to make adaptive choices by posing "before/after" questions to them. These questions invite reflection about what has changed and what has remained constant in family life post loss.

4. *Reinvestment in Other Relationships and Life Pursuits.* Alongside acknowledgment of the loss and sharing of grief, adaptation is facilitated when there is movement, over time, toward forging new relationships in the family, delegating new roles and pursuing meaningful commitments as a family unit. But a fear of being disloyal to

the deceased, or residual conflict and resentment among family members, can often block this process.

The theoretical road map provided previously helps identify where the family needs to go to optimize their adaptation to loss. The road map also helps the therapist organize the vast amount of material that emerges during a family interview. The themes presented by McGoldrick and Walsh readily guide the family therapist or grief counselor as he or she works with a bereaved family across multiple sessions.

How can we recognize vulnerable families prior to a loss? The assessment model proposed by Kissane and colleagues (Kissane et al., 2006; Zaider & Kissane, 2007) focuses on identifying "at-risk" families *before* a loss, thus enabling delivery of a prophylactic intervention leading to prevention of morbidity in bereavement. Their assessment method is empirically derived; uses screening with the Family Relationships Index (FRI; Edwards & Clarke, 2005; Moos & Moos, 1981; see Chapter 1); has been shown to have utility in medical settings; and can be used in a single family meeting—even by practitioners with little or no training in family therapy (Chan, O'Neill, McKenzie, Love, & Kissane, 2004; Del Gaudio, Zaider, Kissane, & Brier, 2012).

In studies of families coping with terminal cancer, Kissane and colleagues observed that certain patterns of family functioning were strongly predictive of psychosocial morbidity in bereavement. Specifically, the qualities of communication, cohesiveness, and/or conflict management were closely linked to depressive symptoms in bereavement (Kissane, Bloch, Dowe et al., 1996; Kissane, Bloch, Onghena et al., 1996). The clinician's inquiry into these areas of functioning aims to highlight habitual styles of relating, so that family members become observers of their own process.

The family's level of cohesiveness appears to be especially important in predicting bereavement outcomes. This finding highlights the importance of the therapist learning about the capacity for solidarity, closeness felt among members, and cooperation in planning and reorganizing family routines and activities. Cohesiveness is assessed through questions such as, "How well do you work as a team?" "Has this loss led you as a family to become closer or more distant?" "How often do you see each other as a family?" "What is similar about your feelings as a group, what is most different?" Families with high cohesiveness easily shore up and maintain support in the aftermath of a loss.

Conflict management is reflected when family members endorse statements on the FRI such as "We fight a lot in our family" or "Family members sometimes get so angry they throw things." Interestingly, the presence of conflict per se is not sufficient to designate a family at risk for distress, as the family's capacity to make repair following conflict can buffer its impact. In assessing conflict, therefore, the clinician should normalize this facet of family life, and then ask how the family typically resolves disagreements, how forgiveness is achieved, which family member is most likely to mediate or compromise, and what role the ill or deceased family member may have played in any long-standing conflicts.

Finally, families with high scores in communication perceive a level of comfort expressing feelings and thoughts in the family, endorsing such items as, "We say anything we want to around the home" or "We tell each other about our personal problems." Assessment of communication seeks to shed light on any constraints that cause family members to withhold or isolate from one another. Relevant questions include, "How easily do you talk with one another about feelings of sadness or grief?" "Who is most likely to talk about difficult feelings, and who is most likely to keep thoughts to him or herself?" or "What helps you talk more openly as a family?"

Historical Responses to Loss across Generations

The family genogram is crucial in understanding and identifying the evolution of a family's response style, members' perceptions of coping, and examples of resilience and strength. Through a genogram assessment, the clinician can elucidate historical influences on a family's response to loss. Among bereaved individuals, a history of prior loss has been shown to be a risk factor for complicated grief (Aranda & Milne, 2000; Burke & Neimeyer, 2012; Rando, 1983). At the level of the family, the clinician looks to make sense of current coping responses by reflecting on prior models of grief that might now be "alive and well."

As described by Kissane and Bloch (2002), the therapist's exploration of family history is often best achieved in early sessions with a family, when it helps to contextualize a family's presenting concerns. The telling of family stories can reduce anxiety, invite compassion around long-standing struggles, and generate stories of pride, as the family reflects on the evolution of their identity over time. In addition to the rich information gleaned, the genogram assessment thereby allows a therapist to build rapport with a family and move away from emotionally laden concerns.

To optimize the therapeutic value of this assessment tool, the therapist is wise to follow certain guidelines:

1. History-taking using a genogram should focus on relevant themes of loss, grief, caregiving, and other key developmental transitions, rather than serve as an obsessional data-gathering exercise. The unfocused collection of excessive factual information, such as recording every name and date, can sometimes derail the process and dilute benefit to the family.
2. If a therapist launches into an inquiry of family history without explanation, certain families can feel threatened, particularly if family secrets, old conflicts, or unspoken sentiments loom large. The therapist enlists the family's collaboration most effectively by introducing the genogram with a rationale for its use and benefit. This includes linking the exercise, when possible, to the particular concerns expressed by the family, such as: "You've shared with me your concern about your father 'falling apart' because of his grief. As we draw your family tree, I'll be interested in learning about any events or patterns that might help us understand how this concern came to be in your family."
3. History taking can be time consuming in general and particularly challenging with a volatile couple or family. De-escalating a highly reactive family and/or establishing emotional safety in session sometimes takes precedent, so that the therapist can ensure a productive discussion and help family members shift to a reflective and non-blaming position.
4. Finally, the benefit of a family genogram ultimately depends on the therapist's ability to synthesize the information provided into a meaningful summary that

can be shared with the family. This ties a family's history to their current patterns. This summary should mention the vulnerabilities that emerged in the family's story—such as prevalence of depression, dependent relationships, intolerance for difference, cutoffs, and family relationships that erode in the aftermath of loss—as well as family strengths including values that survived across the generations, examples of resilience in the midst of trauma, and capacity for caregiving. Significantly, the summary is a powerful tool for achieving consensus in the family around difficult, emotionally threatening topics, as Rolland points out: "Preparing the genogram provides the clinician a way to address family anxieties by beginning to reframe, detoxify and normalize emotionally charged information" (1994, p. 78).

The basic structural map of a genogram typically focuses on three generations of family on both sides of the marital dyad. The therapist draws the genogram on large paper or a mounted board, enabling the family to engage visually in the process. McGoldrick, Gerson, & Shellenberger (1999) offer a comprehensive guide to the technique of constructing and eliciting information for a family genogram. In the setting of bereavement, a genogram assessment should include basic family information such as ages, names, occupations, and critical family events such as prior deaths, illnesses, fractured relationships, migrations, and traumatic events. Additionally, the assessment should map adaptive and maladaptive interaction patterns among family members during and after these events (McGoldrick et al., 1999). A therapist's three key tasks here are to invite the family to reflect on how they become organized as a system in response to adversity, to identify which coping skills proved most effective, and also to identify those behaviors that exacerbated emotional pain. Rolland (1994) further points out the importance of considering how the particular psychosocial demands of a prior crisis are similar to or different from the demands of the family's current predicament.

The following example illustrates how historical patterns of responding to loss can enrich the therapist's understanding of the current challenges.

Case Example

Leonard, age 74, had recently lost his second wife, Caroline, to advanced lung cancer and was invited to a family session by his 51-year-old son, Michael, who expressed concern about Leonard becoming increasingly "clingy" and "depressed." An exploration of the family's genogram revealed several sudden and unexpected losses in Leonard's lifetime. At age 16, he witnessed first-hand the death of his paternal grandfather from a heart attack. Following this traumatic loss, Leonard's father moved the family into a two-family home, to be shared with Leonard's aunts and uncles, so that the families could be closer together. In the summer before leaving for college, Leonard lost a younger sibling to a motorcycle accident and decided afterward to stay home, deferring his education in order to be present for the family. Ultimately, he never started college. In middle age, Leonard's first wife, Sally, left him after she met another man. Within a year, Leonard met and became engaged to Caroline. Leonard reports that Caroline "saved my life." The losses he had encountered in his family of origin were sudden and unexpected, requiring rapid mobilization and adaptation. He experienced great difficulty coping with Caroline's protracted illness and—much to Michael's frustration—had not heeded Caroline's and Michael's requests for more open discussion about her end-of-life wishes before she died. Michael could now appreciate that his father had significant challenges enduring the anticipatory grief, chronicity, and uncertainty that accompanied Caroline's illness and now exhibited a characteristic response to loss in his family of origin, by merging with close family members. Although this was adaptive and protective at various points in his history, it was a coping strategy that did not suit his son, who perceived his father's need for proximity as stifling.

After the therapist first determines the basic family structure and then learns about their responses to critical transitions in the family's history, a third task in conducting a genogram assessment is developing a picture of functional and dysfunctional patterns of relating. The therapist's goal of this exploration is identifying problematic patterns that family members may inadvertently reenact under the strain of loss and empowering the family to make choices previously not apparent to them.

Questions can map onto the key areas of family functioning, including the following:

"What sort of marriage did your parents have?"
"When there was conflict, who became involved and who stayed away?"
"Who in the family was best at giving comfort? Who was turned to for problem solving?"
"What were the expectations for caregiving in your family?"
"How did emotionally charged subjects get talked about?"
"Who shared feelings, and who didn't?"
"What level of caregiving and involvement was expected of women versus men, children versus adults?"

The family's stories of pride and resilience (Sheinberg & Fraenkel, 2001; Walsh, 2002) should be explored with as much emphasis and interest as stories of dysfunction, tragedy, and disconnection. In fact, learning about areas of competence and drawing out examples of family strength in the face of adversity will ultimately be most useful to a therapist and family in formulating intervention goals. For every prior loss or difficult transition with which the family struggled, members should be asked about benefits or renewed priorities that may have consequently emerged. Questions might include: "What resources did the family turn to in times of stress? Were religious institutions or spiritual leaders called upon to aid in providing comfort and support? What sort of caregiving and provision of support did the family observe during difficult periods?" In Kissane and Bloch's Family Focused Grief Therapy model (Kissane & Bloch, 2002), the therapist asks the family to generate a meaningful "family motto" that captures the family's identity, showcases its essential qualities, and highlights sources of pride.

Facilitating an Agenda of Mutual Support: Shared Goals of Therapy

The assessment process concludes with the therapist's crucial task of consolidating the information gleaned and achieving consensus about a plan moving forward. The therapist remains collaborative in checking that his or her understanding of the family's presenting concerns is consonant with their views. The therapist's overview should include what has been learned about multi-generational factors that influence the family's current response patterns and the resources and strengths that are evident in the family's efforts to cope with loss. A sizable portion of families (e.g., those designated supportive, conflict-resolving; see Chapter 1) may not require further support but will benefit nonetheless from feedback that reinforces their capacity for mutual support and identifies how their particular coping styles will likely continue to facilitate adaptation. However, for those families who present with persistent difficulties, it is important that the therapist both recognize areas of vulnerability and present a promising vision of more effective mutual support. Kissane and Bloch (2002) suggest drawing up a list with the family of chief concerns, alongside key family strengths.

As the therapist nears the end of an assessment session, it is important to inquire about any undeclared concerns, for example, "Is there anything we have not yet talked about that you would like us to pay attention to? Are there concerns that have not been discussed yet?" Concerns about alcoholism, substance abuse, extramarital affairs, or suicidal ideation are often more likely to surface after the family's story has been unpacked and rapport has been established with the therapist, rather than early in a session with a new therapist. Acknowledging these issues and including them in the therapist's formulation and summary plan can bring much-needed relief to family members who carry intense and/or covert worry about a vulnerable relative. Specifically, a family member may present with symptoms that warrant a referral for individual psychiatric care. Indeed, when the family members convene as a group, their discussions about their coping can become a catalyst for mobilizing much-needed help for a depressed or at-risk family member. Without undue alarm or scapegoating an individual family member, the protectiveness of family can be highlighted here as a strength. As with any family work, the therapist holds the individual- and family-level perspectives simultaneously, so that one person's need for additional care in no way precludes the role of the family as a potential resource.

Ultimately, a relational assessment leads to a set of recommendations by the therapist, which are intended to address relational concerns. A therapist's common goal is to help a family cultivate or strengthen those qualities of family life that are known to be protective in the long run. Consensus with the family about areas of focus for future support is critical. When divergent views arise about a particular issue, the therapist avoids aligning with one particular perspective and instead reflects back to the family the dilemma they are facing, leaning on them to consider and reconcile the tension between different views. In one family that lost a close grandparent, the mother strongly endorsed the value of talking openly about her grief, urging others to do the same, whereas her husband found little use focusing on sadness, instead preferring to stay active and maintain routines for their children. Rather than suggest a solution or compromise, the therapist can empower the family to generate ideas about how to best serve everyone's needs. The therapist highlights the tension that exists between these positions as a dilemma for the family. The following script illustrates this process:

> On the one hand, some of you recognize the potential benefits and relief that can come from sharing your sadness with one another. On the other hand, I hear a

concern about becoming too stuck in that sadness, so that important family and work tasks would not get done. Both of you want to give your kids the opportunity to heal from this loss in whatever way makes sense for them. Is it possible to do both—to make space for your grief as a family, so that it can be acknowledged and shared, but also to enact protective measures so the grief doesn't become too consuming? How will you know when it's helpful to talk versus helpful to focus on tasks?

Conclusion

Clinically assessing the bereaved family requires an appreciation of the multifaceted and deeply relational nature of grief. In this chapter, I presented a systemic assessment approach that seeks to broaden the lens from the intrapsychic experience of the bereaved individual to the functioning and coping resources of the family as a group. As discussed previously, understanding the bereaved family begins with the story of their loss. The therapist encourages the family to jointly discuss the cherished qualities and roles of the person who died, the legacy left behind, the circumstances of the death itself, and family efforts to memorialize and pay tribute to the life of their beloved. Through this guided narrative, the therapist comes to learn extensively about a family's values and traditions, their beliefs about grief itself, their pattern of organizing and coordinating roles following the loss, and their capacity to tolerate a range of emotional reactions, from anger to sadness to relief. Risk factors related to the nature of a death become evident in this portion of the assessment interview, such as whether the death was unexpected or prepared for, or violent or related to illness.

This chapter has discussed both theoretically grounded and empirically derived methods of assessing family functioning following loss, including the use of routine questions about cohesion, communication, and conflict. These questions can be easily integrated to identify families at risk for psychosocial morbidity. Finally, developing a family genogram was discussed as a powerful means of linking current concerns with patterns "inherited" from prior generations.

The assessment approach presented here promotes understanding the family as a developing, ever-adapting, and self-organizing system, which evolves and shifts with each critical transition. The family group, seen as being "in motion," is a frame that counters the sense of being stuck that can descend on a family post loss. Furthermore, examples of strength, creativity, and mastery always sit alongside challenges, sources of vulnerability, and relational distress. It is with these principles in mind that the therapist weaves a story that is both a snapshot of where the family stands at this point in time and a map that guides its journey into the future. The successful assessment process culminates in insight, clarification, increased empathic attunement, and, ultimately, a sense of choice and empowerment to heal.

References

Aranda, S., & Milne, D. (2000). *Guidelines for the assessment of complicated bereavement risk in family members of people receiving palliative care*. Melbourne: Centre for Palliative Care.
Bowen, M. (1978). *Family therapy in clinical practice*. New York: Jason Aronson.

Burke, L. A., & Neimeyer, R. A. (2012). Prospective risk factors for complicated grief. In M. Stroebe, H. Schut, & J. van den Bout (Eds.), *Complicated grief: Scientific foundations for health care professionals* (pp. 145–161). New York: Routledge.

Chan, E. K., O'Neill, I., McKenzie, M., Love, A., & Kissane, D. W. (2004). What works for therapists conducting family meetings: Treatment integrity in family-focused grief therapy during palliative care and bereavement. *Journal of Pain and Symptom Management, 27*(6), 502–512.

Del Gaudio, F., Zaider, T., Kissane, D., Brier, M. (2012). Challenges in providing family-centered support to families in palliative care. *Palliative Medicine, 26*(8), 1025–1033.

Edwards, B., & Clarke, V. (2005). The validity of the Family Relationships Index as a screening tool for psychological risk in families of cancer patients. *Psycho-Oncology, 14*, 546–554.

Hebert, R. S., Prigerson, H. G., Schulz, R., & Arnold, R. M. (2006). Preparing caregivers for the death of a loved one: A theoretical framework and suggestions for future research. *Journal of Palliative Medicine, 9*, 1164–1171.

Imber-Black, E., & Roberts, J. (1998). *Rituals for our times: Celebrating, healing, and changing our lives and our relationships.* New York: Jason Aronson.

Kissane, D. W., & Bloch, S. (2002). *Family focused grief therapy: A model of family-centered care during palliative care and bereavement.* Buckingham, UK: Open University Press.

Kissane, D. W., Bloch, S., Dowe, D. L., Snyder, R. D., Onghena, P., McKenzie, D. P., & Wallace, C. S. (1996). The Melbourne Family Grief Study, I: Perceptions of family functioning in bereavement. *American Journal of Psychiatry, 153*(5), 650–658.

Kissane, D. W., Bloch, S., Onghena, P., McKenzie, D. P., Snyder, R. D., & Dowe, D. L. (1996). The Melbourne Family Grief Study, II: Psychosocial morbidity and grief in bereaved families. *American Journal of Psychiatry, 153*(5), 659–666.

Kissane, D. W., McKenzie, M., Bloch, S., Moskowitz, C., McKenzie, D. P., & O'Neill, I. (2006). Family focused grief therapy: A randomized, controlled trial in palliative care and bereavement. *American Journal of Psychiatry, 163*(7), 1208–1218.

Klass, D., Silverman, P., & Nickman, S. (1996). *Continuing bonds: New understandings of grief.* Washington, DC: Taylor & Francis.

McGoldrick, M., Gerson, R., & Shellenberger, S. (1999). *Genograms, assessment and intervention* (2nd ed.). New York: W. W. Norton.

McGoldrick, M., & Walsh, F. (Eds.). (2004). *Living beyond loss: Death in the family* (2nd ed.). New York: W. W. Norton.

Moos, R. H., & Moos, B. S. (1981). *Family environment scale manual.* Stanford, CA: Consulting Psychologists Press.

Nadeau, J. W. (2008). Meaning-making in bereaved families: Assessment, intervention, and future research. In M. S. Stroebe, R. O. Hansson, H. Schut, & W. Stroebe (Eds.), *Handbook of bereavement research and practice: Advances in theory and intervention* (pp. 511–530). Washington, DC: American Psychological Association.

Okun, B., & Nowinski, J. (2011). *Saying goodbye: How families can find renewal through loss.* New York: Berkeley Books.

Rando, T. A. (1983). An investigation of grief and adaptation in parents whose children have died from cancer. *Journal of Pediatric Psychology, 8*(1), 3–20.

Rolland, J. S. (1994). *Families, illness, & disability: An integrative treatment model.* New York: Basic Books.

Rosenblatt, P. C. (1996). Grief that does not end. In D. Klass, P. R. Silverman, & S. L. Nickman (Eds.), *Continuing bonds: New understandings of grief* (pp. 45–58). Washington, DC: Taylor & Francis.

Sheinberg, M., & Fraenkel, P. (2001). *The relational trauma of incest: A family-based approach to treatment.* New York: Guilford Press.

Steinhauser, K. E., Christakis, N. A., Clipp, E. C., McNeilly, M., McIntyre, L., & Tulsky, J. A. (2000). Factors considered important at the end of life by patients, family, physicians, and other care providers. *JAMA, 284*(19), 2476–2482.

Walsh, F. (2002). A family resilience framework: Innovative practice applications. *Family Relations, 51*(2), 130–138.

White, M. (1989) Saying hello again: The incorporation of the lost relationship in the resolution of grief. In M. White (Ed.), *Selected papers* (pp. 29–35). Adelaide, Australia: Dulwich Centre Publications.

Zaider, T., & Kissane, D. W. (2007). Resilient families. In B. Monroe & D. Oliviere (Eds.), *Resilience in palliative care*. Oxford: Oxford University Press.

7 Therapist Techniques in Family Work

David W. Kissane and Isabelle Dumont

One recurring criticism of existing clinical research is the startling lack of focus on therapist behaviors that lead to important moments of change in family sessions (Beutler, Williams, & Wakefield, 1993). As Pinsof and Wynne (2000) astutely pointed out, our research thus far offers little guidance to therapists about their in-session decision making. Only a few studies target what is specifically helpful to the ongoing process of therapy (Johnson & Lebow, 2000; Pinsof & Wynne, 2000). Outcome research has emphasized efficacy of a model of therapy rather than building a deeper framework that describes *how* it works.

Fortunately, the family therapy literature has developed conceptual models that can greatly benefit bereavement care. Several authors have described and categorized questions—for instance, circular, reflexive, and strategic—along with illustrations of the purpose and use of such questions (Fleuridas, Nelson, & Rosenthal, 1986; Penn, 1982; Tomm, 1988; White & Epston, 1990). For seasoned therapists, these illustrations favor the assimilation of the different types of interventions (Main, Boughner, Mims, & Schieffer, 2001). However, as such strategies have not been well specified for palliative care and bereavement, clinicians and therapists meeting with the families of advanced cancer patients can find it difficult to develop this style of family session (Kissane & Zaider, 2011).

In this chapter, we examine the clinician's technique of joining with the family, setting an agenda, using questioning style to understand their concerns, and employing integrative summaries in conducting family sessions. More specifically, we draw on Tomm's (1987a, 1987b, 1988) framework to identify, classify, and exemplify questions that can be used by therapists. Successful outcomes for the family as a whole include fundamental elements such as sustaining safety for the family, moving forward at family members' pace and with their permission, highlighting their strengths as a resource, and fostering their involvement in the process.

Before the Therapist Begins: Setting Up a Family Meeting

Families are generally willing to meet for therapy in the hospital or an inpatient hospice setting. Their interest in and worry about the well-being of the ill family member motivates their attendance as a group. Highly supportive families may readily put themselves out. Less functional family units may appear hesitant and need a firm recommendation from the senior clinician that they meet to discuss care plans for the patient.

In the clinic or outpatient setting, the index patient needs to be provided with a rationale for the meeting to offer to his or her relatives. It can be helpful for the therapist and patient to rehearse this request. The therapist asks the patient to repeat it until he or she feels comfortable with the choice of words. Thus, "My doctor asks that we meet as a family to discuss my illness and its management. She believes there may be ways that you can help me and wants to talk with us about my future." Notice that there is no implicit criticism of the family.

In palliative care, just as the nurse goes into the home, we recommend that the family therapist do likewise. This sustains the therapist's involvement with the patient as he or she becomes frail and permits expansion of the family group as needed by the therapeutic work.

During bereavement care, rather than proceed solely with a referred patient, it can be useful if the therapist invites him or her to bring along a relative to assist in understanding of the loss and family (Kissane & Hooghe, 2011). Sometimes this is the relative carrying most concern for the bereaved; at other times, interested offspring will accompany a grieving parent. Whatever the configuration that attends, the therapist's, invitation to move beyond the individual conveys a systemic orientation that will test the family's capacity for support and ensure some focus on reengagement with the living.

Often, the clinician's invitation to a family meeting will yield limited attendance. Invariably, this points to either reduced cohesion among members, their declared protectiveness to avoid burden, their shame at the fractured state of the family, or their direct avoidance of anticipated conflict. The clinician needs to take stock of the patient's concerns, review who is involved, identify reasons for protection of the family, address any perceived fear of being a burden, and thus broker a plan for a meeting. In these circumstances, wisdom dictates that the clinician telephone key family members and extend his or her personal invitation, with rationale for the event. The more dysfunctional the family group, the more the therapist must reach out actively to successfully convene a meeting.

The therapist needs to spell out all practical details for the attendees, including parking options, location of the meeting room, planned start and finish times, who has been invited, and why the meeting is important. Each invited attendee should feel that his or her presence and contribution will be valuable in helping the ill patient and the family as a whole.

Joining with the Family

Although quite basic, the welcome process sets the tone for what follows and is a vital component of a well-run family meeting. The therapist's goal is to put the attendees at ease, help them to introduce themselves, and promote a process of respectful interest in the views of all present. The therapist therefore speaks directly to each person, asking linear questions in a one-to-one manner, and seeks to learn his or her name, relationship to the patient or the deceased, role in the family, and career or hobbies. Retaining memory of this vital material can be aided by a few notes on an initial genogram held on the therapist's lap.

This early investment in five to seven minutes of small talk, unrelated to illness or bereavement, generates remarkable knowledge of the family's talent and spheres of interest. The therapist can use this information later in affirming aspects of the family's accomplishment. Early dynamics also emerge as one family member helps another to share his or her perspective, siblings tease one another, modesty or pride becomes apparent, and family humor or worry begins to be exposed. The golden rule for this section of the family meeting is to help every attendee speak and relax as they express themselves, while the facilitator learns something about each person and builds a sense of safety and trust in the therapy process.

If a physician attends the meeting, he or she may want to talk about the patient, illness, and treatment plan. Rarely will physicians have been taught how to run a family meeting, so they may fail to appreciate the benefits of this joining process. The wise psychosocial clinician will therefore brief them before beginning, seek permission to take the lead, and then guide the family through a welcoming process. If co-facilitators plan to run a meeting, they should agree to divide the introductions and welcome into two, thus ensuring some balance in their joint connection with the family.

Establishing Shared Agendas for the Family Meeting

Common sense and courtesy suggest that value lies in the therapist asking all family members if they have issues or concerns that they bring with them today. Such agenda setting needs to be made explicit as a process. The goal is to literally make a list, which will also include the therapist's agenda as well. The therapist needs sufficient understanding of each issue in order to prioritize its place among the list of concerns, but the "agenda-setting task" is not about hearing the full story. Hence, the therapist welcomes identification of an issue and checks on its name, but deliberately limits any elaboration of detail, while reassuring the advocate that it will receive proper time allocation in due course.

The therapist should take time to declare his or her goal for meeting with the family. In palliative care settings, it is very desirable if the patient can attend the meeting. Then the therapist might say, "My goal for our meeting today is to review where [patient's name]'s illness is at and your family's needs in providing care for and supporting [patient's name]."

If the family is in the bereavement phase, then the therapist might say, "My goal for our meeting today is to learn about your loss, hear the story of [patient's name]'s illness and death, how the funeral went, and where each of you is now at with your grief. I'm very interested in any concerns that you have for one another."

Some families will come together with hopes and expectations, rather than a well-formulated list of concerns. Hence, if the response to an initial question about concerns draws a null response, the therapist can follow up with the query, "What hopes do you hold for what might come from meeting together today?" The therapist's word choice is always critical. To exemplify, families might take offense if the therapist asks, "What problems do you have?" The word "problem" implies a deficit orientation to the family, whereas terms like "issue " or "concern" are more muted and non-judgmental.

Once the therapist has gone around the circle searching for worries, concerns, or hopes from the family members and declared his or her own objectives, a summary comment that reviews the agenda in a ranked order is needed to help the family follow where the therapist plans to go. The therapist judges selection of the order of approach, rather than passively permitting the family to prioritize. This is important for building up a coherent story of all that has occurred. In the process, this also allows the therapist to understand how the family operates, what values they hold, what roles that each party adopts, and eventually where the salient concerns lie. At the same time, the therapist needs to guide development of the family's consensus about the planned agenda. Unless it is ultimately adopted as a shared agenda that will address mutual needs, the joining process will fail, with risk that the family will not return.

Here is an example of an initial summary comment that seeks to draw the joining and agenda-setting process to a close:

Well, thank you so much for coming together for this family meeting today. I appreciate this opportunity to get to know each of you. You've told me that you want to discuss your mother's treatment, your father's distress and how you can support each other more effectively. I also want to learn more about your shared understanding of this illness, its seriousness, and what you perceive the future holds. Therefore, I want to suggest that we talk for 10 to 15 minutes about the illness and its treatment, then move to your future concerns, how each of you is coping, and what you might plan for as a family as a whole. Toward the end of our first hour, once we have clarified in more detail the nature of your stated concerns, we'll take stock of where we are at. Does this sound like a reasonable plan for now?"

Some Theoretical Principles Guiding the Therapist's Further Work

Questions are the primary tool clinicians use to learn about the family's experiences (Main et al., 2001). During palliative care, these questions help gather important information about various issues that concern families, such as care provision, coping, support, and discussion about death and dying. In bereavement, review of the death and funeral, intensity of grief, well-being, sources of support, and quality of life become important.

Before continuing with a discussion of questions that the therapist will now ask, brief consideration of some family therapy theory will help place the ongoing strategies into a worthwhile perspective. A major contribution was made by the Milan school of family therapy (Selvini, Boscolo, Cecchin, & Prata, 1980), which identified three central principles essential to an adequate family interview from a systemic perspective: neutrality, hypothesizing, and circularity (Selvini et al., 1980). Let us briefly consider each of these.

Neutrality refers to the idea of being "allied with everyone and no one at the same time" (Selvini et al., 1980, p. 11). It protects the therapist against unwise alliances with any specific family member, and it fully recognizes that individuals will frequently ask the therapist to endorse the correctness of their perspective over alternative viewpoints. "To stay with the family as a whole" means that the therapist appreciates the diversity of views and strives to understand them all, thus modeling respect and acceptance of differences of opinion.

Sometimes a vulnerable individual may come under too much attack from others in the family, inducing an urge within the therapist to take the side of the "at-risk" person temporarily. Before doing so, the experienced therapist will consider whether someone else in the circle might become a more strategic ally of the vulnerable individual. A question that invites the family to reflect on the emotional response of the vulnerable individual being criticized may prove more effective than simply taking his or her side. Another technique is to summarize the dilemma: "I sense that X feels quite picked on here, while some of you equally display strong feelings about your position. Might there be room for two or more perspectives here?"

Hypothesizing refers to applying one's cognitive resources in order to generate explanations. Through this process, the therapist grows in curiosity as he or she strives to understand the family. A provisional idea is tested, refined, reexamined, and iteratively reframed until the hypothesis is supported and accepted as a consensus view. This models a reflective style and creates a space in which the family can be encouraged to become more mindful of each other's views. Similar to what has been called a *mentalizing* capacity in individual therapy (Bateman & Fonagy, 2006), and the *transitional space* of play and creativity between parent and child (Winnicott, 1971), hypothesizing is an important function for both the therapist and family as a whole. It is the essential process through which new insight is formed about behaviors and lifestyle choices. And many questions are formed through this process of hypothesizing.

Circularity is a process by which the family dynamics are explored and belief systems made explicit via questions that invite family members to comment on what each person thinks and feels about a range of predicaments. As these questions are shifted from one relative to another, a rich exchange of different perspectives promotes deeper understanding of the relational life of the group. Circular processes engage the family as a whole and stand in sharp contrast to linear exchanges where individuals speak about themselves.

To expand on this concept, let us differentiate lineal from circular assumptions about cause and effect. Lineal assumptions break the ongoing flow of events into discrete segments, whereby A causes B, which in turn causes C. This presupposition ignores any greater interrelatedness of behavior, creating a single-minded approach to causality (Weeks & Treat, 2001). As such, it can more easily lead to blaming by focusing the responsibility on a single person or event.

Circular assumptions embody a more holistic perspective, putting emphasis on interconnectedness and any recursiveness present in human actions. In other words, they extend understanding to incorporate the identification of relational patterns, such as reciprocity, mutuality, alliance, polarization, and so on. Often, assumptions are oriented toward a series of small cause-and-effect segments, which when synthesized create a larger integrated pattern. Reciprocally interactional circular assumptions are at the core of systemic approaches.

To capture this depth of understanding in the family's thinking, therapists pose questions that unpack circular assumptions through what is most simply termed a circular questioning process. Circular questions have been supported as essential to adaptive family outcomes (Fleuridas et al., 1986), while also promoting joining to strengthen the therapeutic alliance (Dozier, Hicks, Cornille, & Peterson, 1998; Ryan & Carr, 2001).

The therapist's style of response to the family can also richly exemplify this circular orientation. For instance, if sadness is in evidence clinically, the individual therapist will typically offer an empathic acknowledgment, perhaps normalizing the emotion and, in the process, offering support to the distressed person. Here a linear process has unfolded as found in one-on-one therapy. In the family setting, if the therapist asks other family members how comprehensible the sadness is, who understands it best, who responds most helpfully, and how does any benefit develop, empathic responsiveness may be created between family members. This circular process helps the family become the source of empathy for the distressed relative. The therapist facilitates this development without needing to be the primary source of the compassion.

We begin to see that a fundamental activity of the successful facilitator of family meetings lies in the art of framing questions, in particular through the use of circular questions. Let us turn to a deeper consideration of this approach through consideration of Tomm's model of interventive questioning (Tomm, 1987a, 1987b, 1988).

Questioning Techniques

For the Canadian psychiatrist Karl Tomm (1988), circular questions serve as the foundational skill through which therapists explore family life. He regarded circularity as the "bridge connecting systemic hypothesizing and neutrality by means of the therapists' activity" (Tomm, 1988, p. 33). Questions are designed not only to obtain information for assessment, but also to simultaneously initiate therapeutic change. Thus, they can be investigative or therapeutic in intent.

Tomm distinguished four types of questions in terms of the intentions and assumptions that they embody (see Figure 7.1). Regarding intention, therapists may pose questions in order to *orient* the family through information gathering or to *influence* them and bring about change within the family. Regarding assumptions, therapists may ask questions based on *lineal* (cause-and-effect) or *circular* (cybernetic) assumptions. This ability to differentiate between lineal and circular views is central to systemic thinking.

There are two styles of information-gathering and orienting questions, one based on lineal assumptions (*linear questions*) and the other based on circular assumptions (*circular questions*). By way of definition, *linear questions* take the form of a direct question to an individual about himself or herself, asking for a personal account of the story. These questions have an investigative intent, involve a one-to-one direction, and are used when history or specific information is desired.

Circular questions seek observational information from each family member about others, by asking the respondent to step into the shoes of the others and describe what they think or feel. These questions efficiently solicit information from each person regarding his or her opinion and experience of (1) the family's current concern; (2) sequences of interactions, usually related to relevant issues; and (3) differences in relationships over time (Weeks & Treat, 2001). Circular questioning helps family members to realize that a given issue can be understood differently by various relatives and, in so doing, thus moves the group toward a more "decentered" point of view. Circular questions are especially useful when the clinician believes a family member could benefit from gaining more empathy from others in the family.

Two modes of change-focused or influencing questions emerge from each type of assumption: *strategic questions* tend to be more lineal in nature, whereas *reflexive questions* are more circular. *Strategic questions* are commonly used to invite the family to examine potential solutions to an issue and to bring about change within the family. These questions suggest possible alternatives for action but may have a constraining effect because of the direction offered, which may limit recognition of further options.

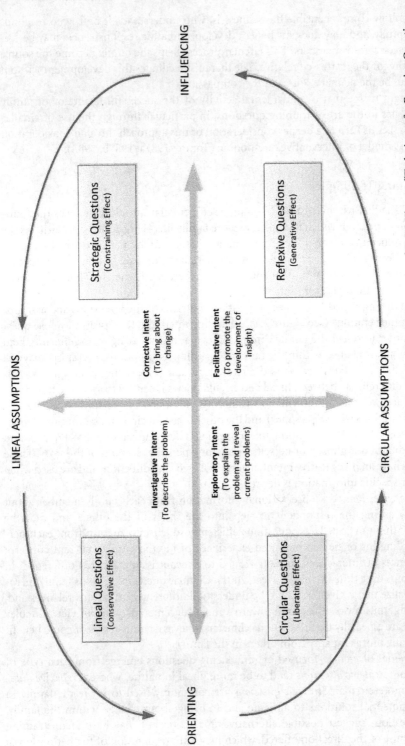

Figure 7.1 Integrative framework of questioning styles. Reprinted with permission from I. Dumont and D. W. Kissane, "Techniques for Framing Questions in Conducting Family Meetings in Palliative Care," *Palliative & Supportive Care, 7*(2009): 166. Adapted with permission.

INFLUENCING

LINEAL ASSUMPTIONS

CIRCULAR ASSUMPTIONS

ORIENTING

Strategic Questions
(Constraining Effect)

Reflexive Questions
(Generative Effect)

Lineal Questions
(Conservative Effect)

Circular Questions
(Liberating Effect)

Corrective Intent
(To bring about change)

Facilitative Intent
(To promote the development of insight)

Investigative Intent
(To describe the problem)

Exploratory Intent
(To explain the problem and reveal current problems)

Reflexive questions invite family contemplation and thus begin autonomous problem solving. These questions help family members to recognize how their various reactions, behaviors, and feelings serve as triggers and dynamically influence the family's interactions. In so doing, they encourage family members to take a step back and look at the issues and patterns from a more disengaged and objective perspective. Reflexive questions are likely to enable the family to generate new insights by embedding a working hypothesis into a question (hypothesis introducing) (Tomm, 1988). In this way, the therapist can draw new options from the family's beliefs system.

An intersection of the two continua of intent (with poles of orienting and influencing styles) and assumptions (with poles of lineal and circular assumptions) offers a comprehensive framework for distinguishing among these four types of questions (see Figure 7.1). Lineal and circular presuppositions should not, however, be considered as mutually exclusive. As Tomm astutely pointed out, "[T]he distinction between lineal and circular may be regarded as complementary, and not just as either/or; these assumptions and their associations may overlap and enrich one another" (1988, p. 4).

Development of Styles of Questions as the Therapy Unfolds

In studying the use of questions during family therapy, we rated therapists' questions according to Tomm's definitions across one sequence of eight sessions of family therapy (Dumont & Kissane, 2009). Early in therapy, the most frequent questions were linear and circular, moving around the family to build up a picture of events from everyone's perspective. Their frequency decreased as sessions unfolded, and they were gradually replaced by reflexive and strategic questions. Thus, the frequency of *orienting questions* (linear and circular) during the assessment phase was 96 percent, compared to 78 percent during the middle phase and 38 percent during the termination phase. As for *influencing questions* (reflexive and strategic), these increased as the therapy progressed, bringing the family to new perspectives. During assessment, they comprised four percent of questions, compared to 22 percent by middle therapy and 62 percent during final sessions. This pattern has been graphed in Figure 7.2. A case illustration will be presented shortly to further exemplify these questioning techniques.

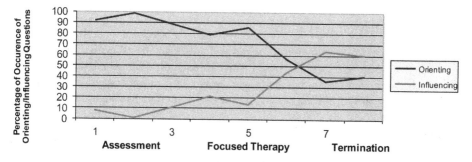

Figure 7.2 Change in questioning style across phases of therapy. Reprinted with permission from I. Dumont and D. W. Kissane, "Techniques for Framing Questions in Conducting Family Meetings in Palliative Care," *Palliative & Supportive Care, 7* (2009): 166. Adapted with permission.

The Role of Summaries as Therapy Unfolds

Beyond this questioning skill, therapists employ one other major technique in running family sessions: summary comments. These help to pace the therapy and ensure that a shared understanding is steadily developing, keeping all members on the same page. In this manner, consensus is established for the family as a whole. A summary is appropriate both before the therapist closes any agenda item and moves on to another issue, and also at the conclusion of each session. In this way, a summary integrates the views that have been shared, balances any differences of opinions, and potentially demonstrates how they can be held concurrently as several views by the family.

In constructing a summary comment, therapists do well to either address the family as a group or, if they choose to mention the perspective of an individual member, preserve neutrality by incorporating the views of several others. Furthermore, care is needed to avoid undue focus on negatives by balancing them with inclusion of family strengths and successes. In this way, summaries are very interventive and serve the important function of affirming the family and its members.

At the conclusion of each session, the family should carefully listen to summaries and carry home key words. The therapist therefore should devote considerable effort to incorporate hope, highlight what he or she likes about the family, emphasize robustness as a resource and potential pathway toward achievement of the family's goals, and point to ways that the family can continue to work together constructively before the next session occurs. Given such importance, the accuracy and focus of the summary is clearly the therapist's responsibility.

A common practice involves inviting family members to contribute collectively to the summary at the end of a session. This clarifies what they derived from their discussions and sometimes sees one member praising something he or she appreciated hearing from another. But if the therapist allows the session to close there, he or she fails the family in not giving them the gift of professional perspective and years of experience. The family expects feedback from the therapist. Moreover, this is a special opportunity to affirm what is good, contain any unsettled feelings (for often there is some unfinished business), reassure about the direction of future work, and arrange to bring the group back again to continue this together.

Sustaining Safety for the Family

Families will quickly withdraw from sessions if any of the members have not felt safe with the therapist. The early working alliance is based on trust, which develops as the family discovers that the therapist not only works hard to understand them, but also holds a deep regard for the wishes and feelings of all present. Through this therapeutic non-critical stance, the therapist builds comprehension by checking in with the family to make sure that he or she understands their perspectives accurately. Then the therapist incorporates views from all to enrich the interlacing tapestry of the system.

Central to this process is the principle of moving forward at the family's pace and with their permission. Respect is needed for avoidant coping styles, recognizing the advantages gained from adopting that position. Much therapeutic wisdom is required to incorporate sensitivity to embarrassment and shame, protection from unbridled criticism, recognition of sources of dispute and rigidity, and understanding the need for gradual revelation of secrets. Likewise, it is also crucial that the therapist have the ability to find things to like about the family, recognize robustness, expound on sources of meaning, and summarize the family's strengths.

The containment of conflict is one basic necessity to sustain safety. Although therapists need to appreciate the sources and processes that underlie disagreements, thus gaining from watching some arguments unfold, they carry responsibility for recognizing family members' limits of tolerability. An inability to contain conflict will quickly lead to the family's withdrawal. Early career therapists do well to accept the co-therapy model as a means to harness support in handling conflictual families. These therapists need to build experience in when to ask for "time out," how to summarize differences with exquisite neutrality, how to refocus attention on the process rather than content, and how to reframe agendas constructively. In summary, they need to know how to be an effective umpire when this is necessary to maintain participants' cooperation.

Certain topics prove a testing ground for safety issues, such as the timing and ability to talk about death and dying; sensitivity in discussing affairs and stories of abuse, alcoholism, and other drug usage; concern for suicidal thoughts or plans; cultural sensitivity; and ways of responding to feelings of disgust and abhorrence. Experience is fundamental in helping families recognize that the clinician has met these issues many times before. Honesty, authenticity, thoughtfulness, sensitivity, and respect prove crucial to sustain an environment in which the family feels secure, understood, and respected, so that family members' deepest fears and concerns can not only be aired but constructively worked through.

Highlighting Family Strengths as a Resource

A therapist's skill in affirming family strengths is central to successful family work. This cannot be false, artificial, or patronizing; it must not miss the mark. As Steinglass and Schuler so aptly laid out in Chapter 4, rather than looking for deficits, the wise therapist endorses resilience. This is built on discovering things about the family that the therapist likes, values that garner respect, achievements that the therapist admires, and roles that prove crucial, although easily taken for granted. For instance, the therapist can track the developmental story of migrant families and the heritage left by ancestors, strive to understand traditions, and be curious about family rituals and mottos. These form the varied pathways that help identify where each family's resources lie and how they might be harnessed to adaptive benefit.

Illustrative Case Example of Therapist Techniques

Mary, an Irish Catholic, was receiving anticancer treatment for progressive and advanced ovarian cancer. She was married to her husband, Peter, for 47 years. Together, they had raised three daughters and two sons, who attended family sessions in the parental home (see Figure 7.3). The family appeared close and protective of each other, but Peter blocked frank discussion of their predicament. They used humor to mask their sadness.

Mary had been the matriarch of this family, always the mediator among her children and the guide to her somewhat more dependent spouse. Peter carried a deep fear of

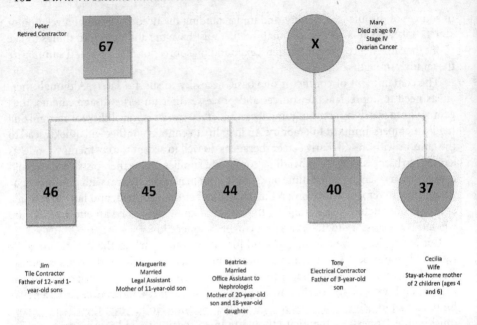

Figure 7.3 Genogram of family presented in the clinical case example. The patient was a 70-year-old Irish Catholic woman diagnosed with a stage IV ovarian carcinoma. Mary had been married to Peter for 47 years. Sessions were held at home. The family members appeared to be close and protective of each other. Reprinted with permission from I. Dumont and D. W. Kissane, "Techniques for Framing Questions in Conducting Family Meetings in Palliative Care," *Palliative & Supportive Care, 7*(2009): 167. Adapted with permission.

her death and the prospect of a lonely life without Mary. The children shared concerns about how they could help their father, recognizing his neediness and vulnerability. Four sessions were possible before Mary died.

Thereafter, Peter became quite demanding of his children who, in turn, felt burdened by his numerous requests. The next six sessions offered a safe place for the family to discuss their feelings; they expressed frustrations, shared grief, and acknowledged differences of opinion.

Early Phase of Therapy: Orienting Questions

During assessment of the family, the therapist sought to connect with each person and encourage his or her participation. Orienting questions (linear and circular) served to gather information about the family, its concerns, and its understanding of Mary's illness. Examples of some of these orienting questions were as follows:

To Mary: "Can you talk a little about your illness?" "How have treatments been going?" "What are the doctors saying?" "Physically, how are you feeling?" "How did you manage your day today?"

To family members: "Can you give me a sense of what you do?" "What would you like to get out of these meetings?" "What are you most concerned about right now?" "How hard is it for you to talk about the illness?" "What have you told your partners and your children about Mary's illness?"

In addition, circular questions deepened understanding of the family's functioning and cohesiveness. Family coping strategies were made explicit, and the predicament was defined as a family matter. Examples of circular questions were the following:

To family members: "Who are you the most worried about?" "Who is especially close within the family?" "How do you connect with each other?" "Can you tell me a little bit about your mom's role and then what your dad does in the family? What similarities and differences do you see?" "How do you think your mom is doing?"

To Peter: "What concerns does Mary have?" "What concerns do your children have?"

Later Phases of Therapy: Influencing Questions

As therapy progressed, the therapist steadily increased the use of reflexive and strategic questions, which promoted insight and change. Families living with illness focus on the difficulties at hand. By asking reflexive questions that were future oriented, the therapist empowered the family to imagine what this might be like. The family members prepared for their loss as they cared for their dying mother. The following examples illustrate this questioning style:

To family members: "What are your hopes and expectations for the future?" "How hard is it to talk about death and what might happen?" "What do you think you would all need from each other?" "What do you think will look different in a year from now?"

To Mary: "As things become harder for you physically, what roles might your children and Peter take on?" "What do you think will happen when they see you become frailer?"

When it is difficult for a family to talk about death and dying, the therapist can seek their permission, thus: "Would it be useful to talk about a time ahead when Mary may not be with us?" Raising the theme of anticipatory grief can also prove helpful (Rolland, 1994) and be approached by asking the family members to share their concerns about the imminence of death. Examples of reflexive questions that helped the family prepare for Mary's death include the following: "In a year, what issues will each one of you need to consider?" "Whose life might be most affected at that time?" "How will those issues be affected by Mary's illness?" "Given Mary's illness, are there certain expectations about how Peter should plan for the next phase of his life?"

When Mary died, Peter felt very alone and became so dependent on his children that they felt burdened by his multiple demands. Peter carried high expectations, looking for care in the manner that Mary had provided for him. It was challenging for Marguerite, one of his daughters, to whom Peter said, "You told your mom that you'd take care of me!" The therapist encouraged Marguerite to talk with her father quite directly about her feelings. Strategic questions helped Marguerite gain new insights and shift her attitude toward her father.

To Marguerite: "Are you able to tell your dad when he does call that it's too much sometimes?" "Is there a way you can just hear your dad talking and yet not get pulled into feeling that way?"

The therapist also challenged Peter's understanding of this.

To Peter: "When you are with the children and you are reminded of something that Mary might have done, can you consider why your children might do this differently?" "How do you think they feel?" "Peter, why don't you reach out to other people besides the children?"

The subsequent questions were powerful in building family solidarity and helping Peter and the children to think differently about the journey.

To the children and Peter: "If Mary (who passed away eight months ago) was here in the session right now, what would she say to you as a family?" "What do you think your mom would want?"

Gradually, Peter was able to step out more with his friends, while his children balanced their involvement with him so that no one individual was overburdened. Harmony grew, and the pain of mourning eased. Therapy thus helped to hold the family together using the memory of Mary's wishes and affirming the children's efforts in their support of their father. In concluding therapy, the therapist summarized:

> I sense that Mary would be proud of her family today, aware of your generosity and mutual care. She'd be grateful for the support that you've given Peter, and the wonderful team effort involved in doing this. And Peter, she'd smile at your gratitude to your family for all they have done for you. Hearing your words of thanks was very touching, letting them know that you appreciate the efforts they put in. I suspect that your teamwork is greater as a consequence of losing Mary, perhaps a hidden benefit despite the pain of her loss. Your grief is easing now, yet you take her memories and values forward with you. It has been a privilege to journey and share this with you. I want to congratulate you on all the work you have done in our meetings. I am confident about the constructive path that you'll take in the future. Good-bye.

Mary's family highlighted the value of each type of question, all of which have a proper place in the course of therapy. Linear questions helped the therapist in joining with the family and defining their concerns. Circular questions deepened their shared understanding of the predicament. Mary's presence and contribution also empowered the subsequent bereavement care.

As the therapy progressed, change-focused questions (reflexive or strategic questions) proved beneficial. Reflexive questions drew upon the family's cognitive and behavioral repertoire to encourage them to problem solve, fostering both their active participation and sense of autonomy. The family also shared grief adaptively after Mary's death. Strategic questions stimulated them to consider new directions by embedding overt suggestions. Difficulties can occur when family members hold tightly to existing beliefs and do not look for new information or perspectives (Robinson, Carroll, & Watson, 2005). This illustration did show both family adaptation and mutual support during bereavement.

Mobilization of the family's strengths and resources creates an environment likely to optimally foster adaptation despite the pain of loss. Multiple data sources and research methods can generate a rich understanding of family therapy processes (Elliott & James, 1989). More work is needed to further clarify what works and why at the process level of therapy (e.g., *client recall*, Elliott & James, 1989; *client reactions system*, Hill et al., 1988).

Dozier et al. (1998) investigated response differences to questions based on circular compared to lineal assumptions. They found that circular and reflexive questions facilitated joining and therapeutic alliance. Ryan and Carr (2001) confirmed this finding. The skill with which the clinician poses questions in therapy may be the critical factor in determining outcome (Dozier et al., 1998, p. 8). Few studies, however, have tested this empirically.

Conclusion

Much of the contemporary education to become a psychotherapist is grounded in a linear way of thinking common to individual therapy. It can be challenging for clinicians to reorient their conceptual framework to assess families in a circular or systemic manner. This chapter offers strategies to help guide this process.

Traditionally, researchers have focused on examining change moments in therapy as one-way interventions delivered by the therapist. Few researchers have investigated how therapists and families co-construct change through the back-and-forth reciprocity of their conversations (Couture, 2006). Family therapists perceive that this construction occurs through non-linear, ongoing circular processes. As we study the therapist's interventions together with the family's reactions, "Over time, it will be difficult to even isolate one person's actions as separate or unconnected from the interaction of the social group" (Gale, Dotson, Lindsey, & Negireddy, 1993, quoted in Couture, 2006, p. 4). In so doing, a more systemic way of thinking is more likely to weave its way through the linear mode of thought that is so deeply ingrained in our implicit or prereflexive epistemology.

References

Bateman, A., & Fonagy, P. (Eds.). (2006). *Mentalization based treatment: A practical guide*. Oxford: Oxford University Press.

Beutler, L. E., Williams, R. E., & Wakefield, P. J. (1993). Obstacles to disseminating applied psychological science. *Journal of Applied and Preventive Psychology, 2*, 53–58.

Couture, S. J. (2006). Transcending a differend: Studying therapeutic processes conversationally. *Contemporary Family Therapy, 28*, 285–302.

Dozier, R. M., Hicks, M. W., Cornille, T. A., & Peterson, G. (1998). The effect of Tomm's therapeutic questioning styles on therapeutic alliance: A clinical analog study. *Family Process, 37*, 189–200.

Dumont, I., & Kissane, D. W. (2009). Techniques for framing questions in conducting family meetings in palliative care. *Palliative & Supportive Care, 7*, 163–170.

Elliott, R., & James, E. (1989). Varieties of client experience in psychotherapy: An analysis of the literature. *Clinical Psychology Review, 9*, 443–468.

Fleuridas, C., Nelson, T. S., & Rosenthal, D. M. (1986). The evolution of circular questions: Training family therapists. *Journal of Marital and Family Therapy, 12*, 113–127.

Hill, C. E., Helms, J. E., Spiegel, S. B., & Tichenor, V. (1988). Development of a system for categorizing client reactions to therapist interventions. *Journal of Counseling Psychology, 35*, 27–36.

Johnson, S., & Lebow, J. (2000). The "coming of age" of couple therapy: A decade review. *Journal of Marital and Family Therapy, 26*, 23–38.

Kissane, D. W., & Hooghe, A. (2011). Family therapy for the bereaved. In R. A. Neimeyer, D. L. Harris, H. R. Winokuer, & G. F. Thornton (Eds.), *Grief and bereavement in contemporary society: Bridging research and practice* (pp. 287–302). New York: Routledge.

Kissane, D. W., & Zaider, T. I. (2011). Focused family therapy in palliative care and bereavement. In M. Watson & D. Kissane (Eds.), *Handbook of psychotherapy in cancer care* (pp. 185–197). Chichester, West Sussex: Wiley-Blackwell.

Main, F. O., Boughner, S. R., Mims, G. A., & Schieffer, J. L. (2001). Rolling the dice: An experiential exercise for enhancing interventive questioning skill. *The Family Journal, 9*, 450–454.

Penn, P. (1982). Circular questioning. *Family Process, 21*, 267–280.

Pinsof, W. M., & Wynne, L. C. (2000). Toward progress research: Closing the gap between family therapy practice and research. *Journal of Marital and Family Therapy, 26*, 1–8.

Robinson, W. D., Carroll, J. S., & Watson, W. L. (2005). Shared experience building around the family crucible of cancer. *Families, Systems, & Health, 23*, 131–147.

Rolland, J. S. (1994). *Families, illness, & disability: An integrative treatment model.* New York: Basic Books.

Ryan, D., & Carr, A. (2001). A study of the differential effects of Tomm's questioning styles on therapeutic alliance. *Family Process, 49*, 67–77.

Selvini, M. P., Boscolo, L., Cecchin, G., & Prata G. (1980). Hypothesizing—circularity—neutrality: Three guidelines for the conductor of the session. *Family Process, 19*, 3–12.

Tomm, K. (1987a). Interventive interviewing: Part I. Strategizing as a fourth guideline for the therapist. *Family Process, 26*, 3–13.

Tomm, K. (1987b). Interventive interviewing: Part II. Reflexive questioning as a means to enable self healing. *Family Process, 26*, 167–183.

Tomm, K. (1988). Interventive interviewing: Part III. Intending to ask lineal, circular, strategic, or reflexive questions. *Family Process, 27*, 1–15.

Weeks, G. R., & Treat, S. R. (2001). *Couples in treatment: Techniques and approaches for effective practice* (2nd ed.). New York: Brunner Routledge.

White, M., & Epston, D. (1990). *Narrative means to therapeutic ends.* New York: Norton.

Winnicott, D. W. (1971). *Playing and reality.* London, Tavistock Publications.

8 Culture and Grief in Families

*David W. Kissane, Bridgette Boucher, and
Francesca Del Gaudio*

Although ethnology points to the biological underpinnings of grief, the major determinant of the form of expression of grief—shaped by the ethnic background, social
traditions, and norms—is culture (Klass & Chow, 2011). It often guides the manner of
response, whether in facial reaction, demeanor, clothing, customs, or behaviors. Cultural sensitivity is therefore an essential clinical orientation in supporting and seeking to
understand the bereaved. It always behooves the clinician to make sense of any cultural
dimension of mourning. This maxim is never truer than when one turns to the family—
the significant social group that is likely to be the major transmitter of cultural norms.

In this chapter, we review some major cultures and consider from the family perspective some key values and traditions into which clinicians need insight. We acknowledge
an inability to deal comprehensively with each and every culture that is included and an
inability to include every prominent culture. Rather we seek to illustrate the importance
of the family's culture to therapeutic work, offering a glimpse of the manner in which it
is woven into the fabric of each family's story.

Latino Cultural Values

Therapists need to be familiar with the cultural values of Latinos, who are projected to
represent some 25% of the U.S. population by 2029 (US Census Bureau, 2010; Betacourt, Green, Carrillo, & Ananeh-Firempong, 2003). A culturally sensitive practice
should have an understanding of *familismo*, the gender roles of *machismo* and *marianismo*, and the strength of tradition, caretaking, and religion (Del Gaudio et al., 2012).

Familismo

Many Latino families carry a deep orientation to family loyalty, known as *familismo*.
This is characterized by a remarkable solidarity within families, which transcends multiple generations and values familial relationships with a striking devotion and mutuality (Marin, 1993; Marin & Triandis, 1985; Sabogal, Marin, Otero-Sabogal, Marin, &
Perez-Stable, 1987). This aids family work considerably and can lead to large gatherings
of family members when a loved one is dying.

But instances of marital breakdown, separation, and divorce can lead to fragmen-
tation and consideration of whether lost relationships can be repaired. We have seen
numerous examples of previously estranged couples assisting in care provision when
one is ill and perhaps dying, such as when a mother helps her daughters care for their

father, from whom she is divorced. The extended family, with grandparents, aunts, and uncles, may be utilized in these circumstances.

Gender Roles

Manliness is a prominent characteristic, known as *machismo*, with the expectation that the man will be physically strong and courageous and assume responsibility to protect and provide for his family (de Rios, 2001; Falicov, 1998; McGoldrick, Preto, Hines, & Lee, 1991; Vega, 1990). One corollary is an avoidance of emotional discourse and talk of death. The sick male may shun sharing personal feelings about his illness; therapists need to exercise great sensitivity to not cause embarrassment here. Likewise, males may avoid displays of grief and distress at funerals, but this stereotype is not universal, and many Latino men will be overtly emotional and distressed.

The complementary female role is *marianismo*, whereby a woman is self-sacrificing, religious, and responsible for running the household and raising children (Bean, Perry, & Bedell, 2001). Caregiving can be generously provided in this way to the sick. Yet when the family caretaker gets sick, she may find it difficult to let other people step in to help (Miranda et al., 2005).

Tradition—What Families Do Together

Sometimes due to a sense of *familismo* and sometimes out of perceived gender roles, family tradition can be strongly upheld in many Latino families. Expectations may be very strong that family attends specific meals and certain outings or gatherings and participates in religious rituals celebrated across the generations. If the family deems closeness important, family members may also expect the therapist to be personable and willing to join with them on a shared journey (Minuchin, 1974). Bean and colleagues (2001) described the potential for idealization of the therapist as a form of *personalismo*, wherein the Latin culture may glorify a family member. Wycoff and Chavez Cameron highlighted the acceptance of co-parenting by Latinos as another reason why clinicians may be expected to relate warmly to the family, feel they belong, and be willing to offer guidance and support (Wycoff & Chavez Cameron, 2001). When a family upholds this tradition, it can display great respect for authority and would look to be valued in a reciprocal manner (Ho et al., 2004).

Religion

Aligned with respect and tradition, acceptance of the will of God can be a central value predicting the outcome of the illness (de Rios, 2001). Older family members in the Latino culture may be churchgoing and use prayer as an active coping approach. Families may have high regard for rituals, such as anointing of the sick, which they believe reflects the seriousness of the illness at hand. Importantly, religion can also be a valuable resource as a source of comfort through trust in God.

At other times, religion can impede the person's capacity to face the gravity of the illness and prepare for death. Trust in God's mercy might be so strong that denial of alternative outcomes prevails. If family work is continued over time, these beliefs and focus can change (de Shazer et al., 1986). After a family member's death, many Latinos find that religion provides a major comfort as the family speaks of their loved one in heaven.

Case Example

Carlos was a 52-year-old Puerto Rican, who had been divorced from his wife and estranged from his two children for several years. Now sick with advanced lung cancer, Carlos had recently broken off from his girlfriend and returned to live with his elderly mother and her sister in a three-bedroom house. Hospice nurses were visiting to help with pain control. With a history of substance abuse and dependence on welfare, Carlos had been identified as an at-risk person; the nurses often considered him angry and uncooperative.

The therapist met at the home of Carlos's 84-year-old mother, Theresa. Her English was limited, so she was helped by her younger sister, Rosa, aged 66 (see Figure 8.1). These women loyally cooked and cared for Carlos, emphasizing that "He is family!" They struggled to understand his illness, and Carlos was not readily forthcoming about what was happening to him. Often angry, Carlos accused them of insufficient care and lack of respect. They sidestepped his outbursts and sustained their efforts.

Across several sessions, the therapist was able to encourage family outreach to Carlos's children. His daughter, Alexa, became involved, attending sessions and helping with his care. In turn, Alexa brought her mother, Maria, along to help and to contribute to the family sessions. The female kinship network was thus strengthened around Carlos, opening up communication and mutual support. The therapist noted that Carlos remained irascible and difficult until the end of his life, but a family benefit was for those left behind. Although his relationship with his son, Louis, was not rekindled, Carlos was reconciled with Alexa. The stable base provided by Carlos's mother and the cultural emphasis on family unity empowered this family therapy to be generative at the end of his life.

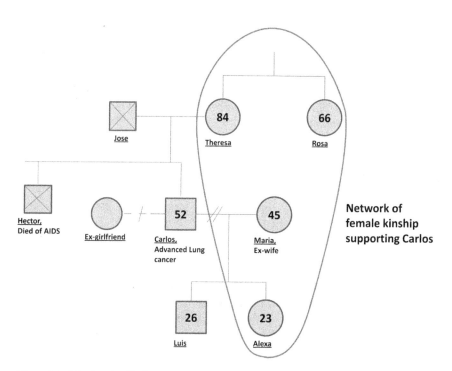

Figure 8.1 A Latino family from Puerto Rico, where family loyalty strengthened the female kinship as they cared for Carlos, who was ill.

For generations, the structure of Latin American family life has been affected by a U.S. congressional act of 1917 that granted automatic American citizenship to all Puerto Ricans, to which other Latino groups were not privy. The movement of people between the mainland United States and Puerto Rico became known as circular migration (Meléndez, 1993). It created a potential cycle of family ruptures along with dependence on the extended family for accommodation and financial support. This occurred as people moved from one country to the other, while needing to reconstruct social networks. The principle of family loyalty, however, ensured that relatives welcomed their kin. In the previous family illustration, Carlos returned to Puerto Rico during the final months of his life, further demonstrating the potential role of family unity, honor, and welfare in the Latino culture.

Asian Cultural Values

Some prominent themes that may arise in therapy with families from Asian backgrounds include familial hierarchy, lack of balance in gender-based power, conflict across intergenerational relationships, preoccupation with shame, and the limits of emotional expression (Mondia et al., 2011). To facilitate communication and empower gains for these families, therapists must recognize the potential role of these cultural values and know how to properly manage any resultant tensions.

Power Hierarchy

Although no generalization can suffice, a common family structure in Chinese families respects a line of authority that extends from the father to the mother to the first-born son to the last child (Kim, 1985). This hierarchy of power highlights the importance of filial piety in many Chinese families. In some families, male dominance may be common, especially in older couples, where the wife may appear submissive (McGoldrick, Giordano, & Preto, 2005), but conflict may occur and can lead to domestic violence and abuse (Chung, Tucker, & Takeuchi, 2008).

Cultural Beliefs

Family cohesion in some Asian families can be decreased in other ways, too. Immigrant parents, for instance, do not necessarily acculturate to life in a new country in the same way as their children (Tsai-Chae & Nagata, 2008). Immigrants tend to ally with the traditions of their home country, whereas subsequent generations adopt the customs of the host country. When these clash, conflict readily appears. Consider, for example, that intergenerational misunderstanding can arise when an older member recommends adherence to Eastern practices such as taking daily herbs and mushrooms, which is rooted in Taoism, to balance the "yin" and "yang" through natural means (Chen, 1996). Another belief is the attribution of blame for illness, whereby certain actions can lead to consequences such as the development of cancer

(Ratanakul, 2004). Knowledge of such cultural beliefs can be crucial to address these intergenerational issues.

Shame and Inhibited Emotional Expression

Therapists need to understand the concept of shame and its relationship to the lack of overt emotional expression in Asian cultures. The risk of losing face in front of strangers through the expression of too much emotionality may lead some families to avoid family meetings. For instance, in Filipino culture, the concept of *hiya*, or shame, signifies embarrassment and fear of perceived inferiority, which can impede sharing feelings (Root, 1985; Tiu & Seneriches, 1995). This shame is not unlike *machismo*, whereby Filipino men may be expected to be hyper-masculine and prideful (Nadal, 2009). Therapy that is generally supportive-expressive in style needs to accommodate and respect this *machismo* concept. For example, some mothers, in suggesting that their sons not cry in bereavement but rather remain silent to maintain a masculine composure, might proclaim, "They're not girls; they don't show emotions."

Case Example

Huang, a single, Chinese woman, 57, worked as a school counselor until she received a diagnosis of metastatic gastric cancer for which she received palliative chemotherapy. She was sensitive to extreme temperatures, felt weak, and had started to lose her hair. She was irritable and emotionally explosive with her family, causing people to either withdraw from her or to criticize her harshly. Though she appeared optimistic about her future in the initial family session, she began to sob because she could not fulfill her brother Ping's expectation that she exercise. In light of this, all of the family wanted to improve communication and harmony.

The therapist was a female Caucasian psychologist, who sought to defuse conflict that arose from miscommunication. She encouraged the family members to explore their ancestral and cultural bases for this strife, hoping to strengthen familial bonds.

A high degree of conflict, coupled with low levels of cohesiveness and communication, pervaded the sessions (see Figure 8.2). Arguments developed from the family's tendency to speak but not listen to each other; this pattern was most evident in Huang's relationship with her elder sister, Yan, for whom she carried long-lasting grudges. Huang's nieces, Emily and Vicky, felt detached from these battles between their aunts, but they were curious to understand what caused them.

The sisters, Huang and Yan, resented their father's negative influence in fostering their distrust of men. They never married, for which they blamed him. Their father was abusive, both physically and emotionally, creating fear in them that a husband could likewise dole out abuse. Moreover, the sisters were not adept at facing failure. In childhood, Huang had been told that her main priority was to "be perfect for everyone." The therapist focused on the connection between the family's unhealthy communication and the father's influence. She allowed Huang and her siblings to explore this and openly share the experiences they had with their father, creating the possibility that they could begin to trust more and relate better.

112   *David W. Kissane, et al.*

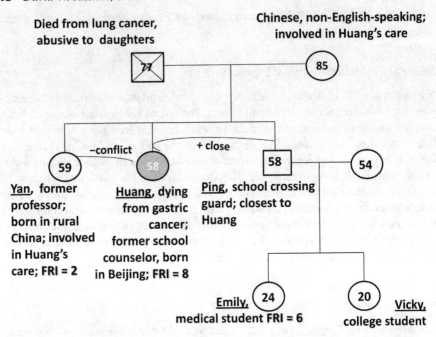

Figure 8.2 A family from China with a pattern of male dominance, preferential treatment of sons, and rivalry between sisters. FRI = Family Relationships Index, where the optimal score is 12.

The father appeared to have exercised power to leave them feeling regret and resentment. He was very demanding of his daughters, which stemmed from his preference for his son. His children were set up to compete unhealthily with each other; they strived to gain his approval at the cost of personal fulfillment. Wang and Heppner (2002) showed that any discrepancy between perceived parental expectations and one's performance generated distress, including depression and anxiety. Huang and Yan's inability to please their father and their tendency to compete may have sparked the dysfunctional communication evident during therapy. Intergenerational strain was also apparent in the family, where Emily and Vicky were second-generation descendants of immigrant grandparents. Their alliance with Western beliefs and lifestyles led to a gap in understanding their parents' experience. They also felt shame, which in turn contributed to emotional suppression, lest it be seen as weakness and a loss of face.

African American Families

Strong emotional ties tend to exist not only with the immediate family but also with the extended family of African Americans. Therapists therefore need to be open to the involvement of whoever is considered important. The culture may place great importance on "going out in style," wherein the funeral conveys respect for the deceased. African Americans may customarily turn up in large numbers. The wake and church ceremony reflect the influence of African philosophy and Christianity upon their mourning. In the South, "sitting up" to receive visitors in the days before the funeral has been traditional. The eulogy and music may be designed to evoke emotional release, such as the practice of opening the casket for a final viewing (Carter, 2001).

For African Americans who have a high regard for family, attendance at family bereavement sessions can be common. Unfinished business, whether because of prior conflicts or family secrets, may be attended to at this time (Boyd-Franklin, 2003). The therapist can facilitate this and encourage open communication, curiosity, respect, and concern for the needs of all. Families tend to want to be helpful to one another, show flexibility in roles and provision of support, and generally prioritize this at this time of grief and mourning (Moore Hines, 2004).

African American families can sometimes see the invitation to a family meeting with a therapist as prying and have struggled historically to trust the medical system (Hines, 1999; Shelton et al., 2010; Thompson, Valdimarsdottir, Winkel, Jandorf, & Redd, 2004). They may conceive of therapy as not for them. Genogram work may need to be delayed until the therapist has developed an alliance with the family (Hines, 1999). African American women can be more religious than men and tend to be perceived as the strength of the family (Boyd-Franklin, 2003), as will be seen in the subsequent case example (see Figure 8.3). Engagement with the women can be the secret to engaging the family's commitment to therapy.

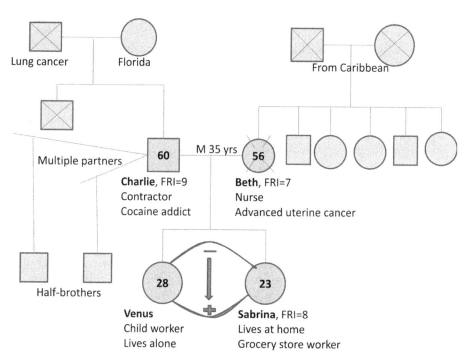

Figure 8.3 An African American family, in which the mother, Beth, died from cancer and family therapy fostered communication between Charlie and his daughters. The therapy also helped to reduce conflict and enhance mutual support between the sisters. FRI = Family Relationships Index, where the optimal score is 12.

Case Example

Beth, a 56-year-old African American mother of two daughters, was dying from advanced uterine cancer. She was concerned about her daughters' relationship, which was sometimes conflictual. She also strove to find forgiveness for Charlie, her husband of 35 years, who had used cocaine throughout his life and had been unfaithful to her with several women, including two with whom he had fathered sons. Despite the fractured relationships in the family, they still strove to be loyal because of their Christian values. As very regular church attendees, they were connected to a broad circle of congregants, who came in and out of the family home like extended family.

Beth was the eldest of a family of six, who had migrated from the Caribbean. Charlie's family came from harsh poverty in the American Deep South and had lost knowledge of its ancestral roots. Beth, a nurse, was the family matriarch, connecting siblings and extended family, welcoming one and all to her home in Queens. Echoing her strong beliefs, Beth expressed that "God watches over us." This contrasted with the views of her younger daughter, who blamed her mother's hospital for delay in diagnosing the cancer. The daughters, Venus, 28, and Sabrina, 23, had fought often through the years. Venus worked in child protection services and lived independently of the family. Sabrina still lived at home and worked in a local grocery store. They agreed that effective communication was their family's greatest challenge.

Before Beth died, three sessions took place in the family home with a psychologist. The acknowledgement of the seriousness of her illness opened the door for good-byes to begin. Charlie, a 60-year-old maintenance worker, apologized for "using drugs" and his "wanderings in the past," and thanked Beth for being a generous mother to their girls. When Beth died, the church and its rituals helped the family share its grief with their community. Three further family sessions over the next six months helped define the future relationship between the daughters and their father. Frank exchanges occurred about loyalty and protection, with Sabrina demanding that Charlie be more selective about which men he brought home—that his daughters were not to be seen as "available women" for his friends to proposition.

Sabrina moved temporarily into Venus's apartment, and the two strengthened their relationship and mutual support. The therapist affirmed this as the fulfillment of their mother's wishes. As their grief at losing their mother was intensely expressed, they bonded and helped one another. Both talked frequently by phone with their father, and eventually Sabrina felt safe and returned to the family home. Charlie started dating a female congregant from their church as life began to move forward again for this family.

The work done with African American women is well exemplified here. Because they can put the needs of the family first and strive for its benefit, some will display both tolerance and forgiveness for prior wrongs (Boyd-Franklin, 2003). Their spirituality is also striking as an expression of their values and wider connection with their community (Boyd-Franklin, 2003). When they share their stories of church rituals, therapists can develop a deeper appreciation of the importance of these beliefs, which can offer consolation in bereavement.

In another African American family in therapy, music became a poignant part of the family's mourning ritual. The young woman, 35, and her husband had played in gigs professionally. As she was dying of cancer, her husband could not easily share his sadness except through music, which became a source of deep comfort to his bereaved mother-in-law. She was intensely distressed at the untimely death of her daughter but could draw solace from the beauty of this music. The young couple also told their story of the cancer on Facebook, sharing many photos about each phase of illness with their friends. The music was also posted and created a means to unite family and friends in a supportive network in bereavement. It became helpful to equip the mother with Internet access and thus allow her to experience the breadth and depth of appreciation that her daughter's friends had for her creative life. As an enriched understanding of the meaning of her daughter's life and marriage emerged, this facilitated some healing in bereavement.

Cultural Variations in Islam

Muslims will generally follow the religious rule of their country concerning death and mourning. Clinicians might consider inviting an imam to visit the patient who is dying and provide support for the patient's family (Abudabbeh, 2005). Prayers that embrace a profession of their faith may be desirable close to death, after which the family washes the deceased body, wraps it in a shroud, with burial in the ground, usually within 24 hours (Jonker, 1996). Cremation is forbidden because of belief in the resurrection of the dead. There is wide variation in emotional expression of grief, usually governed by the tradition of their country of origin and ranging from loud cries of lamentation and the singing of dirges to quiet and contained grief, where stoicism is valued (Jonker, 1997).

Within Islamic traditions, religious dictates include prayers at the graveside, where the male relatives answer five questions of faith asked of the deceased that will determine his or her eventual resurrection on the last day (Sheikh, 1998). Further prayers can be said, usually at the mosque, by the family on the third, seventh, and fortieth days after death. At the one-year anniversary, a stone is traditionally placed on the grave. Children can be protected from involvement with these rituals. North African women may be seen traditionally mourning in white clothes, Middle Eastern in black, and Turkish in subdued clothing. The young might wear mourning clothes for three months, and the elderly for one year (Gardner, 1998).

These traditions within the Muslim culture point to the centrality of the family during mourning (Abudabbeh, 2005). They are guided by the wisdom of many centuries of Islamic custom, and grief may be shared with the family and community, the *Ummah*. Family life may be patriarchal, where communication may be directed vertically from those in authority to others in the family. Many strains on Muslim families today result from education, urbanization, war, and Westernization. A family approach to clinical support would understand the potential for such traditions, with respect offered to the father in keeping with the hierarchical nature of family life, necessitating some linear questions to understand his point of view.

Haitian Families

The Francophile Republic of Haiti was the first nation in the Caribbean to achieve its independence, which was won in 1804 after a slave-led revolution (Laguerre, 1981). Occupying the western, smaller side of the island it shares with the Dominican Republic, Haiti is densely populated, yet very poor. Its people speak French or Creole and are predominantly Catholic. After long periods of political conflict, its people have been spread across the Caribbean and the United States, especially along the East Coast. The devastating earthquake in 2010 brought much destruction to Haiti, necessitating major humanitarian efforts.

Haitian culture tends to emphasize spirituality, a great love of music, and a deep faith in God (Desrosiers & St. Fleurose, 2002). Illness can unite their large families, and they may turn to prayer for help. As the mother of a dying son said in the subsequent example, "God is good. He may still bring us a great surprise!" Haitians present a ready example of how a Catholic belief system can operate in the face of a cancer death.

Case Example

Pierre was only 25 when his widely metastatic bowel cancer was first discovered. He had been ill with ulcerative colitis for several years, and his symptoms had been attributed to that disease, leading to some delay in his cancer diagnosis. Although treated with chemotherapy, eventually his cancer progressed, and by the time Pierre was 27 years old, his family recognized that his demise was close. Pierre had planned to marry his Jamaican girlfriend, Martine, but given the demands of his treatment, some family conflict broke out over the timing of this wedding. Unbeknownst to the family, Pierre and Martine wed in secret. Pierre was close to his elder sister, Dominique, while Martine confided in the younger sister, Sophie (see Figure 8.4). Typical of families with a young cancer patient, Pierre's family became steadily more involved in his care, with his mother taking up the role of main caregiver.

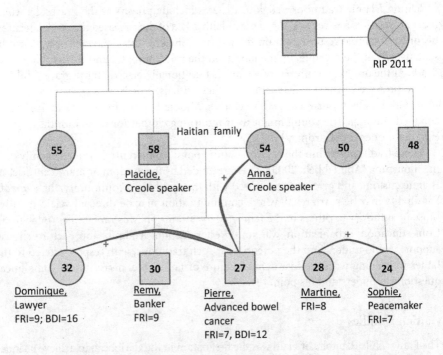

Figure 8.4 A Haitian family whose third child, Pierre, had his diagnosis of bowel cancer delayed through an extended focus on ulcerative colitis. He had secretly married his Jamaican girlfriend, Martine. Pierre's family wanted to care for him at home as he was dying, with some tension developing between their wishes and Martine's. FRI = Family Relationships Index, where an optimal score is 12; BDI = Beck Depression Inventory short form, where a normal score is <5.

The family found it difficult to talk about Pierre's cancer and avoided any discussion of a negative outcome. His parents carried their distress privately or confided in the older generation, whereas the siblings turned to somewhat awkward humor. Gradually, Pierre became anxious about the burden he had become to everyone, expressing guilt to the medical team over what was happening to his family. This prompted the setting up of a family meeting. When they met with a psychologist, the emotional pain they all carried was blatantly clear, yet their protective stance created tension as they struggled to support one another. Sophie said, "We float along independently, instead of floating toward one another!" Martine added, "We're flying by the seat of our pants, as there is no road map for this experience." Showing great courage, Pierre asked each relative to tell him how his illness was affecting them. Amid freely flowing tears, the family began to unite as they shared their fears and distress. Although Martine acknowledged finding it hard to feel welcomed by Pierre's family, she accepted Anna and Placide's invitation to bring Pierre home to their house.

This relocation entailed a hospital bed being established for Pierre in the family room, where subsequent family meetings also occurred. Discovering that Martine and Pierre had wed, the family welcomed Martine as a daughter-in-law, and all grew closer as they cared for the frail Pierre. The family recited hymns and prayers collectively as he died.

Often the therapist can harness the goodwill and mutual support of a family through the mechanism of a family meeting. And when this momentum is aligned with the family's religious tradition or belief system, grief can be shared beneficially. The spiritual meaning of the loss that is adopted by the family as a whole, for example, "Pierre's death was God's will," helps with the eventual resolution of this grief over time.

Hinduism and India

This ancient civilization is comprised of vast diversity, which is separated hierarchically by its caste system—*Brahmans*, or intelligentsia; *Kshatriyas*, or administrators; *Vaisyas*, or traders; and *Sudras*, or servants (Sharma, 2004). Hinduism is the religious philosophy embraced by more than 80 percent of the population (India Census, 2001), whereby one's life can undertake many journeys through rebirth until its soul (the *atman*) eventually merges with God (Sharma, 2004). Four holy texts, the *Vedas*, relate beliefs about the deities, whereas other texts, the *Upanishads*, explore the workings of the inner self. Through knowledge, constructive action, and devotion, a person gains steady reincarnation at higher levels.

Within the Hindu worldview, individualism can be subjugated to a more community-oriented way of life where the family occupies primacy (Hodge, 2004). Large extended families can permit the easy movement of relatives among different extensions of the family. The festival of *Rakhi* celebrates a brother-sister relationship and represents a deep sense of filial duty and affection that the culture can bestow on sibling relationships (Sonawat, 2001). To celebrate, sisters tie silken threads onto the wrists of their brothers as a wish of success and health but in return for a promise of protection. This annual ritual can help to sustain familial bonds. Acceptance of arranged marriages between families is another symbol of the potential power of the family within the culture. Underpinning many of these ancient customs is a religious respect for women, including female divinities and the worship of God as the Divine Mother (Kurien, 2001).

At times of illness, Indian tradition commonly recognizes the family as the source of healing and support. The family educates, nurtures, bonds people together, and socializes people. Traditionally, the mother-in-law has been respected and the daughter-in-law understands that she may be expected to accommodate the wishes of her mother-in-law. This three-generational family life can be common. Nonetheless, as societies change, conflict can arise intergenerationally, especially over who is in charge. Therapists need to understand expectations that may exist regarding such hierarchies in a society that for many centuries has placed the needs of the family well ahead of the aspirations of any individual.

Case Example

Krishna was a 63-year-old banker who turned to his sister for help when his pancreatic cancer was diagnosed. He had divorced his wife some years before, was childless, and turned back to his family of origin for support. Well-versed in the old ways, his sister, Veena, readily took him in. She delighted in feeding and caring for her brother, both to the amusement of her husband and the curious surprise of her Westernized daughter.

The previous generation had known much hardship; Veena and Krishna's father was raised in an orphanage (see Figure 8.5). He had ensured that in the annual festival of Rakhi, his children understood their filial duties and loyal commitment to each other. This underscored the confidence with which Krishna reached out to his sister in his time of personal challenge. Although the family had lived in various states and was infrequently in contact with its relatives, the cultural tradition and expectations of family life worked favorably.

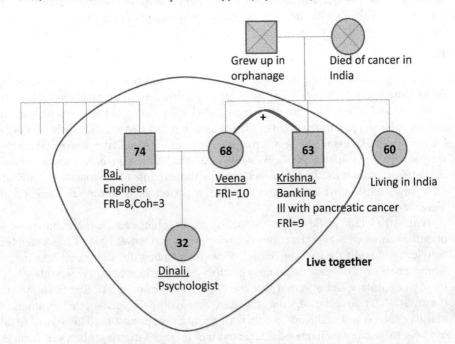

Figure 8.5 A Hindu family where the cultural tradition of a strong brother-sister relationship informed their commitment to family loyalty. FRI = Family Relationships Index; Coh = cohesiveness of the family. The maximum FRI score is 12, and maximum Coh score is 4.

A therapist with a Western cultural upbringing must take care not to assume that contemporary secular norms should guide family behaviors and attitudes. This brings an additional level of complexity to the therapeutic principle of neutrality: cultural sensitivity necessitates that the therapist respect family customs that may not appear immediately sensible to him or her (Kissane & Bloch, 2002). Although intergenerational clashes are frequent when immigrant parents want to adhere to the old culture of their country of origin and their children want to engage in the culture of the new country, the therapist wisely avoids taking a side. The therapist might express fascination for the rationale that underpins different traditions and wonder aloud about how this family will tolerate its differences constructively.

The Judaic Tradition

The Judaic emphasis on life, its preciousness, and the ethical pursuit of this can bring a distinctive outlook (Grollman, 1993; Lamm, 2000). The family may rally around their sick relative, visiting and helping as best they can. Jewish people bring a long history of customs to guide their response to family grief, whereby these traditions foster a deep level of mutual support (Lamm, 2000). When death occurs, the custom after the burial of "sitting shiva" (literally, seven days, as Joseph mourned the death of his father, Jacob, for seven days in Genesis 50:1–14) means that the bereaved are visited by their extended family and friends, who not only console but provide instrumental care (Rosen & Weltman, 2005). Today, of course, many families who observe shiva will only receive visits for two or three days or nights. This visitation can be seen as a mark of respect, displaying kindness and compassion and fostering the correct tenor for mourning.

Ritual supports mourning, including regular temple visits and prayer recitation for those who are more religiously inclined (Lamm, 2000). The custom of designating the mourning period as 12 months for close relatives allows for the gradual easing of grief and the completion of mourning, thereafter moving on (Lamm, 2000). The anniversary would typically include unveiling of the tombstone. Importantly, these rituals can be pursued as a family, both guiding and normalizing processes that care for the bereaved.

Conclusion

Our coverage of these cultures has illustrated varied ways in which customs and traditions can be adopted by the bereaved. In no way do we mean to stereotype any cultural or ethnic group. Rather, we advocate for a culturally sensitive approach in which the clinician asks each particular family about any practices that are important to them (Kissane et al., 2006).

As we take stock of these varied cultural contributions to the process of mourning, we can appreciate the wisdom of these practices from a sociological viewpoint in guiding what to do and how to mourn. By being curious about cultural norms for each group, clinicians can then invite the family to consider the potential benefit they might gain by following any available rituals. Given that the world has become more secular in its orientation, endorsement of rituals can highlight their potential to help the mourning process (Imber-Black, 1992). Furthermore, by conveying both interest in and respect for these traditions, the therapist adopts a stance of cultural sensitivity that will strengthen the therapeutic alliance. Culture can be so intimately expressed and lived through the family that it forms a crucial lens through which family grief can be observed.

Further Reading

McGoldrick, M., Giordano, J., & Garcia-Preto, N. (Eds.). (2005). *Ethnicity and family therapy* (3rd ed.). New York: Guildford Press.
This edited text of 54 chapters provides an extensive description of culture-related family issues relevant to mental health care.
Neimeyer, R. A., Harris, D. L., Winokuer, H. R., & Thorton, G. F. (Eds.). (2011). *Grief and bereavement in contemporary society.* New York: Routledge.
This internationally edited recent text with its emphasis on contemporary society provides insight into the diversity and universality of bereavement care.
Parkes, C. M., Laungani, P., & Young, B. (Eds.). (1997). *Death and bereavement across cultures.* London: Routledge.
This edited handbook focuses on the world's major religions as a lens to understand rituals and beliefs that influence both the dying process and bereavement.

References

Abudabbeh, N. (2005). Arab families. An overview. In M. McGoldrick, J. Giordano, & N. Garcia-Preto (Eds.), *Ethnicity and family therapy* (3rd ed., pp. 423–436). New York: Guilford Press.
Bean, R., Perry, B., & Bedell, T. (2001). Developing culturally competent marriage and family therapists: Guidelines for working with Hispanic families. *Journal of Marital and Family Therapy, 27,* 43–54.
Betacourt, J. R., Green, A. R., Carrillo, J. E., & Ananeh-Firempong, O. (2003). Defining cultural competence: A practical framework for addressing racial/ethnic disparities in health and health care. *Public Health Report, 118,* 293–302.
Boyd-Franklin, N. (2003). *Black families in therapy: Understanding the African American experience* (2nd ed.). New York: Guilford Press.
Carter, J. H. (2001). *Death and dying among African Americans: Cultural characteristics and coping tidbits.* New York: Vantage.
Chen, Y. D. (1996). Conformity with nature: A theory of Chinese American elders' health promotion and illness prevention processes. *Advances in Nursing Science, 19,* 17–26.
Chung, G. H., Tucker, M. B., & Takeuchi, D. (2008). Wives' relative income production and household male dominance: Examining violence among Asian American enduring couples. *Family Relations, 57,* 227–238.
Del Gaudio, F., Hichenberg, S., Eisenberg, M., Kerr, E., Zaider, T. I., & Kissane, D. W. (2012). Latino values in the context of palliative care: Illustrative cases from the family focused grief therapy trial. *American Journal of Hospice and Palliative Medicine, 30*(3), 271–278.
de Rios, M. D. (2001). *Brief psychotherapy with the Latino immigrant client.* New York: Haworth Press.
de Shazer, S., Berg, I. K., Lipchik, E., Nunnally, E., Molnar, A., Gingerich, W., & Weiner-Davis, M. (1986). Brief therapy: Focused solution development. *Family Process, 25,* 207–221.
Desrosiers, A., & St. Fleurose, S. (2002). Treating Haitian patients: Key cultural aspects. *American Journal of Psychotherapy, 56,* 508–522.
Falicov, C. J. (1998). *Latino families in therapy.* New York: Guilford Press.
Gardner, K. (1998). Death, burial and bereavement among Bengali Muslims. *Journal of Ethnic Migration Studies, 24,* 507–521.

Grollman, E. A. (1993). Death in Jewish thought. In K. J. Doka & J. D. Morgan (Eds.), *Death and spirituality* (pp. 21–32). New York: Baywood.

Hines, P. (1999). The family life cycle of African American families living in poverty. In B. Carter & M. McGoldrick (Eds.), *The expanded family life cycle: Individual, family and social perspectives* (3rd ed., pp. 327–345). Boston: Allyn & Bacon.

Ho, M. K., Rasheed, J. M., & Rasheed, M. N. (2004). *Family therapy with ethnic minorities.* Thousand Oaks, CA: Sage.

Hodge, D. R. (2004). Working with Hindu clients in a spiritually sensitive manner. *Social Work, 49,* 27–38.

Imber-Black, E. (1992). *Rituals for our times.* New York: Harper Collins.

India Census. (2001). Indian population. Retrieved from http://www.hinduism.about.com/population.htm

Jonker, G. (1996). The knife's edge: Muslim burial in the diaspora. *Mortality, 1,* 27–45.

Jonker, G. (1997). The many facets of Islam. In C. M. Parkes, P. Laungani, & B. Young (Eds.), *Death and bereavement across cultures* (pp. 147–165). London: Routledge.

Kim, S. C. (1985). Family therapy for Asian Americans: A strategic structural framework. *Psychotherapy Theory, Research, Practice, Training, 22*(2S), 342–348.

Kissane, D. W., & Bloch, S. (2002). *Family focused grief therapy: A model of family-centred care during palliative care and bereavement.* Buckingham, UK: Open University Press.

Kissane, D. W., McKenzie, M., Bloch, S., Moskowitz, C., McKenzie, D. P., & O'Neill, I. (2006). Family focused grief therapy: A randomized, controlled trial in palliative care and bereavement. *American Journal of Psychiatry, 163,* 1208–1218.

Klass, D., & Chow, A. Y. M. (2011). Culture and ethnicity in experiencing, policing, and handling grief. In R. A. Neimeyer, D. L. Harris, H. R. Winokuer, & G. F. Thornton (Eds.), *Grief and bereavement in contemporary society* (pp. 341–353). New York: Routledge.

Kurien, P. (2001). Religion, ethnicity and politics: Hindu and Muslim Indian immigrants in the United States. *Ethnic and Racial Studies, 24,* 263–293.

Laguerre, M. S. (1981). Haitian Americans. In A. Harwood (Ed.), *Ethnicity and medical care* (pp. 172–210). Cambridge, MA: Harvard University Press.

Lamm, M. (2000). *The Jewish way in death and mourning* (2nd ed.). New York: Jonathon David.

Marin, G. (1993). Influence of acculturation on familialism and self-identification among Hispanics. In M. E. Bernal & G. P. Knight (Eds.), *Ethnic identity* (pp. 181–196). New York: SUNY Press.

Marin, G., & Triandis, H. C. (1985). Allocentrism as an important characteristic of the behavior of Latin Americans and Hispanics. In R. Diaz-Guerrero (Ed.), *Cross-cultural and national studies in social psychology* (pp. 85–104). Amsterdam: North-Holland.

McGoldrick, M., Giordano, J., & Preto, N. (2005). *Ethnicity & family therapy* (3rd ed.). New York: Guilford Press.

McGoldrick, M., Preto, N. G., Hines, P. M., & Lee, E. (1991). Ethnicity and family therapy. In A. Gurman & D. Kniskern (Eds.), *Handbook of family therapy* (Vol. 2, pp. 546–582). New York: Brunner/Mazel.

Meléndez, E. (1993). *Los Que Se Van, Los Que Regresan.* New York: Center for Puerto Rican Studies.

Minuchin, S. (1974). *Families and family therapy.* Cambridge, MA: Harvard University Press.

Miranda, J., Siddique, J., Der-Martirosian, C., & Belin, T. R. (2005). Depression among Latina immigrant mothers separated from their children. *Psychiatric Services, 56,* 717–720.

Mondia, S., Hichenberg, S., Kerr, E., & Kissane, D.W. (2011). The impact of Asian-American value systems on palliative care: Illustrative cases from the Family Focused Grief Therapy trial. *American Journal of Hospice and Palliative Care.* doi: 10.1177/1049909111426281

Moore Hines, P. (2004). Mourning in African-American culture. In F. Walsh & M. McGoldrick (Eds.), *Living beyond loss: Death in the family* (2nd ed., pp. 125–130). New York: W. W. Norton.

122 *David W. Kissane, et al.*

Nadal, K. L. (2009). *Filipino American psychology: A handbook of theory, research, and clinical practice.* Bloomington, IN: Authorhouse.

Ratanakul, P. (2004). Buddhism, health and disease. *Eubios Journal of Asian and International Bioethics, 15,* 162–164.

Root, M. P. P. (1985). Guidelines for facilitating therapy with Asian American clients. *Psychotherapy Theory, Research, Practice, Training, 22*(2S), 349–356.

Rosen, E. J., & Weltman, S. F. (2005). Jewish families: An overview. In M. McGoldrick, J. Giordano, & N. Garcia-Preto (Eds.), *Ethnicity and family therapy* (3rd ed., pp. 667–679). New York: Guildford Press.

Sabogal, F., Marin, G., Otero-Sabogal, R., Marin, B. V., & Perez-Stable, E. J. (1987). Hispanic and acculturation: What changes and what doesn't? *Hispanic Journal of Behavioral Sciences, 9,* 397–412.

Sharma, A. P. (2004). *Hinduism redefined.* New Delhi: Vedam Books.

Sheikh, A. (1998). Death and dying: A Muslim perspective. *Journal of the Royal Society of Medicine, 91,* 138–140.

Shelton, R. C., Winkel, G., Davis, S. N., Roberts, N., Valdimarsdottir H., Hall, S. J., & Thompson, H. S. (2010). Validation of the group-based medical mistrust scale among urban black men. *Journal of General Internal Medicine, 25,* 549–555.

Sonawat, R. (2001). Understanding families in India: A reflection of societal change. *Psicologia Teoria e Pesquisa, 17,* 177–186.

Thompson, H. S., Valdimarsdottir, H. B., Winkel, G., Jandorf, L., & Redd, W. (2004). The group-based medical mistrust scale: Psychometric properties and association with breast cancer screening. *Preventive Medicine, 38,* 209–218.

Tiu, A. T., & Seneriches, J. S. (1995). *Depression and other mental health issues: The Filipino American experience.* San Francisco, CA: Jossey-Bass Publishers.

Tsai-Chae, A. H., & Nagata, D. K. (2008). Asian values and perceptions of intergenerational family conflict among Asian American students. *Cultural Diversity and Ethnic Minority Psychology, 14,* 205–214.

U.S. Census Bureau. (2010). Overview of race and Hispanic origin: 2010. Retrieved from http://www.census.gov/newsroom/releases/archives/2010_census/cb11-cn125.html

Vega, W. A. (1990). Hispanic families in the 1980s: A decade of research. *Journal of Marriage and the Family, 52,* 1015–1024.

Wang, L., & Heppner, P. P. (2002). Assessing the impact of parental expectations and psychological distress on Taiwanese college students. *Journal of Counseling Psychology, 30,* 582–608.

Wycoff, S., & Chavez Cameron, S. (2010). The Garcia family: Using a structural systems approach with an alcohol-dependent family. *Family Journal, 8,* 47–57.

9 An Account of Family Therapy in Bereavement

One Mother's Dying Legacy for Her Family

Su Jin Kim

Here the story of therapy as it unfolded across 10 sessions is shared by an experienced family therapist. The family took part in a randomized trial of family therapy starting in palliative care and continuing into bereavement. After initial screening, the family was identified as being at some risk for a morbid bereavement outcome, but any disturbance in their functioning was only mild. Using Kissane's typology of family functioning, their classification was *intermediate* (Kissane et al., 1996).

Though the family was seemingly close, relationships varied: there was a strong kinship among the females, the family was led by a matriarch, and the husband was dependent on her. Her death presented a considerable bereavement risk to her spouse, often difficult to deal with preventatively while the key relationship continues.

In this chapter, the therapy illustrated is a typical and fairly straightforward example of how this work is addressed. A session-by-session account is presented with reflections after each session to orient the reader and to share the reactions of the therapist and supervisory peer group. All names and identifying features have been altered to preserve their anonymity.

The Family

Nessa, a 70-year-old grandmother, received a diagnosis of stage IV colon carcinoma in February 2003 (see Figure 9.1). She was told that because of secondary spread of her cancer, there was no hope of cure, but treatment would seek to optimize her quality of life. She underwent hemicolectomy surgery (removal of half her large bowel containing the primary cancer) and then received chemotherapy. Nessa was a fighter, vocal about her optimism from the very start. Just a few months after chemotherapy, she was told that her tumors had grown back, but she battled on, undergoing seven further regimens of differing medications and multiple surgeries. For some time, this approach worked, but after three years, her physicians told her to get her affairs in order. Chemotherapy was putting her life at greater risk of infection than helping limit progression of her cancer. The goal of care now was to sustain quality of life by effective symptom management.

During an appointment at her physician's office with one of her daughters, Bella, they heard about family therapy and were interested in participating. Prior to the first session, we learned that Nessa and Vernon had been married for 47 years and had raised

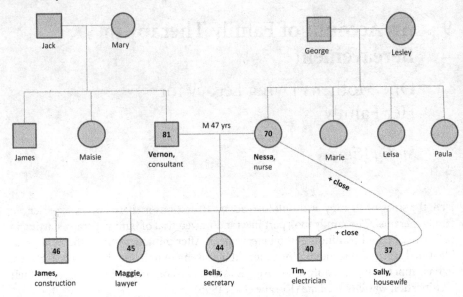

Figure 9.1 Family genogram showing key relationships in Nessa's family.

five children together. Nessa had been a school nurse. Vernon, her husband, had worked as a consultant for the county welfare office and previously in manufacturing but now was retired. The parents hoped that all their adult children would be involved in sessions, but it was decided that they would come without their spouses and children because otherwise there would be too many people in the room. The family consisted of Nessa, Vernon, James, Maggie, Bella, Tim, and Sally. They were slated by the study's randomization process for 10 sessions of therapy.

For the sake of clarity, the word "children" is used to describe Nessa and Vernon's grown offspring. Their family functioning scores were measured with the Family Relationships Index, wherein each person gave their personal perception of family relational life (see Table 9.1). These scores showed mild reduction in communication and some conflict perceived by two of the children, Bella and Tim. These perceptions brought the family into care.

Session 1—Held in September

Therapy was scheduled in the parental home. The therapist was greeted at the door by Vernon, and it was clear that Nessa had prepared the family in advance. She had designated the living room as the place to meet, forming a circle with extra chairs for everyone. The therapist introduced herself, thanking the family for letting her into their lives during a difficult time. She began by getting to know each family member a little.

To join with the family and build an alliance, the therapist asked the family members about their goals and what they each wanted to get out of these sessions together. Uniformly, they said, "to deal with what is happening with Mom." Some added that Maggie, who is supportive and "for family therapy," was "emotional" and had "difficulty facing things or facing crisis."

Table 9.1 Family Functioning Scores on Initial Screening Using the Family Relationships Index (FRI)

Family Member	Age (in years)	FRI*	Cohesiveness**	Expressiveness**	Conflict Resolution**
Nessa	70	10	4	3	3
Vernon	81	9	4	2	3
James	46	12	4	4	4
Maggie	45	–	–	–	–
Bella	44	8	4	2	2
Tim	40	9	4	3	2
Sally	37	10	4	3	

*FRI scores are out of a maximum of 12.
**Cohesiveness, expressiveness, and conflict resolution are each out of a maximum of 4. FRI scores are the sum of the subscale scores for cohesiveness, expressiveness, and conflict resolution. The initial conflict scores are reversed so that subscale addition involves scores rated in a consistent direction. Maggie did not complete the FRI.

The therapist questioned why Nessa wanted the family to participate. She declared that she "had always taken care of everything" and still wanted to help her family as much as possible. Vernon worked two jobs throughout their lives, providing money for the family. Nessa was a stay-at-home mother for the first 15 years and then went back to study to become a school nurse. She considered herself an independent woman, who enjoyed being active and "in charge."

The therapist explored the story of Nessa's illness. Nessa expressed her wish to stay positive and strong but added that her chemotherapy treatments had not been working and that there was "nothing more to do to stop the cancer now, making it important for the family to get together to talk." Nessa's matter-of-fact style and directness were impressive. The therapist asked Nessa what her biggest worry was right now. Nessa replied, "Leaving everybody!" Sadness was palpable, but Vernon and the children were silent as she volunteered this. The therapist validated how difficult it must be to hear this, asking each of them, "Who are you most worried about?" The children appeared uniformly to be concerned about their father, and Nessa agreed, saying, "I just want to be sure that he will be alright when I'm gone." As a counterpoint, Vernon declared that he was worried about Nessa and what was happening to her physically and emotionally, saying, "Some days I know she's having a hard time and I feel bad."

Nessa and Vernon described the recent shift in their roles. Vernon had been trying to take on more in the house (e.g., laundry, dishes, bills, and calling the children), a role that Nessa had looked after all their lives but that was now proving too difficult to continue on her own.

Moving to an exploration of their family dynamics, the therapist asked, "What words come to mind to describe your mother?" One by one, they called her "the counselor," "the rock," "the strong one," and "the go-to person." On hearing these words, Nessa reflected, "I've never thought of myself that way. I just am who I am!" The therapist acknowledged Nessa's modesty but affirmed her strength and leadership—the person whom the children looked up to. Nessa smiled reassuringly.

Exploring closeness and alliances in the family further, the therapist asked, "Who are closest among you?" and "Who gets along with whom?" Sally and Tim, who were close in age, shared a strong bond, but they quickly described that they were a close-knit family unit overall, living near each other and seeing one another often. Everyone seemed to nod in agreement. Nessa then shared that because Sally stayed home with her kids, Nessa confided in Sally, naturally sharing a little more with her.

The therapist asked, "Just as families can be close, from time to time, there are also conflicts in every family. Can you tell me how arguments are usually resolved in your family?" They looked curiously at one another. Maggie thought that fights were resolved "naturally and quickly." The rest nodded in agreement. When disagreement was growing, Nessa would say "knock it off," and the tension would just resolve on its own. Asked if there were times when differences didn't get resolved as quickly, the siblings expressed harmony, that arguments never continued longer than necessary. In fact, Nessa would not allow it. The therapist noted how impressive this was.

During the session, Sally, Tim and James described this idea of "being strong," saying, "When someone feels they are in trouble, another person forges ahead, not breaking down, so that we are there for each other." Again, the therapist validated what a strength this was for the family.

As the session came to a close, the therapist summarized some themes that had emerged. She described the family's strengths as "your closeness, openness, humor and your honesty. One of the striking themes is your family's unity and your ability to be strong in tough times. This is so helpful and worth keeping in mind."

Another theme that emerged was the family's use of silence and holding back on any sadness or tears. This could be understood as providing protection and care for one another. At the same time, it blocked members expressing their distress or fears directly and openly. Using a well-practiced family therapy technique of "both/and," the therapist asked the family whether there was room for *both*.

Before concluding, the therapist declared that in the second session, she would be exploring their family history through a genogram (creating a family tree) to identify significant themes across the generations and to better focus their work together.

Therapist's Reflections on Session 1

The first session created a warm and comfortable environment. There were prominent coping strengths, such as readily coming together as a family, using humor at times of tension, and displaying strong cohesiveness. Nessa clearly was the matriarch in bringing the family together and serving as the "glue" that connects Vernon with the children. Collectively, they were struggling with feelings of sadness, grief, and concern about Nessa's illness and their future together. They seemed ready to talk about this. Many of their sad emotions went unexpressed, as they were feeling the need to protect one another, a common behavior in this setting.

Reflecting on session 1, the therapist wrote, "I wanted to further explore the meaning of support and strength in this family and what that looks like for each of them. Some questions I wished to explore were: When is it okay to cry? What would happen if some of the family expressed sadness and tears more openly, such as Maggie, who had been labeled the 'emotional one?' And how will they support Vernon in bereavement?"

Session 2—Held Two Weeks Later

Nessa, Vernon, Maggie, Tim, and Sally attended this session. The therapist began by asking how each thought the first session had gone. Nessa spoke for the family in saying that everyone had acknowledged that they would not normally sit and talk like that. She appreciated having heard more from her sons, James and Tim, at the first session. The siblings noted that Maggie was able to talk without breaking down. The family wanted to cope better, but it was unclear what that would look like. The therapist affirmed that they were off to a good start in talking more openly about what might be scary. Most of the second session was devoted to creating a family genogram, tracking three generations and their stories of courting, loss, illness, closeness, and distance.

Nessa and Vernon first met while working at a hospital. Nessa noticed Vernon's "sharp dress and that he was fun." Vernon fell in love with Nessa's caretaking, saying she was "always good company." He had appreciated her organization and devotion across so many years.

Nessa's mother had died of lung cancer at 70, right around the age Nessa was now, while Vernon's mother had also died of cancer, lymphoma. Both Vernon and Nessa became self-sufficient and were independent by age 18. Nessa described not having been able to say good-bye to her father or grieve his death. There were several losses that, for the most part, went unexpressed. Being the oldest of the family, Nessa was the mother figure in her family of origin, taking care of her siblings.

One theme that emerged was the strong role of women in their family, their determined stoicism and way of keeping the family together. The family started to discuss the manner in which Sally picked up on her mother's wishes and most easily took over Nessa's role, as they now realized Nessa had done in her family. Nessa agreed that the route of communicating through Sally was most comfortable for her. Indeed, Sally cooperated willingly with her mother in this role. And as Nessa described her own mother, she talked with pride about how her mother had "never complained" and did not want help during her last days. Nessa hoped to follow her mother's example and maintain her dignity during her dying.

At the end of this session, Nessa turned to Sally and asked her to be the "scheduler" of the next session. Symbolically, it was Nessa's way of indicating to her family that it was time for her to step down as director, passing this role to her daughter. Her daughters, without overtly discussing it, appeared to know that this transition was taking place and welcomed it while staying loyal and honoring their mother. During this genogram work, the therapist found herself thinking about their style: "Just do it!"—a motto that got them through hard times. She drew attention to this in her summary.

Therapist's Reflections on Session 2

This session was lively and everyone seemed to appreciate reminiscing about their family stories and themes of strength, illness, and relationships across the generations. An important part of the work is helping the family express feelings and emotions with each other while still maintaining their overall strength and protection. Nessa was the "director" of this family, and the children were looking for her lead in allowing more responsibility to be shared. Nessa looked to the women to take up her roles in a similar way that she took over from her mother.

Session 3—Held in October

All were present. Nessa had been hospitalized for approximately five days and had just come home. Everyone appeared tired and worried about her. Her decline was visible. She had difficulty walking and getting up out of her seat; bodily discomfort resulted from swollen abdomen and legs. Vernon and the children were doing all they could to help.

Discussion focused on the meaning of "fighting an illness." Nessa felt she was "giving in" by asking for help, wondering if frailty would then develop more rapidly. The therapist highlighted her fighting spirit, "just pulling through and doing it" when times were tough. Nessa nodded in agreement. Crying at that point, Sally summarized, "We are all fighting with you, Mom, and I'm selfish—I have no intention of giving up on you so easily!" Family consensus prevailed.

In talking about the hospitalization, Bella began to cry, declaring that when she found out about her mother's recent hospitalization, her first reaction was fear that Nessa would die. This comment gave permission for others to agree. Vernon, Sally, and Tim were then able to cry together.

The therapist asked about different communication styles, becoming curious about what worked best when. Vernon acknowledged that he would get anxious, often wanting things done right away and sometimes not considering his children's needs and schedules.

Therapist's Reflections on Session 3

There was a real shift in the family here in sharing their emotional distress. The therapist reflected that this appeared to be a strength, as it engendered mutual care and support. Not only were they pragmatic in their approach of "just do it," but their solidarity showed through as they considered how to best support each other. It seemed helpful for Nessa to witness Vernon and the children talking more directly about what may be hard for them.

Session 4—Held in November

Nessa was not doing well, now unable to walk without assistance. Sally said that "everyone was feeling it" and recognized that Nessa's death was imminent. Nessa stayed on the couch throughout the meeting, her lower body very swollen, her demeanor weak, but she still made her effort to engage.

From the outset, it was clear that Nessa had an agenda, wanting to express her wishes to the family before she died. She began by talking about her grandchildren, what they understood and how they might be feeling. She had done her best to talk with them and give each a gift to remember her by.

Then Nessa turned to Tim, observing that "it is hard for you." As Nessa began to cry, Tim came across to comfort her. "I'm okay," he said, crying. "I'm going to be fine, one day at a time." The therapist gently acknowledged the distress of the whole family. They nodded in acquiescence. Tim talked about how upset he was, adding, "I'm coping in my own way." He found himself angry at people for little reason. Bella reassured him about the naturalness of his emotions. Sally gave examples of her anger and then returned to her sadness, recalling all the special things that her mother and she had shared.

Most of the session was devoted to Nessa's wishes for the family. The therapist invited Nessa to speak directly with Vernon in front of the children about her wishes for him after she was gone. She wanted him to continue to spend time doing the things he enjoyed and asked that all of her children support him in his grief. She told the family that she wanted them to visit her grave only on special occasions, as it was important to her that they got on with their lives. In dying, as in living, Nessa continued to guide and counsel her family.

Therapist's Reflections after Session 4

Sally phoned the therapist just before Thanksgiving to say that Nessa had died. The family had been gathered together near her bed. Bella and Sally phoned back a couple of more times that day to discuss the obituary and their wish to donate money to cancer research in lieu of flowers. The therapist attended the wake to pay her respects, connecting with each member of the family. They expressed appreciation for the last session, which had empowered them to say their good-byes to Nessa. The supervisory team congratulated the therapist on what fine work she had done thus far with the family.

Session 5—Held in Late December

All family members were present at the family home. An empty seat symbolized where Nessa had been. Vernon welcomed the therapist, expressing appreciation for the family meetings. This session was devoted to talking about their grief. After reviewing her death, wake, funeral, and the time since, the children and Vernon recognized the sadness they all shared. They telephoned each other often to connect and reminisce. Sally felt angry at having lost her mother sooner than expected. Bella said that she felt her mom in the room. Vernon lit a candle every day and talked regularly with her. James saw a rainbow at the cemetery, thinking, "I knew it was Mom."

Halfway through the session, Maggie broke down and began to cry, reporting that sometimes it became too much for her to spend time with her father. She expressed feelings of guilt when her father would call and request her help, for instance, with a bill or a meal, or he would ask if she would come over that evening. There was palpable tension as the children spoke about meeting their father's expectations. Sally worried that he called too often. Vernon became somewhat defensive, fearing he might lose his children, while Bella became more protective, highlighting that he was going through a hard time.

Therapist's Reflections on Session 5

The family's grief was overt, mixed feelings abided, and Vernon declared his dependence on his children. Therapy had become a safe space in which to discuss matters that could otherwise prove too hard to speak about. The children sought further sessions as they grieved and struggled to respond adequately to their father's needs.

Session 6—Held in February

By this session, Vernon was the concern for all. Bella began, volunteering that her father was coping as best as he could, maintaining his activities in the house, getting together with friends, and trying to continue to be social in some way. Sally quickly proffered a different opinion, reporting that Vernon carried high expectations that were "unrealistic." Sally talked about having taken her father to Florida with her husband and children. She said the vacation was tense and Vernon "kept reminding me that he was alone." Vernon carried a photo of Nessa everywhere, which he showed to many, though it upset Sally.

James complained that his father had created a "shrine" on a chair in which Nessa used to sit. The chair was covered by their mother's picture, some candles, a sweater, and Nessa's slippers. The shrine had grown bigger each week. Sally vocalized how sad the shrine left her feeling. Vernon gave voice to a fear that his children would go on with their lives, leaving him alone. His children sustained the message that they loved him. James, however, recalled the difference in Vernon's and Nessa's communication styles, in which their father "expects everything to be done right away."

In an effort to keep the discussion safe, the therapist spoke about the challenges present when family members carried different levels of grief. The children had a clear sense of how deeply their father missed his wife's care, knew how much she had done for him, and feared that he expected them to take over. Sally offered a compromise, "Dad, we don't mind taking care of things for you, but you can't expect that everything will be done on your time."

Vernon voiced his fear that after six months, "everyone will no longer come over" and that he would be alone. The therapist asked where he got this feeling from. "It's what I hear and see in other families," he said. The children chuckled and remarked to their father that they were not like other families and were close. They expressed that their father was a worrier and always had been.

The therapist summarized that Vernon's children wanted to make things better for him so he felt less alone but also acknowledged that he was grieving the loss of his wife of 47 years. Time would be needed for a new level of trust to develop. Vernon nodded in agreement, sharing that he missed Nessa deeply.

Therapist's Reflections on Session 6

Vernon's children all took some risks in expressing their honest feelings directly to their father. Although there were some tense moments, Vernon was able to hear that his children were also grieving the loss of their mother. They thought his fears were excessive. This tension seemed necessary as Nessa had been the buffer. Vernon and his children were learning to communicate with each other more directly, which they had not done for most of their lives.

Session 7—Held in March

Before this session, the therapist received calls from Sally and Bella, each voicing concern about the family's status. Sally was worried about Maggie, who seemed frustrated by her father's many phone calls and requests. Maggie could not attend this session. Sally also felt that her father was feeling blamed, recalling that after the last session, he said that the sessions were getting "too personal." Bella declared that the others, especially Sally, were "ganging up" on their father during this fragile time. Bella feared that the sessions could prove harmful if they were unsupportive of her father. The therapist validated their feelings and encouraged them to raise these concerns at the start of therapy the next day. Both Bella and Sally shared some discomfort about the risk of "stirring the pot" if it made things worse. They were reassured that at times, in therapy, there are disagreements and tension, as there are in all families, and that it would be important to share this with the family rather than in isolation with the therapist. The therapist expressed faith in the values of the family to cope with this discussion.

At the meeting, family concerns started with Maggie, who seemed to be overwhelmed with work and anxious about the responsibility she carried as holder of her father's power of attorney. The family's protectiveness came out very strongly during this discussion.

The therapist observed that whenever disagreements developed, the family qualified these with statements like "It's no big deal" or "We're all okay, we're going to all chip in." She wondered whether such issues were really explored thoroughly. The family seemed to appreciate that trying to forget about something did not ever resolve it. Greater efforts were needed.

Therapist's Reflections on Session 7

This was an unsettling session for the therapist. She carried the family's distress, which seemed to be coming to a head. Ambivalence had been growing in certain family members without ready resolution. With only three sessions remaining, it seemed prudent that the therapist focus on the family's avoidance of conflict, aiming to encourage more active problem solving. This required some shift from the "just do it" attitude to something more creative. Might more open communication be necessary given the authentic values of care and genuine connection evident in this family?

Session 8—Held in April

The session focused on the children's communication with Vernon and areas where his expectations were unrealistic about what the children could provide. The therapist became curious about how the family dealt with hurt feelings. All intuitively agreed that they often did not talk directly to the person who had hurt them. The therapist noted that this made it difficult to be more direct with each other. In the past, they spoke to Nessa about this, and she worked behind the scenes. Each recalled that Nessa had been the mediator, and they missed her buffering comments. Sally was attempting to fill this role but with limited effect.

The therapist supported Vernon by validating the difficulty of sitting with hurt feelings. Vernon shared how sometimes he could say things that others found hurtful, but that he did not really mean this. Without Nessa to correct him, it felt easier to forget about it. Vernon recognized that he needed to apologize at these moments. The tone of the family lightened as if some new insight had been gleaned. Others gave examples of walking away with mixed feelings. The price of silence and just getting on with it became more apparent.

The therapist affirmed the family's persistent effort to find a better way that seemed to depend on more open and authentic communication. She expressed optimism in the love and mutual concern evident in the family, encouraging their exploration of direct communication about what really mattered.

Therapist's Reflections on Session 8

Vernon and the children continued to forge new ground in communicating with one another, tolerated more of their differences, and problem solved in response to Vernon's concrete needs. The children remained positive in seeking ways to better communicate with their father in their time of grief, and thus realized Nessa's wishes for the family to find a solution rather than remain in conflict.

Session 9—Held in June

The family reported dreaming more about Nessa, which intrigued them. There was sadness as summertime had been Nessa's favorite season. Tradition included rituals like visits to their summer house. They recalled that Nessa liked to sing in the car during the summer.

The primary focus of the session was exploration of continued tensions between the children and their father. All rallied and supported Maggie, allowing her to speak openly about feeling hurt by her father. Maggie and Vernon became argumentative, both getting very angry and upset. Eventually, Maggie walked out of the room. Sally got up to console Maggie, asking her to persevere with their conversation, which Maggie did.

There were some deeper tensions between the children and Vernon, a key difficulty with their overall communication. The therapist asked everyone, "If Nessa were here, what would she be saying to all of you?" This seemed to jolt the family. They replied that she would say, "Cut it out." The therapist wondered if Nessa would reprimand some subtle self-centeredness and asked how the family could take her values and love forward in the years ahead.

The session ended with a fresh commitment to be generous, keeping Nessa's words in the room, close to their hearts, as they were searching for a way of communicating constructively with one another. The therapist emphasized this orientation to keep Nessa's values and wishes alive as a worthwhile way beyond therapy. They planned to meet for the final session in three months.

Therapist's Reflections on Session 9

This is a family that felt confident about sticking together and remaining close, despite recent tension between the father and the children. The children seemed to be gradually accepting that Vernon "may never change," giving slight voice to this reality in this session, but more importantly, they recognized their commitment to be there for each other and for their father—family loyalty prevailed, as Nessa would have wanted. Maggie seemed more able to express her anger and hurt feelings. Sally and others were supportive of Maggie in her struggle and dilemma of both wanting to be there for her father to carry out her mother's wishes but also feeling angry and hurt at some of her father's words and actions. Vernon's personal insights and comments came as a surprise, yet offered hope.

Session 10—Held in October

It had been more than three months since the prior session; this session was the last. The therapist checked in with Vernon and with Maggie, wondering how the past months had been for the family.

The family appeared well and reported that although family dynamics had not changed much, they were coping better and handling their father's care. His real estate and finances were better. Maggie shared that Vernon had been more cooperative, less blaming, and indeed "nicer" to her. The siblings were continuing to utilize one another in constructive ways. Vernon agreed.

The family talked about how difficult it had been to enjoy the summer without Nessa. Next month would be the one-year anniversary of her death. Sally, Bella, and Maggie wondered what to do to commemorate the anniversary of Nessa's death and how to organize Thanksgiving. The holiday had always been organized by Nessa and celebrated in the parental home.

Having needed to take care of so much when their mother died seemed to have left less room for the children to just be with their sadness. The therapist acknowledged these feelings and asked how the family might plan the concrete pieces of Thanksgiving, while taking care to not have one person take on too much.

The family reviewed their different feelings concerning visiting Nessa at the mausoleum. Sally wondered if the family wanted to go to California. Tim talked about the custom of visiting the cemetery, and Vernon expressed his wish to visit Nessa's grave on the anniversary of her death. When asked what Nessa would say in this instance, they chorused, "Don't stop your life for me and go on."

The therapist reminded the family that this was the last session, bringing to a close 11 months of working together. Sterling work had been done across these 10 sessions. The family's strength in staying united and connected was admirable. They recognized the importance of sharing their grief to sustain mutual support. Although there had been some tension between Vernon and his children, they sought solutions rather than becoming entrenched in the problem. Vernon continued to report some anxiety, difficulty sleeping, and ongoing grief. Sustained support would prove helpful for him. This session ended with hugs between the family and therapist, and with good wishes being conveyed to the family.

Therapist's Reflections upon Closing Therapy

This family proved cohesive and planned to remain close and protective of one another. The family had initially identified themselves as not needing therapy but welcomed a space to talk together and grieve their losses, sadness, memories, and family conflicts.

The agreed goal in meeting was to optimize sharing, and at the end of these sessions, although there were still areas of family conflict, the overwhelming opinion was that it had become more manageable. The family realized that by more authentic communication, they could sustain generous values that accommodated family needs without anyone being overly burdened. They accepted their father's needs. They rallied together to maintain their mother's love, confident in their teamwork and commitment to help one another. Overall, the therapist felt pleased with what the family had accomplished.

Discussion

The goal of this chapter has been to exemplify how the Family Focused Grief Therapy model works by illustrating the therapy delivered to a family from beginning to end. By use of regular reflections as discussed in the peer-group supervision sessions, the reader is helped to follow the challenges and difficulties that arose for the family members and how the therapist attempted to respond to these.

The patient and family presented here gained considerably from their work. The presence of the patient for the first four sessions is a noteworthy component of this model, enabling her perceptions and concerns to be included as targets of the work, empowering discussion of her dying and helping the family to say good-bye. The therapist came to know and understand the patient pre-death in a manner that is distinctively helpful to bereavement care.

This is a preventive model of care delivered to at-risk families that have been identified by a simple process of screening during palliative care. The resultant continuity of care that begins in the palliative phase and segues into bereavement is seen as optimal for its cost-effectiveness and ability to support several people at the same time. It is premised on the notion that the family is the primary source of support to the bereaved and that harnessing the family as a resource is not only pragmatic but very strategic as a therapeutic model of care.

Reference

Kissane, D. W., Bloch, S., Dowe, D. L., Snyder, R. D., Onghena, P., McKenzie, D. P., & Wallace, C. S. (1996). The Melbourne Family Grief Study, I: Perceptions of family functioning in bereavement. *American Journal of Psychiatry, 153*, 650–658.

Part III

Family Grief Therapy in Particular Circumstances

Therapy needs to be adapted to the specific circumstances of the death, whether from trauma, suicide, or another form of ambiguous loss. Likewise, the clinician should consider the timing of the death within the different stages of the life cycle—whether the loss was perinatal or a child or parent. Attention should be paid to the unique needs of the elderly in bereavement.

10 Family Therapy in the Context of Traumatic Losses

Darcy Harris and Stephanie Rabenstein

Most of the literature on trauma and grief focuses on caring for individuals after exposure to a trauma or death. Many of these descriptions draw upon symptoms that are listed in the criteria for post-traumatic stress disorder (PTSD), as found in the *Diagnostic and Statistical Manual of Mental Disorders* (*DSM*; American Psychiatric Association [APA], 2000). In this chapter, we wish to expand the way in which trauma is defined and thereby widen the scope from an orientation toward the individual to the shared experience of the family system. We begin by exploring the defining features of traumatic losses, followed by reviewing the literature that deals with trauma within the family context and then describing some of the therapeutic considerations for working with families where this has occurred.

Traumatic Loss

Ten-year-old Danny[1] was referred to a child and adolescent mental health care outpatient program from the pediatric emergency department, where he was seen for breathing problems and chest pains. During triage, the emergency staff learned that Danny's father, Tom, a kidney transplant recipient, had suddenly died six months previously. One day, when Danny and his 13-year-old sister Maggie were home alone with Tom, he lost consciousness and fell in the bathroom against the door. While Maggie tried to force her way into the bathroom, Danny ran to a neighbor's home for help. The neighbor then called for an ambulance and contacted their mother, Sylvie, at work. One day later, in the hospital, Tom died.

I (S. R.) saw Danny with his mother and sister in the initial session (see Figure 10.1). As he and Maggie sat together on the couch, periodically, Maggie would try to take Danny's hand. But he remained passive and seemed unaware that she was there. Sylvie sat on a chair nearby. Danny and Maggie were tearful throughout the interview. When Danny answered a question, his voice trembled and was barely audible. Sylvie, who was also tearful, gave a clear account of seven years of Tom's decline in health, his time on the waiting list for a kidney transplant, and then five years of good health after the transplant. However, over the nine months before his death, Tom's health again began to fail. Privately, Sylvie revealed that the couple had informally separated at Tom's initiative and lived in separate bedrooms, but she thought the children were unaware of the reason for this household change.

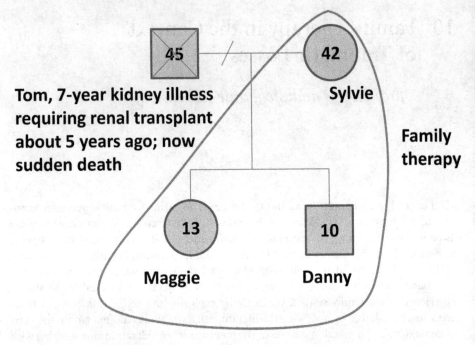

Figure 10.1 Genogram of Danny's family. Danny presented to an emergency room with chest pain and breathing difficulty, which could be traced to witnessing his father's sudden death.

What Is Traumatic Loss?

A common definition of a traumatic event is one that occurs outside the range of most people's normal life experiences or expectations (Walsh, 2006). Although this description is certainly helpful, we believe that whether or not an experience is traumatic is centered upon the perceptions and interpretations made by those who experience it. A traumatic loss may be the violent death of a family member, but it may also be any loss that significantly undermines one's sense of safety or that stretches the boundaries of one's assumptions about how the world should work to the point that one experiences profound feelings of senselessness, helplessness, powerlessness, and distress (Carlson & Dalenberg, 2000; Janoff-Bulman, 1992; Kauffman, 2002). The key aspect of the trauma pertains to a sense of threat to the individual or to someone who is embedded into the attachment system of that individual, along with an inability to protect and to prevent harm. Importantly, the threat is not limited to the possible loss of physical existence through death; it may also include loss of one's sense of psychological and emotional integrity. We are careful in our practices to listen to how our clients describe their experiences, allowing them to tell us not only their stories about what happened, but, more importantly, *how they perceive and interpret the event(s) that occurred.*

Although deaths that are untimely, sudden, or violent are cited as the most common sources of trauma, other experiences include incidents of physical harm or disability, natural disasters, sudden absence, abduction, relationship dissolution, job dismissal, refugee plights, immigration, and abuse or violence that is sexual, emotional, or physical

(Walsh, 2007). It is also important at this juncture to make a distinction between the use of the terms *traumatic loss, traumatic death,* and *traumatic grief.*

- *Traumatic loss* is any loss experience that involves *shattering* one's core assumptions about how the world should work, how people should act, and/or one's core view of himself or herself (Janoff-Bulman, 1992; Kauffman, 2002). Common examples of traumatic losses may include violent, untimely, or sudden deaths; events involving prolonged suffering (especially when attempts to try to alleviate suffering are ineffective); losses that are ambiguous or stigmatized; the cumulative experience of loss; and experiences that trigger memories of prior traumatic events (Walsh, 2007; Webb, 2004). Traumatic losses do not necessarily involve the death of another. Some of our clients who experience non-death-related traumatic losses will sometimes describe feeling that what died was something "inside" them, rather than a person (Harris, 2010). These losses may be symbolic or may be experiences that diminish safety and security, create anxiety about the future, and invoke an inability to trust others or oneself (Webb, 2004). The degree of traumatic overlay is related to the depth in which one's assumptive world is challenged or rendered meaningless. Loss experiences may also encompass more than a single, finite event. The literature on nonfinite loss and chronic sorrow describes losses that are ongoing and without a foreseeable end (Boss, Roos, & Harris, 2011; Schultz & Harris, 2011). Persisting uncertainty, vulnerability, and the need for vigilance prevail.
- *Traumatic death* refers to bereavement that occurs after an extreme or horrific event, such as a mass disaster involving violence, destruction, and mutilation or similar consequences (Chapple, Swift, & Ziebland, 2011). Such deaths invoke traumatic symptomatology in the bereaved. The therapist must ascertain whether this event actually experienced by an individual or the individual's family was a traumatic loss by listening carefully to the survivors' perceptions and reactions to see if family members were involved.
- *Traumatic grief* is sometimes referred to as a "loss trauma," with heightened distress and resultant difficulty arising from the separation, wrenching away a central figure (Weisaeth & Eitinger, 1993). The trauma in this descriptor is the impact of the loss itself on the individual or family, rather than how the loss occurred. The loss of a primary attachment figure could lead to a sense of heightened vulnerability and lowered sense of safety.

In the literature on children's responses to traumatic loss, Cohen, Mannarino, and Deblinger (2012) assert that childhood traumatic grief results from the death of an important person in a child's life under circumstances that he or she perceives as traumatic. Memories of the deceased trigger overwhelming trauma responses that, in turn, make it impossible for the child to grieve. At the far end of the continuum, this predicament, if left untreated, can prompt the onset of depression, substance abuse, suicide attempts, psychiatric hospitalizations, and relationship difficulties (American Academy of Child and Adolescent Psychiatry, 2010).

Similarly, in research with adults, Holland and Neimeyer (2011) found differences in how grief is experienced when events surrounding the loss are shockingly traumatic

(traumatic distress) versus when the loss itself is the triggering stimulus (separation distress). Additionally, it is important to note that (1) traumatic distress may coexist with separation distress, (2) both descriptions involve significant upset and may be experienced as a threat to the individual or family integrity, and (3) the focus of therapy should remain on how the loss is experienced and interpreted.

Value of a Family Approach

As refugees, the Ramirez family was referred to the outpatient clinic by their community support worker for trauma assessment and treatment. The family, consisting of Luisa, 7; Carlos, 11; Janina, 13; and their mother Maria (see Figure 10.2), was new to the area when the referral was made. Three years previously, the family's home had been violently invaded by a gang, who dragged Juan, who was the children's father and Maria's husband, into the garage and executed him. Although told not to follow, Maria ran to her husband's side as he lay dying. Unbeknownst to Maria, the children followed her. The family was relocated to another community for protection.

In the initial assessment, the whole family first sat still and tense, though gradually they relaxed and even smiled. The children were asked to draw a picture of their family and set about this task. When the therapist asked Maria for her husband's name, she volunteered that Janina and her father were so close that as a toddler, she called him "Juan" instead of Papa. With this statement, Janina made eye contact with her mother and smiled again. Seeing this opening, the therapist asked, "Janina, can you tell us something special about Juan?" At this point, Janina's face and body froze; she lowered her head and covered her face with her hair. Carlos looked up from his drawing and peered in to see his sister's face. When she did not respond, he seemed paralyzed and immobile. Their mother, Maria, began to weep, rocking back and forth where she sat. The youngest, Luisa, looked at her family, paused, and returned studiously but dry-eyed to her drawing. Raw emotions dominated this family with horrific memories blocking easy sharing of the story. A more gradual approach using artwork and play therapy was needed. We will return to the Ramirez family later.

Historical Perspective

A family systems approach to the treatment of trauma began right after World War II (Hill, 1949) and continued with veterans returning from the Vietnam War (Walsh, 2007). Numerous models of family therapy have been applied to traumatic loss (Coulter, 2011), including when one family member has been exposed to trauma and the "ripples" from this experience affect the whole system (Dinshtein, Dekel, & Polliack, 2011; Ein-Dor, Doron, Mikulincer, Solomon, & Shaver, 2010; Monson, Taft, & Fredman, 2009). Indeed, the family can be profoundly affected by traumatic events that individual members have experienced, but the family can also moderate the impact of such events. Of further interest is Cohen, Mannarino, and Deblinger's (2012) trauma-focused cognitive behavioral therapy for children, where parental involvement in their child(ren)'s treatment has been found to alleviate symptoms in both children and parents. These researchers have emphasized that relieving parents' distress likewise mitigates children's distress.

Catherall (2004) and Figley (1998) described the relational stresses within families after war, catastrophes, violence, and abuse. Barnes (2005) and Matsakis (2004)

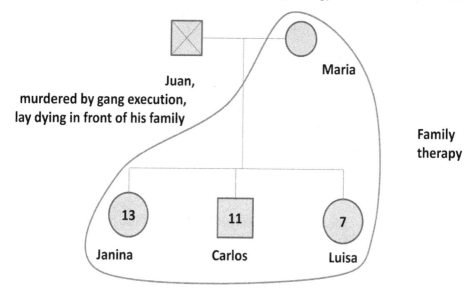

Figure 10.2 Genogram of the Ramirez family, which experienced the violent murder of their father.

documented the impact on the family when the traumatized needed them for subsequent support. Family members are often the "hidden victims" of trauma because their lack of direct exposure may be seen as protective when, in fact, they share feelings of powerlessness, helplessness, and threat transferred to them by the direct witness (Briere & Scott, 2006). With reciprocal relationships that are caring, a supportive family can mitigate some of the effects of the trauma, but unpredictably, others may be traumatized by the very sharing of the story (Carlson & Dalenberg, 2000; Coulter, 2011; Ozer, Best, Lipsey, & Weiss, 2003).

Attachment Relationships as Sources of Support

The attachment system aims to preserve our sense of safety and security in the world. Attachment is usually cultivated in primary familial relationships in infants and young children. It is reinforced by close relationships as we mature and forms the basis for development of our schemas and perceptions of the world, others, and the self, which tend to remain stable through one's lifetime (Janoff-Bulman, 1992). The core of the attachment system is usually the family, which forms the foundation for how individuals navigate change, loss, and transition. Typically, the attachment system exists below the level of conscious awareness; most individuals are not aware of its importance until a perceived threat activates attachment behaviors and motivates them to seek proximity and contact with close, supportive figures (Webb, 2004). For example, when adults in North America are asked what they did upon learning of the events of September 11, 2001, the vast majority respond that they immediately contacted a loved one, even though their loved one was not directly involved with the events that were unfolding. The desire to establish connection with key figures at this time exemplifies the activation of attachment behavior in response to a perceived threat that creates fear for one's safety.

The effects of trauma are moderated by the degree to which those who are wounded can find comfort, reassurance, and safety with others (Walsh, 2007; Webb, 2004). This very activation of the attachment system in response to trauma highlights the therapeutic potential through harnessing support. Yet paradox may arise: though the sense of vulnerability may heighten proximity-seeking behaviors and need for closeness with attachment figures, on the other hand, trusting others may be difficult, especially if someone caused the traumatic event (Ein-Dor et al., 2010). In families that do not function well, disorganized attachment style, characterized by behaviors that are erratic, avoidant, or inconsistent, has been linked to any unresolved trauma or losses within the family (Liotti, 2004).

Recent research indicates that mourning is often best facilitated when the therapist encourages the family to continue the bond with the deceased rather than encouraging letting go. This continuing bond theory highlights the importance of finding ways to remain connected through rituals, memories, stories, and actions, and objects (Klass, Nickman, & Silverman, 1996; Stroebe, Schut, & Boerner, 2010). This bond with the deceased can draw families together at a time of great pain and confusion. Walsh (2007) states that families need to be involved in "making meaning [together] of the trauma, putting it in perspective, and weaving the experience . . . into the fabric of collective identity and life passage" (p. 210).

Secondary Traumatization

Those closest to the traumatized individual are not immune to sharing the related emotions and developing feelings of helplessness and powerlessness from the interaction and from hearing the stories. Indeed, the current proposed revisions to the criteria for PTSD in the *DSM-V* include:

Exposure to actual or threatened (1) death, (2) serious injury, or (3) sexual violation, in one or more of the following ways:

1. Directly experiencing the traumatic event(s).
2. Witnessing, in person, the traumatic event(s) as it occurred to others.
3. Learning that the traumatic event(s) occurred to a relative or close friend; cases of actual or threatened death must have been violent or accidental.
4. Experiencing repeated or extreme exposure to aversive details of the traumatic event(s) (e.g., first responders collecting human remains; police officers repeatedly exposed to details of child abuse); this does not apply to exposure through electronic media, television, movies, or pictures, unless this exposure is work related (APA, 2012).

These proposed revisions suggest profound implications for families coping with a traumatic loss. Parents of traumatized children can themselves be traumatized by watching their loved ones struggle and by their awareness of their children's exposure. Thus family members may be at increased risk for PTSD.

According to Briere and Scott (2006), social support is one of the most important determinants of the effects of trauma upon an individual. And for most individuals, the family is the primary source of that support. Working with families in this way creates the opportunity for the therapist to support them so that the risk of secondary traumatization is minimized. In therapy, members are helped to be mutually supportive, creating a safe haven for those who need to discuss traumatic material, and providing a means to integrate the experiences in a helpful manner.

Traumatic loss experiences can combine significant grief responses with intense feelings of anxiety, hypersensitivity, withdrawal, jealousy, verbal abuse, anger, and destructiveness. The person who is traumatized might seem very disconnected from the outer world and might not be available to his or her family. At times, he or she may even seem to behave in bizarre ways through, for example, flashbacks or extreme startle responses. If the individual shows accompanying avoidance symptoms associated with the loss, then routine daily activities, such as visiting with friends or taking part in family or children's functions, can be complicated and difficult (Dekel & Monson, 2010). Emotional numbing can diminish one's attachment to children and intimate partners. Irritability and anger associated with living in a heightened state of physiological arousal can add tension and stress to close relationships: family members report that they "walk on eggshells" due to fear of upsetting their traumatized loved one. These types of responses are commonly reported by families whose loved one has returned from military service in areas of war or armed conflict (Dekel & Monson, 2010; Ein-Dor et al., 2010; Milliken, Auchterlonie, & Hoge, 2007; Monson et al., 2009).

Inclusion of Children in the Process

A family-based approach is often considered ideal when children are involved in a traumatic loss, even though less experienced family therapists may be intimidated by including them at a family session. However, since they often act out the stresses of the family system, if the child who is reacting to such stress is treated in isolation, little headway might occur with that child's therapy unless the underlying family dynamics are addressed. Children's reactions can be closely related to their parents' and other relatives' stress, and most children who feel uncertainty or stress rely upon their parents for a sense of safety and security (Webb, 2004). Lund, Zimmerman, and Haddock (2002) state that family therapists may not include children in the therapeutic work because (1) the therapist is uncomfortable handling children in the therapy sessions or has had no training in work with children; (2) the therapist is concerned about difficulties engaging children who are at different developmental levels; (3) very few child-oriented therapies have been adapted to a family context; (4) the therapist is concerned about exposing children to adult issues or perceives that children may be distracting in the session; and (5) only sparse literature is available to provide examples and descriptions of family therapy with younger children. Although parents may choose wisely to protect young children, adolescents are readily involved in family meetings.

Traumatic losses that affect a parent's ability to provide appropriate care and stability in the home may also impede a child's ability to cope. Reactions within the family may include increased parental conflict, family disorganization, and stress from disparate reactions or dyssynchrony of grieving styles, which may all have a negative impact upon children (Cohen et al., 2012). Although children may not be directly exposed to a traumatic event or experience a loss as traumatic, their risk for anxiety, depression, social impairments, and secondary traumatization increases when they are exposed to a parent who is experiencing difficulties coping (Bernardon & Pernice-Duca, 2010; Brown, 2005; Pynoos, Steinberg, & Goenjian, 1996). Parents may not be aware of the stress and symptoms of the children if they are engulfed by their own reactions. Systemically oriented interventions that are aimed at stabilizing and reorganizing the family system constructively—while supporting the experiences of both the parents and children in a safe environment—tend to provide the best outcome for children (Bernardon & Pernice-Duca, 2010; Cohen, Mannarino, & Deblinger, 2006; Pernicano, 2010; Tarrier, Sommefield, & Pilgrim, 1999).

Clinical Considerations

The Intersection of Grief and Trauma

A loss experience that has an overlay of trauma may trigger flashbacks that are cognitive, emotional, or physiological. This may occur when the individual perceives heightened vulnerability, powerlessness, or helplessness. At these times, acute physical signs of arousal, intense anxiety, panic, or anger may incapacitate him or her. On the other side of the spectrum, such a person may also experience cognitive and emotional numbing and avoid people, places, or any other triggers for the traumatic material. In addition, individuals who struggle with exposure to traumatic material often report feeling aroused and hypervigilant; difficulties with sleep, concentration, and regulating emotions such as anger and rage; and exaggerated startle responses to stimuli (Cohen et al., 2012; Coulter, 2011; Nader, 1997; Pernicano, 2010; Rynearson, 2010; Simpson, 1997). When the trauma is accompanied by significant loss, this intersection causes an unusual "dance." Although typical bereavement responses overlap with some reactions to trauma, grief tends to draw individuals into a need for immersion into the loss, manifested by the commonly described behaviors of searching, yearning, and a desire to reminisce, search for meaning, and share memories (Holland & Neimeyer, 2011; Nader, 1997).

Traditional grief therapy and support, which may involve actively remembering the person, talking about memories, sharing feelings, and going deeply into the grief, can cause emotional flooding if traumatic overlay is present. Though the avoidance of stimuli appears protective, it prevents an individual from integrating the loss through these normal grieving responses. Indeed, it may intensify the attachment wound that is left by the loss. As exemplified in the case study with young Janina, reminiscing about the loved one, even through happy memories, may potentially lead to a reexperiencing of the trauma (Nader, 1997). It is a catch-22 for many individuals, but pacing the therapy gently is the key. Therapists who work with families in which children are dealing with traumatic grief must recognize when trauma is present and make sure that the work is going sufficiently slowly, without flooding the child, while still touching upon everyone's grief (Cohen et al., 2012; Nader, 2008). This clinical judgment requires a great deal of wisdom and sensitivity.

When both grief and trauma symptoms exist, the initial therapeutic focus should be upon finding a way to contain the trauma symptoms with the related anxiety before more grief-focused interventions are initiated (Nader, 1997; Rynearson & Salloum, 2011).

Establishing Safety within the Family Context

Given the heightened level of vulnerability and need for safety after trauma, the therapeutic setting needs to provide a "container" where the family members feel safe with the therapist and each other. This safety concerns not just the traumatic events, but also how the family processes its feelings about the loss, themselves, and each other. The concept of safety encompasses three broad areas:

1. Physical and environmental safety, which involves protection from external threats or further harm.
2. Safety within the family system, which includes how members process what has occurred and relate respectfully to each other, and how the therapist facilitates the therapy if the family has been the source of the trauma (e.g., sexual abuse or domestic violence). This encompasses psychological safety for any individual where one member cannot engage due to fear, shame, or concern about potential negative consequences if he or she shares openly.
3. Safety related to each individual's intrapsychic threshold of tolerance due to the potential for triggering or flooding, thus reexperiencing the trauma harmfully.

When the response of one family member has the potential to destabilize other relatives, the therapist takes responsibility for creating safety by (1) providing clear boundaries about how much material is covered and how quickly, (2) explaining the ground rules for how the sessions are conducted, (3) making explicit mechanisms for disengagement if members begins to feel unsafe, and (4) modeling respectful accommodation for members who are more vulnerable. The therapist may offer some sessions to groups of individuals and other sessions to couples and should thoughtfully consider who will benefit from hearing what. The therapist acknowledges and contextualizes the change in the equilibrium of the family, while normalizing all the diverse responses that family members use.

Nader (1997) describes difficulties for children coping with trauma if a parent is unavailable or unable to be engaged with them due to the parent's symptomatology. Cohen et al. (2006) state that when a parent's symptoms impinge on "his or her emotional availability or judgment to the point that the therapist believes it is interfering with adequate parenting practices, the parent needs to be referred for his or her own therapy" (p. 36).

Family Resilience and Reality

In her work with families who have experienced traumatic events, Walsh (2007) states that therapy should focus on "[a] multisystem, resilience-oriented approach that recognizes the widespread impact of major trauma, situates the distress in the extreme experience, attends to ripple effects through relational networks, and aims to strengthen family and community resources for optimal recovery" (p. 207).

Although the level of resilience can vary, even disorganized families can display many strengths and coping skills. The emphasis here is for the therapist to recognize the positive attributes, including attempts to cope with a very difficult experience, even when the family appears overtly dysfunctional. Calhoun and Tedeschi (2006) highlighted the development of new strengths, untapped potential, creative expression, and innovative solutions after participants experienced trauma of various types. Families have a great deal of potential to mediate and transform how they respond.

Intervention Strategies

Assessment

Assessment is the basis of strong clinical intervention in family therapy (see Table 10.1). Therapists find it valuable to work with the family as a whole whenever possible because, as the axiom goes, the whole is greater than the sum of its parts. This is particularly important when the family is traumatized *and* grieving. The family begins to construct a coherent narrative of the loss whereby each member's experience becomes part of the shared family story, especially if the trauma is the sudden, graphic death of a loved one. When terrible events occur, treatment may be provided to combinations of individuals, in subgroups such as the parent alone, child alone, or parent and child together where one child among siblings has been identified as distressed (Lehmann & Rabenstein, 2002). The therapist who sees the family together as a whole for assessment can generate information about whether the system is paralyzed by the loss or if some are actively grieving, while others are frozen by trauma. An astute therapist recognizes that a young child who leaves his or her play to crawl into the lap of the weeping father is as important to understanding the family as the mother's story of how the family's older son died in a hit and run on his way to school.

When traumatic loss or grief is known or suspected, a carefully conducted, thorough assessment of the family is vital for several reasons:

1.   When the family includes very young children up to six years old, the therapist must work sensitively. The developing coping strategies of a young child may be compromised by the traumatic loss, especially if the deceased is a parent (National Child Traumatic Stress Network, 2012).
2.   A child will be distressed by a traumatized caregiver/parent who is incapacitated by his or her grief. Depending on the age of the child, this parent/caregiver may even be inattentive to the emotional or physical needs of the child at critical stages of development (Cohen et al., 2006; Hennighausen & Lyons-Ruth, 2007).
3.   Abuse in families has the potential to isolate members and fragment the collective story. The legal system may perpetuate this by prohibiting members from talking to each other when criminal charges are laid. Crisis intervention services in domestic violence programs and adult mental health services often work with adults and children separately. In these instances, the family as a unit may never talk together about the events leading to the loss (Lehmann & Rabenstein, 2002).

Table 10.1 Assessment Questions for Traumatized Families with Children

---

Starting the interview with the children can orient the conversation to their understanding of the event(s) and begins to identify their emotional tolerance of the subject. It also recognizes the importance of their role and story in the family.

Children:

• Why do you think you and your family are here today?

• What will your [parents/caregivers] say about why your family is here?

• I know that something bad has happened in your family. It may be hard to talk about. Can you tell me a bit about what happened?

• Can you draw me a picture of what happened?

• Can you show me in the sand/in the dollhouse, using the toys, what happened?

Parents/Caregivers:

• Can you tell me in a way that feels comfortable with the whole family present why you are here today?

• Can you draw me a picture/show me with the toys what happened?

• What is your biggest concern for your family?

• What needs to happen here today for this interview to be helpful for your family?

Assessment Questions That Draw Out Family Strengths

Children:

• What helped you most when you had to:

  ◦ talk to the police?

  ◦ go to the funeral?

  ◦ go back to school?

• Who helped you? What did they do that made it easier for you?

• How did you help yourself when you felt sad, angry, confused, or scared? Draw a picture or show me with the toys. Did you surprise yourself?

• What helps when you think about [X]?

• What has your family done that has helped you all manage as a family?

Parents/Caregivers:

• What has helped you as a family cope with [death of family member/this event]?

• What have you done to survive that you couldn't have imagined doing before this happened?

• What strengths have you seen from the family that have helped everyone manage?

• What have you learned about your family through all of this that you didn't know before?

• What has been the most positive surprise through this for you?

• What has kept you going even when you were exhausted or felt you had nothing left to give?

Family therapy provides a forum for relatives to hear each other's perspective of events and feelings, correct misconceptions, and create a coherent narrative. This allows the family to move forward together through development of a deeper wisdom and understanding of the trauma that occurred.

Configurations of Traumatic Loss in the Family System

The complex interplay of any event—along with an individual's proximity to it, meanings attributed, and the role of close relationships—has led us to develop three configurations that prove helpful when initially considering family therapy after traumatic loss (see Table 10.2). These definitions provide guidance throughout the assessment and treatment process.

Table 10.2 Assessment of Traumatic Grief in Families

Configuration	Definition	Considerations	Assessment Options
Traumatized Families	All family members have experienced the death of someone intimate in a sudden, horrific way.	Children and adolescent family members can be viewed as vulnerable; capacity of adults to manage their own grief and trauma should be assessed.	Parents, without children, first to hear story essentials. Ascertain parents' ability to attune to the children's needs while they also manage their own trauma and grief. Or Family as a whole meet with goal of joining with family members and assessment of individual and collective tolerance of traumatic grief story.
Families with Traumatized Parents	Parents experienced traumatic loss, but not children.	If family dynamics have changed, children may not know why. Children may be harmed by exposure or secondarily traumatized by material.	May meet with parents alone first, or with whole family, because injured parent may not know that children are aware of parent's distress. Session with the entire family provides verbal and nonverbal information about roles, alliances, and sharing of each member's story about what has happened and why.
Families with Traumatized Children	Children experienced trauma, but parents not traumatized.	Parents at risk for secondary traumatization. Parents may or may not be capable of being attuned to children in session.	Meet with family together; clinician and parents pace according to children's needs.

1. *Traumatized Families:* These have collectively experienced the traumatic loss first-hand. The Ramirez family is one such example (see Figure 10.2). Maria and her children had strong, positive relationships with Juan as husband and father. They witnessed his murder and were themselves threatened by gang members and physically injured by ricocheting gunfire.

2. *Families with Traumatized Children:* The parents may or may not have directly experienced the loss that their child(ren) has experienced, but they do not have the complicating overlay of trauma. Sylvie was not present when Tom collapsed (see Figure 10.1), although she was very concerned for and sensitive to her children's horror and panic that they could not reach their father behind the bathroom door. When the therapist met with Sylvie alone, she declared her belief that Tom knew he was dying even though he did not tell her at the time, and that his withdrawal from her was his way of preparing for his impending death. Grieving the breakdown of her marriage had, at some level, prepared Sylvie for the death of her husband. However, she was not prepared to watch her children's distress and felt powerless to protect and comfort them. In this instance, she experienced some secondary traumatization (Briere & Scott, 2006).

   In another example, eight-year-old Shannon was inconsolable after a classmate died suddenly from meningitis. For weeks thereafter, Shannon cried freely, was afraid to go to sleep, and did not want to attend school. She became distraught when she was separated from her mother, obsessed about bodily functions, and adamantly refused to attend the funeral or discuss her friend. At the same time, Shannon's mother, Michelle, reported feeling sad and anxious. Michelle was having problems sleeping and was hypervigilant when Shannon coughed, sneezed, or complained about aches and pains. Michelle told the therapist, "I feel like I'm going crazy! I never used to be so overprotective. I have no idea why I am this upset all the time." She needed professional support for her confusion over her inability to relieve Shannon's prolonged, intense distress. Michelle benefited from brief intervention that focused on understanding her own vicarious stress, so that she could provide the structure and nurture necessary throughout Shannon's treatment for her grief. These case studies underscore the importance of assessing and supporting the parents of traumatized children because we may erroneously assume that parents, who did not experience a traumatic event directly, are emotionally available and can nurture and support their grieving, traumatized child(ren).

3. *Families with Traumatized Parents:* Here the parent has experienced a traumatic loss, but the children have not. In one case example, a father who returned from military deployment as an army medic in Afghanistan was plagued by nightmares of soldiers in his unit who were killed or seriously injured. His shouts and moans at night would wake the household. During the day, he was moody and preoccupied, not the man that his wife or their adolescent sons remembered. The entire family dynamic was thus affected by his suffering.

Perspective of the Clinician

Because of the contagion of distress, secondary traumatization is a potential hazard for therapists hearing these accounts (Ben-Porat & Itzhaky, 2009; Figley, 1995; McCann & Pearlman, 1990). Training in therapeutic work typically involves a focus on change as the cornerstone underlying the resolution of difficulties. Therapists also have their own assumptions about the world, themselves, and their work, which typically entail their desire to help relieve the suffering of others. However, in problematic situations where suffering is prolonged, or injustices continue and cannot be remedied, all good intentions and training can seem to be ineffectual.

In horrific circumstances, therapists are confronted with patients' issues concerning cruelty, abuse, injustice, and violation. The therapist may identify with the stance of victimization and powerlessness that clients feel. Gerhart and McCollum (2007) state that although all good therapists desire to help their clients, they must also understand that there is inevitable suffering in life: "It is tempting for us to subtly join [with clients] in their search for the mythical state of pain-free living and embark on an effort to change what is unchangeable" (p. 215).

Acceptance of suffering as a normal part of life can be a valuable position in family therapy. Cultivation of mindfulness and compassion-based practices can open the growth that may result from suffering. Gellar and Greenberg (2002) recommend the stance of "being with" rather than "doing to." Clinicians can cultivate the ability to be fully present, engaged, and attuned. Therapeutic presence also adds to the relationship conditions a sense of grounding, which includes therapists trusting their own felt and expressed experience. With presence, the therapist is as close as possible to the client's experience while maintaining a sense of self as separate and whole (Gellar & Greenberg, 2002).

Therapists utilizing mindful awareness are fully present and appropriately empathic in response rather than jumping in to reframe what might otherwise be overwhelming for families.

Conclusion

Therapists who work with families that have experienced traumatic loss must understand how the individual experience of traumatic loss is embedded within the family system, which is also shaped by the structural and political context of the family. Therapists must also be adept at understanding relational dynamics and developmental factors specific to children. In addition, they must be able to recognize traumatic symptomatology and be sensitive to the "dance" that occurs when grief and trauma intersect. Finally, therapists need to know how to create safety within the therapeutic environment, and they should be well versed in the literature and recent findings related to both trauma and grief.

Note

1. In the case studies presented in this chapter, scenarios and names have been changed and adjusted to protect the identities, confidentiality, and privacy of clients.

References

American Academy of Child and Adolescent Psychiatry. (2010). Practice parameter for the assessment and treatment of children and adolescents with posttraumatic stress disorder. *Journal of the American Academy of Child and Adolescent Psychiatry, 49*(4), 414–430.
American Psychiatric Association. (2000). *Diagnostic and statistical manual of mental disorders* (4th ed. rev). Washington, DC: Author.

American Psychiatric Association. (2012). *DSM-V development: Proposed changes to G 03, posttraumatic stress disorder.* Retrieved from http://www.dsm5.org/ProposedRevision/Pages/proposedrevision.aspx?rid = 165

Barnes, M. F. (2005). When a child is traumatized or physically injured: The secondary trauma of parents. In D. R. Catherall (Ed.), *Specific stressors: Interventions with couples and families* (pp. 73–90). New York: Brunner-Routledge.

Ben-Porat, A., & Itzhaky, H. (2009). Implications of treating family violence for the therapist: Secondary traumatization, vicarious traumatization, and growth. *Journal of Family Violence, 24,* 507–515.

Bernardon, S., & Pernice-Duca, F. (2010). A family systems perspective to recovery from posttraumatic stress in children. *Family Journal: Counseling and Therapy for Couples and Families, 18*(4), 349–357.

Boss, P., Roos, S., & Harris, D. (2011). Grief in the midst of ambiguity and uncertainty: An exploration of ambiguous loss and chronic sorrow. In R. Neimeyer, D. Harris, H. Winokuer, & G. Thornton (Eds.), *Grief and bereavement in contemporary society: Bridging research and practice* (pp. 163–176). New York: Routledge.

Briere, J., & Scott, C. (2006). *Principles of trauma therapy: A guide to symptoms, evaluation, and treatment.* London: Sage.

Brown, E. J. (2005). Efficacious treatment of stress disorder in children and adolescents. *Pediatric Annals, 34,* 139–146.

Calhoun, L. G., & Tedeschi, R. G. (2006). The foundations of posttraumatic growth: An expanded framework. In L. G. Calhoun & R. G. Tedeschi (Eds.), *Handbook of posttraumatic growth: Research and practice* (pp. 1–23). Mahwah, NJ: Lawrence Erlbaum Associates.

Carlson, E., & Dalenberg, C. (2000). A conceptual framework for the impact of traumatic experiences. *Trauma, Violence, and Abuse, 1,* 4–28.

Catherall, D. R. (2004). *Handbook of stress, trauma, and the family.* New York: Brunner-Routledge.

Chapple, A., Swift, C., & Ziebland, S. (2011). The role of spirituality and religion for those bereaved due to a traumatic death. *Mortality, 16*(1), 1–19.

Cohen, J. A., Mannarino, A. P., & Deblinger, E. (2006). *Treating trauma and traumatic grief in children and adolescents.* New York: Guildford Press.

Cohen, J. A., Mannarino, A. P., & Deblinger, E. (2012). *Trauma-focused CBT for children and adolescents: Treatment applications.* New York: Guildford Press.

Coulter, S. (2011). Systemic psychotherapy as an intervention for post-traumatic stress responses: An introduction, theoretical rationale and overview of developments in an emerging field of interest. *Journal of Family Therapy, 41*(3), 502–519.

Dekel, R., & Monson, C. (2010). Military-related post-traumatic stress disorder and family relations: Current knowledge and future directions. *Aggression and Violent Behavior, 15,* 303–309.

Dinshtein, Y., Dekel, R., & Polliak, M. (2011). Secondary traumatization among adult children of PTSD veterans: The role of mother–child relationships. *Journal of Family Social Work, 14*(2), 109–124.

Ein-Dor, T., Doron, G., Mikulincer, M., Solomon, Z., & Shaver, P. (2010). Together in pain: Attachment-related dyadic processes and posttraumatic stress disorder. *Journal of Counseling Psychology, 57*(3), 317–327.

Figley, C. R. (1995). Compassion fatigue as a secondary traumatic stress disorder: An overview. In C. R. Figley (Ed.), *Compassion fatigue: Coping with secondary traumatic stress disorder in those who treat the traumatized* (pp. 1–20). New York: Brunner-Mazel.

Figley, C. R. (1998). *The traumatology of grieving.* Philadelphia: Brunner/Mazel.

Gellar, S. M., & Greenberg, L. S. (2002). Therapeutic presence: Therapists' experience of present in the therapeutic encounter. *Person-Centered and Experiential Psychotherapies, 1*(1/2), 71–86.

Gerhart, D. R., & McCollum, E. E. (2007). Engaging suffering: Towards a mindful re-visioning of family therapy practice. *Journal of Marital and Family Therapy, 33*(2), 214–226.

Harris, D. (2010). Introduction. In D. Harris (Ed.), *Counting our losses: Reflecting on change, loss, and transition in everyday life* (pp. xi–xviii). New York: Springer.

Hennighausen, K., & Lyons-Ruth, K. (2007). Disorganization of attachment strategies in infancy and childhood. In R. E. Tremblay, R. G. Barr, & R. Peters (Eds.), *Encyclopedia on early childhood development* [online]. Montreal, Quebec, Canada: Centre of Excellence for Early Childhood Development. Retrieved from http://www.child-encyclopedia.com/documents/Hennighausen-yonsRuthANGxp_rev.pdf

Hill, R. (1949). *Families under stress.* New York: Harper.

Holland, J., & Neimeyer, R. (2011). Separation distress and traumatic distress in prolonged grief: The role of cause of death and relationship to the deceased. *Journal of Psychopathology and Behavioral Assessment, 33,* 254–263.

Janoff-Bulman, R. (1992). *Shattered assumptions: Towards a new psychology of trauma.* New York: Free Press.

Kauffman, J. K. (2002). Safety and the assumptive world. In J. Kauffman (Ed.), *Loss of the assumptive world: A theory of traumatic loss* (pp. 205–212). New York: Routledge.

Klass, D., Nickman, S., & Silverman, P. R. (1996). *Continuing bonds: New understandings of grief.* Washington, DC: Taylor & Francis.

Lehmann, P., & Rabenstein, S. (2002). Children expose to traumatic violence: The role of impact, assessment, and treatment. In A. R. Roberts (Ed.), *Handbook of domestic violence intervention strategies* (pp. 343–364). New York: Oxford.

Liotti, G. (2004). Trauma, dissociation, and disorganization: Three strands of a single braid. *Psychotherapy: Theory, Research, Practice, Training, 41*(4), 472–486.

Lund, L. T., Zimmerman, T. S., & Haddock, S. A. (2002). The theory, structure, and techniques for the inclusion of children in family therapy: A literature review. *Journal of Marital and Family Therapy, 28*(4), 445–454.

Matsakis, A. (2004). Trauma and its impact on families. In D. R. Catherall (Ed.), *Handbook of stress, trauma, and the family* (pp. 12–26). New York: Brunner-Routledge.

McCann, L., & Pearlman, L. A. (1990). Vicarious traumatization: A framework for understanding the psychological effects of working with victims. *Journal of Traumatic Stress, 3,* 131–149.

Milliken, C. S., Auchterlonie, J. L., & Hoge, C. W. (2007). Longitudinal assessment of mental health problems among active and reserve component soldiers returning from the Iraq war. *JAMA, 298,* 2141–2148.

Monson, C., Taft, C., & Fredman, S. (2009). Military related PTSD and intimate relationships: From description to theory-driven research and intervention development. *Clinical Psychology Review, 29,* 707–714.

Nader, K. D. (1997). Childhood traumatic loss: The intersection of trauma and grief. In C. Figley (Ed.), *Death and trauma: The traumatology of grieving* (pp. 17–41). New York: Brunner-Mazel.

Nader, K. D. (2008). *Understanding and assessing trauma in children and adolescents: Measures, methods, and youth in context.* New York: Routledge.

National Child Traumatic Stress Network. (2012). *Understanding child traumatic stress.* Retrieved from http://www.nctsnet.org

Ozer, E. J., Best, S. R., Lipsey, T. L., & Weiss, D. S. (2003). Predictors of posttraumatic stress disorder and symptoms in adults: A meta-analysis. *Psychological Bulletin, 129,* 52–73.

Pernicano, P. (2010). *Family-focused trauma interventions.* Plymouth, UK: Jason Aronson.

Pynoos, R. S., Steinberg, A. M., & Goenjian, A. (1996). Traumatic stress in childhood and adolescence: Recent developments and current controversies. In B. A. van der Kolk & A. C. McFarlane (Eds.), *Traumatic stress* (pp. 331–358). New York: Guildford Press.

Rynearson, E. K. (2010). The clergy, the clinician, and the narrative of violent death. *Pastoral Psychology, 59,* 179–189.

Rynearson, E. K., & Salloum, A. (2011). Restorative retelling: Revisiting the narrative of violent death. In R. Neimeyer, D. Harris, H. Winokuer, & G. Thornton (Eds.), *Grief and bereavement in contemporary society: Bridging research and practice* (pp. 177–188). New York: Routledge.

Schultz, C., & Harris, D. (2011). Giving voice to nonfinite loss and grief in bereavement. In R. Neimeyer, D. Harris, H. Winokuer, & G. Thornton (Eds.), *Grief and bereavement in contemporary society: Bridging research and practice* (pp. 235–248). New York: Routledge.

Simpson, M. A. (1997). Traumatic bereavements and death-related PTSD. In C. Figley (Ed.), *Death and trauma: The traumatology of grieving* (pp. 3–16). New York: Brunner-Mazel.

Stroebe, M., Schut, H., & Boerner, K. (2010). Continuing bonds in adaptation to bereavement: Toward theoretical integration. *Clinical Psychology Review, 30,* 259–268.

Tarrier, N., Sommerfield, C., & Pilgrim, H. (1999). Relatives' expressed emotion and PTSD treatment outcomes. *Psychological Medicine, 29,* 801–811.

Walsh, F. R. (2006). *Strengthening family resilience* (2nd ed.). New York: Guildford Press.

Walsh, F. R. (2007). Traumatic loss and major disasters: Strengthening family and community resilience. *Family Process, 46*(2), 207–227.

Webb, N. B. (2004). The impact of traumatic stress and loss on families. In N. B. Webb (Ed.), *Mass trauma and violence: Helping families and children cope* (pp. 3–22). New York: Guildford Press.

Weisaeth, L., & Eitinger, L. (1993). Posttraumatic stress phenomena: Common themes across wars, disasters, and traumatic events. In J. P. Wilson & B. Raphael (Eds.), *International handbook of traumatic stress syndromes* (pp. 69–77). New York: Plenum Press.

11 Family Therapy following Suicide

Diana C. Sands and Julian L. North

When a loved one dies through suicide, a distressing aftermath may extend throughout the entire immediate and extended family and their work-related and social organizations. The death of a family member through suicide may provoke shock, trauma, and a range of intense grief responses that change irrevocably the family's assumptive world (Janoff-Bullman, 1992). These beliefs and ideas about "how life should be" are challenged, reorganized, and forever altered through the family's relational, communicative, and meaning-making processes (Kaslow & Gilman, 2004; Sands, Jordan, & Neimeyer, 2011). For those bereaved by suicide, unlike other causes of death, the deceased seemingly made a decision to die rather than remain with loved ones. The volitional intent of the family member who chooses suicide violates on many levels relational bonds of care and trust, and meaning-making efforts are fraught with difficulties that complicate adaptive grieving (Neimeyer & Sands, 2011; Sands et al., 2011). Death, a conceptually difficult topic, becomes even more inexplicable.

This chapter reviews the challenges of suicide grief for families and discusses the pertinent clinical application of family therapy, with examples and discussion of case material. For those bereaved by suicide, therapy focuses on creating safety and neutrality for family members to listen and provide emotional comfort and support for each other as they reflect, review, reconstruct, and restore healing familial grief narratives.

Suicide, Grief, and Trauma

Suicide is an awful way to die, and concerns related to the manner of death pose unique challenges for the survivors. The damage and state of the deceased's body, whether seen or imagined, and the sudden, shocking, violent, and volitional nature of the death are risk factors for trauma symptoms, complicated grief, increased suicidal ideation, and even possible suicide itself (Brent, Moritz, Bridge, Perper, & Canobbio, 1996; Currier, Holland, & Neimeyer, 2006; Jordan, 2011; Kim et al., 2005; Mitchell, Kim, Prigerson, & Mortimer, 2005; Runeson & Asberg, 2003). The scene of the death is a crime scene, with no allowances for the micro-transitional death rites of sitting, holding, and touching the deceased. Individuals and families may feel so overwhelmed that they silence the experience because there can be no resolution. But unarticulated trauma corrodes the ease of trust and family communication. Rynearson (2001) found that the disparity between the killing action of the deceased and the caring actions of the bereaved destabilized the narration of the dying story, creating "a structural dead end that fundamentally complicates retelling" (p. 21).

Indeed, the deceased's lonely, violent ending can challenge the limits of family meaning-making efforts. Currier et al. (2006) found a significant relationship between the inability to make sense of suicide death and complications in grieving including suicidal ideation. These and other issues are implicated in the development of a maladaptive relationship with the deceased (Sands, 2009; Sands et al., 2011). Klass (1999, 2006) termed the bereaved person's post-loss attachment to the deceased as the "continuing bond between griever and deceased" and noted that this bond could be adaptive or maladaptive.

Boerner and Heckhausen (2003) conceptualized the development of the continuing bond, or relationship with the deceased, as a transformative process that involved disengagement from the living person and reconnection with an imaginal mental representation. Neimeyer, Baldwin, and Gillies (2006) found that when the griever has a high post-loss attachment to the deceased and low meaning making, there is an increased risk of bereavement complications. The challenged family system of trust, compromised communication, meaning-making difficulties, trauma, and relational repair issues tend to complicate the development of an adaptive relationship with the deceased (Hedtke & Winslade, 2004; Walter, 1996).

Suicide, Grief, and Family Therapy

Family therapy conceptualizes family members as connected together in patterns—including some that are long term and intergenerational—that have been interwoven through myriad complex systemic processes (Nadeau, 1998; Walsh & McGoldrick, 1995). Family therapy can be beneficial in strengthening family cohesion, supporting problem solving, and deconstructing negative narratives and unhelpful beliefs (Cerel, Jordan, & Duberstein, 2008; Jordan, 2011; Kaslow, Samples, Rhodes, & Gantt, 2011; Linn-Gust, 2010; Nadeau, 1998).

Family therapy commences with early goals to understand the story of the suicide and its impact upon all involved. In unraveling this tale of the death, understanding who the deceased was, his or her strengths and accomplishments, alongside any struggles and illness, seeks a balanced perspective. In like manner, the family history, its patterns of care and trust, alongside challenges with separations and quest for independence, provide insight into the familial context in which the tragedy has occurred. Seeking the family's permission to retell the story of illness and loss helps to make explicit an agenda to understand more deeply all that occurred. An unspoken notion here may be to help over time with some reframing of this story. And, of course, the experience of the bereaved, their reactions, concerns, and coping need to be mapped out. This initial road map of how to assess the family may take two or three sessions and leads eventually to the therapist's summary of where the family is at, what concerns persist, what the goals of continued therapeutic work are, and how the therapist perceives that this will help all involved.

Every family and each member within the family will grieve in their own unique way. The assault on the family's system of mutual care and trust is particularly significant with parental suicide, while a child's suicide can traumatize parents' belief in their ability to sustain healthy relations and keep remaining children safe (Demi & Howell, 1991; Parrish & Tunkle, 2005). Grief processes are influenced by factors such as the pre-existing patterns of family relationships, roles, functions, and significance within the family of the person who has died. The therapist should also consider the antecedent conditions, circumstances, and method of death; the specific relationships that existed with the deceased; and preexisting communication patterns (Sands et al., 2011). Also relevant is the life cycle stage of the family, other family stressors, and family experiences, beliefs, and tolerance for different ways of coping with stressful events (Kaslow et al., 2011; Nadeau, 1998).

Although family therapy encompasses a diverse collection of theories, the unifying principle is support of adaptive processes among the various elements that comprise the family system (Boscolo, Cecchin, Hoffman, & Penn, 1987; Walsh & McGoldrick, 1995). Unlike individual therapy approaches that are concerned with the individual's internal experiences, family therapy is primarily concerned with relationships between and among people within family systems. Family therapy does not require every member to attend; typically, sessions include various members in combinations and sub-groups, plus individual sessions and extended family, including social and peer-group members. For example, if a parent committed suicide, the children would attend only some, not all, of the sessions with the surviving parent.

Evaluation of a family bereavement program that incorporated caregivers with children for sections of the program found a decrease in adverse grief effects (Sandler et al., 2008). While attending family therapy, members can also be directed to informative Web sites. They can elect together or separately to attend an adult, young people's, or children's suicide bereavement group. The therapist should decide the number of counseling sessions in discussion with the family, to meet their individual requirements. Family therapy should take place over an extended period of time covering significant grief anniversaries.

Let us now illustrate this process through a case study. The outline that follows is based on case intake notes, summaries of sessions to provide contextual information, discussion notes, and excerpts from sessions. Although every family is different and requires therapy tailored to its unique circumstances, the 10 sessions reviewed here provide insight into the benefits of a family-centered approach.

Case Example

Jill sought grief counseling for her 17-year-old stepdaughter, Sophie, whose mother, Cindy, had died through suicide. Two months earlier, Cindy had attempted suicide by overdose and was hospitalized. Subsequently, Cindy went to convalesce at the home of her parents, where a further attempt resulted in her death by suicide.

After her mother's first suicide attempt, Sophie was placed with her biological father, Paul, and her stepfamily: his wife, Jill, and siblings Phoebe, 8, and Mark, 6. This temporary living arrangement was a major change for Sophie, who had been living with her mother and had only infrequent contact with her father and stepfamily since the divorce when she was 4. However, with the death of Sophie's mother, this new living arrangement became permanent.

Sessions 1 and 2: Engagement, Reassurance, and Family Care

Paul and Jill attended an initial session which focused on Cindy's death and practical changes in the family to accommodate Sophie (see Figure 11.1). They also reviewed emotional changes related to Sophie settling into the family, Sophie's grief, and the estranged relationship between father and daughter. As the story was elicited by the therapist, information about individual and family meaning making became clearer. It became obvious that Jill was very fond of and concerned for Sophie. Also apparent was the issue of the "ghost" of Paul's ex-wife, Cindy, who was brought back into Paul's new family through Sophie and her grief. Though Paul remarked that he was saddened by Cindy's death, he added that they were "kids" when they married, and living with Cindy was "one drama after another." He confirmed that "Jill is the love of my life," and Jill noted that they were lucky to have "a good marriage."

At session 2, which focused on the different ways in which people grieve, Paul talked of his parents, who were both deceased. Jill said she was only 16 when her mother died after a long struggle with cancer, and that it was important to share her grief with her sister. Jill was worried that Sophie was "bottling it up." Sophie explained that she did not "like talking about Mum. It's all mixed up and feels like a big lot of stuff stuck inside." Frequently, she said, she tried "not to think about Mum being dead" and felt "kind of tired and sick."

Both Jill and Paul were worried that they did not know the right way to talk about it. Jill admitted that "telling the children and speaking with the school was difficult," and Sophie added that she did not "know what to say to her friends about Mum." The therapist suggested that the whole family, including Sophie's two step-siblings, attend the next session and watch a film in which children discuss losing a loved one through suicide, to help with "how to talk about it." This second session ended with the "Butterfly Story" (see more detail in the section "Session 3 Excerpts"), which emphasizes through

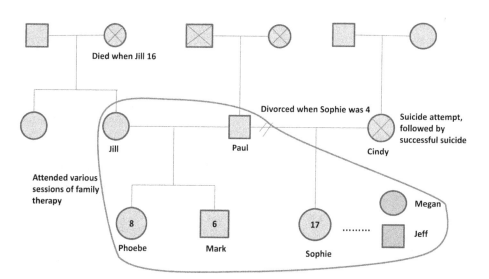

Figure 11.1 Genogram of a blended family following suicide.

the metaphor of the butterfly life cycle that grieving is an adaptive coping process that unfolds over time, not a state that can be simply "fixed."

Discussion about Sessions 1 and 2

Initial sessions are important for therapists to engage families; build trust, safety, and reassurance; and elicit their understanding about issues of concern. The parameters of family identity are being challenged, and it is essential to decrease anxiety through reassurance and support of the existing family care system. Although the suicide took place on the other side of the country, and Cindy had never lived with this family, her death is very present in the family through Sophie. The family is "trying on the shoes" as they engage with the self-volition of the death (Sands, 2009). It takes courage to engage with these issues. Often families move in and out of accepting the terrible reality and implications of the manner of death. The therapist noted that Sophie was withdrawn and invited her to bring photos of her mother to the next session. Although therapists acknowledge the pain and difficulties, therapy seeks to facilitate both self-care and family care and the mobilization of mutual support.

A bereaved parent with children has many practical and financial issues to negotiate and resolve. One mother said that finding enough time to love her children, "to compensate for the love they have lost from their dad," was the most difficult challenge since the suicide and that it was an emotional and practical time-solving problem (Sands, 2008). In Sophie's family, issues concern the shared bedroom and different bedtimes, as well as conflicting relational loyalties for the whole family.

Tools such as the family genogram (Walsh & McGoldrick, 1995; see Figure 11.1) can help the family to better understand its system and gather information that can aid positive connation (O'Brian & Bruggen, 1985) in highlighting family strengths alongside family members' concerns. For example, Sophie's grief and presence in the family is understood through a family-centered, systemic lens which requires each member of the family to help the family as a whole to support and negotiate changes. The therapist's attitude is respectful, curious, multi-positional, and aligned with all members, with the aim of facilitating family processes and new information into the family system that can increase everyone's understanding and choices. Questioning forms the bedrock of family counseling, with the use of circular and other styles of questions to stimulate and increase communication within the family (MacKinnon, 1988). This process provides relevant information, often termed "news of difference," for family members about emotional and behavioral responses, meaning making, communication patterns, perceived roles, and rules within the family. For example, Jill could be asked by the therapist to comment on the relationship between Paul and Sophie: "Why do you think Dad leaves the room when Sophie is looking upset? Is it (1) because Dad believes Sophie would prefer to be on her own? Or is it (2) more because Dad is worried he may not be good at comforting Sophie? Or (3) does Sophie's upset remind him of his own upset feelings, or something else?" This exemplifies what can be called an other-oriented, forced-choice, triadic question and is intended to stimulate reflection and discussion.

To explore different grief styles, a therapist may discuss the idea of members of the family using masks to deal with grief. For example, an "I'm busy" mask or an "I'm angry" mask may both have the effect of pushing people away (Sands, 2013).

In session 2, the therapist has punctuated the issue of not knowing how to talk about the suicide, inviting the family to watch a psycho-educational film, *Red Chocolate Elephants for Children Bereaved by Suicide*, designed to engage children in family grief conversations (Sands, 2010). Sharing grief is a relational process, and Sophie's family needs reassurance, education, and support for responding in helpful ways. The therapist hopes that the film will boost the family's ability to offer support for one another and open up communication about suicide.

Session 3 Excerpts—Psycho-education to Mobilize Mutual Care, Trust, and Communication

The whole family arrived. Phoebe and Mark were excited and pleased to be included. They were curious about what was happening in therapy and clearly adored their "new" big sister. Each family member selected a puppet: a dog for Paul; a fairy with a wishing wand for Jill; a turtle for Sophie; a rabbit for Phoebe; and for Mark, a puppet that can be turned from a caterpillar to a cocoon, which opens to become a butterfly. Each person commented on his or her puppet. Jill said she wished she had a wand to make things better; Sophie talked about wanting to go inside her turtle shell and stay there. Phoebe remarked that the rabbit was soft and cuddly; Mark recalled the butterfly story their mother had shared about Sophie, and said that "you can't just make sad feelings go away." Using circular, dyadic, and triadic questions, the therapist explored the qualities of each puppet. Various family members contributed: for example, Paul said that dogs can bark loudly and keep the family safe from bad people; they are loyal and always love you. Using the same circular questioning method, family members considered how it was for Sophie in her turtle shell. Mark volunteered that it would be safe but dark; Phoebe added that you could get lonely. Sophie looked sad, and Phoebe responded by moving closer to Sophie.

After playing the educational DVD about suicide grief, the therapist noted that Phoebe had moved to cuddle next to Sophie, while Mark was sitting on the floor leaning against his mother. Sophie became visibly upset, referring to a comment in the film, "I think they might blame my Dad . . . but they don't know the full story . . . they can't judge him" (Sands, 2010, p. 17). Sophie said she felt people were judging her mother. She looked at Jill and Paul as they digested this information silently. Mark wanted to share what he noticed in the DVD, in which a boy said, "But if I lose my Mum . . . I'm going to have to just take care of myself" (Sands, 2010, p. 18). Mark wanted Sophie to know, "You can live at our house and share our Mum." Paul added, "Sophie, you have a home with us always!" Jill nodded her head in agreement, with tears in her eyes as she cuddled her son. Paul, looking at the floor, said he noticed how much on the DVD the kids talked about funerals, and that Sophie's mother had none because of the travel distance, and Cindy's elderly parents were in poor health and "couldn't anyway have afforded a funeral." The therapist introduced the idea that the family could assist Sophie with a remembrance ceremony for her mother.

The session ended with the therapist laying a heart-shaped pillow in the middle of the floor and commenting on how much love and strong family heart this family possessed. Each of them was then invited to place in the family heart something special to help it grow and stay strong. Phoebe placed her "really good cuddles" into the family heart, and Sophie said she was feeling a little safer to come out of her turtle shell. The others respected her need to withdraw in her own time frame. The session ended with a sense of caring, understanding, and increased connection among family members. Sophie decided to invite a couple of her best friends to the next session.

Discussion about Session 3

Puppets are one way of engaging and reducing anxiety, while at the same time providing information about family relationships, such as the alignment between Sophie and Phoebe. Play therapy and expressive art exercises can be sensitively introduced into family settings. For example, "talking sticks" (for details, see Sands, 2010, p. 28), can help family members talk about matters that are difficult to discuss (Hooghe, Neimeyer, & Rober, 2011). Psycho-educational DVDs can increase the family's understanding of grief post suicide and provide different ways to think and talk about the experience. As Sophie shared some of her grief, family members responded with empathy and care. Sophie made an important statement that she does not want anyone judging her mother for having taken her own life. The therapist hypothesized that the positive connotation of the family heart as growing and strengthening would support mobilization of the family's care and trust of each other.

Planning a commemorative ritual can be very significant. In suicide bereavement, often the nature and circumstances of the death prevent the usual rituals. Recognizing the benefits of strengthening family relationships, the therapist also proposed "homework" talks between Dad and Sophie on drives to and from the sessions.

Sessions 4 and 5: Relational Networks and Family Life Cycle

Session 4 focused on engaging Sophie's peer relational network for support. Sophie invited her boyfriend, Jeff, and her best friend, Megan, to attend. The therapist used a creative artwork intervention with visual prompts to assist the young people in identifying resilience within their relational network (Sands, 2013). For example, Sophie received support in talking on the phone with her maternal grandparents, whom she had never met. The therapist coached Sophie about how to talk with her peers about her grief. This helped Sophie to consider how much information she chose to share about her mother.

Paul, Jill, and Sophie attended session 5, which focused on the family life cycle, with overt discussion of the developmental differences between Sophie and her stepsister and stepbrother. The therapist gave Sophie guidance about how to negotiate with Jill and her father regarding rules and limits more appropriate to her age. This set up a process by which future differences could be more readily resolved.

Sessions 6 and 7: Relational Repair and Communication

As Sophie trusted the family more, she revealed how often her mother had talked about wanting to die. Sophie would regularly come home from school and find her mother in bed. Feeling responsible, Sophie would then stay home to look after her. Significantly, her mother's mental illness was not formally diagnosed, nor was it understood by Sophie. Mental illness is often managed within families this way.

Building on the family heart metaphor, Sophie and her father explored what would happen if they told people they trusted more about the hurt they held within their hearts. They then took tentative, thoughtful steps with this process to thus reveal the beginnings of relational repair and forgiveness.

Session 8 Excerpts: The Body of Trust, Trauma, and Relational Repair

The therapist invited Sophie and her father to select a colored material that made them feel relaxed and comfortable. A soft pink material reminded Sophie of a blanket she had on her bed when she was little. She wrapped it around herself, commenting that the material reminded her of her mother's love. Her father selected a deep blue, which reminded him of the quiet flow of the river where he would fly-fish. Sophie's body outline was traced by the therapist onto a large sheet of paper, and, as Sophie's story unfolded, both her father and the therapist added words, drawings, and symbols reflecting her embodied experience on to the paper (for details, see Neimeyer & Sands, 2011; Sands, 2012). Sophie recalled that the last time she talked with her mother; Sophie was still upset with her and did not say, "I love you" at the end of the phone call. This was a matter of deep regret for Sophie. Her father then drew a heart on the body, inserting the words "I love you so much, Mum." The therapist guided Sophie's attention to her bodily responses. She said, "It's all jagged pieces broken inside me!" She recalled the day she came home from school to find her mother had overdosed: "She wouldn't wake up . . . I was scared and screaming at Mum to wake up and shaking all over . . . I thought she was dead." Shaky lines captured Sophie's bodily response and screams on the body drawing. Sophie paused and used self-soothing strategies to reduce anxiety.

Sophie explained that the day her mother killed herself and her earlier suicide attempt were "all mixed together." She shook her head and added, "I just couldn't believe Mum would do that." Sophie mentioned a black, heavy lump in her stomach. As the therapist explored what this was like, Sophie's hurt and anger came to the fore, prompting her to say, "I'm so angry at Mum." Sophie sobbed, "Maybe she didn't really love me?" As Sophie shared more of her feelings, she wondered, "If I had been with Mum . . . maybe I could have stopped it happening." The therapist gently questioned these unhelpful ideas. Sophie's father echoed his own guilt about Cindy's death: "I feel really bad about what happened . . . that somehow I should have done something." Finally, he put his arms around Sophie and rocked her, saying, "The way Mum did it, there was nothing anyone could have done . . . You couldn't have done anything to stop it, Sophie." Father and daughter cried together. After a long pause, Sophie asked, "I wonder whether Mum knows how much I miss her?" This question was followed by a lengthy pause and a shift in the feelings within Sophie. Hesitantly, she reminisced about hearing her mother's favorite song at the shopping mall—Cher singing, "I Believe in Love." Sophie thought it was her mother's way of sending her love. The therapist wrote "I believe in love" on the drawing, and, using the color pink, her father drew a blanket all around Sophie's body drawing, saying, "This is Mum's love for you, Sophie."

Previous sessions with Sophie and her father had explored resilience and taught self-soothing and beneficial strategies to reduce distress, such as the use of coping cards (Granello, 2010; Levine, 1997). In this session, an "anchoring" strategy that made use of colored materials was used to build trust in one's own internal feelings. Called the "body of trust" intervention, it is supported by research using narrative and body-focused methods to facilitate integration of traumatic sensory, emotional, and cognitive material and thus assist adaptive meaning reconstruction (Neimeyer & Sands, 2011; Ogden, Minton, & Pain, 2006; Sands, 2012). Sophie's ongoing relationship with her mother had been saturated with issues of guilt, blame, and abandonment. These were further compounded by frightening thoughts about her mother's actions and death imagery about the pain of her mother's dying alone, without Sophie there to get help. These issues complicated grief processes and the development of a more nurturing, adaptive relationship with her mother (Sands et al., 2011).

Sophie's statements highlighted the ambivalent ideas generated by a suicide, shifting from questioning her mother's intention to die, her love for Sophie, and Sophie's anger at her mother, and guilt and self-blame for not being able to save her. Such mixed feelings create tremendous difficulties in meaning making. During the session, the therapist prompted Sophie's reflection by asking, "Where did you get the idea that one person could be responsible for keeping another person alive?" and "All those times Mum was unwell, who was looking after you, Sophie?" The trauma of her mother's death is deeply associated with her past coping experience of looking after and caring for her mother.

Discussion about Session 8

This was a significant session for both Sophie and her father, providing opportunities for trauma deconstruction and relational repair, while also helping to adaptively integrate the reality of death. Moules, Simonson, Prins, Angus, and Bell described the process of developing the relationship with the deceased as "a walk backwards, while keeping a sure foot in living forward" (2004, p. 99). The therapist was seeking development of an adaptive relationship with the deceased for both father and daughter, as well as an enhanced relationship between father and daughter, so that eventually Cindy would become a more benevolent presence in the family. These concerns were further explored in session 9, which is not included here.

Session 10: Commemoration and Growth

The family reported a commemorative gathering at a river parkland. Sophie, wrapped in her mother's blue pashmina shawl that had been sent to her by her grandparents, spoke about her mother's life, while family and friends listened. Sophie had found a place to hold her mother safely in her heart. Paul said a few words about Cindy and the gift of Sophie in the family. Sophie played "I Believe in Love," while the family and friends threw flower petals into the river. The family read together a prayer of blessing over Cindy's life.

Follow-up sessions continued to encourage the family's growth, promoting their shared understanding that the work of mourning can be refashioned over a lifetime. Sands et al. (2011) noted that healing narratives included a range of themes that helped to rebuild safety and trust within the family.

Having illustrated the complexity that unfolds as a therapist works with a family bereaved by suicide, let us now consider further theory to better explain all that transpired.

The Family Care and Trust System

The family's assumptive world is defined as their co-constructed implicit and explicit expectations of relational bonds of love, care, trust, and intimacy, which form the basis of their safety, cohesion, and stability. We call this particular set of ideas and beliefs the *family care and trust system* (FCTS) (Sands, 2008). The shock that a loved one would end his or her life tends to traumatize these beliefs at their very foundation, leaving family members to question the way they experience themselves as a family (Attig, 2002; Cerel et al., 2008; Neimeyer et al., 2002). This constellation of issues impels the family to investigate why and how their FCTS failed to keep them safe. For some family members, this process begins with police questioning at the death scene (Aguirre & Slater, 2010; Parrish & Tunkle, 2005). Linn-Gust (2001) noted that "parents are fearful for the safety of family members; siblings are secretly concerned that 'they, too, will die by suicide'" (p. 120). Often family members become concerned with whether the suicide was a rational or irrational choice, though this brings little relief from the terrible knowledge that the deceased was suffering (Shneidman, 2001).

Many families bereaved by suicide find this assault on relational care, trust, and family intimacy extremely painful, hindering their ability to mobilize their natural resources, resilience, and coping capacity. A loved member leaving the family so violently and unexpectedly provokes family members to question if they could have provided better care that would have prevented this death (Jordan, 2011; Linn-Gust, 2001, 2010; Parrish & Tunkle, 2005). Almost inevitably, a sense of guilt and responsibility emerges for the family. In the "tripartite model of suicide bereavement" (Sands, 2009; Sands et al., 2011), Sands explained how this investigative process involved "walking in the shoes" of the deceased and identified how therapy can facilitate repair and restoration of the family and help develop an adaptive relationship with the deceased through narrative reconstruction processes (Neimeyer & Sands, 2011; Sands, 2009; Sands et al., 2011).

When suicide occurs, the family unit, which is usually the primary source of comfort and care for family members in times of stress, is often compromised in fulfilling these functions. A bereaved sister recalled, "Everyone in the family looked around and blamed either themselves or someone else in the family" (Sands, 2008). A bereaved mother lamented, "I will never stop searching for what I could have done to save him" (Sands, 2008). These reactions of guilt or responsibility, or implied attributions of blame and shame, erode the FCTS and isolate family members (Neimeyer & Sands, 2011; Neimeyer et al., 2002). Linn-Gust (2001) noted that family members withdraw from each other, "trying to save themselves from guilt and blame" (p. 121). Nadeau (1998) observed that when the family identified the death as preventable, their energy tended to be expended on this issue, often compromising adaptive family grief processes.

When the suicide raises mental health issues, the family attempts to understand not only whether the choice was rational or irrational, but how and why this death happened at this particular moment in time (Rappaport, 2009). At the same time, as distressed family members investigate their role in the death, they also question the violation of FCTS assumptions that those whom we care about will not place their life at risk.

Suicide can be construed as a compromise of trust, and the family struggles to make meaning of what is experienced by many as betrayal, rejection, and abandonment by their loved one (DePrince & Freyd, 2002; Rynearson, 2001; Sands & Tennant, 2010; Wertheimer, 1991). This can be summed up in a bereaved child's question, "Why did he do that to us?" (Sands, 2010, p. 14). The traumatizing assault on the family's founda-tional sense of trust and care has been linked with persistent negative grief effects, family breakdown, disrupted meaning-making processes, and impaired family communication and social processes (Cerel et al., 2008; Janoff-Bullman, 1992; Lohan & Murphy, 2002; Murphy, 1996; Neimeyer, 2000; Riches & Dawson, 2000).

Family Communication and Social Processes after Suicide

The FCTS is developed and sustained through family members engaging in meaning-making communications. Narratives of overt and covert family self-stigmatization—namely, guilt, responsibility, and blame—are further compounded by real or perceived negative responses from within the extended family, friendship networks, and the com-munity. Not surprisingly, these same networks are also described by many family mem-bers as a primary source of comfort and support (McMenamy, Jordan, & Mitchell, 2008). However, bereaved families may interpret inconsistent or absent responses as blame and rejection, and thereby feel shame, guilt, and a sense of extended family and commu-nity censure (Barlow & Morrison, 2002; McMenamy et al., 2008). Research has noted the flow-on effect from these issues in distorted, decreased, and silenced family com-munications (Cerel et al., 2008; Kaslow et al., 2011). Feigelman, Gorman, and Jordan (2009) found that those bereaved by suicide experienced three key forms of stigmatiza-tion: (1) "a wall of silence," (2) an "absence of caring interest," and (3) "unhelpful advice" (p. 603). Research confirms that despite education to increase social awareness, stigma and negative attitudes regarding suicide persist within the community and beyond, thus increasing the intensity and complexity of suicide bereavement (Barlow & Morrison, 2002; Cerel et al., 2008; Feigelman et al., 2009; Jordan, 2011; McMenamy et al., 2008).

Hedtke and Winslade (2004) wrote about the socio-cultural contexts within which language is positioned, explaining that the language of grief is permeated with historical and socio-cultural discourses. Social commentary about suicide is often negative, which inhibits expression of grief and appropriate responses. There is an "absence of clear-cut social norms in how to relate to survivors" of suicide (Feigelman et al., 2009, p. 606), which can limit confidence in those people offering support (Doka, 2002). Range (1998) com-mented, "When people misunderstand the bereavement experience, their support attempts may be inappropriate or harmful" (p. 215), causing those bereaved to reduce social inter-actions. Perceived community stigma tends to reduce family help-seeking behaviors (Aguirre & Slater, 2010; Cerel et al., 2008; Jordan, 2001, 2011; Provini, Everett, & Pfeffer, 2000). A child bereaved by her father's suicide expressed her awareness of community censure: "I would rather him die of a heart attack because it's more understandable than killing yourself . . . him doing that makes me a bit embarrassed to other people" (Sands, 2010, p. 16). This sense of social censure can also cause the bereaved to keep secret the circumstances of death (Range, 1998). Walsh and McGoldrick (1995) noted the adverse effects to the FCTS when conversations relating to the suicide are silenced.

Family members may also experience discomfort and confusion about socially unac-ceptable grief responses like relief, anger, perceived responsibility, or betrayal of trust and abandonment issues. Moreover, intrusive death trauma imagery may manifest itself in the guise of concerns about pain the deceased suffered when dying, whether death came quickly or whether they changed their mind during dying. In light of these difficult topics, communication decreases, leaving a heavy silence. Family members also seek to protect others from these conversations (Kaslow & Gilman, 2004), sometimes fearing that talking about suicide might implant the idea of suicide in another (Linn-Gust, 2001). These beliefs increase stress and hyper-vigilance within the family (Linn-Gust, 2001). For example, a daughter bereaved by suicide commented, "I thought about suicide all the time . . . and worried that my sisters must be thinking about it too . . . but I couldn't ask them" (Sands, 2008).

Family Assessment and Cultural Considerations

For those bereaved through suicide, assessment screening is worthwhile to discern any risk of complicated grief (also termed prolonged grief disorder), trauma symptoms, suicidal thinking, or other mental health issues (Jordan, 2008, 2011; Kaslow & Gilman, 2004; Parrish & Tunkle, 2005). Postvention, an intervention offered after suicide to support the bereaved, is about providing a variety of services, support, information, and choices. Family therapy might not be a comfortable experience in light of a family's socio-cultural, religious, or spiritual beliefs; style of communication; or other complicating family concerns. For example, individual counseling may be preferable when mental health issues are involved (Jordan, 2008, 2011; Linn-Gust, 2010). Further, McMenamy et al. (2008) noted the range of different services available and cautioned against "a one-size-fits-all" approach (p. 385). Kissane and Lichtenthal (2008) suggested longer-term therapy for families with low cohesiveness and expressiveness, or with high conflict.

Assessment may also identify socio-cultural, religious, and spiritual dimensions that make linking families to religious and culturally appropriate community resources worthwhile. For example, Australia has a large population of immigrant and refugee families who present special concerns in terms of accumulated grief, trauma, and depleted relational systems and resources. Some Australian Indigenous groups and Torres Strait Islanders have cultural taboos against saying the name of the deceased or talking about the family grief, especially if the death was due to suicide. Moreover, police photographs of the deceased taken for coronial inquiries add another layer of distress. Significantly, Wingard (2001) has noted how, as a result of colonization, accumulated intergenerational and unacknowledged historical grief and trauma in Australian Indigenous communities complicates family and community grief processes in an ongoing conspiracy of silence.

How Can Family Therapy Help Suicide-Bereaved Families?

The family may experience a loss of agency and control when suicide occurs, often reinforced by medical, police, and coronial investigation processes. Personal items belonging to the deceased are removed for investigation, the police interview family and friends, and funerals have to wait for the completion of forensic autopsy procedures (Rynearson, 2001). This may be especially distressing for religious groups that require burial within 24 hours of death.

Family therapy can provide support for families coping with an overwhelming array of complex issues and themes including abandonment, guilt, responsibility, blame, shame, lowered self-esteem, anger, relational withdrawal, and the intense search to make meaning of the death (Jordan, 2001; Linn-Gust, 2001; Neimeyer & Sands, 2011; Wertheimer, 1991). The idea of passing light through a crystal prism and observing how the light is refracted into several colors is helpful in explaining the value of each family member's contribution to healing, restoration, and reinvestment in the FCTS.

Psycho-education can normalize and increase understanding of grief by providing a language to communicate grief experiences within the family (Kaslow et al., 2011). Moreover, psycho-education can be imparted through family conversations, therapist-introduced examples and metaphorical stories, creative play activities, expressive art interventions, pamphlets, books, DVDs, and films (Sands, 2013). Restorative resilience interventions can be used to promote exploration and identification of individual and family resilience styles, resources, and past coping strategies, using visual images, enactments, play therapy, expressive artwork, poetry, story, and journal and letter writing (Sands, 2013). Therapy can encourage family members to access resources within the extended family and social networks system, thereby reducing their isolation and helping to protect against risk of suicide (Aguirre & Slater, 2010). The therapist can coach family members in how to communicate their grief with concerned others in ways that increase the likelihood of appropriate responses.

Family map interventions can introduce alternative understandings of family members' responses, within both the immediate and extended family (Sands, 2013). Practical problem-solving strategies are of central importance, and solution-focused programs that foster resilience to address practical and emotional problems can help families coping with suicide (de Castro & Guterman, 2008). Therapy can help families develop reflective, cognitive, emotional, and behavioral functioning to foster flexible, open communication that challenges and deconstructs external and internal negative narratives. Research confirms that family-based cognitive-behavior programs for those bereaved by suicide are particularly effective in reducing maladaptive grief reactions and possibly preventing complicated grief (de Groot, Neeleman, van der Meer, & Burger, 2010).

Families often tell the story of trauma from one frozen perspective. Therapy can help them access alternative explanations to deepen understanding. When the emotional experience of trauma has been intense, teaching families how to comfort and soothe one another promotes greater mutual support (Levine, 1997; Totton, 2003). In drawing perspectives from several family members, the therapist may use several representational systems for somatic, sensory, and cognitive responses to eventually integrate these into a more complete picture (Neimeyer & Sands, 2011; Totton, 2003). Narrative methods suit families, with the therapist helping to reconstruct the material into a meaningful account (de Castro & Guterman, 2008; Neimeyer, 2000; Sands et al., 2011; Walter, 1996). When the relationship with the deceased has been conflicted, estranged, or ambivalent, the bereaved may require help to repair this relationship through the grief work (Neimeyer & Sands, 2011; Sands et al., 2011). This therapeutic process involves deconstructing trauma associated with the death and developing a narrative that helps the family begin to integrate the loss (Neimeyer & Sands, 2011; Sands, 2012), including the potential for post-traumatic growth (Calhoun & Tedeschi, 2006; Sands et al., 2011). The transformative shift that takes place through this retelling has been called "taking off the shoes" (Sands & Tennant, 2010; Sands et al., 2011). For many, growth follows relational repair and restoration of the capacity for trust and love, leaving the family with a narrative that now honors the deceased's life. Commemorative rituals at anniversaries can aid this greatly.

Conclusion

The loss of a family member to suicide can leave families adrift in unknown territory, with the foundations of their assumptive beliefs and their relational care, trust, and intimacy systems challenged and overwhelmed. Families often experience guilt and feelings of responsibility, hyper-vigilance, and increased anxiety, and they withdraw from each other in ways that compromise the giving and receiving of comfort and sharing of grief. Efforts to make meaning of the volitional nature of the death alongside understanding any perceived failure of trust and care within the family can be exhausting. The family's sense of identity may be irrevocably altered. These challenging issues mutually interact and grow exponentially in complexity. They often result in negative meaning-making narratives about the death, which further compromises trust and communication to the detriment of family processes and developing an adaptive relationship with the deceased. Family therapy can provide safety, reassurance, and support for families as they navigate the changes demanded by these particularly complex grief processes.

References

Aguirre, R. T., & Slater, H. (2010). Suicide postvention as suicide prevention: Improvement and expansion in the United States. *Death Studies, 34,* 529–540.

Attig, T. (2002). Questionable assumptions about assumptive worlds. In J. Kauffman (Ed.), *Loss of the assumptive world: A theory of traumatic loss* (pp. 55–68). New York: Brunner-Routledge.

Barlow, C., & Morrison, H. (2002). Survivors of suicide: Emerging counseling strategies. *Journal of Psychosocial Nursing and Mental Health, 40,* 28–40.

Boerner, K., & Heckhausen, J. (2003). To have and have not: Adaptive bereavement by transforming mental ties to the deceased. *Death Studies, 27,* 199–226.

Boscolo, L., Cecchin, G., Hoffman, L., & Penn, P. (1987). *Milan systemic family therapy: Conversations in theory and practice.* New York: Basic Books.

Brent, D. A., Moritz, G., Bridge, J., Perper, J., & Canobbio, R. (1996). Long term impact of exposure to suicide: A three-year controlled follow-up. *Journal of American Academy of Child and Adolescent Psychiatry, 35,* 646–653.

Calhoun, L., & Tedeschi, R. G. (Eds.). (2006). *Handbook of posttraumatic growth.* Mahwah, NJ: Lawrence Erlbaum.

Cerel, J., Jordan, J. R., & Duberstein, P. R. (2008). The impact of suicide on the family. *Crisis, 29,* 38–44.

Currier, J. M., Holland, J. M., & Neimeyer, R. A. (2006). Sense-making, grief, and the experience of violent loss: Toward a mediational model. *Death Studies, 30,* 403–428.

de Castro, S., & Guterman, J. T. (2008). Solution-focused therapy for families coping with suicide. *Journal of Marital and Family Therapy, 34,* 93–106.

de Groot, M., Neeleman, J., van der Meer, K., & Burger, H. (2010). The effectiveness of family-based cognitive-behavior grief therapy to prevent complicated grief in relatives of suicide victims: The mediating role of suicide ideation. *Suicide and Life-Threatening Behavior, 40,* 425–437.

Demi, A. S., & Howell, C. (1991). Hiding and healing. *Archives of Psychiatry and Nursing, 5,* 350–356.

DePrince, A. P., & Freyd, J. J. (2002). The harm of trauma: Pathological fear, shattered assumptions or betrayal? In J. Kauffman (Ed.), *Loss of the assumptive world* (pp. 71–82). New York: Taylor and Francis.

Doka, K. J. (2002). How could God? Loss and the spiritual assumptive world. In J. Kauffman (Ed.), *Loss of the assumptive world: A theory of traumatic loss* (pp. 49–54). New York: Brunner-Routledge.

Feigelman, W., Gorman, B. S., & Jordan, J. R. (2009). Stigmatization and suicide bereavement. *Death Studies, 33,* 591–608.

Granello, D. H. (2010). A suicide crisis intervention model with 25 practical strategies for implementation. *Journal of Mental Health Counseling, 32,* 218–235.

Hedtke, L., & Winslade, J. (2004). *Re-membering lives: Conversations with the dying and the bereaved.* Amityville, NY: Baywood.

Hooghe, A., Neimeyer, R. A., & Rober, P. (2011). The complexity of couple communication in bereavement: An illustrative case study. *Death Studies, 35,* 905–934.

Janoff-Bullman, R. (1992). *Shattered assumptions: Towards a new psychology of trauma.* New York: The Free Press.

Jordan, J. R. (2001). Is suicide bereavement different? A reassessment of the literature. *Suicide and Life-Threatening Behavior, 31,* 91–102.

Jordan, J. R. (2008). Bereavement after suicide. *Psychiatric Annals, 38,* 679–685.

Jordan, J. R. (2011). The principles of grief counseling with adult survivors. In J. R. Jordan & J. L. McIntosh (Eds.), *Grief after suicide* (pp. 179–223). New York: Routledge.

Kaslow, N. J., & Gilman, A. S. (2004). Recommendations for family interventions following a suicide. *Professional Psychology: Research and Practice, 35,* 240–247.

Kaslow, N. J., Samples, T. C., Rhodes, M., & Gantt, S. (2011). A family-oriented and culturally sensitive postvention approach with suicide survivors. In J. R. Jordan & J. L. McIntosh (Eds.), *Grief after suicide* (pp. 301–323). New York: Routledge.

Kim, C. D., Seguin, M., Therrien, N., Riopel, G., Chawky, N., Lesage, A. D., & Turecki, G. (2005). Familial aggregation of suicidal behavior: A family study of male suicide completers from the general population. *American Journal of Psychiatry, 162,* 1017–1019.

Kissane, D. W., & Lichtenthal, W. G. (2008). Family focused grief therapy: From palliative care into bereavement. In M. S. Stroebe, R. O. Hansson, H. Schut, & W. Stroebe (Eds.), *Handbook of bereavement research and practice: Advances in theory and intervention* (pp. 485–510). Washington, DC: American Psychological Association.

Klass, D. (1999). *The spiritual lives of bereaved parents.* Philadelphia, PA: Brunner/Mazel.

Klass, D. (2006). Continuing conversation about continuing bonds. *Death Studies, 30,* 843–858.

Levine, P. A. (1997). *Waking the tiger healing trauma – The innate capacity to transform overwhelming experiences.* Berkeley, CA: North Atlantic Books.

Linn-Gust, M. (2001). *Do they have bad days in heaven? Surviving the suicide loss of a sibling.* Albuquerque, NM: Chellehead Works.

Linn-Gust, M. (2010). *Rocky roads: The journeys of families through suicide grief.* Albuquerque, NM: Chellehead Works.

Lohan, J. A., & Murphy, S. A. (2002). Family functioning and family typology after an adolescent or young adult's sudden violent death. *Journal of Family Nursing, 8,* 32–49.

MacKinnon, L. (1988). Openings: Using questions therapeutically. *Dulwich Centre Newsletter,* Winter, 15–18.

McMenamy, J. M., Jordan J. R., & Mitchell A. M. (2008). What do suicide survivors tell us they need? Results of a pilot study. *Suicide and Life-Threatening Behavior, 38,* 375–389.

Mitchell, A. M., Kim, M., Prigerson, H. G., & Mortimer, M. K. (2005). Complicated grief and suicidal ideation in adult survivors of suicide. *Suicide and Life-Threatening Behavior, 35,* 498–506.

Moules, N. J., Simonson, K., Prins, M., Angus, P., & Bell, J. M. (2004). Making room for grief: Walking backwards and living forward. *Nursing Inquiry, 11,* 99–107.

Murphy, S. A. (1996). Parent bereavement stress and preventive intervention following the violent deaths of adolescent or young adult children. *Death Studies, 20,* 441–452.

Nadeau, J. W. (1998). *Families making sense of death.* Thousand Oaks, CA: Sage.

Neimeyer R. A. (2000). Searching for the meaning of meaning: Grief therapy and the process of reconstruction. *Death Studies, 24,* 541–558.

Neimeyer, R. A., Baldwin, S. A., & Gillies, J. (2006). Continuing bonds and reconstructing meaning: Mitigating complications in bereavement. *Death Studies, 30,* 715–738.

Neimeyer, R. A., Botello, L., Herrero, O., Pacheco, M., Figueras, S., & Werner-Wilder, L. A. (2002). The meaning of your absence: Traumatic loss and narrative reconstruction. In J. Kauffman (Ed.), *Loss of the assumptive world: A theory of traumatic loss* (pp. 31–47). New York: Brunner-Routledge.

Neimeyer, R. A., & Sands, D. C. (2011). Meaning reconstruction and bereavement: From principles to practice. In R. A. Neimeyer, D. L. Harris, H. R. Winokuer, & G. F. Thornton (Eds.), *Grief and bereavement in contemporary society: Bridging research and practice* (pp. 9–22). New York: Routledge.

O'Brien, C., & Bruggen, P. (1985). Our personal and professional lives: Learning positive connotation and circular questioning, *Family Process, 24,* 311–322.

Ogden, P., Minton, K., & Pain, C. (2006). *Trauma and the body: A sensorimotor approach to psychotherapy.* New York: W. W. Norton.

Parrish, M., & Tunkle, J. (2005). Clinical challenges following an adolescent's death by suicide: Bereavement issues faced by family, friends, schools, and clinicians. *Clinical Social Work Journal, 33,* 81–102.

Provini, C., Everett, J., & Pfeffer, C. (2000). Adults mourning suicide: Self-reported concerns about bereavement, needs for assistance, and help-seeking behavior. *Death Studies, 24,* 1–19.

Range, L. (1998). When a loss is due to suicide: Unique aspects of bereavement. In J. H. Harvey (Ed.), *Perspectives of loss: A sourcebook* (pp. 213–220). Philadelphia, PA: Brunner/Mazel.

Rappaport, N. (2009). *In her wake: A child psychiatrist explores the mystery of her mother's suicide.* Basic Books: New York.

Riches, G., & Dawson, P. (2000). *An intimate loneliness: Supporting bereaved parents and siblings.* Buckingham, UK: Open University Press.

Runeson, B., & Asberg, M. (2003). Family history of suicide among suicide victims. *American Journal of Psychiatry, 160,* 1525–1526.

Rynearson, E. K. (2001). *Retelling violent death.* Philadelphia, PA: Brunner-Routledge.

Sandler, I. N., Wolchik, S. A., Ayers, T. S., Tein, J. Y., Coxe, S., & Chow, W. (2008). Linking theory and intervention to promote resilience in parentally bereaved. In M. S. Stroebe, R. O. Hansson, H. Schut, & W. Stroebe (Eds.), *Handbook of bereavement research and practice: Advances in theory and intervention* (pp. 531–550). Washington, DC: American Psychological Association.

Sands, D., & Tennant, M. (2010). Transformative learning in the context of suicide bereavement. *Adult Education Quarterly, 60,* 99–121.

Sands, D. C. (2008). *A study of suicide grief: Meaning making and the griever's relational world.* Unpublished doctoral thesis, University of Technology, Sydney, Australia. Retrieved from http://utescholarship.lib.uts.edu.au/iresearch/scholarship-works/handle2100/777

Sands, D. C. (2009). A tripartite model of suicide grief: Meaning-making and the relationship with the deceased. *Grief Matters: The Australian Journal of Grief and Bereavement, 12,* 10–17.

Sands, D. C. (2010). *Red chocolate elephants: For children bereaved by suicide.* Sydney, Australia: Karridale.

Sands, D. C. (2012). The body of trust. In R. A. Neimeyer (Ed.), *Grief therapy: Creative strategies for counseling the bereaved.* New York: Routledge.

Sands, D. C. (2013). Restoring the heartbeat of hope following suicide. In B. Thompson & R. A. Neimeyer (Eds.), *Grief and the expressive arts: Practices for creating meaning.* New York: Routledge.

Sands, D. C., Jordan, J. R., & Neimeyer, R. A. (2011). The meanings of suicide: A narrative approach to healing. In J. R. Jordan & J. L. McIntosh (Eds.), *Grief after suicide* (pp. 249–282). New York: Routledge.

Shneidman, E. S. (2001). Introduction. In E. S. Shneidman (Ed.), *Comprehending suicide: Landmarks in 20th-century suicidology* (pp. 3–9). Washington, DC: American Psychological Association.

Totton, N. (2003). *Body psychotherapy: An introduction.* Philadelphia, PA: Open University Press.

Walsh, F., & McGoldrick, M. (1995). Loss and the family: A systematic perspective. In F. Walsh & M. McGoldrick (Eds.), *Living beyond loss: Death in the family* (pp. 1–29). New York: W. W. Norton.

Walter, T. (1996). A new model of grief: Bereavement and biography. *Mortality, 1,* 7–25.

Wertheimer, A. (1991). *A special scar: The experiences of people bereaved by suicide.* London: Routledge.

Wingard, B. (2001). Grief: Remember, reflect, reveal. In B. Wingard & J. Lester (Eds.), *Telling our stories in ways that make us stronger* (pp. 45–55). Adelaide, South Australia: Dulwich Centre Publications.

12 Family Therapy for the Unresolved Grief of Ambiguous Loss

Pauline Boss and Carla M. Dahl

Families often experience an irresolvable type of loss called "ambiguous loss." Through no fault of their own, their grief process is frozen and remains unresolved, sometimes for a lifetime. This unique kind of loss was first described by Boss through research with families of persons missing physically or psychologically, and subsequently introduced to family therapists (Boss, 1999, 2006; Boss & Greenberg, 1984) and the general public (Boss, 2011). Here we review the concepts of ambiguous loss for family therapists, identify its effects on family systems, and present guidelines for therapy and intervention for more global application. Finally, we focus on the person of the therapist, because in order to help families with ambiguous loss, we as therapists must first increase our own tolerance for ambiguity.

The Nature of Ambiguous Loss

Ambiguous loss is a loss that remains unclear to the family. There is no official verification of the loss, no ritual of support, and thus no possibility of resolution or closure. In the first of the two types of ambiguous loss, a family member is lost *physically* but kept psychologically present: there is no clarity about the lost person's whereabouts or status as dead or alive. For example, close to 3,000 individuals perished, many with no body ever recovered, due to the Sept. 11, 2001 terrorist attacks on the U.S. Today, around the world, family members continue to disappear from terrorist attacks as well as from circumstances such as war and being lost at sea. In the second type of ambiguous loss, a family member is lost *psychologically—absent in mind*—but present physically. Examples are family members with Alzheimer's disease or other dementias, coma, traumatic brain injury, autism, depression or other chronic mental illnesses, and addiction (see Figure 12.1).

Both types of ambiguous loss can occur simultaneously in one family—for example, a woman struggles at the same time with a husband lost at sea and a mother lost to dementia (Boss & Carnes, 2012). In this chapter, we use examples of both kinds of ambiguous loss to illustrate the unrelenting grief that results for families.

Linking Ambiguous Loss to Unresolved Grief

Whether an ambiguous loss is physical or psychological, families are not offered rituals of support that ordinarily comfort the bereaved. They suffer in isolation without the

Ambiguous Loss

Two Types

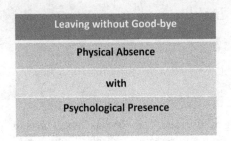

Leaving without Good-bye	Good-bye without Leaving
Physical Absence	Physical Presence
with	with
Psychological Presence	Psychological Absence

Family member is physically lost but kept psychologically present, as there is no body to bury or assurance of finality.

Family member is physically here but mind and memory are lost.

Examples
Missing from war, terrorism
Disappeared, kidnapped
Vanished from man-made or natural disaster
Lost at sea
More common: moved due to immigration, divorce, or adoption

Examples
Can occur in certain cases of:
Alzheimer's disease and other dementias
Depression
Autism
Coma
Addictions
More common: unresolved grief, homesickness

Figure 12.1 Two types of ambiguous loss.

balm of community support. Those who were attached to the lost person are on their own in a kind of limbo, where their grief is blocked because, as "people may" say, "Nobody died." Their grief remains unresolved because the loss experience continues indefinitely.

Why Family Therapy?

Because ambiguous loss is a relational loss, family therapy is the treatment of choice. Although there may be individual symptoms, it is not an individual disorder. The problem is systemic; everyone in the family is affected in some way. Although the systemic view may also be valid when there is a death in the family, families experiencing ambiguous loss face more confusion amongst themselves about the loss as well as misunderstanding and isolation from society. Individual therapy may certainly be helpful with people suffering ambiguous loss, but the building of resilience for the long haul is most easily achieved with family- or community-based therapies and interventions. This is because those suffering from ambiguous loss need relational therapy or interventions with family, peers, or friends—in other words, someone whom they love or can connect with between sessions so they do not feel alone. Therapy ideally is an experience of deepened connection within the family and social systems because those relationships continue after therapy ends. Our task then, as family therapists, is to set the stage for family members to strengthen new and lasting human connections. For unlike spouses, siblings, other relatives, friends, and neighbors, a therapist's role in the family is temporary.

A ripple effect of unresolved loss keeps the family system and the individuals in it immobilized. The family as a team does not know what to do or what decisions to make. They cannot shift gears permanently because the loss may not be permanent; a missing person may recover or return. Family members may independently cope by prematurely extruding the missing person, considering them dead; or at the other extreme, they may even deny that anything is wrong. Neither of these absolutes is functional. The resiliency to live with this kind of loss lies in the middle ground. The goal is to get the system on track again despite ongoing ambiguity.

In the absence of clear, factual information, it is natural that individual perceptions vary. But for the family to function, there must be both some tolerance for difference and some congruence in how they see themselves as a team moving forward despite uncertainty. They may never agree on what happened to their loved one, but they need to agree on how to move forward—and not let the mystery divide their family.

After labeling the loss, our first task as family therapists is to prevent family rifts or cutoffs. As early as possible, we tell the family (or a group of families): "What you are experiencing is ambiguous loss—one of the most difficult kinds of loss because of its lack of information. Because of this, family members may disagree on what is happening. It is all right for you to see the situation differently right now." We repeat this statement many times during a session because it gives families permission to disagree. Paradoxically, this calms the family.

As we normalize their differing perceptions about how to see their loss and what to do, we lower the family's conflict and increase tolerance for one another's views. By preventing family schisms early on, we strengthen the family's natural resilience—a necessity, as it is likely that their loss will remain ambiguous for a long time, if not a lifetime.

The Psychological Family

Sometimes gathering one's biological family for therapy is not possible, so for us, the definition of family is not limited to legal or biological parameters (Boss, 1992, 1999, 2006; Dahl & Boss, 2005). Because of high mobility resulting from factors such as employment, migration, immigration, or rifts, people need a "psychological family"—a group of like-minded people who share a history and future together. They often share a similar experience. If, for example, we are treating the parents of a child who is in a coma, or a child who has been kidnapped, we must early on determine "Who is family?" in order to bring in their support system. It may include extended relatives, but often it includes friends, neighbors, fellow workers or worshipers, and even pets. Or it may be symbolic, like the presence of a deity or an ancestor. When people call for therapy, we ask them to bring along whomever they consider "family." It is not practical for us to decide *for* them who that should be.

The Effects of Ambiguous Loss on Family Systems

When a loved one is ambiguously lost, systemically, the ambiguity and lack of information immobilize the family by blocking both coping and grief processes. Decisions are delayed, grief is frozen, conflict erupts, and relationships are in a holding pattern. The family's traditional celebrations and rituals may be canceled because members feel guilty about enjoying themselves without the missing person or feel disinterested in having fun. Conflict might increase across the generations as members disagree on whether the lost person is irretrievably lost. In the confusion, effective communication diminishes and interactions triangulate as people take sides.

Although the effects are systemic, individual symptoms may also develop. Depression, anxiety, ambivalence, guilt, substance abuse, suicidal ideation, lack of self-care, and stress-related illnesses are common with ambiguous loss. However, what diagnostic manuals label as pathology can be normal reactions to an abnormal type of loss. When psychological meaning is blocked, behavioral adaptations are often maladaptive. Mostly, with ambiguous loss, pervasive sadness ensues.

To help identify the magnitude of loss, we ask family members to tell us, in the presence of others, about their perceptions of what they have lost. Typically, in addition to the person who is missing, they list points such as the following:

- Loss of my loved one as he or she was
- Loss of certainty about my future and his or hers
- Loss of control over my life and my loved one's
- Loss of my loved one's dream and mine
- Loss of hope for a good future for my family
- Loss of my identity. Am I still a wife if my husband is missing? Am I still a son or daughter if I am "parenting" my mother or father who has dementia?

Once we identify such invisible losses and relational uncertainties, we begin to understand the complexity of its impact.

Although sadness is inevitable after loss of a loved one, depression is not. Rather than using the word "depression" inappropriately, some professionals select more benign diagnoses like "adjustment disorder" or "relational problem." Above all, we should not pathologize family members, as this situation is not their fault. If a diagnosis of clinical depression must be given, this should be explained to the patient. Not all people feel negatively about this diagnosis, but many have resented being labeled as "sick." It makes them feel weak and thus erodes their confidence.

Across the generations, ambiguous loss leaves its mark of profound sadness. Many who are bereaved still carry the legacy of ambiguous loss from genocide due to political terror, the Holocaust, slavery, tsunamis, earthquakes, airplane explosions, sunken ships, and of course, wars in which many soldiers are never found. Diane Campbell, the wife of a pilot who had gone missing in 1969 during the Vietnam War, wrote: "I grieved the heck out of everything, except, of course, Clyde's death. Without a credible determination to provide the certainty that Clyde was really dead, it seemed a betrayal to grieve him, as though by doing so, I would have condemned him myself" (D. Campbell, personal communication, September 26, 2012).

And then after 43 years, she received evidence of his death. She then wrote:

> Once the certainty was in place, grieving his death came quickly, but so much gentler and kinder . . . no, the word is mercy . . . more mercifully, than what I experienced over the years. So for me, I think rather than lacking the ability to grieve, it was the freedom to grieve that I lacked until I was no longer a captive of ambiguous circumstance. Some people never get certainty at all, and I have such a heart for them.
>
> What I found most curious was the process from lingering doubts, when I learned there was no viable DNA, to realization and comfort with the knowledge that the remains are my husband's, and finally, at the burial, the beginning of "normal" grieving for the loss of this man who was the love of my life. There has been grieving all these 43 years, but I believe it to be grief over the split of the self that occurs with ambiguous loss, at least in these circumstances for me. Part of me kept vigil in the past, waiting for him to come home, or to know with certainty that he would not, so I could know how best to live, because that is the expectation. We expect that there is nothing between dead and alive, that one is or is not alive. (D. Campbell, personal communication, September 26, 2012)

Like Diane, those who suffer ambiguous loss can still manage to have good lives. They teach us that we as professionals must have more patience with this unique kind of loss. Ambiguous loss inherently complicates grief. Especially with physical ambiguous loss, when there is no body to bury, doubt becomes the constant. The anxiety may be lifelong or longer as descendants continue to struggle with the remnants of not knowing. This is why supportive grief therapy is insufficient.

What is needed instead of conventional grief therapy is therapy that will increase: (1) a family's freedom to grieve a loss that occurs before or without proof of death, and (2) the family's (and the therapist's) tolerance for being able to simply hold the ambiguity. Neither of these is easy to achieve in a culture that values solutions, yet we must strive toward these goals, for in any culture, ambiguous loss has painful consequences.

Paradoxical Thinking

For families living with ambiguous loss, holding two opposing ideas at the same time becomes a necessary tool for resiliency. Here are some examples of "both-and" thinking:

- My loved one is both here and gone.
- I can both stay attached and let go.
- Embracing the ambiguity—rather than fighting it—is both painful and enlivening.
- I am both suffering from loss and discovering new opportunities to move forward in life.

Once we provide families with a sample or two, they quickly identify their own. "Both-and" thinking thus becomes a central tool for the family and therapist throughout therapy.

Six Key Guidelines for Therapy with
Families Experiencing Ambiguous Loss

We begin by explaining why we present guidelines for treating ambiguous loss and not a manual of specific treatment strategies. First, families that experience ambiguous loss come from diverse cultures and belief systems, so that specific strategies would not be universally applicable. Second, we who work with ambiguous loss come from different disciplines with differing goals, so each of us needs to fit our intervention to our discipline and professional work, while also tailoring treatment to fit a family's culture, development stage, and type of loss. Thus, rather than prescribing set strategies, we offer guidelines that are readily adapted to each family. These guidelines were formulated on the basis of research, clinical experience, and field testing (for details, see Boss, 1999, 2004, 2006; Boss, Beaulieu, Wieling, Turner, & LaCruz, 2003). Therapists should not use the guidelines in a linear, cookbook order, but rather flexibly in a circular way that is informed by professional judgment and the family's need.

1. Finding Meaning

Although families may never make sense *of* the loss, resilience requires that they find meaning *in* the loss. Naming the problem is a part of this, as is talking with others who are experiencing ambiguous loss, accessing spiritual resources, practicing family rituals, and accepting the both-and realities of paradox. A particularly powerful set of questions that allows the family to begin to notice paradox is: What have you lost? What do you still have? What have you gained? Because isolation, secret keeping, martyrdom, and accusation hinder the discovery of new meaning, making new human connections becomes essential. Family- and community-based therapies are thus ideal for finding meaning after ambiguous loss (see Boss, 2006, chapter 4).

2. Tempering Mastery

In cultures that value mastery and control, families are more likely to demand closure by either denying the loss or prematurely considering the lost person as dead. Behind this second guideline is the need to moderate this desire for control and its accompanying absolute certainty. Perfectionism (believing one can and should do everything) and passivity (believing one can and should do nothing) are the extreme poles of mastery. Therapists must point out places of a family's past and present resiliency where family members live well despite ambiguity and uncertainty. It is helpful for people to know that someone in their family came to the realization that one cannot always control what happens, and in response, balances acceptance with mastery or control. While resilient people find ways to control much of their lives, they also know that things will not always go their way and that the world is not always a fair and safe place. Families gain strength from hearing their own stories of resiliency and knowing that bad things can happen even to good and hardworking people (see Boss, 2006, chapter 5).

Although mastery must be tempered in most cases, sometimes a family member's use of mastery must be increased, not lowered. In order to function despite a missing husband, for example, a wife may need more empowerment, not less, if she comes from a culture where women have had little power or agency (Robins, 2010, 2013).

3. Reconstructing Identity

As families redefine their support systems (including the "psychological families" described earlier), they will most likely find it necessary to renegotiate family roles and boundaries. Identifying and connecting with supportive family members will provide important assistance in developing a new sense of identity, both individually and in relationships. Determining "who is in" and "who does what" in the family provides stability in the changing dimensions of ambiguous loss. As with making meaning, isolation and disconnection hinder this important reconstructive task. So, too, does a belief that identity shifts are somehow abnormal, though in reality, human identity and experience are quite malleable over time even apart from ambiguous loss (see Boss, 2006, chapter 6).

4. Normalizing Ambivalence

Ambivalence is a natural outcome of not knowing if a loved one is here or gone. The more that families can be open regarding any mixed emotions about the loss and the ambiguously lost person, the more they can helpfully integrate the experience into their family story. With the ambiguous loss of deep dementia, for example, family members may wish that the experience were over. Then they feel guilty and wish their loved one to live on. Because persons not acquainted or comfortable with loss might find it unsettling to hear this ambivalence, it might be most productively attended to with family professionals. Bowlby (1980) wrote that the loss of a loved person is one of the most intensely painful experiences a human can suffer. Few would disagree. But when he wrote about the complexities of ambivalence in bereavement and the stress that motivates letting go in order to lower this anxiety, he did not refer to losses that remain ambiguous. Ambiguous loss inherently increases ambivalence—but its cause is sociological, not psychiatric (see Boss, 2006, chapter 7).

5. Revising Attachment

Family members, such as adult children of a parent with dementia or parents of a child who ran away from home, report confused attachment, as they no longer know how to relate to the lost person. Are they connected or not? Parents say they no longer have the relationship they had emotionally, socially, and cognitively. Spouses say they no longer have the intimacy they once had. The attachment as they knew it is gone. What is left is confusion about the relationship, as they still experience some caring. One has to embrace the both-and paradox: a loved one is gone but still here.

Expecting or desiring "closure" is not as useful as maintaining an ongoing internal relationship with the ambiguously lost person, while also investing emotional energy in new ventures and relationships. We discourage disconnection: there is a fear of forgetting (or even worse, betraying) the lost one by living fully in his or her absence. This fear can end up inhibiting the reinvestment of emotional energy into new relationships (see Boss, 2006, chapter 8).

6. Discovering Hope

Despite the ongoing nature of ambiguous loss, it is possible—and important—that the bereaved find ways to discover and sustain hope. Some families learn that humor—including the ability to laugh at what is absurd—helps them deal with the meaninglessness of ambiguous loss. Some family members discover that working for justice embodies hope, particularly when working in an area related to the loss. Others find that renewing and deepening spiritual resources enable them to tolerate the ambiguity with less discomfort and even to celebrate paradox. Understanding that hope does not end suffering but enables them to move forward despite the pain of unresolved grief becomes a valuable family resource. It helps them to develop confidence that good can come from something so painfully unknown.

These six guidelines, reviewed briefly here, embody the therapeutic core needed to restore meaning and hope despite ambiguous loss (see Boss, 2006, for more details). With these guidelines, we work systemically to challenge the idea that unresolved grief is always pathological. People see that if others are feeling as they do, their still raw and unresolved grief cannot be that abnormal. For this reason, traditional grief therapies are not effective with ambiguous loss. Instead, we recommend the previously discussed guidelines to foster dialectical thinking and the idea that sometimes, through no deficit of one's own, grief will remain unresolved.

Therapist Techniques

Because families as well as the nature of ambiguous losses differ, we begin by asking questions to learn more about the family's perceptions about its loss, its culture, and its processes of interaction. Whereas traditional grief therapies focus on grief, we focus on the *inability to grieve*. Table 12.1 lists a series of questions that prove helpful during assessment of these families.

Table 12.1 Questions to Ask during Family Therapy for Ambiguous Loss

---

Questions about Family Perceptions

1. What does this situation mean to you? How do you see this loss?
2. Is there disagreement in the family about the lost person?
3. What do you still retain of this person?
4. What have you lost as a result of this situation (e.g., loss of family's dreams and plans, loss of trust in the world as fair and just, and so on)?

Questions about Family Roles

1. What family roles and tasks have you lost as a result of the loss?
2. What family roles and tasks have you gained?
3. How do you manage these changes? What would help?
4. How do you see your roles in the family now?
5. How do you feel about this change? What would help?

Questions about Family Rules

1. What were your family rules about loss and grief and ambiguity, and have they changed now?
2. Do family rules about race, religion, gender, class, and age create more stress for you as you try to cope with your loss?
3. Who is allowed to do what in your family? Has this changed?
4. Is there a "family team" approach, or does the work (or blame) fall to one person?

(Continued)

Table 12.1 (Continued)

Questions about Family Rituals

1. What family rituals did you celebrate before your ambiguous loss?
2. Now?
3. How might you reshape your family rituals and celebrations to fit the circumstances now? (Note: This is a good theme to explore early in family therapy for ambiguous loss.)

Questions about Community Support

1. Whom do you see as your community support system now?
2. Have new people become "like family" to you?
3. Does your community offer spiritual, recreational, respite, and informational support?

In addition to therapists asking key questions to explore the family's response to ambiguous loss, several other leading principles will help therapists to structure their work with these families. A practical checklist of these principles is presented in Table 12.2.

Table 12.2 Practical Principles and Tips for Therapists Undertaking Family Therapy with Families That Have Experienced Ambiguous Loss

---

1. Gather the family as they define themselves.
2. Label the family's problem as ambiguous loss, and clarify that the culprit is the ambiguity, not any one family member.
3. Normalize differing perceptions of what has occurred and what to do. Tell families that it is all right for them to see the situation differently now; repeat often.
4. Expect conflict, and assume the existence of more than one narrative within the family about the loss. It is natural for family members to interpret the situation differently. Normalize differences early and often to minimize family rifts and alienation and to increase their patience and respect for one another.
5. Focus on meaning, not closure. Eventually making some sense of a loss despite ambiguity is a key factor for resilience and hope.
6. Focus on strengthening the family's natural adaptability. Rather than cure or closure, the goal with ambiguous loss becomes resilience over the long haul, which means tolerance for ambiguity. This is not easy in a culture that values mastery, yet it is surprisingly possible (see Boss, 2006, 2011, 2012).
7. Acknowledge the paradoxes inherent in ambiguous loss, and practice "both-and" thinking with the family.
8. Challenge the family's expectation about closure and timelines for grief after loss. With ambiguous loss, there is no closure and no timeline; it may go on forever. The goal is to live with the ambiguity.
9. Make explicit the "family gamble" to keep hoping or give up, and encourage family conversations about the ambivalence inherent in even trying to construct an ending to their story.
10. Help the family "hold" the ambiguity rather than arbitrarily constructing a clear ending to their ambiguous loss story.
11. As therapists, we must attend to our own tolerance for ambiguity. This may be the greatest challenge.

Although various theories of family therapy abound, our work with ambiguous loss rests primarily on social construction (Berger & Luckmann, 1966; Gergen, 2001). From this perspective, families heal by telling their story of traumatic loss and then reconstructing that story to allow better functioning and moving forward. In other words, the collective reconstruction of their story encourages change. Although "healing through story" is considered postmodernism, the narrative methodology is rooted in ancient tribal storytelling to treat suffering. Narrative therapy is especially effective with families and communities experiencing ongoing ambiguous loss because the emphasis is on reconstructing meaning and hope, not on finding a solution.

The Challenge: Developing Our Own Tolerance for Ambiguity and Unresolved Loss

Using a systemic approach means that we, as clinicians, are also part of the family's system, albeit temporarily. Joining that system suggests that as we help families tolerate their ambiguity, we must increase our own tolerance for it. Yet we are trained to heal, and many of us live and work in mastery-oriented settings. Accordingly, it is not easy to make our own peace with ambiguous loss. Therein lies our challenge: Can we become more mindful of our own unresolved losses? Can we find peace with those losses without demanding artificial "closure"? The process of accompanying families on this painful journey is paralleled by "being with" ourselves. Again the goal is not to find answers, but rather, to find meaning in even unanswered questions.

Loss, whether clear or ambiguous, is a universal human experience. We regularly find ourselves invited into the bereavement experiences of clients at the same time we are experiencing the immediacy and pain of our own losses.

This parallel process is inevitable in clinical work and manifests itself in particular ways for therapists. For example, one therapist who had multiple miscarriages and stillbirths, despite apparently healthy pregnancies, experienced a fresh wave of grief when a couple with whom she had been working for several months decided to discontinue fertility treatments and pursue adoption. The shift they described in their approach to gaining their wanted child triggered a revision of the therapist's own feelings toward her lost children.

As a family struggles to make meaning of their loss, so we as therapists are challenged to construct our own meaning and reaffirm the sources of that meaning making: the sacred, the scientific, self-efficacy, or some combination thereof. As a client learns to temper his or her need for mastery and control, we must do the same (which can be countercultural in a profession that tempts its practitioners to fix and manage). Continually revising one's identity in response to one's own losses requires time and energy that are often in short supply for helping professionals.

Similarly, therapists must manage any ambivalence they may feel toward these families. Frustration, impatience, and irritation with families are signals to family therapists—not of our inadequacy as helping professionals, but of our human need to attend to self-care and our own relational health. Accordingly we revise our need for absolute clarity in our relationships, right along with our clients.

Perhaps especially for grief therapists, developing and sustaining hope is a challenge within the parallel process of this work. One social worker whose wife had suffered a traumatic brain injury while serving in the military in Iraq found it increasingly difficult to maintain a sense of purpose and optimism as he worked with refugee families. Pursuing his own therapy and renewing a relationship with a trustworthy group of peers provided him with opportunities to acknowledge and process his ambiguous loss and develop strategies for self-care and self-compassion. He learned he could live with the paradox and make peace with the inevitable unresolved grief. As with this social worker, our personal understanding of ambiguous loss increases our professional effectiveness. We can become more fully present to the pain and despair of families with whom we journey.

In addition to personal experience with loss, how can we as clinicians increase our capacity for holding paradox and tolerating ambiguity and resist our own temptations to mastery? Some of us find that simply paying attention to the complex realities of parenting or partnering enlarges that capacity—particularly the reality that so much in those relationships is beyond our control. Others intentionally try having less control by engaging in activities that demand both receptivity and effort to embrace ambiguity: fishing, sailing, white-water rafting, hiking without a map, knitting without a pattern, or improvising in music or theater. We learned from Carl Whitaker's grandchildren that when he was still able, he would, to their delight, ask them to join him in the car to "go and get lost" (personal communication, Spring 1995). Such activities without agenda could be of great benefit in allowing ourselves to surrender to serendipity and temper our need for control. Some of us may need to start this process by scheduling time for spontaneity—an apparent oxymoron but helpful in containing the anxiety we may feel when we have not planned every moment.

Conclusion

If we as professionals can temper our need for certainty, if we can acknowledge our own ambiguous losses, then we can help families live well despite this unique kind of loss and grief. If we see it personally, we will more likely see it professionally. Compassionate, mindful self-reflection is essential.

The parallel process of working with families experiencing ambiguous loss has changed us. We, too, walk with the tensions of unresolved loss and grief, coexisting with daily joys and passions. Our personal and professional lives remind us constantly that a family member's absence or presence is rarely, if ever, absolute. We can—and do—live with relational imperfection.

References

Berger, P. L., & Luckmann, T. (1966). *The social construction of reality: A treatise in the sociology of knowledge* (1st ed.). Garden City, NY: Doubleday.

Boss, P. (1992). Primacy of perception in family stress theory and measurement. *Journal of Family Psychology, 6,* 113–119.

Boss, P. (1999). *Ambiguous loss: Learning to live with unresolved grief.* Cambridge, MA: Harvard University Press.

Boss, P. (2004). Ambiguous loss research, theory, and practice: Reflections after 9/11. *Journal of Marriage & Family, 66*(3), 551–566.

Boss, P. (2006). *Loss, trauma, and resilience: Therapeutic work with ambiguous loss.* New York: W. W. Norton.

Boss, P. (2011). *Loving someone who has dementia: How to find hope while coping with stress and grief.* San Francisco, CA: Jossey-Bass.

Boss, P. (2012). Resilience as tolerance for ambiguity. In D. S. Becvar (Ed.), *Handbook of family resilience* (pp. 285–297). New York: Springer.

Boss, P., Beaulieu, L., Wieling, E., Turner, W., & LaCruz, S. (2003). Healing loss, ambiguity, and trauma: A community-based intervention with families of union workers missing after the 9/11 attack in New York City. *Journal of Marital & Family Therapy, 29*(4), 455–467.

Boss, P., & Carnes, D. (2012). The myth of closure. *Family Process, 51,* 456–469.

Boss, P., & Greenberg, J. (1984). Family boundary ambiguity: A new variable in family stress theory. *Family Process, 23*(4), 535–546.

Bowlby, J. (1980). *Loss: Sadness and depression: Vol. 3. Attachment and loss series.* New York: Basic Books.

Dahl, C., & Boss, P. (2005). The use of phenomenology for family therapy research: The search for meaning. In D. Sprenkle & F. Piercy (Eds.), *Research methods in family therapy* (2nd ed., pp. 63–84). New York: Guilford Press.

Gergen, K. (2001). *Social construction in context.* London: Sage.

Robins, S. (2010). Ambiguous loss in a non-Western context: Families of the disappeared in post-conflict Nepal. *Family Relations, 59,* 253–268.

Robins, S. (2013). *Families of the missing: A test for contemporary approaches to transitional justice.* New York/London: Routledge Glasshouse.

13 Perinatal Loss

Unforeseen Tragedy with Ongoing Grief Trajectories

Nicole Alston and Valerie R. Samuels

Children are not supposed to die . . .
Parents expect to see their children grow and mature.
—J. H. Arnold & P. B. Gemma (1994, pp. iv, 9)

With the loss of an infant, in one moment, parents must shift gears from preparing for a new birth to mourning a death. It is a devastating, life-changing event for expectant or new parents. This unanticipated tragedy transforms the joy and expectations associated with bringing a new life into existence into anger, shock, confusion, guilt, inadequacy, and distress (Horchler & Morris, 1997). Significant data from thousands of population-based studies around the world demonstrate the psychological morbidity associated with prenatal and perinatal loss. Women exhibit notably elevated levels of depression and anxiety in the weeks and months following the loss—and even after the subsequent birth of a healthy child (Blackmore et al., 2011).

Perinatal loss is common throughout the world (Kersting & Wagner, 2012) and is a public health issue that has gained momentum over the years. Despite the millions of perinatal deaths that occur globally each year, international leadership, visibility, and resources are still lacking (Frøen et al., 2011). The infant mortality rate is formally defined as the number of resident newborns in a specified geographic area dying under one year of age divided by the number of resident live births for the same geographic region, multiplied by 1,000 (MacDorman & Kirmeyer, 2009). In this chapter, we will examine the nature of these losses and then explore the impact of perinatal loss upon the family's grief, including some consideration of cross-cultural perspectives.

Types of Perinatal Loss

The lack of a universally adopted definition for perinatal loss leads to some ambiguity and inconsistency. Varied definitions consider infant weight, length, and gestational age. According to the World Health Organization (WHO), the perinatal period extends from the twentieth gestational week to the first month post-birth (DeBackere, Hill, & Kavanaugh, 2008). However, researchers studying perinatal loss differentiate "early"— which occurs during the first 12 weeks following conception—from "late," which is greater than 20 weeks' gestation (Scotchie & Fritz, 2006). Of all recorded pregnancies, an estimated 12 to 20 percent end in an early fetal loss (Scotchie & Fritz, 2006). Rates of late perinatal loss vary considerably across countries, with low socio-economic countries having much higher death rates. Fortunately, women who suffer perinatal loss typically have an 80 percent chance of becoming pregnant again within 18 months (DeBackere et al., 2008).

In discussing family grief associated with perinatal and infant death in this chapter, we will categorize these losses into three domains: (1) stillbirth and miscarriage, (2) neonatal death, and 3) sudden infant death syndrome (SIDS). Let us take each of these forms of loss in turn.

Stillbirth

Stillbirth occurs when an infant has been conceived and dies in the womb after the first 20 weeks of pregnancy, but before delivery. Physicians typically perform ultrasound examinations to hear the baby's heartbeat at various stages of pregnancy and during labor. Oftentimes, the stillborn's death is realized in utero, but before labor. In other instances, the death might occur while the mother is in labor. Mothers endure the same excruciating pain of delivering a live-born baby as having a stillborn—yet without the satisfaction of forgetting the pain and experiencing the elation connected with birthing a new life into the family. Stillbirth differs from miscarriage, which, as colloquially used, occurs before the twentieth week of pregnancy.

Neonatal Death

In neonatal death, an infant dies during the first 28 days of its life (Heron et al., 2009). Over 40 percent of all infant deaths in the world are attributed to neonatal death (Jehan et al., 2009). Although most of the causes are known, in some instances the cause is not clearly understood. Women carry greater risks for having a neonatal death if they (1) had a previous premature birth, (2) are pregnant with multiple babies, or (3) have uterine or cervical problems (Martin et al., 2009). Infants born very prematurely and those with multiple severe congenital abnormalities are also at risk of early demise.

SIDS

Sudden infant death is defined as the death of a healthy infant from the neonatal period through to age one. Many of the causes of SIDS deaths remain unexplained after several decades of investigations and, of course, routine autopsies. In 1994, a national "Back to Sleep" campaign was implemented as a joint effort between the First Candle Organization, the American Academy of Pediatrics, and the National Institute of Child Health and Human Development. This approach entails that infants be placed on their back (not prone, as on their stomach) to permit safe sleep, thus preventing an obstructed airway in infants less able to adequately move their head if an airway became blocked. SIDS rates have declined by more than 50 percent since the introduction of this "Safe to Sleep" practice.

We will examine each of these three causes of loss in turn, considering etiology, family impact, and principles of bereavement care in turn.

Stillbirths

Stillbirths are regarded as a "hidden loss" due to uncounted and varied data collection systems, and the lack of global priorities and policies (Stanton, Lawn, Rahman, Wilczynska-Ketende, & Hill, 2006). According to recent world estimates, at least 3.2 million infants are born dead each year (Lawn et al., 2009). The highest absolute number of stillborn babies occurs in South Asia, due to the large population there, while the incidence is highest in sub-Saharan Africa when cited as the rate per 1,000 births. Recent data also show large variation between high-income countries where stillbirths are below 5 per 1,000 births, compared to approximately 32 per 1,000 births in South Asia and sub-Saharan Africa (Lander, 2006). Approximately 98 percent of stillbirths occur in low- to middle-income countries (LMIC) (Stanton et al., 2006). Millions of deaths go unrecorded for social and religious reasons. Stillbirths are not recognized on the world's health agenda; they are not included in the categorized health crises such as the Global Burden of Disease or as part of the United Nations Millennium Development Goals (Frøen et al., 2011). There are approximately 4,000 stillbirths every year in the United Kingdom; 1 in every 200 births ends in a stillbirth (NHS Choices, 2013). Thus 11 babies are stillborn every day in the United Kingdom (Frøen et al., 2011). In the United States, fetal mortality affects 1 in every 160 pregnancies (MacDorman et al., 2009). In Australia, 6 babies are stillborn each day, which equates to more than 2,000 per year (Frøen et al., 2011).

What Causes Stillbirth?

Despite technological advances in medicine, in nearly half of all stillbirths, physicians fail to discover the direct cause of the baby's death, or, if they suspect a cause, they omit to communicate this clearly to the parents (Frøen et al., 2011). Not knowing what has caused the baby's death compounds the parents' anger, frustration, and grief.

To date, known obstetric causes for stillbirth include the following: (1) poor fetal growth in utero, where the infant receives inadequate nourishment through the placenta; (2) birth defects, which can involve chromosomal or genetic abnormalities; (3) placenta abruption, where hemorrhage behind the placenta separates it from the uterus, cutting off blood supply to the baby; (4) umbilical cord accidents, where knots or tears in the umbilical cord interfere with the requisite flow of blood, oxygen, and nutrients to the baby; and (5) maternal conditions like diabetes, hypertension, renal impairment, or preeclampsia, which in turn can interfere with the infant's nourishment (Bukowski et al., 2011). Although some of these, such as placental abruption, can occur suddenly and without warning, others can reflect some failure of obstetric monitoring and induced delivery, thus raising the potential for anger and blame in bereavement.

In 2006, the Eunice Kennedy Shriver National Institute of Child Health and Human Development funded a very large multi-center, prospective, population-based study of stillbirth in the United States, with the hope of addressing important scientific gaps (Bukowski et al., 2011). Across the globe, the *Lancet*'s international Stillbirth Steering Committee drafted *Stillbirths: The Vision for 2020* (Goldenberg et al., 2011). In this report, physicians and educators called for stillbirth inclusion as a recognized outcome in all relevant international health reports and initiatives. In addition, the committee asked countries to develop and implement plans to reduce the prevalence of stillbirths and to count stillbirths in their vital statistics and other health outcome surveillance systems. More importantly, the committee requested increased investment in stillbirth-related research (Goldenberg et al., 2011).

Impact on the Family

A stillbirth shatters the dreams and hopes of the mother and father as they await their child. The loss feels intense and deeply painful. Through several months, a relationship has grown from the initial moments of excitement at being pregnant, through the many changes that develop in the mother's body, the movements felt as the child grows, to the reverie of wonderment in which mothers typically engage as they think about their developing child. The family commonly selects names, buys clothing, and perhaps prepares a nursery. As antenatal care unfolds, the father may be drawn into attending classes and invited to hold his partner's stomach to feel the baby; he is steadily drawn into the expectant excitement about what this future will bring. This process of attachment develops during the pregnancy, deepening with every month that unfolds. This creates a safe parental unit into which the baby can be born and nurtured. These bonds reflect the relationship, which in turn may be shared with the broader family. The strength of attachment is typically greatest for the mother, then the father, and may be relatively weaker for others in the family, accounting for differential experiences of grief intensity in the family when the stillbirth occurs.

Bereavement care has matured today in midwifery practices that fully honor and celebrate the baby as a person. Optimally, the stillborn baby will be named, bathed and clothed, and held by available family members, with photographs taken to consolidate memories and empower review of this baby's image in the years that follow. The use of ritual is to be encouraged. In some traditions, christening may occur as a naming ceremony, and funerals may be considered an important recognition of this child within the family. Yet fundamentally, the differential rate of grief can make this bereavement difficult for families as the parents continue to mourn, while others are ready to move on. Unless addressed preventively, bereavement can become awkward for the family, harder to acknowledge by those less involved over time, and thus a cause of parental withdrawal to a silent and lonely space, where their pain continues without family support.

Much progress has occurred in supporting parents and their families bereaved by stillbirth in the Western world. A look back in time can nevertheless remind us how poorly these deaths were handled, and continue to be handled in less well-developed parts of the world.

Case Example

Debra, a 15-year-old African American, was just shy of eight months pregnant when she received the devastating news that her unborn son, Kyle, no longer had a heartbeat. Labor needed to be induced. Hours after her painful delivery, Debra sat in the recovery room, attempting to make sense of what had happened and writing Kyle's obituary. A nurse observed Debra and, laughing sarcastically, asked, "What on earth are you doing that for? Your baby is dead!"

Today, at age 61, Debra's unparalleled grief still lingers. The aftermath of Kyle's death was a time of vicious, unrelenting emotional struggle for her. Immediately following his death, Debra withdrew from family and friends. She lost interest in school and extracurricular activities. Fortunately, a forward-thinking aunt encouraged her to attend psychotherapy. A psychiatrist diagnosed her condition as depression and prescribed anti-depressants. But even with this management, memories of Kyle consumed her.

When Kyle's death occurred during the 1960s, many practices for perinatal bereavement had yet to be established. Debra was robbed of the opportunity to take a photograph of Kyle, dress or bathe him, or just hold him, all of which are typically afforded mothers in Western cultures today.

Debra, who has a vague memory of Kyle, acknowledges him in her own way: "I do fantasize he would've been a cocoa-color brown, a no-nonsense guy. Maybe he would've grown to be strong and protective of me. I'll never know." In the more than 45 years since Kyle's death, Debra has succumbed to the lure of drugs and even landed in jail.

This case illustration reveals how poorly both society and families in general have been prepared to handle the stillborn loss and the resultant burden of chronic grief that can follow. Sadly, in many parts of the world, this outcome is still commonplace. Stillborn grief can be disenfranchised; families can collude with the resultant neglect of compassion and support. We now know that the care model can be very different.

Information and Support

Many sources of support are available today to assist women and their families to better deal with a stillborn child. The following are reputable resources:

1. www.firstcandle.org (United States)
2. www.facesofloss.org (International)
3. www.stillbirthalliance.org (International)
4. www.stillbirthfoundation.org.au (Australia)

Neonatal Deaths

The first four weeks of an infant's life are the most critical, and the risk of death is higher than at any other time in the human life span (Lawn, Cousens, Zupan, & Lancet, 2005). Today, newborn deaths account for 41 percent of all child deaths before the age of five accounting for nearly 8 million each year (Oestergaard et al., 2011). Physicians and educators acknowledge that a large proportion of children who die during the neonatal period do so from preventable or treatable diseases (Oestergaard et al., 2011). To address this morbid crisis, world leaders created the Millennium Development Goal 4 (MDG 4) in 2000—with the goal of reducing the childhood mortality rate by two-thirds. In 2011, the WHO, Save the Children, and the London School of Hygiene and Tropical Medicine completed the most comprehensive study on neonatal deaths spanning the past 20 years, with data provided from all 193 WHO member states (Oestergaard et al., 2011). Although the results showed some improvement, much more needs to be accomplished to achieve the MDG 4 goal.

For several years, research and aid earmarked to address the reduction of infant mortality were targeted toward high-income countries (HIC), even though the magnitude of the problem affects the LMIC. Countries are classified by their income level as assessed by the World Bank List of Economics. According to the 2011 WHO study, almost 98 percent of neonatal deaths occurred in LMIC, with 31 million in Southeast Asia, 21 million in Africa, and 1 million in HIC (Oestergaard et al., 2011).

Moreover, in 2009, 3.3 million babies died during the neonatal period, compared to 4.6 million in 1990. More than half of the deaths in 2009 occurred in five countries: India, Nigeria, Pakistan, China, and the Democratic Republic of Congo. Millions of children's lives could have been saved with simple hygiene advice and breast-feeding guidance (Oestergaard et al., 2011).

Neonatal Deaths: Known Causes

Experts agree that three main causes account for 75 percent of neonatal deaths in the world: preterm delivery (29 percent), asphyxia (23 percent), and severe infections, such as sepsis and pneumonia (25 percent) (percentages do not sum as multiple etiologies occur) (Oestergaard et al., 2011). To elaborate further, key causes include the following:

1. Premature birth: delivery of an infant before 37 weeks of pregnancy
2. Respiratory distress syndrome: infant breathing problems during or after delivery (asphyxia)
3. Intraventricular hemorrhage: bleeding in the brain
4. Necrotizing enterocolitis: intestinal problems; serious inflammation of the bowel
5. Infections: premature infants have immature immune systems and readily develop infections like pneumonia, sepsis, and meningitis

Socioeconomically Deprived Countries: A Century Behind

At a dismal reduction of 1 percent per year, Africa has seen the slowest progress of any region in the world. Among the 15 countries with more than 39 neonatal deaths per 1,000 live births, 12 were from the WHO African Region (Angola, Burundi, Chad, Central African Republic, Democratic Republic of the Congo, Equatorial Guinea, Guinea, Guinea-Bissau, Mali, Mauritania, Mozambique, and Sierra Leone) plus Afghanistan, Pakistan, and Somalia. Based on the current rate of progress, Africa would need more than 150 years to catch up with U.S. or UK newborn survival levels (Oestergaard et al., 2011).

Case Example

Multiple and high exposure of the spinal cord signaled a grave abnormality for a newly delivered baby. This so-called "spina bifida" had not declared itself during the pregnancy. The severity of his abnormalities with complete lower limb paralysis and the perceived absence of any prospect for control over bladder or bowel brought the verdict of "inoperable." The family's task was to provide love and care, even as they were told that infection was inescapable, meningitis inevitable, and death predictable. Two to three weeks were provisionally available to get to know this baby more, even as he was growing frailer.

Impact of Neonatal Death on the Family

Families may find cause for worry due to prematurity and may find themselves in a neonatal intensive care unit with all of its monitoring, incubation cribs, and lights— a setting that lends itself to uncertainty and anticipation of an unwelcome outcome. The family becomes involved in a journey, with the infant visible, prayed for, and much talked about as the neonatal period unfolds.

Mourning after neonatal loss is fundamentally related to the length and strength of attachment that develops to the infant. The capacity for different degrees of attachment is still very apparent, with consequential differential grief.

Multiple levels of loss alternate with phases of hope and later despair, which unfold throughout this journey. Resilient families rally with mutual support and consolation. However, families that are more readily stressed find that cumulative loss events become increasingly taxing, potentially with escalating conflict, relationship fracture, and mounting distress. Family meetings become essential for the care team and can provide vital support and assistance to these readily stressed families.

SIDS and Sudden Unexpected Infant Deaths (SUID)

Every year in the United States, more than 4,500 babies die suddenly and unexpectedly (SUID). Of these, more than 2,300 are diagnosed as SIDS. Most SIDS deaths occur when a baby is between two and four months old, and 90 percent of all SIDS deaths occur before six months of age (First Candle Organization, 2012).

SIDS/SUID Causes

In developed countries, SIDS is still the leading cause of death amongst babies one month to one year of age (Moon, Horne, & Hauck, 2007). African American and Native American babies are two to three times more likely to die of SIDS than Caucasian babies (First Candle Organization, 2012). In addition, 60 percent of SIDS victims are male.

Based on epidemiological studies, causes of SIDS include (1) prone and side positions for infant sleep, (2) smoke exposure, (3) soft bedding and sleep surfaces, (4) overheating, (5) inherited metabolic disorders, (6) genetic cardiac disorders, (7) accidental and intentional suffocation, and (8) some undetermined factors (Moon et al., 2007).

Case Example

In a family that included three daughters, the birth of a son brought special joy. The baby's prematurity and small size brought the girls curiosity and delight. His father was especially proud to have a son at last. The mother took delight in the joy this little man brought to all. Friendly competition was strong to take turns in helping to feed him, changing the diapers, and assisting with the daily bath. This new addition quickly became the central focus of the family.

One morning, a sudden scream erupted from his mother when he was found to not be moving. His body was cold. Death came unexpectedly and brutally, taking all joy from this family group. The doctor arrived but could not offer explanations. The baby's body was transferred to the local coroner's office, and a postmortem was needed to assess what had gone wrong. The words "sudden infant death syndrome" were introduced to this shocked family: a bereft mother, a pale and tearful father, and three young girls weeping as they confronted the tragic shroud of SIDS.

Not only is the sudden and unanticipated nature of SIDS a shocking life event for all involved, but it comes after a steadily deepening bond of attachment has been developing for the family. The unexplained cause of death evokes heart-searching efforts to understand; questioning and even blame may quickly develop. Parents, children, grandparents, aunts, and uncles from the clan get involved, and many need to make sense of what has occurred. Here we see the value of a family-centered approach to care provision. For all need to have their grief validated and supported; all need help to understand what SIDS is; all will join in a search as they grapple with the horror of what has occurred.

Coordination of the clinical team also brings its challenges here. The pediatrician often takes the lead. But involvement of the coroner, police, and related services may help yet confound the predicament. Not all clinicians have experience with this life event, and the community may be lost for words, finding comfort hard to offer. Indeed, many may avoid any expression of consolation. Isolation and social avoidance can bring a sense of stigma to the bereaved as they struggle with their profound loss. How can these parents restore a happy and secure childhood to their surviving children? Who can guide them in the months ahead?

Family Responses to Infant Death

Grief is a binding experience; it universality binds sufferers together. More is shared than is different.

—J. H. Arnold & P. B. Gemma (1991, p. 55)

Parental grief is a boundless emotion that may touch every aspect of the parent's being (Arnold & Gemma, 1991). Mourning is a complex and evolving human process that affects everyone on different levels. Perinatal loss produces a unique kind of mourning because the infant is a large part of the parental identity (Callister, 2006). It is commonly said that death of a child is not part of the natural order, as parents are expected to predecease their children. Societal knowledge and confidence about how to assist those mourning perinatal grief have been limited in the past. Psychologists, social workers, physicians, and nurses have studied the impact of perinatal loss and related grief in order to educate and heal the bereaved parents and their families.

Capitulo (2005) and other educators have offered growing evidence suggesting that perinatal grief produces all of the expected physical, psychosocial, emotional, and cognitive expressions of grief. A recurring theme is the extent to which society recognizes the need to grieve from such loss. Kenneth Doka has described a community's failure to recognize the need to mourn in predictable situations, like the death of a pet or an abortion. Doka (1989) terms this "disenfranchised" grief. Here society denies the mourner's "right to grieve" by not truly acknowledging the loss. Stillborn, neonatal and SIDS deaths are often examples of disenfranchised grief.

Doka has helped us understand how such grief clashes with the expectations of others. He observed that instrumental grievers can fail to show a strong, affective response to loss; alternatively, intuitive grievers may seem to demonstrate excessive emotion. Then there are the ways in which community members might recognize culturally ingrained response styles, whether stoicism or wailing—they could easily be seen to violate the grieving norms of any given society.

Evolution of Family Grief Programs

The study of grief and loss has evolved across 40 years, whereas most research on perinatal loss has spanned the past 20 years (Callister, 2006). Theoretical models have matured over this period, from the traditional model of "letting go" to the contemporary emphasis on "holding on" to the emotional relationship with the child (Davies, 2004). Throughout this time, the primary focus has remained on the maternal perspectives of perinatal loss.

In addition, most survival-extending research programs have targeted diseases affecting children over one month old. Scientific progress involved reducing or preventing pneumonia, malaria, diarrhea, and other vaccine-preventable diseases. There have also been safe motherhood programs, which focused on the mother and not her infant (Tinker, ten Hoope-Bender, Azfar, Bustreo, & Bell, 2005). International organizations provided train-the-trainer models to assist local instructors in educating birth attendants from rural communities deemed vital by the WHO, such as various countries in Africa, as well as India and Pakistan. This type of program offered help through means including routine neonatal care, resuscitation, and breast-feeding (Carlo et al., 2010).

Along the way, various scales to measure grief have also been developed for this population: the Perinatal Bereavement Scale, Perinatal Grief Scale, and Perinatal Grief Intensity Scale (Hutti, DePacheco, & Smith, 1998). These have helped to deepen understanding of the trajectory of grief over time.

Grief Kits

Today, medical institutions and private organizations around the world provide patients with standardized grief kits after perinatal and infant deaths. These usually contain brochures, journals, and caregiver insight into comforting the bereaved. The United Kingdom has a standardized approach that encourages parents to hold their stillborn and to have photos and footprints taken. The majority of parents want to grieve their baby despite the emotional burden of doing so. Parents may want to remember what their child's face, hands, and feet looked like. Many parents agree that although creating memories may prolong or ignite grief, it would be outweighed by regret if they never again saw the baby.

Grief Gender Differences

Researchers have spoken of "incongruent grief" to highlight some gender differences in perinatal loss experienced by respective parents. Mothers may experience longer periods and higher levels of grief because women are generally more emotionally expressive and more likely to share their feelings via grief support groups than men (Capitulo, 2005). Fathers, on the other hand, may experience a deep sense of loneliness and isolation (Armstrong, 2001). Still, longitudinal studies show that both men and women have similar levels of grief (Swanson, 2007).

Perinatal loss may create an added strain on the couple's relationship if there is discordance in the grieving process. For others, the loss may bring the couple closer. Men may find it difficult to emotionally support their partner when they are dealing with their own grief response (Corbet-Owen, 2003).

The "Forgotten Mourners" in Families

Siblings and grandparents also experience grief after perinatal and SIDS losses. They have been termed the "forgotten mourners" (Thomas, 1998). The limited research in this area demonstrates that children's understanding of death varies according to their cognitive development and age. Siblings may feel left out, neglected, guilty, and sad. Immediate responses may include sadness, frustration, disappointment, and anger. Long-term effects may include residual sadness coupled with a sense of helplessness (Thomas, 1998).

Grandparents typically quickly join the excitement of an expected child, share the journey of pregnancy, and hold high hopes for the outcome. They not only grieve for the lost baby but also care deeply about the distress and disappointment of their own child. As the family members most typically involved in providing support, the grandparents can provide the setting in which grief is most naturally shared. However, when there has not been ready acceptance of their child's partner, the dynamics of the grandparents may conflict with the needs of the bereaved parents. Challenges then unfold in how the family as a whole approaches its grief.

Cultural Differences in Grief

Culture is a central determinant of how grief is expressed emotionally. Where a couple has blended cultural backgrounds, the potential for misunderstanding exists. Fortunately, most cultures highly value having children, and perinatal loss is thus universally painful and significant. Clinicians need to strive to understand culturally diverse traditions and rituals; comprehending the meaning of the loss to the parents and family is crucial. For example, in Jewish culture, bearing and rearing children are considered a great blessing. When a child is lost perinatally, its naming will occur at the burial, so that the baby is included in family records. Jewish families may select a name that will be associated with comfort.

The rate of perinatal and infant loss for African American women is twice the rate for Caucasian women (Shaefer, 2010). Urban and less educated African American women experience a higher rate of infant loss (Shaefer, 2010). Moreover, women in this population may find it awkward to articulate their feelings, with resultant potential for isolation and lack of support. Additional contemporaneous issues that African American mothers may face while grieving the loss of their baby include other personal losses, economic losses such as unemployment and lack of funds for a burial, and social losses such as fear of the loss of the relationship with the baby's father.

In Native American culture, including Navajo values, families can be quite stoic in bereavement and grieve privately. In contrast, many Asian families may express deeply felt emotion when grieving. Hsu and colleagues reported that Taiwanese women after the birth of a stillborn child felt a strong sense of loss of control and felt shattered, with all their dreams lost, wondering if something was wrong with them (Hsu, Tseng, & Kuo, 2002). Within the Hmong culture, after miscarriage, the belief that the soul of the baby cannot be reincarnated with the family impacts family members' sense of family lineage, which is so important to their ancestral traditions (Rice, 1999).

In Islamic culture, if death is thought to be imminent for a Muslim infant, the father may whisper in the child's ear the *Shadah*, "There is no God but Allah." In a study of Islamic women who lost a neonate, naming proved essential because of their belief that in paradise, this child and its mother would eventually be united. The deceased Muslim newborn should be bathed and wrapped in a seamless white sheet and buried within 24 hours (Lundqvist & Dykes, 2003).

For Iranian women, fetal loss is typically grieved in silence. Pregnancy is customarily not publicized or discussed with family. This relates to the fear that if one talks about unwelcome tragedy, more terrible things will follow (Shaefer, 2010). As in other Shiite Muslim countries, when a death occurs in Iran, burial ought to occur within 24 hours. After the third, seventh, and fortieth days, family and friends visit the graveside for a religious ritual. Women wear black during mourning; the later change of outfit becomes an indication that a woman has moved on from grief. The first anniversary of the death is the last time family and friends formally gather to acknowledge their loss (Shaefer, 2010).

For Mexican Americans, the family is customarily the major source of support in bereavement. Many Puerto Ricans believe that spiritual assistance is generally required for the journey to the next life. They therefore may invite faith healers and spiritualists to help. There are many variations among other Hispanic groups. Mormons, those espousing the beliefs of the Church of Jesus Christ of Latter-day Saints, believe that families are eternal and that parents will have the opportunity of reunion in the next life with children who die prematurely (Callister, 2003). Christianity also offers believers the hope of seeing their child in the afterlife. Therapists need great cultural sensitivity in responding to bereaved families, asking them about their customs, alongside therapists' personal efforts to use resources to enhance their knowledge and understanding of each ethnic group.

Scope of Programs

A range of services is needed to meet the needs of families suffering stillbirth, neonatal, and SIDS deaths. Community support groups may be difficult to organize for lack of sufficient numbers identifying these types of deaths, though hospitals specializing in obstetrics may be able to offer such periodic groups. In general, the use of family meetings to help the bereaved is underdeveloped among this population. Yet the needs of the couple and often their parents are clear. More could be done to offer family-centered models of support.

Program Improvements

Organizations that support the bereaved should carefully evaluate their programs to sensitively gauge whether they adequately address the needs of parents and families.

Health care providers and other stakeholders need to undergo specialized grief training in order to comfort grieving parents. It is important to understand the cultural nuances of a family's expectations and traditions for mourning. Some key principles include ensuring that the mother does not blame herself, that the family does not blame the mother, and that the paternal family does not expel the mother as inherently evil.

One new field of study involves understanding what it means to be a "companion" to a bereaved individual. Companioning has paved the way to educate key stakeholders in handling parents and family members who have experienced perinatal loss. Thus, Alan Wolfelt's (2009) work, *The Handbook for Companioning the Mourner: Eleven Principles*, specifies key areas for caretakers to consider when dealing with the bereaved:

> Companioning is about honoring the spirit;
> It is not about focusing on intellect.
> Companioning is about learning from others;
> It is not about teaching.
> Companioning is about walking alongside;
> It is not about leading or being lead.
> Companioning is about listening with the heart;
> It is not about analyzing with the head.
> Companioning is about being present to another person's pain;
> It is not about taking away or relieving the pain.

Conclusion

Perinatal and infant death inevitably involves the family. Not only are the mother and father impacted, but distress extends to siblings and grandparents, making a family-centered model of care optimal. Yet clinical programs have done relatively little family work in response to such bereavement distress, perhaps most commonly because of the sheer dominance of the individual care paradigm. We hope that as a result of the concepts and examples presented here, clinicians will ask more family-directed questions and begin to harness the support available from the family as a whole.

References

Armstrong, D. (2001). Exploring fathers' experiences of pregnancy after a prior perinatal loss. *MCN: American Journal of Maternal/Child Nursing, 26*(3), 147–153.

Arnold, J. H., & Gemma, P. B. (1991). Grief on the death of an infant. In C. A. Corr, H. Fuller, C. A. Barnickol, & D. M. Corr (Eds.), *Sudden infant death syndrome: Who can help and how* (pp. 45–56). New York: Springer.

Arnold, J. H., & Gemma, P. B. (1994). *A child dies: A portrait of family grief.* Philadelphia, PA: Charles Press.

Blackmore, E. R., Côté-Arsenault, D., Tang, W., Glover, V., Evans, J., Golding, J., & O'Connor, T. G. (2011). Previous prenatal loss as a predictor of perinatal depression and anxiety. *British Journal of Psychiatry, 198*(5), 373–378.

Bukowski, R., Carpenter, M., Conway, D., Coustan, D., Dudley, D. J., Goldenberg, R. L., & Pinar, H. (2011). Causes of death among stillbirths. *JAMA: Journal of the American Medical Association, 306*(22), 2459–2468.

Callister, L. C. (2003). A perspective from the Church of Jesus Christ of Latter-Day Saints. In M. L. Moore & M. K. Moos (Eds.), *Cultural competence in the care of childbearing families* (pp. 68–70). White Plains, NY: March of Dimes.

Callister, L. C. (2006). Perinatal loss: A family perspective. *Journal of Perinatal & Neonatal Nursing, 20*(3), 227–234.

Capitulo, K. L. (2005). Evidence for healing interventions with perinatal bereavement. *MCN: American Journal of Maternal/Child Nursing, 30*(6), 389–396.

Carlo, W. A., Goudar, S. S., Jehan, I., Chomba, E., Tshefu, A., Garces, A., . . . Derman, R. J. (2010). Newborn-care training and perinatal mortality in developing countries. *New England Journal of Medicine, 362*(7), 614–623.

Corbet-Owen, C. (2003). Women's perceptions of partner support in context of pregnancy loss(es). *South African Journal of Psychology, 32*(1), 19–27.

Davies, R. (2004). New understandings of parental grief: Literature review. *Journal of Advanced Nursing, 46*(5), 506–513.

DeBackere, K. J., Hill, P. D., & Kavanaugh, K. L. (2008). The parental experience of pregnancy after perinatal loss. *Journal of Obstetric, Gynecologic, & Neonatal Nursing, 37*(5), 525–537.

Doka, K. (1989). Disenfranchised grief. In K. Doka (Ed.), *Disenfranchised grief: Recognizing hidden sorrow* (pp. 3–11). Lexington, MA: Lexington Books.

First Candle Organization. (2012). Facts on sudden infant death syndrome/sudden unexpected infant death. Retrieved from http://www.firstcandle.org/grieving-families/sids-suid/about-sids-suid/sids-facts-faq

Frøen, J. F., Cacciatore, J., McClure, E. M., Kuti, O., Jokhio, A. H., Islam, M., & Shiffman, J. (2011). Stillbirths: Why they matter. *Lancet, 377*(9774), 1353–1366.

Goldenberg, R. L., McClure, E. M., Bhutta, Z. A., Belizán, J. M., Reddy, U. M., Rubens, C. E., & Darmstadt, G. L. (2011). Stillbirths: The vision for 2020. *Lancet, 377*(9779), 1798–1805.

Heron, M., Hoyert, D., Murphy, S., Xu, J., Kochanek, K., & Tejada-Vera, B. (2009). Deaths: Final data for 2006. *National Vital Statistics Reports, 57*(14), 1–135.

Horchler, J. N., & Morris, R. R. (1997). *The SIDS survival guide: Information and comfort for grieving family and friends and professionals who seek to help them.* Hyattsville, MD: SIDS Educational Services.

Hsu, M. T., Tseng, Y. F., & Kuo, L. L. (2002). Transforming loss: Taiwanese women's adaptation to stillbirth. *Journal of Advanced Nursing, 40*(4), 387–395.

Hutti, M. H., DePacheco, M., & Smith, M. (1998). A study of miscarriage: Development and validation of the Perinatal Grief Intensity Scale. *Journal of Obstetric, Gynecologic, & Neonatal Nursing, 27*(5), 547–555.

Jehan, I., Harris, H., Salat, S., Zeb, A., Mobeen, N., Pasha, O., McClure E. M., Moore, J., Wright, L. L., & Goldenberg, R. L. (2009). Neonatal mortality, risk factors and causes: A prospective population-based cohort study in urban Pakistan. *Bulletin of the World Health Organization, 87*, 130–138.

Kersting, A., & Wagner, B. (2012). Complicated grief after perinatal loss. *Dialogues in Clinical Neuroscience, 14*(2), 187–194.

Lander, T. (2006). *Neonatal and perinatal mortality: Country, regional and global estimates.* Geneva, Switzerland: World Health Organization.

Lawn, J., Yakoob, M., Haws, R., Soomro, T., Darmstadt, G., & Bhutta, Z. (2009). 3.2 million stillbirths: Epidemiology and overview of the evidence review. *BMC Pregnancy and Childbirth, 9*(Supplement 1), S2.

Lawn, J. E., Cousens, S., Zupan, J., & Lancet, N. S. S. T. (2005). 4 million neonatal deaths: When? Where? Why? *Lancet, 365*(9462), 891.

Lundqvist, A., & Dykes, A. K. (2003). Neonatal end of life care in Sweden: The views of Muslim women. *Journal of Perinatal and Neonatal Nursing, 17*(1), 77–86.

MacDorman, M. F. & Kirmeyer, S. (2009). Fetal and perinatal mortality, United States, 2005. *National Vital Statistics Reports, 57*(8), 1–19.

Martin, J., Hamilton, B., Sutton, P., Ventura, S., Menacker, F., & Kirmeyer, S. (2009). *Births: Final data for 2006*. Hyattsville, MD: U.S. Department of Health and Human Services, CDC, National Center for Health Statistics.

Moon, R. Y., Horne, R. S. C., & Hauck, F. R. (2007). Sudden infant death syndrome. *Lancet, 370*(9598), 1578–1587.

NHS Choices. (2013). Stillbirth. Retrieved from http://www.nhs.uk/conditions/Stillbirth/Pages/Definition.aspx

Oestergaard, M. Z., Inoue, M., Yoshida, S., Mahanani, W. R., Gore, F. M., Cousens, S., & Mathers, C. D. (2011). Neonatal mortality levels for 193 countries in 2009 with trends since 1990: A systematic analysis of progress, projections, and priorities. *PLoS Medicine, 8*(8), e1001080.

Rice, P. L. (1999). When the baby falls: The cultural construction of miscarriage among Hmong women in Australia. *Women & Health, 30*(1), 85–103.

Scotchie, J. G., & Fritz, M. A. (2006). Early pregnancy loss. *Postgraduate Obstetrics & Gynecology, 26*(9), 1–7.

Shaefer, J. (2010). When an infant dies: Cross cultural expression of grief and loss IV. *NFIMR Bulletin.* Washington, DC: ACOG.

Stanton, C., Lawn, J. E., Rahman, H., Wilczynska-Ketende, K., & Hill, K. (2006). Stillbirth rates: Delivering estimates in 190 countries. *Lancet, 367*(9521), 1487–1494.

Swanson, K. M. (2007). Nursing as informed caring for the well-being of others. *Journal of Nursing Scholarship, 25*(4), 352–357.

Thomas, J. (1998). The death of a baby: Siblings and memories. *Journal of Neonatal Nursing, 4*(5), 25–29.

Tinker, A., ten Hoope-Bender, P., Azfar, S., Bustreo, F., & Bell, R. (2005). A continuum of care to save newborn lives. *Lancet, 365*(9462), 822–825.

Wolfelt, A. (2009). *The handbook for companioning the mourner: Eleven essential principles.* Fort Collins, Colorado: Companion Press.

Wolfelt, A. D. (1999). *Companioning philosophy.* Retrieved from http://www.newpathcenter.org/resources/CompanioningPhilosophy.pdf

14 Family Bereavement Care after the Death of a Child

Lori Wiener and Cynthia A. Gerhardt

Life is like a road,
The road is often not straight,
or clear,
and sometimes the road splits,
and we must choose what direction to go.
Sometimes we can walk this road with friends,
other times we must walk alone.
But when you get to the end of the road,
and all is said and done,
nothing really matters anymore,
except for the journey,
and the love you've shared and received during it,
and the fact that this love will stand the test of time,
and go on forever.

—A patient, Evan (2012)

From the moment they are born, with their intense helplessness and need for interaction, babies invite us into a mutually loving relationship. This evolves into something new with each developmental milestone, as parents envision and plan for their child's future. No matter the region, culture, or cause of death, parents typically feel they are simply not supposed to bury their child. Likewise for siblings, the disruption of this unique and powerful bond is significant. Siblings, after all, share a lifetime of experiences and serve many roles for one another, such as teacher, competitor, antagonist, and friend. Thus, the loss of this attachment can have lasting effects on the development of surviving children.

The death of a child cuts across families' lives in a path that is much broader than any other loss and typically robs parents, siblings, and grandparents of their future expectations. Each can be left bereft, experiencing a grief that can be wrenching, disabling, and life-altering (Rosof, 1994). What are parents to do with that special parent-child bond that developed with such intensity as their child grew? How does the extended family grieve this loss? How can grandparents witness their own child's profound suffering while simultaneously grieving the loss of their grandchild? How does the death affect the parents' relationship, their physical and emotional health, and interactions with surviving children?

We begin this chapter with an overview of the prevalence of childhood death and the adaptive factors that govern how a family mourns that loss. We cover descriptions of bereavement phenomena and presentations of grief, including anticipatory, pathological, and prolonged grief, and factors that can ease suffering. Further, we present a clinical approach to care, with accompanying timelines and interventions. We conclude with the challenges faced when working with bereaved parents and siblings, and we discuss future directions for intervention.

Prevalence

The number of deaths worldwide for children under age five has declined from more than 12 million in 1990 to 7.6 million in 2010. According to the United Nations Children's Fund (2011), in 2010, nearly 21,000 children under age five died every day. The highest rates of childhood mortality are still in sub-Saharan Africa (where 1 in 8 children dies before age five) and in South Asia (1 in 15 children). As under-five-year-old mortality rates are 20 times lower and have fallen more sharply in industrialized countries (1 in 167), the disparity between these two regions and the rest of the world has grown. In the United States, childhood mortality from both trauma and complex chronic health conditions has declined (Feudtner, Hexem, & Rourke, 2011). Part of this decrease results from the longer life span of children with chronic health conditions, as deaths among 20- to 24-year-olds actually rose by 11.6 percent over an 18-year period (1979–1997) (Feudtner et al., 2001). Thus, many young adults die from congenital conditions or conditions with childhood onset, which has important implications for bereavement care from infancy to early adulthood (Feudtner et al., 2011).

The Grief Experience

Early theorists conceptualized mourning as a linear process, involving a number of stages leading to the resolution of grief (Freud, 1917; Kubler-Ross, 1969; Raphael, 1984). More contemporary understandings describe parental grief as intense and enduring (deCinque et al., 2006; Rando, 1985; Sanders, 1995; Schwab, 1992). Certainly, the death of a child from any cause can be traumatic, devastating, and life-altering. It challenges the expected family trajectory and threatens the parents' sense of identity, purpose, and anticipated legacy.

For parents who lose their child to illness, grief certainly does not begin when the last breath is taken: it is already present when parents realize that their hopes and dreams of the future with their child will need to be radically altered. Grieving occurs repeatedly along the journey of illness. The loss of the child's hair, limb, and ability to walk and attend school—and even the death of another child with a similar condition—comprise part of a series of cumulative losses that the family may face, leading eventually to their own child's death.

Coping and adaptation differ tremendously for each parent and family. The intensity of grief ebbs and flows, dependent on the nature and length of the dying process, as well as individual psychological and cultural factors (Contro, Kreicbergs, Reichard, & Sourkes, 2011). For siblings, the death may have been preceded by months or years when the family's attention and resources were directed toward saving the ill child. Some siblings also assume adult roles in the home, caring for younger children or participating in medical care. After the death, siblings are often described as the silent mourners: they may face the double loss of a brother or sister plus parents who may be consumed by grief and unavailable to them.

Normative and Adaptive Responses

Grief can present with a range of "normal" symptoms, and therefore it can be damaging to judge the bereaved, especially within the first 6 to 12 months after a child's death. Moreover, the death of a child can be traumatic, and parental grief is more intense and persistent than distress following other losses (Arnold, Gemma, & Cushman, 2005; Kreicbergs, Lannen, Onelöv, & Wolfe, 2007). Bereaved parents are at increased risk for psychological morbidity (e.g., anxiety, depression, and poor quality of life; Kreicbergs, Valdimarsdóttir, Onelöv, Henter, & Steineck, 2004a; Li, Laursen, Precht, Olsen, & Mortenson, 2005; Rosenberg, Baker, Syrjala, & Wolfe, 2012); physical problems (e.g., hypertension, colitis, obesity, and somatic complaints); and mortality (Espinosa & Evans, 2013; Li, Precht, Mortensen, & Olsen, 2003). Similarly, bereaved siblings may experience more social, emotional, and behavioral difficulties, especially in the first two years after the death (Birenbaum, Robinson, Phillips, Stewart, & McCown, 1989; Hutton & Bradley, 1994; McCown & Davies, 1995). However, most family members eventually come to terms with the child's death and restore a potentially satisfying and meaningful life (Bonanno, Moskowitz, Papa, & Folkman, 2005). One of our bereaved parents eloquently stated, "In time, whether we think we want to or not, we learn to survive, and we can even experience guiltless enjoyment. The hole will never go away, but it becomes passable and a beautiful place of remembrance." Indeed, knowledge of the boundaries of adaptive grief can allow for recognition of complicated or prolonged grief as well as effective treatment of clinically important problems (Zisook & Shear, 2009). The understanding of clinical presentations of grief is therefore crucial.

Clinical Presentations of Grief

Anticipatory. Family members who know the child's death is unavoidable may experience many of the same symptoms while the child is alive as those experienced after the death. This process has been coined "anticipatory grief" (Aldrich, 1974). Parents may find themselves in deep despair while thinking about all that will be missed, the reactions of others, and how they will survive without their child. Anticipatory grieving is an adaptive coping mechanism that allows some of the work of grieving to start even before the death (Schonfeld, 2012). Yet, when excessive, anticipatory grief can leave some parents later wishing they had been more emotionally present while the child was still alive.

Acute. The *acute grief* that occurs in the early aftermath of death can be intensely painful and is often characterized by behaviors and emotions that would be considered unusual in everyday life. A parent may experience disorganization, emptiness, listlessness, heightened startle reactions, poor sleep and appetite, flashbacks of their child, and sudden waves of painful longing and sadness. Unfamiliar emotions and responses can include looking for their child in a crowd, seeing their child's face in others, sensing their child's presence, talking to their child, vivid dreams of their child, wondering how one can feel so much pain and survive, transient thoughts of suicide, wondering how others can go on as if nothing has happened, no longer fearing death, difficulty concentrating, and disinterest in other people and activities (Zisook & Shear, 2009). In addition, family members may feel guilty for failing to save the child from death and suffering.

Integrated. In time, grief becomes more integrated into daily functioning (Zisook & Shear, 2009). As grief has no formal expiration date, sadness and yearning lessen but may never be completely relinquished. However, the thoughts and memories of the deceased are no longer as preoccupying or disabling—equanimity gradually develops. Periods may surface when acute grief reawakens. This can occur around holidays, birthdays, anniversaries, the first day of school, another loss, or a particularly stressful time. Siblings can also experience re-grief when they process the loss from different vantage points as they grow and mature. For some, time helps heal; for others, it can bring deeper anxiety. As one mother said 18 months after her child's death, "I hate every New Years because it is getting further and further since she was here. I hate the 30th of every month. I even hate every Thursday. In fact, I hate every day at 3:30."

Prolonged. Grief does not always dissipate with time and may persist for several years (Lichtenthal, Cruess, & Prigerson, 2004; Prigerson, Vanderwerker, & Maciejewski, 2008; Shear, Frank, Houck, & Reynolds, 2005). Enduring feelings of guilt, envy, bitterness, or anger can lead to complicated grief reactions. About 7 percent of bereaved people (Kersting, Brähler, Glaesmer, & Wagner, 2011) cannot cope adaptively with bereavement. Instead, they become entangled in grief and find themselves helplessly on endless waves of acutely painful emotion. This pathological reaction to bereavement has been termed "prolonged grief disorder" (PGD), which includes symptoms of separation distress; avoidance of reminders of their loved one; difficulty accepting the loss; and feeling shocked, bitter, numb, meaningless, and distrustful for at least six months after the death (Prigerson et al., 2008). Bereaved parents are at heightened risk for PGD (Ginzburg, Geron, & Solomon, 2002); less is known about this phenomenon in children. Thus, assessing the severity of grief is important.

Factors that Contribute to Variability in Outcome

Although some families are shattered by grief, others emerge strengthened and more resourceful. Resilience—the ability to withstand and rebound from disruptive life challenges—involves dynamic processes fostering positive adaptation within the context of significant adversity (Luthar, Cicchetti, & Becker, 2000). Central here is personal relationship transformation through which families grow and recover (Boss, 2001). Several factors may ease the intensity of sadness, reduce morbidity, and improve adaptation. These include clear communication with the child's medical team, strong family relationships (Kreicbergs et al., 2007), faith, and an ability to find meaning despite death (Kubler-Ross & Kessler, 2005). Each of these factors is reviewed subsequently. A timeline for interventions that support families and help facilitate adaptation is discussed in the section "Family Therapy after the Death of a Child."

Communication within a Medical Environment

Family communication with the medical team about realistic outcomes affects decision making at the end of life and helps to prevent regrets. Parents rarely elect to discontinue cancer-directed therapy without an explicit physician recommendation to do so (Bluebond-Langner, Belasco, Goldman, & Belasco, 2007). When there is no realistic chance to extend life, most parents still choose anti-cancer treatment—but those who felt their child suffered from such a course were particularly unlikely to recommend that others with advanced cancer do so (Mack et al., 2012). Similarly, parents informed about the imminence of demise are better prepared and are more likely to talk about death with their child, often tailoring care to their child's wishes (Valdimarsdóttir et al., 2007). On the downside, the grief process can be negatively affected by absence of accessible clinicians at the moment of a child's death and a poor relationship with the medical team, particularly if the child's or parents' wishes were not respected (Kreicbergs et al., 2005).

Communication with the Ill Child

Unfortunately, when parents have children who are very young, nonverbal, or who die unexpectedly, the chance to say good-bye may be missed. Kreicbergs, Valdimarsdóttir, Onelöv, Henter, and Steineck (2004b) found universally that bereaved parents who had talked to their dying child about death did not regret doing so, whereas 27 percent of parents who did not talk with their child felt regret, particularly when they sensed their child was aware of his or her imminent death. Furthermore, parents with regret reported greater anxiety or depression four to nine years later, compared to parents who were content with their decision (Kreicbergs et al., 2004a). Although discussing death with all children may not be appropriate or feasible, communicating openly can help facilitate adjustment, as illustrated by the following case scenario.

A 15-year-old girl with multiply relapsed leukemia shared with her therapist that she did not want any more treatment—but was worried because her mother was working hard to search for new therapies. The therapist first worked with the mother, helping her to communicate with her daughter about their respective wishes. This was followed by joint sessions where mother and daughter were able to share their concerns and fears. Together they made the decision to go home and not pursue more treatment. After her daughter's death, the mother's letter to the therapist exemplifies the meaning offered by such open communication: "Thank you for the enlightened guidance that opened us up to talk about so many vital things that have really given me the peace of mind I cling to. Nothing was left unsaid and so many pitfalls avoided because all of her wishes were spelled out for me to follow."

Communication with Siblings

Because of the intense parental involvement with the ill child, the needs of healthy siblings may pale in comparison. Siblings are often left with extended family members or friends and may not learn about a child's illness or death until many others have been informed. Parents often want to protect children from the pain of watching their brother or sister die. However, even young children can understand death, and some protective measures can leave siblings feeling less important, excluded, abandoned, invisible, and angry (Alderfer et al., 2010), thus hampering the grief process (Giovanola, 2005). Because bereaved siblings have also reported less communication, availability, and support from parents after the death (Rosen, 1985), clinicians should educate parents about the value of addressing children's needs, including having family meetings

Table 14.1 Indicators That Surviving Siblings May Need Professional Help

- Persistent anxiety about their own death
- Changes in appetite or sleep patterns
- Destructive outbursts, self-destructive behavior, or acting out
- Threats of hurting self or others
- Compulsive caregiving
- Euphoria
- Unwillingness to speak about their deceased relative, especially if a conflicted relationship existed
- Expression of only positive or only negative feelings about their sibling
- Suppression of all feelings about the death
- Inability or unwillingness to form new relationships
- Daydreaming, resulting in poor academic performance
- Stealing or hoarding household items
- Excessive separation anxiety and/or school phobia
- Withdrawal from peers or previously enjoyable activities
- Sudden unexplained change in behavior, attitude, or mood
- History of multiple losses or trauma
- Alcohol or substance use
- Fragile or stressed family relationships

to communicate directly with all involved from the beginning. Table 14.1 lists indicators that suggest surviving siblings may need professional help, and Table 14.2 provides interview questions for a comprehensive assessment of a sibling's grief reactions and adaptation.

Table 14.2 Interview Questions for a Sibling Whose Brother or Sister Died

Relationship with Deceased

1. Can you tell me a little something about your brother or sister?
2. What was your relationship like with him or her?
3. What kind of things did you do together?
4. Had you known that he/she had (e.g., cancer, depression)?
5. If yes, when had you learned this information?
6. Who told you?
7. What was your response when you first learned this?
8. Were you able to share this with anyone else?
9. When you had worried, whom did you talk to?
10. Can you tell me a little something about his or her death?
11. Were you there? (If not) What had you heard?
12. Did you realize that he/she was sick enough to die?
13. Who knew the truth about your brother's/sister's illness?
14. Are you concerned that you might get (e.g., cancer, depression)?

(Continued)

Table 14.2 (Continued)

15. Were there things you wanted to tell your relative before he or she died? (If the sibling didn't know the death was imminent, are there things the sibling wishes he or she could now say?)

16. Is there anything that you wanted to do together that you didn't have a chance to do?

17. Do you have any of your brother's or sister's things that you hold on to? (If yes) Can you tell me about them?

18. Some brothers/sisters feel that they may have said something or done something that caused their sibling to get sick. Is there anything that you have thought to yourself that you might have done even if you know it is not really true?

19. Do you feel your family understands what the loss of your brother or sister is like for you?

Adjustment

1. Since your brother/sister died, what has life been like for you?

2. What has life been like for your family (go through each significant person individually) since your brother/sister died?

3. Other children who have lost a brother or sister have said that sometimes, when something bad like this happens, other things can also be difficult for them either at school, with friends, or at home. Has anything else not been going well for you?

4. (If yes) Tell me about (each one).

5. Have you been through any other bad times like this before? (Traumatic memories) Any other losses?

6. (If yes) Tell me about them—what helped you get through those times?

7. Tell me about your friends. (Trying to get a sense of quality of relationships and how these might have changed since the death.)

8. Now can you tell me about how you have been eating?

9. And sleeping? Has your sleeping changed? (If yes) Tell me about how it has changed. (Also get a sense of the kind of dreams he or she is having, especially frightening images.)

10. Do you get sad a lot? (If yes, ask what he or she does when sad and about frequency/intensity and assess for depression.)

11. Do you find yourself sometimes getting scared but not sure why? (If yes, assess further for separation anxiety, generalized anxiety, specific phobias, and post-trauma symptoms.)

12. Tell me about your teacher(s). Do they know about your brother's/sister's death?

13. How are you doing with your schoolwork? Homework? Grades? (Assess for changes.)

14. Have you been seeing a doctor for any health problems of your own?

15. (If yes) Tell me about that.

16. Do you have a faith belief (belief in God or a higher being). If so, does this help you? Has your faith changed since your brother/sister died?

17. Is there something else that I haven't asked about?

18. Is there anything else you think I should know about how you are getting along?

19. (If yes) Tell me about that.

20. Do you have any questions that you would like to ask me? (If yes) Go ahead.

21. Would you be interested in (books, counseling, groups, bereavement camps)?

22. Thank you for talking to me and for sharing this information. At this point, I would like to (refer you to ..., provide my card if you have questions or would like to talk to me at any time, etc.).

*SuperSibs in the USA: Offers two $5,000 college scholarships to high school seniors that are siblings of children with cancer. Visit http://www.supersibs.org.

Family Relationships

When a child is seriously ill, family dynamics are influenced. Family roles are altered. Parents and siblings assume increased responsibilities at home, with potential for caregiver burden (Wiener, Alderfer, & Hersh, 2011). A meta-analysis of the influence of pediatric cancer on parent and family functioning demonstrated that mothers report a small but significantly increased level of family conflict compared to healthy controls (Pai et al., 2007). Family conflict can spill over to relationships with extended family members, neighbors, and the health care team.

Disruption in family relationships can directly affect the adjustment of bereaved siblings, as well as account for the transmission of distress within families. Considerable evidence supports that a parent's distress, particularly maternal depression, increases a child's risk for adjustment problems, primarily through negative parent-child interactions (Foster et al., 2008; Garber & Cole, 2010). These influences are likely bidirectional. As bereaved parents and siblings are changed by a child's death, they may also struggle with how to relate to one another in new ways (Foster et al., 2012; Gilmer et al, 2012). For example, a bereaved father may find it challenging to now parent his daughter who is more mature, withdrawn, or otherwise different.

Studies have examined whether family conflict leads to subsequent divorce, but findings have been inconsistent due to methodological issues. Some marriages may stay intact because the couples do not want to inflict another loss on the surviving children. For others, existing bonds may be strengthened as parents grieve together the loss of their child—especially if the relationship was good at the outset (Sloper, 2004; Vrijmoet-Wiersma et al., 2008). Moreover, couples' values may change, and they may become more conscious of certain qualities in the relationship (Neff & Karney, 2005; Thompson, 1993). Marital conflicts may be seen as small compared to what they have already endured (Sabbeth & Leventhal, 1984). This highlights the importance of researchers not focusing on divorce as the outcome so much as the quality of the parents' relationship and their ability to communicate and respect each other's coping styles. A tremendous hurdle for bereaved parents is learning to live with multiples griefs: their own, their partner's, and their surviving children's. Openness to each other's differences is critical.

Complex family structures can also add complications to grieving. A parent may have been the sole caregiver, engaging in lone parenting, regardless of marital status (Brown et al., 2008). Blended family members may be uncertain of their roles and could feel judged by biological family members due to different levels of sadness. Families who lose an adopted child or foster child may face insensitivity to their grief: some people mistakenly believe that parents can only deeply love a child who was born to them. Grandparents often question their role in decision making, fear for their own child's emotional well-being, and grieve the anticipated loss of their grandchild (Ponzetti & Johnson, 1991). Clinicians need an awareness of the complex family structure and dynamics so that the appropriate support system can be identified.

Finding Sense and Meaning

Parents can experience a crisis in meaning while trying to make sense of the death of a child (Lehman, Wortman, & Williams, 1987; Murphy, Johnson, & Lohan, 2003; Wheeler,

2001; Wu et al., 2008). But finding positive consequences after the death can ease suffering (Keesee, Currier, & Neimeyer, 2008). What helps sustain families in their quest for meaning is maintaining a sense of connection with the child, holding a deep belief that their bond continues and that the child's life and existence will never be forgotten (Arnold & Gemma, 1994). Although continuing bonds may be associated with both positive and negative effects for bereaved individuals, many parents and siblings find comfort in maintaining their relationship with the child after the death (Foster et al., 2011). They may be aided by keeping linking objects such as clothing, writings, or the child's favorite possessions. Others sustain the relationship through living legacies, such as carrying out a mission in honor of the child (e.g., Alex's Lemonade Stand Foundation for Childhood Cancer), making donations or volunteering for a cause connected to the child's death (e.g., Mothers Against Drunk Drivers), providing emotional support to other bereaved families, or contributing to a clinical trial or postmortem examination that might advance science (Foster et al., 2009). Commemorative activities like visiting the grave, releasing a message inside a balloon to a child, or lighting candles may likewise help sustain memories.

Faith

Many families find strength, comfort, and guidance through connections with their cultural and religious traditions (Walsh, 1999). Particular beliefs about heaven have been noted to help parents grieve the loss of their child. Spiritual resources and faith-based practices such as prayer, meditation, and religious/congregational affiliation can be wellsprings for resilience (Werner & Smith, 1992). Other bereaved family members find spiritual nourishment outside of formal religion through a deep personal connection with nature, music, or a higher power (Walsh, 2003). To effectively optimize this as a source of support, health care professionals must understand each family's personal belief system (deCinque et al., 2006). This includes asking what helps each person make sense of his or her world. Believing in something, anticipating something good, being cared for and caring for others, relying upon something or someone—these are all somewhat theological concepts that are common to medicine and spirituality (Brooks & Ennis-Durstine, 2011). For one mother of Hindu faith, a vision experienced at the time of her son's death has continued to bring significant comfort.

> As NB was taking his last breaths (there were four breaths left), there were about 30-odd people around his bed—family, friends, teachers. Some were saying, "We love you, NB." A few were saying the Hindu mantras, some were just watching. . . . I was saying, "Go, NB, go towards the Light."
>
> Well, when he took his fourth to last breath, I was looking as his face intently, and I saw these strings that came from the Heavens and were attached to the earth. Then NB took another breath, and I saw an imaginary scissor cutting the strings. I could almost see the stings thwang as they got cut and half went towards the Heavens and half towards Earth. Then as he kept taking his third and second breath, I kept seeing the strings getting cut. It was the most amazing sight. Then there was one string left. I could see that it was the "fattest" one—one with the most diameter to it. And the thought occurred to me that this was his last tie to Earth—it may be the one to the girls and me. Then NB took his last breath, and that last string got cut.

Then, all of a sudden, I felt a "WHOOOSH"! His spirit got lifted up, up, up and went up to the ceiling. The first thing he said to me was, "Wow, no pain!!!!" And I realized he was in so much pain for the past two years that was the first thing he could tell me. Then I just felt bliss from him and I felt him on top of us all just watching us. You know what—I could not even cry that night because the bliss of NB being pain free was a LOT more than me missing him. I am blessed to have had this vision because when I feel really sad/cry, then I think back to it and I have to tell myself NB is so much happier and pain-free. [Extracted with permission from her clinical history]

Pre-death Suffering

The severity of physical and emotional suffering throughout the child's illness and at the time of death can lead to cumulative parental exhaustion. Bereaved parents who reported that their child experienced anxiety or disturbed sleep due to pain were at increased risk of long-term morbidity (Jalmsell, Kreicbergs, Onelöv, Steineic, & Henter, 2010). Bereavement reactions may also be affected by such factors as previous losses or trauma, prior psychiatric difficulties, substance abuse, fragile or stressed family relationships, poor social support, and other co-existing crises including financial woes and illness of family members (Arnold & Gemma, 1994).

Age and Gender

A Swedish study found fathers of children older than eight at the time of death were at greater risk of anxiety and depression than fathers of younger children (Kreicbergs et al., 2004a). Psychological distress is generally higher among bereaved mothers. Although fewer fathers than mothers had resolved their grief at four to six years post-death, more fathers had come to terms with the loss after seven to nine years (Kreicbergs et al., 2007). The time between intellectual realization that a disease is fatal and emotional awareness has also been examined. Fathers with shorter emotional awareness had an increased risk of depression, absence from work, and early retirement (Valdimarsdóttir et al., 2007). This pattern was not evident for mothers. In spite of trends for deeper paternal involvement, men are often not taught that it is necessary to grieve and may be discouraged from open expression of mourning. For siblings, it appears that bereaved girls and adolescents may have more emotional and behavioral difficulties (Fanos & Nickerson, 1991; Worden, Davies, & McCown, 1999), whereas bereaved boys and younger children may evidence more social difficulties (Gerhardt et al., 2012).

Place of Death

The place of death has been the focus of a few pediatric reports. In an Australian study conducted with 25 parents after the death of their child from cancer, fathers but not mothers reported significantly higher levels of depression, anxiety, and stress if the child died in the hospital rather than at home (Goodenough, Drew, Higgins, & Trethewie, 2004). In another study, end-of-life home care was comparable to hospital care for satisfactory pain relief, access to pain medication, and treatment for other physical symptoms (Surkan, Dickman, Steineck, Onelöv, & Kreicbergs, 2006). In a more recent cross-sectional study of 140 parents who lost a child to cancer at two U.S. pediatric hospitals, parents who planned end-of-life care reported high-quality palliative care, even among non-home deaths, suggesting the actual location of the child's death is less important than the opportunity to plan the location of death (Dussel et al., 2009).

In bereavement studies, the country where the research was conducted influences quality of care and financial contribution to stress. Several studies that report on mental health and family outcomes have been carried out in countries where health care is free of charge to all citizens. Leaves of absence and various economic welfare benefits are commonly given to parents with chronically ill children. These families may therefore experience a modest financial impact from their child's medical care, compared to those who have less extensive social programs (Blekesaune & Øverbye, 2003). Even more well-adjusted families can be tipped into stress overload by mounting medical bills, the risk of losing one's job and hence health insurance, and the fear of losing one's home. Therefore, clinicians should be cautious about making generalizations from available studies and should inquire about lingering financial stressors.

Family Therapy after the Death of a Child

After a child dies, access to bereavement care can be challenging. Families enrolled in hospice may elect to receive periodic home visits from a chaplain or social worker for two years after the death. However, the majority of children die in the hospital, and consequently, many families are reluctant to return for services. Some families may have previously relied on psychosocial services provided as part of their child's treatment, only to return home to few, if any, professionals skilled in working with bereaved families in their community. There are increasing numbers of self-help books, online resources, and community-based support groups (e.g., the Compassionate Friends, a U.S.-based organization with chapters worldwide), but many bereaved families report that such resources do not address the unique needs of grieving parents and siblings (Levy & Derby, 1992). Furthermore, there is evidence that bereaved individuals in general underutilize grief resources (Cherlin et al., 2007; Lichtenthal et al., 2011).

This highlights the inherent challenge in providing quality care for grieving parents and siblings. Although research has examined the efficacy of various grief interventions (see Table 14.3), some controversy persists as to the overall benefit, and it is difficult to know if differential effects for bereaved parents and siblings may exist relative to other bereaved populations. Recent meta-analyses of grief interventions for adults and children suggest the most benefit occurs when offered to highly distressed or prescreened individuals early in the grieving process (e.g., Currier, Holland, & Neimeyer, 2007; Currier, Neimeyer, & Berman, 2008; Rosner, Kruse, & Hagl, 2010). These interventions are often group sessions with a therapist that focus on psychoeducation, sharing memories of the death and deceased, such as exposure treatments, and teaching coping skills (e.g., relaxation and cognitive restructuring).

Growing evidence indicates that models of coping and cognitive-behavioral approaches can inform empirically based bereavement care (Compas, Connor-Smith, Saltzman, Thomsen, & Wadsworth, 2001; Currier, Holland, & Neimeyer, 2010; Folkman,

Table 14.3 Timeline of Events and Interventions

	Siblings	Parents	Extended Family	Community
Prior to Death	□ Describe what the dying process might look like. □ Inform that lack of communication does not reflect lack of desire to speak with the sibling. □ Whenever possible, help sibling to have a chance to say good-bye. □ Assess for feelings of guilt, anger, and fear, and provide counseling as needed. □ Prepare for burial/funeral if the siblings wish to have a part (read or say something).	□ Describe what the dying process might look like. □ If possible, help choose the location. Encourage child input and communication. □ Discuss and help with funeral planning (including selection of an undertaker, who will guide the various funeral arrangements). □ Explore and consider ethnic, cultural, and spiritual beliefs and practices. □ If in the hospital, prepare for being able to spend time with the body and the body needing to leave the room. If at home, prepare for the hearse coming and the body bag being closed. □ Encourage saying good-bye, or provide words parents may feel comfortable saying. □ Identify a contact person who can contact others with changes and family needs.	□ Encourage grandparents and other key family members to visit with the child and family (avoid if conflict or poor family cohesion is present). □ Inform them of the emotional needs of the parents and siblings and how they can help. □ Normalize their own deep emotions.	□ Work closely with teachers to prepare the classroom for the child's death. They may wish to write cards, make a videotape to share with the child and family or reach out via e-mails or social media methods. □ Neighbors and local organizations might be able to provide support to the family (e.g., meals, cleaning services, and lawn care).
Within First Weeks after Death	□ Inquire about their psychosocial well-being.	□ Assess reactions of each individual in the family. □ Assess sleep, eating, and mood. □ Provide information on books and local support organizations. □ Write condolence note.	□ Inquire about their psychosocial well-being.	□ Offer to talk with the child's classroom about death, loss, and "normal" responses and when additional support is appropriate.

	Siblings	Parents	Extended Family	Community
Within Three Months	□ Inquire about their psychosocial well-being. □ Recommend age-appropriate reading material. □ Inform about support systems (e.g., through local hospices).	□ Contact the family when you have time, without interruption, allowing time for parents to describe and reminisce. □ Inquire about their psychosocial well-being. □ Inform them that bereavement is without a timeline, highly individual.	□ Inquire about their psychosocial well-beingo □ Make referrals, as indicated for bereavement counseling, support groups, and online resources.	□ Same as above.
Six to Nine Months	□ Inquire about their psychosocial well-being. □ Perform assessment if indicated (Table 14.1), and make appropriate referrals. □ Refer to camp programs for bereaved siblings (counselor and/or leadership opportunities). □ Inform about sibling college scholarship programs, as appropriate.*	□ Same as above. □ Inquire about family dynamics/relationships, substance use/abuse, and parental coping. □ Make referrals, as indicated for family therapy, couples counseling, and individual treatment. □ Minority families are less likely to obtain bereavement services. Dispel myths and barriers, if needed (Lichtenthal et al., 2012).	□ Same as above.	□ Encourage the pediatrician of the well children in the family to assess for grief reactions (including somatic complaints) and the need for additional intervention.

(Continued)

Table 14.3 (Continued)

	Siblings	Parents	Extended Family	Community
At One Year	□ Same as above.	□ Same as above. □ Contact the family around the anniversary of the child's death. This is an especially difficult day, and contact is greatly appreciated.	□ Same as above. □ For grandparents in particular, contact around the anniversary of the child's death to share your thoughts of their grief can be greatly appreciated.	□ Contact with grandparents around the anniversary of the child's death is greatly appreciated.
Yearly	□ Same as above. □ If possible, remember the sibling on his or her birthday and on the anniversary of the deceased child's death. Many siblings feel forgotten and fear that they too may die at the age their sibling died.	□ Depending on how the family is doing, family members may wish to learn about ways they can get involved with other non-profits.	□ Same as above. □ The family may need help in planning remembrance events (from simple dinners, to cemetery visits, candlelight ceremonies, balloon or butterfly release, etc.).	□ If the family finds comfort from this, encourage community groups (e.g., spiritual or school to have some kind of remembrance on the anniversary of the child's death).

2001; Skinner, Edge, Altman, & Sherwood, 2003). Despite calls to integrate these types of models with contemporary grief theory, there is still much to learn regarding how bereaved individuals, particularly children, come to find meaning in their experience, integrate the death in their lives, and gain acceptance of the loss. Furthermore, the family's co-construction of this process is important and may evolve over time, particularly for children as they grow and mature. These major tasks of bereavement may require accommodative coping strategies, such as cognitive restructuring and positive reframing, which can be particularly effective in response to uncontrollable events such as the loss of a family member. Studies of bereaved parents indicate that more active and externally directed strategies (e.g., teaching problem solving) are associated with better outcomes, whereas passive and internal strategies (e.g., blocking intrusive thoughts and ruminating) are associated with distress (Folkman, 2001; Lepore, Silver, Wortman, & Wayment, 1996).

A therapist's work with bereaved siblings also requires appreciating the developmental aspects of grief and psychopathology, the family context in which the child is grieving and the normative tasks or demands of typical children their age. Despite calls to conceptualize interventions from a family systems perspective in response to a child's death (Kazak & Noll, 2004), few studies have used such an approach. Grief interventions may be more challenging for younger children who have fewer cognitive and social resources on which to rely while processing the death. Alternate forms of communication and expression may be useful, such as music or art therapy (Rosner et al., 2010). It is also important for the therapist to consider what the sibling knows or understands, which may be quite different from what they were told about the illness or death. Family work may require decisions about when and how often sessions occur with parents or children separately in order to manage appropriate sharing of information and to tailor the teaching of specific skills.

Sensitivity to different perceptions and grief responses within a family is necessary. Therapists must meet the family where they are emotionally and allow an opportunity to hear their story in a manner that is non-judgmental (Kazak & Noll, 2004). Clearly, it is important to learn about the child who died, so that he or she can be openly discussed with the family. Exposure techniques that include revisiting circumstances surrounding the illness and death may allow families to process these events and manage any feelings of guilt or regrets. Psychoeducation should review common presentations of grief—including its duration and typical and complicated forms—as well as validate individual experiences.

Part of facilitating the co-construction and integration of grief is to help bereaved families recognize the changes that have occurred in individual family members and relationships since the illness and death. These changes can be positive or negative. In therapy, family difficulties can be identified and solutions generated to increase cohesion, reduce conflict, and improve communication (Kissane et al., 2006). Aspects of resilience, such as the development of other competencies and personal growth, might be explored. Increased maturity, compassion, and recognition of different priorities may bring purpose back to the individual's life. Family members can come to identify the child's legacy by sharing memories of the child's character, values and beliefs, life choices, and suffering. By continuing this legacy and thus keeping the memory of the child alive, families may find comfort in remaining connected to their loved one.

Conclusion

Although we still have much to learn from grieving families, this chapter highlights how a family mourns the loss of a child, explicates different presentations of grief, and pinpoints some of the adaptive factors that can ease suffering. What we know without doubt is that the grieving process often encompasses the survivors' entire world and affects their emotional, cognitive, spiritual, and physical selves, often in unexpected ways. Grief can be a lifelong process. Families may need to be reminded to have patience with themselves and each other. However, many families can begin to make sense of a seemingly nonsensical death and, with time, gain acceptance of their changed world to live a life with purpose again.

Selected Resources for Grieving Parents and Surviving Children

Children's Lifecycle Books

Agee, J. (1969). *A death in the family.* New York: Bantam.

Al-Chokhachy, E. (1988). *The angel with the golden glow.* Marblehead, MA: The Penny Bear.

Blackburn, L. B. (1991). *The class in room 44: When a classmate dies.* Omaha, NE: Centering.

Boulden, J. (1992). *Saying goodbye.* Kansas City, MO: Boulden.

Breebart, J., & Breebart, P. (1993). *When I die, will I get better?* Belgium: Peter Bedrick Books.

Brown, L., & Brown, M. (1996). *When dinosaurs die.* Boston: Little, Brown.

Buscaglia, L. (1982). *The fall of Freddie the leaf.* Thorofare, NJ: Charles B. Slack.

Carlstrom, N. (1990). *Blow me a kiss, Miss Lilly.* New York: HarperCollins.

Coerr, E., & Young, E. (1993). *Sadako and the thousand paper cranes.* New York: G. P. Putnam & Sons.

Crawford, C. P. (1974). *Three-legged race.* New York: Harper & Row.

Dodd, M. (2004). *Oliver's story: For "sibs" of kids with cancer.* Kensington, MD: Candelighters Childhood Cancer Foundation.

Fahy, M. (1989). *The tree that survived the winter.* New York: Paulist.

Fitzgerald, H. (2000). *The grieving teen: A guide for teenagers & their friends.* Lady Lake, FL: Fireside Press.

Gootman, M. E. (1994). *When a friend dies.* Minneapolis, MN: Free Spirit.

Greene, C. C. (1976). *Beat the turtle drum.* New York: Viking.

Grollman, E. A. (1993). *Straight talk about death for teenagers: How to cope with losing someone you love.* Boston: Beacon Press.

Hichman, M. (1983). *Last week my brother Anthony died.* Nashville, TN: Abingdon.

Johnson, J., & Johnson, M. (1982). *Where's Jess?* Omaha, NE: Centering.

Lee, V. (1972). *The magic moth.* New York: Seabury Press.

Levy, L. E. (1982). *Children are not paper dolls: A visit with bereaved siblings.* Caryl, IL: Publishers Mark.

Mellonie, B., & Ingpen, R. (1983). *Lifetimes: The beautiful way to explain death to children.* New York: Bantam.

Mills, J. C. (1993). *Gentle willow.* New York: Magination Press.

Peterkin, A. (1992). *What about me? When brothers and sisters get sick.* New York: Magination Press.

Putter, A. M. (1997). *The memorial rituals book for healing and hope.* Amityville, NY: Baywood.

Richter, E. (1986). *Losing someone you love.* New York: Putnam.

Rofes, E. (1985). *The kids' book about death and dying.* Boston: Little, Brown.

Romain, T. (1999). *What on earth do you do when someone dies?* Minneapolis, MN: Free Spirit.
Sanders, P. (1990). *Let's talk about death and dying.* London: Aladdin Books.
Sasso, S. E. (1999). *For heaven's sake, what is heaven? Where do we find it?* Woodstock, VT: Jewish Lights.
Shriver, M. (1999). *What's heaven?* New York: Golden Books.
Sims, A. M. (1986). *Am I still a sister?* Slidell, LA: Big A & Company Starline Printing.
Sonnenblick, J. (2004). *Drums, girls and dangerous pie.* San Francisco: DayBue.
Starkman, N. (1988). *Z's gift.* Seattle, WA: Comprehensive Health Education Foundation.
Varley, S. (1992). *The badger's parting gifts.* New York: Mulberry Books.
Viorst, J. (1971). *The tenth good thing about Barney.* New York: Atheneum.
White, E. B. (1952). *Charlotte's web.* New York: Harper and Row.
Wild, M. (1995). *Old pig.* New York: Penguin Books.
Williams, M. (1971). *The velveteen rabbit.* Garden City, NY: Doubleday.
Zim, H., & Bleeker, S. (1970). *Life and death.* New York: Morrow.

Books for Parents

Apple, D. L. (2008). *Life after the death of my son: What I'm learning.* Kansas City, MO: Beacon Hill Press.
Bernstein, J. R. (1998). *When the bough breaks: Forever after the death of a son or daughter.* Kansas City, MO: Andrews McMeel.
Fitzgerald, H. (1992). *The grieving child: A parent's guide.* New York: Simon & Schuster.
Grollman, E. (1976). *Talking about death.* Boston: Beacon Press.
Kander, J. (1990). *So will I comfort you.* Cape Town, South Africa: Lux Verbi.
Kushner, H. (1994). *When bad things happen to good people.* New York: Anchor Books.
LeShan, E. (1976). *Learning to say goodbye.* New York: Macmillan.
Livingston, G. (2004). *Too soon old, too late smart.* New York: Marlowe.
Mitchell, E. (2009). *Beyond tears: Living after losing a child* (Rev. ed.). New York: St. Martin's Press.
Redfern, S., & Gilbert, S. K. (2008). *The grieving garden: Living with the death of a child (22 parents share their stories).* Charlottesville, VA: Hampton Roads.
Rosof, B. D. (1994). *The worst loss: How families heal from the death of a child.* New York: Henry Holt.
Schaefer, D., & Lyons, C. (1988). *How do we tell the children? Helping children understand and cope when someone dies* (Rev. ed.). New York: Newmarket.
Schiff, H. (1979). *The bereaved parent.* New York: Crown Publishing.
Stillwell, E. E., Behme, T. J., Pierce, G. F. A., (eds). (2004). *The death of a child: Reflections for grieving parents.* Chicago, IL: ACTA Publications.
Walton, C. (1996). *When there are no words. Finding your way to cope with loss and grief.* Ventura, CA: Pathfinder.

Internet Resources

Space does not allow us to include all potentially useful resources, and therefore, this list is not exhaustive. New and additional resources may be available.

Cancer Care Inc.

http://www.cancercare.org
   Services: Programs include group, individual, family, and bereavement counseling (in person, online, and through telephone). Information and referral to local community resources.

Centering Corporation

http://www.centering.org
   Address: P.O. Box 3367, Omaha, NE 68103; Phone: 402-553-1200
   Services: Provides guidance for families experiencing grief. Can request a copy of their catalog describing many books, pamphlets, and videos that focus on healing and grief.

Compassionate Friends

http://www.campassionatefriends.org
   Phone: +1-630-990-0010 for referral to local chapter
   Services: National network of support groups that focus on assisting parents who have lost a child of any age, from any cause. Offers publications for parents and siblings.

Death and Dying and Grief Support

http://www.death-dying.com
   Services: Web site that offers information and support for families that are living with terminally ill children. Offers sections on grief, memorializing, coping, and self-care.

The Dougy Center

http://www.dougy.org
   Services: A place for children, teens, young adults, and their families that are grieving a death to share their experiences through peer support, groups, education, and training. Grief resources available.

National Center for School Crisis and Bereavement

https://www.cincinnatichildrens.org
   Phone: +1-513-803-2222
   Services: Provides guidance to parents and schools in order to understand and meet the needs of children, families, and peers.

New York Life Grief Guide

http://www.newyorklife.com/nyl/v/index.jsp?contentId = 143448&vgnextoid = 1572a2b341f32310VgnVCM100000ac841cacRCRD
   Phone: +1-212-576-7341
   Services: Provides resources that can help a family navigate a loss.

Supersibs.org

http://www.supersibs.org
   Services: Goal is to reach out to siblings of more than 10,000 children who are diagnosed with cancer each year. Siblings of children diagnosed with cancer are sent

a welcome packet and periodic packages throughout the year. Support guides are also offered to medical staff, teachers, and parents.

References

Alderfer, M. A., Long, K. A., Lown, E. A., Marsland, A. L., Ostrowski, N. L., Hock, J. M., & Ewing, L. J. (2010). Psychosocial adjustment of siblings of children with cancer. *Psycho-Oncology, 19*(8), 789–805.

Aldrich, C. N. (1974). Some dynamics of anticipatory grief. In B. Schoenberg (Ed.), *Anticipatory grief* (pp. 143–156). New York: Columbia University Press.

Arnold, J., Gemma, P. B., & Cushman, L. F. (2005). Exploring parental grief: Combining quantitative and qualitative measures. *Archives of Psychiatric Nursing, 19*, 245–255.

Arnold, J. H., & Gemma, P. B. (1994). *A child dies: A portrait of family grief* (2nd ed.). Philadelphia, PA: Charles Press.

Birenbaum, L. K., Robinson, M. A., Phillips, D. S., Stewart, B. J., & McCown, D. E. (1989). The response of children to the dying and death of a sibling. *OMEGA—Journal of Death and Dying, 20*, 213–228.

Blekesaune, M., & Øverbye, E. (2003). *Family change, health and social security: Four longitudinal studies.* NOVA Report No. 22. Oslo: NOVA.

Bluebond-Langner, M., Belasco, J. B., Goldman, A., & Belasco, C. (2007). Understanding parents' approaches to care and treatment of children with cancer when standard therapy has failed. *Journal of Clinical Oncology, 25*, 2414–2419.

Bonanno, G. A., Moskowitz, J. T., Papa, A., & Folkman, S. (2005). Resilience to loss in bereaved spouses, bereaved parents, and bereaved gay men. *Journal of Personality and Social Psychology, 88*(5), 827–843.

Boss, P. (2001). *Family stress management. A contextual approach.* Newbury Park, CA: Sage.

Brooks, J., & Ennis-Dustine, R. K. (2011). Faith, hope, and love: An interdisciplinary approach to providing spiritual care. In J. Wolfe, P. S. Hinds, & B. M. Sourkes (Eds.), *Textbook of interdisciplinary pediatric care* (pp. 111–118). Philadelphia, PA: Elsevier Saunders.

Brown, R. T., Wiener, L., Kupst, M. J., Brennan, T., Behrman, R., Compas, B. E., . . . Zelter, L. (2008). Single parenting and children with chronic illness: An understudied phenomenon. *Journal of Pediatric Psychology, 33*(4), 408–421.

Cherlin, E. J., Barry, C. L., Prigerson, H. G., Green, D. S., Johnson-Hurzeler, R., Kasl, S. V., & Bradley, E. H. (2007). Bereavement services for family caregivers: How often used, why, and why not. *Journal of Palliative Medicine, 10*, 148–158.

Compas, B. E., Connor-Smith, J. K., Saltzman, H., Thomsen, A. H., & Wadsworth, M. E. (2001). Coping with stress during childhood and adolescence: Problems, progress, and potential in theory and research. *Psychological Bulletin, 127*, 87–127.

Contro, N., Kreicbergs, U., Reichard, W. J., & Sourkes, B. (2011). Anticipatory grief and bereavement. In J. Wolfe, P. S. Hinds, & B. M. Sourkes (Eds.), *Textbook of interdisciplinary pediatric care* (pp. 41–54). Philadelphia, PA: Elsevier Saunders.

Currier, J. M., Holland, J. M., & Neimeyer, R. A. (2007). The effectiveness of bereavement interventions with children: A meta-analytic review of controlled outcome research. *Journal of Clinical Child and Adolescent Psychology, 36*, 253–259.

Currier, J. M., Holland, J. M., & Neimeyer, R. A. (2010). Do CBT-based intervention alleviate distress following bereavement? A review of current evidence. *International Journal of Cognitive Therapy, 3*, 77–93.

Currier, J. M., Neimeyer, R. A., & Berman, J. S. (2008). The effectiveness of psychotherapeutic interventions for bereaved persons: A comprehensive quantitative review. *Psychological Bulletin, 134*, 648–661.

deCinque, N., Monterosso, L., Dadd, G., Sidhu, R., Macpherson, R., & Aoun, S. (2006). Bereavement support for families following the death of a child from cancer: Experience of bereaved parents. *Journal of Psychosocial Oncology, 24*(2), 65–83.

Dussel, V., Kreicbergs, U., Hilden, J. M., Watterson, J., Moore, C., Turner, B. G., . . . Wolfe, J. (2009). Looking beyond where children die: Determinants and effects of planning a child's location of death. *Journal of Pain and Symptom Management, 37*(1), 33–43.

Espinosa, J., & Evans, W. N. (2013). Maternal bereavement: The heightened mortality of mothers after the death of a child. *Economics & Human Biology, 11*(3), 371–381.

Fanos, J. H., & Nickerson, B. G. (1991). Long-term effects of sibling death during adolescence. *Journal of Adolescent Research, 6,* 70–82.

Feudtner, C., Hays, R. M., Haynes, G., Geyer, J. R., Neff, J. M., & Koepsell, T. D. (2001). Deaths attributed to pediatric complex chronic conditions: national trends and implications for supportive care services. *Pediatrics, 107*(6), E99.

Feudtner, C., Hexem, K., & Rourke, M. (2011). Epidemiology and care of children with complex conditions. In J. Wolfe, P. S. Hinds, & B. M. Sourkes (Eds.), *Textbook of interdisciplinary pediatric care* (pp. 7–17). Philadelphia, PA: Elsevier Saunders.

Folkman, S. (2001). *Revised coping theory and the process of bereavement.* Washington, DC: American Psychological Association.

Foster, C. E., Webster, M. C., Weissman, M. M., Pilowsky, D. J., Wickramaratne, P. J., Talati, A., . . . King, C. A. (2008). Remission of maternal depression: Relations to family functioning and youth internalizing and externalizing symptoms. *Journal of Clinical Child & Adolescent Psychology, 37,* 714–724.

Foster, T. L., Gilmer, M. J., Davies, B., Barrera, M., Fairclough, D. L., Vannatta, K., & Gerhardt, C. A. (2009). Bereaved parents' and siblings' reports of legacies created by children with cancer. *Journal of Pediatric Oncology Nursing, 26,* 369–376.

Foster, T. L., Gilmer, M. J., Davies, B., Dietrich, M., Barrera, M., Fairclough, D. L., . . . Gerhardt, C. A. (2011). Comparison of continuing bonds reported by parents and siblings after the death of a child from cancer. *Death Studies, 35,* 420–440.

Foster, T. L., Gilmer, M. J., Vannatta, K., Barrera, M., Davies, B., Dietrich, M. S., . . . Gerhardt, C. A. (2012). Changes in siblings after the death of a child from cancer. *Cancer Nursing, 35,* 347–354.

Freud, S. (1917). Mourning and melancholia. In S. Freud, *Collected papers* (Vol. 4). London: Hogarth Press.

Garber, J., & Cole, D. A. (2010). Intergenerational transmission of depression: A launch and grow model of change across adolescence. *Developmental Psychopathology, 22,* 819–830.

Gerhardt, C. A., Fairclough, D. L., Grossenbacher, J. C., Barrera, M., Gilmer, M. J., Foster, T. L., . . . Vannatta, K. (2012). Peer relationships of bereaved siblings and comparison classmates after a child's death from cancer. *Journal of Pediatric Psychology, 37,* 209–219.

Gilmer, M. J., Foster, T. L., Vannatta, K., Barrera, M., Davies, B., Dietrich, M. S., . . . Gerhardt, C. A. (2012). Changes in parents after the death of a child from cancer. *Journal of Pain & Symptom Management, 44,* 572–582.

Ginzburg, K., Geron, Y., & Solomon, Z. (2002). Patterns of complicated grief among bereaved parents. *OMEGA: Journal of Death and Dying, 45,* 119–132.

Giovanola, J. (2005). Sibling involvement at the end of life. *Journal of Pediatric Oncology Nursing, 22*(4), 222–226.

Goodenough, B., Drew, D., Higgins, S., & Trethewie, S. (2004). Bereavement outcomes for parents who lose a child to cancer: Are place of death and sex of parent associated with differences in psychological functioning? *Psycho-Oncology, 13,* 779–791.

Hutton, C. J., & Bradley, B. S. (1994). Effects of sudden infant death on bereaved siblings: A comparative study. *Journal of Child Psychology and Psychiatry, 35*(4), 723–732.

Jalmsell, L., Kreicbergs, U., Onelöv, E., Steineic, G., & Henter, J. I. (2010). Anxiety is contagious—symptoms of anxiety in the terminally ill child affect long-term psychological well-being in bereaved parents. *Pediatric Blood & Cancer, 54,* 751–757.

Kazak, A. E., & Noll, R. B. (2004). Child death from pediatric illness: Conceptualizing intervention from a family/systems and public health perspective. *Professional Psychology: Research and Practice, 35,* 219–226.

Keesee, N. J., Currier, J. M., & Neimeyer, R. A. (2008). Predictors of grief following the death of one's child: The contribution of finding meaning. *Journal of Clinical Psychology, 64,* 1145–1163.

Kersting, A., Brähler, E., Glaesmer, H., & Wagner, B. (2011). Prevalence of complicated grief in a representative population based sample. *Journal of Affective Disorders, 131*(1–3), 339–343.

Kissane, D. W., McKenzie, M., Bloch, S., Moskowitz, C., McKenzie, D. P., & O'Neill, I. (2006). Family-focused grief therapy: A randomized controlled trial in palliative care and bereavement. *American Journal of Psychiatry, 163,* 1208–1218.

Kreicbergs, U., Lannen, P., Onelöv, E., & Wolfe, J. (2007). Parental grief after losing a child to cancer: Impact of professional and social support on long-term outcomes. *Journal of Clinical Oncology, 25*(22), 3307–3312.

Kreicbergs, U., Valdimarsdóttir, U., Onelöv, E., Björk, O, Steineck, G., & Henter, J.-I. (2005). Care-related distress: A nationwide study of parents who lost their child to cancer. *Journal of Clinical Oncology, 23,* 9162–9171.

Kreicbergs, U., Valdimarsdóttir, U., Onelöv, E., Henter, J. I., & Steineck, G. (2004a). Anxiety and depression in parents 4–9 years after the loss of a child owing to a malignancy: A population-based follow-up. *Psychological Medicine, 34,* 1431–1441.

Kreicbergs, U., Valdimarsdóttir, U., Onelöv, E., Henter, J. I., & Steineck, G. (2004b). Talking about death with children who have severe malignant disease. *New England Journal of Medicine, 351*(1), 175–186.

Kubler-Ross, E. (1969). *On death and dying.* New York: Touchstone.

Kubler-Ross, E., & Kessler, D. (2005). *On grief and grieving.* New York: Scribner Press.

Lehman, D. R., Wortman, C. B., & Williams, A. F. (1987). Long-term effects of losing a spouse or child in a motor vehicle crash. *Journal of Personality and Social Psychology, 52*(1), 218–231.

Lepore, S. J., Silver, R. C., Wortman, C. B., & Wayment, H. A. (1996). Social constraints, intrusive thoughts, and depressive symptoms among bereaved mothers. *Journal of Personality & Social Psychology, 70,* 271–282.

Levy, L. H., & Derby, J. F. (1992). Bereavement support groups: Who joins; who does not; and why. *American Journal of Community Psychology, 20,* 649–662.

Li, J., Laursen, T. M., Precht, D. H., Olsen, J., & Mortenson, P. B. (2005). Hospitalization for mental illness among parents after the death of a child. *New England Journal of Medicine, 352,* 1190–1196.

Li, J., Precht, D. H., Mortensen, P. B., & Olsen, J. (2003). Mortality in parents after death of a child in Denmark: A nationwide follow-up study. *Lancet, 361,* 363–367.

Lichtenthal, W. G., Cruess, D. G., & Prigerson, H. G. (2004). A case for establishing complicated grief as a distinct mental disorder in *DSM-V. Clinical Psychology Review, 24,* 637–662.

Lichtenthal, W. G., Nilsson, M., Kissane, D. W., Breitbart, W., Kacel, E., Jones, E. C., & Prigerson, H. G. (2011). Underutilization of mental health services among bereaved caregivers with prolonged grief disorder. *Psychiatric Services, 62,* 1225–1229.

Lichtenthal, W. G., Wiener, L., Sweeney, C., Roberts, K., Farberov, M. (2012). Disparities in prolonged grief, mental health service use, and barriers to use in racial/ethnic minority parents bereaved by cancer. Oral presentation at the American Psychosocial Oncology Society 9th Annual Conference, Miami, FL, 2/12.

Luthar, S. S., Cicchetti, D., & Becker, B. (2000). The construct of resilience: A critical evaluation and guidelines for future work. *Child Development, 71,* 543–562.

Mack, J. W., Joffe, S., Hilden, J. M., Watterson, J., Moore, C., Weeks, J. C., & Wolfe, J. (2008). Parents' views of cancer-directed therapy for children with no realistic chance for cure. *Journal of Clinical Oncology, 26,* 4759–4764.

McCown, D. E., & Davies, B. (1995). Patterns of grief in young children following the death of a sibling. *Death Studies, 19,* 41–53.

Murphy, S. A., Johnson, L. C., & Lohan, J. (2003). Finding meaning in a child's violent death: A five-year prospective analysis of parents' personal narratives and empirical data. *Death Studies, 27,* 381–404.

Neff, L. A., & Karney, B. R. (2005). Gender differences in social support: A question of skill or responsiveness? *Journal of Personality and Social Psychology, 88,* 79–90.

Pai, A. L., Greenley, R. N., Lewandowski, A., Drotar, D., Youngstrom, E., & Peterson, C. C. (2007). A meta-analytic review of the influence of pediatric cancer on parent and family functioning. *Journal of Family Psychology, 21*(3), 407–415.

Ponzetti, J. J. & Johnson, M. A. (1991). The forgotten grievers: Grandparents' reactions to the death of grandchildren. *Death Studies, 15,* 157–167.

Prigerson, H. G., Vanderwerker, L. C., & Maciejewski, P. K. (2008). A case for inclusion of prolonged grief disorder in *DSM-V.* In M. S. Stroebe, R. O. Hansson, H. Schut, & W. Stroebe (Eds.), *Intervention* (pp. 165–186). Washington, DC: American Psychological Association.

Rando, T. A. (1985). Bereaved parents: Particular difficulties, unique factors, and treatment issues. *Social Work, 30*(1), 19–23.

Raphael, B. (1984). *The anatomy of bereavement: A handbook for the caring professions.* London: Hutchinson.

Rosen, H. (1985). Prohibitions against mourning in childhood sibling loss. *OMEGA: Journal of Death and Dying, 15,* 307–316.

Rosenberg, A. R., Baker, K. S., Syrjala, K., & Wolfe, J. (2012). Systematic review of psychological morbidities among bereaved parents. *Pediatric Blood Cancer, 58*(4), 503–512.

Rosner, R., Kruse, J., & Hagl, M. (2010). A meta-analysis of interventions for bereaved children and adolescents. *Death Studies, 34,* 99–136.

Rosof, B. (1994). *The worst loss: How families heal from the death of a child.* New York: Henry Holt.

Sabbeth, B. F., & Leventhal, J. M. (1984). Marital adjustment to chronic childhood illness: A critique of the literature. *Pediatrics, 73*(6), 762–768.

Sanders, C. M. (1995). *Grief of children and parents.* Washington, DC: Hospice Foundation of America.

Schonfeld, D. (2012). Providing support for families experiencing the death of a child. In J. Wolfe, P. S. Hinds, & B. M. Sourkes (Eds.), *Textbook of interdisciplinary pediatric care* (pp. 223–230). Philadelphia, PA: Elsevier Saunders.

Schwab, R. (1992). Effects of a child's death on the marital relationship: A preliminary study. *Death Studies, 16,* 141–154.

Shear, K., Frank, E., Houck, P. R., & Reynolds, C. F., III. (2005). Treatment of complicated grief: A randomized controlled trial. *Journal of the American Medical Association, 293*(21), 2601–2068.

Skinner, E. A., Edge, K., Altman, J., & Sherwood, H. (2003). Searching for the structure of coping: A review and critique of category systems for classifying ways of coping. *Psychological Bulletin, 129,* 216–269.

Sloper, P. (2004). Predictors of distress in parents of children with cancer: A prospective study. *Journal of Pediatric Psychology, 25*(2), 79–91.

Surkan, P. J., Dickman, P. W., Steineck, G., Onelöv, E., & Kreicbergs, U. (2006). Home care of a child dying of a malignancy and parental awareness of a child's impending death. *Palliative Medicine, 20*(3), 161–169.

Thompson, L. (1993). Conceptualizing gender in marriage: The case of marital care. *Journal of Marriage and Family, 55*(3), 557–569.

United Nations Children's Fund. (2011). *Levels & trends in child mortality: Report 2011.* Retrieved from http://www.childinfo.org/files/Child_Mortality_Report_2011.pdf

Valdimarsdóttir, U., Kreicbergs, U., Hauksdóttir, A., Hunt, H., Onelöv, E., Henter, J. I., & Steineck, G. (2007). Parents' intellectual and emotional awareness of their child's impending death to cancer: A population-based long-term follow-up study. *Lancet Oncology, 8*(8), 706–714.

Vrijmoet-Wiersma, J. C. M, van Klink, J. M., Kolk, A. M., Koopman, H. M., Ball, L. M., & Maarten Egeler, R. (2008). Assessment of parental psychological stress in pediatric cancer: A review. *Journal of Pediatric Psychology, 33*(7), 694–706.

Walsh, F. (1999). *Spiritual resources in family therapy.* New York: Guilford Press.

Walsh, F. (2003). Family resilience. Strength forged through adversity. In R. Walsh (Ed), *Normal family processes* (3rd ed., pp. 399–423). New York: Guildford Press.

Werner, E., & Smith, R. (1992). *Overcoming the odds: High-risk children from birth to adulthood.* Ithaca, NY: Cornell University Press.

Wheeler, I. (2001). Parental bereavement: The crisis of meaning. *Death Studies, 25,* 51–66.

Wiener, L., Alderfer, M., & Hersh, S. P. (2011). Psychiatric and psychosocial support for child and family. In P. A. Pizzo & D. G. Poplack (Eds.), *Principles and practice of pediatric oncology* (6th ed., pp. 1322–1346). Philadelphia, PA: Lippincott.

Worden, J. W., Davies, B., & McCown, D. (1999). Comparing parent loss with sibling loss. *Death Studies, 23*(1), 1–15.

Wu, L., Bonanno, G., Duhamel, K., Redd, W. H., Rini, C., Austin, J., . . . Manne, S. (2008). Pre-bereavement meaning and post-bereavement distress in mothers of children who underwent haematopoietic stem cell transplantation. *British Journal of Health Psychology, 13,* 419–433.

Zisook, S., & Shear, K. (2009). Grief and bereavement: What psychiatrists need to know. *World Psychiatry, 8*(2), 67–74.Table 14.3 (Continued)

15 Care of Families with Children Anticipating the Death of a Parent

Anna C. Muriel

The death of a parent creates grief, distress, and change for surviving children and their families at any age. However, when children are adolescents or younger, or are dependent, the death of a parent typically results in unique stressors and developmental challenges. Medical and mental health clinicians working with these families may play important roles in providing anticipatory guidance, facilitating communication, identifying families at risk, and offering intervention for favorable psychosocial outcomes. Yet clinicians who interact with dying parents may not have expertise in working with children and adolescents. Therefore, this chapter provides background and a basic approach for helping patients who are actively parenting while facing life-limiting illness. Attention to the children's developmental stage and specific needs can help clinicians and surviving family members to support children during the patient's end-of-life period and into bereavement. Specific psychosocial interventions may be useful to higher risk families during palliative care and into bereavement.

Background

Child Coping with Parental Illness

The terminal phase of a parent's illness is a vulnerable time for children as they may experience more anxiety, depression, lower self-esteem, fears, misconceptions, and accompanying behavior changes (Christ et al., 1993; Christ, Siegel, & Sperber, 1994; Siegel, Karus, & Raveis, 1996). Children living with a parent with cancer have more anxiety associated with an inability to discuss the illness, decreased time spent in age-appropriate activities, and ongoing worries about the cancer (Nelson, Sloper, Charlton, & While, 1994). These anxieties may be mediated by increased communication because children who are given specific information about the illness have been shown to have lower anxiety (Rosenheim & Reicher, 1985).

However, these family conversations may not happen readily; even parents who are generally rated highly as communicators by their children are no more likely to disclose the probability of death than parents with low general communication ratings (Siegel et al., 1996). Therapists who facilitate family communication before a parent's death may improve children's ability to cope with the illness and loss. Children at different developmental stages can benefit from specific approaches that accommodate their unique emotional and cognitive needs (Christ & Christ, 2006).

Parent and Family Factors

Parental depression and family dysfunction are also important predictors of children's emotional and behavioral problems in the context of a parent's illness (Thastum et al., 2009). Families may be additionally vulnerable to parents' and children's difficulties in coping due to the well parent's physical and emotional preoccupation with the dying spouse (Saldinger, Porterfield, & Cain, 2004). Of course, parents and children also have differences in their cognitive understanding and therefore their anticipation of the death, which may have implications for children's coping and outcomes (Saldinger, Cain, Kalter, & Lohnes, 1999). The child may exhibit a range of responses to the graphic experience of a parent's terminal illness, with attendant changes in appearance, function, and dependence on medical equipment, which can sometimes, but not always, be mediated by overwhelmed adult caregivers (Saldinger, Cain, & Porterfield, 2003).

Parents with serious illness may benefit from specific attention from their medical providers regarding their role as parents, and targeted interventions may help mediate parental, family, and child distress. Some parents may have higher levels of concern about their children, including mothers, single parents, or those with metastatic or recurrent cancer, a subjective understanding of incurable disease, and mental health concerns (Muriel et al., 2012). Not surprisingly, parents with advanced cancer who have dependent children have higher rates of anxiety than those without dependent children. This population of parents also tends to prefer more aggressive treatment and is less likely to engage in advanced care planning (Nilsson et al., 2009).

Family-focused therapeutic approaches during palliative care have been shown to reduce distress and depression in bereavement in high-risk families with adolescent and adult children (Kissane et al., 2006). Among families with younger children who seek preventive bereavement services, family intervention has been shown to improve parenting, coping, and caregiver mental health, and to reduce internalizing and externalizing problems in children with increased psychological difficulties at presentation (Sandler et al., 2003).

Childhood Bereavement

Descriptive studies of childhood bereavement find that children naturally make active efforts to maintain a connection to their deceased parents and construct an ongoing relationship that may shift with developmental stages to support effective coping with the loss (Silverman, Nickman, & Worden, 1992). The surviving parent can give the child important opportunities to remember and memorialize the deceased parent and can facilitate integration of the loss throughout different phases of growth and development (Nickman, Silverman, & Normand, 1998).

Clinicians and families often fear that parental loss during childhood will necessarily create mental health problems in adulthood. Although such a loss has echoes throughout life, studies show that most bereaved children do not develop psychiatric disorders. Though many children may demonstrate non-specific, sub-clinical, and transient behavioral disturbances (Black, 1998; Vida & Grizenko, 1989) in the year following a parent's death, only one in five children has a formal psychiatric disorder (Dowdney, 2000).

Epidemiologic studies highlight that preexisting psychosocial risk factors in families with an ill parent are an important predictor of bereaved children's increased rates of subclinical problems and decreased global function (Kaplow, Saunders, Angold, & Costello, 2010). Earlier studies of typology of family functioning during palliative care and bereavement also note that dysfunctional families have higher rates of depression and psychosocial morbidity during early bereavement (Kissane et al., 1996).

Parental loss in and of itself does not necessarily predict future psychopathology in adulthood, and studies also show that the quality of the surviving parent's care (Bifulco, Brown, & Harris, 1987; Harris, Brown, & Bifulco, 1986) or general home life (Breier et al., 1988) are better predictors of subsequent adult depression. Other factors that may mediate depression in adulthood are warmth and empathy in surviving parents and, importantly, the opportunity to participate in the mourning process (Saler & Skolnick, 1992).

Developmental Context

How Children at Different Ages Understand Death

Clinicians who seek to support families during end of life and bereavement need a basic developmental framework from which to work. Children's understanding of death is influenced by their general level of cognitive and emotional development, as well as their exposure to death in their community. Individual variation in children's temperaments and development must be considered, and parents should be respected as experts on their own children. A clinician's understanding of basic needs at different ages provides a useful guide for the general support of children during the parent's terminal phase and can be the foundation for anticipatory guidance and general psychosocial intervention.

Infants and Toddlers (Newborns to 2 Years Old)

Infants and toddlers work on the complex tasks of attachment, basic self-regulation, and trust in their environment and caregivers. These youngsters have no understanding of time or the finality of death. They are, however, sensitive to separations and will feel the absence of a familiar caregiver. They may be distressed by changes in routines and will likely be affected by the emotional distress of grieving adults around them.

Although familiarity and structure are helpful for people of all ages during difficult times, they are even more essential for the youngest children. During the stressful months or weeks approaching a parent's death, infants and toddlers can best be cared for by a limited number of familiar caregivers who can get accustomed to a child's routine and provide care as consistently and predictably as possible.

Preschoolers (3 to 6 Years Old)

Preschool children have a wider range of social interactions than infants and toddlers. Their understanding of parental illness and death is influenced by developmentally expectable egocentrism, associative logic, and magical thinking. These self-referential ideas can be mediated to help prevent misunderstandings and guilt about what is happening in their family. Children of this age do not yet understand the irreversibility of death, so they may also offer "solutions" for it and for serious illness.

Because young children may attribute the grief and distress of adults to their own behavior, they may benefit from regular reminders that nothing they say or do can make a parent ill or die. Adults need to inquire about how the child thinks their parent got sick or died and dispel misconceptions repeatedly. In addition, caregivers may need to be patient with a natural disconnection of feelings and content, whereby a child might talk about the death very matter-of-factly or create a song about it, yet become cranky or experience difficulties with routine activities or changes in schedule. Parents of pre-schoolers can also expect behavioral regression under stress: a fully toilet-trained child may have trouble using the bathroom, or a child may get upset when being dropped off at a previously beloved day care center.

In discussing death with young children, it is important to be concrete and use observable examples. Parents' descriptions of death as "going to sleep" can make children worry about bedtime and not awakening. A child may conceptualize heaven as a place that one can visit and come back from. Adults may begin this conversation by asking a young child what they think death is like. This allows the conversation to focus on a child's misperceptions, and the adult can use simple language and examples that the child can relate to. Concrete explanations may ease worries about pain or everyday needs after death. For example, adults may talk about death as meaning that "the body doesn't work anymore," that the person can't move or breathe or think or feel, and so forth. Adult survivors are sometimes surprised and disturbed by how often young children may get confused or upset, and need this explanation.

School-Age Children (7 to 12 Years Old)

School-age children are immersed in mastering academic, physical, and social skills, and they are working to understand the logic of cause and effect. They are often invested in fairness and are sensitive to things that set them apart from their peers.

By age six or seven, children consistently understand the permanence of death and may be distressed by the separation and loss that it entails. Their conceptions may still be very concrete; they may have difficulty understanding more abstract or spiritual issues. In fact, they can be preoccupied with the factual, medical, or physical aspects of death and dying that adults find challenging to discuss. The uncertain time frame for the death may be particularly hard for younger children to grasp, so anticipating the death itself may become distorted. For example, a 10-year-old who hears that a parent is getting sicker and "coming home to die" may think the parent will die that very night.

Because so much of a child's day is spent at school, it is important that appropriate school personnel be kept up to date about the status of an ill parent. Although children may not want teachers to approach them about the parent's illness at school, it is helpful for children to know to whom they can turn if they are having a difficult day. Although school personnel's expectations for the child's schoolwork may need to change temporarily, most children benefit from regular tasks and routines so that they understand that their life continues, notwithstanding a parent's illness and death. Families may come to rely on other families in their communities to support their children's participation in age-appropriate activities. School-age children are also vulnerable to worries about their own health or the health of their surviving family members, for which they need consistent reassurances. They may express emotional distress via complaints of physical ailments and need reassurance.

Adolescents (13 Years Old and Older)

Teenagers are in the process of identity formation and separation from parents and are caught up in the changes of puberty and a wider social environment. Although they have more adult capacities for abstract thinking, their brains are not fully mature until they are into their twenties.

Adolescents understand that death is final, irreversible, and universal, and they may think actively about existential and spiritual issues. They may also vacillate between abstract ideas about their parent's death and preoccupation with very specific and self-oriented ways in which it affects their life, worrying about continuing without their parent and anticipating milestones that their parent will not witness.

Surviving adult caregivers may struggle to understand adolescent self-involvement as developmentally normal; they may need reminders not to attribute it to negative character flaws. Adolescents may be at risk for more independence than they can handle and will continue to need consistent adult support and guidance surrounding a parent's illness and death. Families should be mindful of teenagers who take on too many adult responsibilities or even engage in risky behaviors such as substance abuse or illegal activity.

Older adolescents and young adults also need specific details about a parent's illness and probability of death as they make decisions about moving away from home for employment or education. Although parents may want to give them significant freedom, these young adults need accurate information in order to make decisions comfortably and minimize any possible regrets about being too close or too far away during the end of a parent's life.

General Support for Families

Anticipatory Communication with Children

Taking into account child development, family style, and parental coping to date, clinicians can address parental concerns about helping their children through this difficult time. The approach that clinicians take for these discussions is influenced by the family's communication style in general, the adults' capacities to integrate end-of-life care, and the expected progression of disease.

Clinicians can begin by assessing the adults' understanding and expectations of the illness and death:

* What is the adults' understanding about the expected time course?
* What do they know about the expected symptomatology?
* What do they hope for in terms of location and medical circumstances of the death?

The stage is then set to explore with the parents the children's understanding of the illness to date:

* What language has been used with the children?
* What do the children understand about the outcome of the illness?
* What experiences have the children had with major life changes or death in their community or family?
* How have they managed these experiences as a family?

- Do the parents have particular concerns about their children's ability to cope with the illness so far?
- What are the parents' particular concerns about their children coping with death?

The answers to these questions provide scaffolding for families and help parents to have honest conversations with their children while addressing worries and misconceptions along the way. Parents should be encouraged to use straightforward and age-appropriate language, checking frequently for the children's understanding and welcoming questions as they arise. If the children have not yet been told the specific name of the illness, it is important to do so now to minimize confusion and anxiety about illness in general.

Given careful clinical discussion with parents and adult caregivers, it may not be necessary for clinicians to meet directly with the children. In some settings, a meeting is not possible, and for most children, information mediated by their parents is most easily integrated and discussed in an iterative process over time. However, when children are present during medical encounters by chance or by design, they should be welcomed into the discussion so that their questions can be addressed. Likewise, when children are at home during hospice visits, they can be invited to join parts of the conversation and ask questions. Some older children may ask to participate in meetings with medical providers in order to feel more fully included in the family experience. In some instances, children may challenge clinicians or parents with questions that are anxiety provoking or out of the blue. Asking a child, "What got you thinking about that?" may help clarify exactly what makes the child curious or worried and allows adults to provide specific answers without adding more detail than the child wishes or can process.

Timing of Discussions with Children

Families often wonder when to talk about the terminal nature of a parent's illness with children. Of course, sometimes it is hard for parents to talk openly, even when children have already observed the parent's deteriorating status or have overheard that death is likely. Other times, parents have trouble holding back the fact that care is transitioning from curative to palliative treatment, even if there is no observable change in the parent's appearance or function and death is likely many months away.

The worst way for a child to hear news is by overhearing it, and many children will experience well-intentioned protection as exclusion. Children left to their own conclusions about a parent's terminal illness may also be vulnerable to misconceptions about why the illness is progressing or how their life will change after a parent dies. On the other hand, it is difficult for younger children to understand that a parent may live for some time even in the terminal phase, and they may get confused when anticipating death for a prolonged period.

Concrete changes in a parent's appearance or functional status may be important time points to discuss with school-age or older children that death may occur within a certain time frame. Indeed, many children will ask about death directly in the context of seeing a parent getting more ill or less functional. To encourage children to articulate their worries, a parent can ask, "Do you know what could happen if Mom gets even sicker or different parts of her body stop working?" For the youngest children, acknowledging the functional changes as they pertain to their interactions with the parent may be enough: "Dad used to be able to take walks with us and play with you, but now he can't because he is sicker, so he stays in bed a lot." Although they may be aware of the distress in the home, younger children will have the greatest need for consistency, reassurance, and dispelling of misconceptions—even more than the anticipation of death. Conversations with pre-school-age or younger children may be most meaningful after the death has occurred.

Decisions about the Setting for End-of-Life Care in a Family Context

One of the most important decisions for families anticipating a parent's death is where they would choose that the death occur. There is no one answer that will suit every family, and the ill adult may have experiences or personal wishes that will dictate whether he or she wishes to die at home, in the hospital, or in an inpatient hospice setting. If families have choices, they should, if and when reasonable, consider the needs of the children in addition to the medical or personal needs of the dying parent.

Sometimes an inpatient hospice or hospital setting makes the most sense for families. But the well parent will have to divide his or her time between the inpatient setting with the spouse and home with the children. Having thoughtful, familiar adults at home can ease this strain and allow the children to continue with their usual home and school activities. Visiting by the children should be facilitated whenever possible and is discussed subsequently.

If families are interested in home hospice services and expect a parent to die at home, attention to certain logistical details can increase the children's comfort. For example, whenever possible, keeping the dying parent in a room with a door, as opposed to an open or family area, allows the children to titrate their own exposure to the ill parent and medical equipment. The advantage of having everyone at home is that the children can maintain more of their usual routines and likely have more access to their well parent. If other adults stay in the home to help, they should be aware of older children's needs for privacy and daily routines.

If the ill parent remains at home, it becomes even more important that the family discuss changes in medical status and check for children's questions or misconceptions about what is happening. Children may have particular fears about the death itself, and clinicians can help both adults and curious children by anticipating symptoms and treatments for pain, secretions, shortness of breath, and so forth, and for children who are curious, or who are likely to be present for the death, explaining what the physical process of dying might look and sound like. This also allows older children to consider how much they want to be around during the final days and hours. When a parent dies at home, parents should consider where the children will be when the funeral home arrives to remove the body.

Visits between Ill Parents and Children

If a parent is expected to die in an inpatient or hospice setting, visits from children should be facilitated whenever possible. Children who are reluctant may have specific worries, such as seeing blood or seeing their parent die, and can usually be reassured with explanations and contingency plans. It is best to avoid an agitated or delirious parent who may be frightening, though a child can still visit a sedated parent. Older children and adolescents who are reluctant to visit may benefit from opportunities to discuss their concerns and make a decision for themselves with which they feel comfortable over time.

Most importantly, children need to be prepared for the visit, with descriptions of the setting, medical equipment, and roommates, as well as the physical and functional status of the parent. For younger children, these descriptions may need to be concrete comparisons to the last time they saw their parent. An additional supportive adult should accompany the child so that they can leave when the child is ready, even if the well parent would like to stay longer. Younger children may tolerate only brief visits or might need structured, quiet play or drawing activities to do in the room. Touching a sick parent should never be forced but can be modeled and supported if the child is willing. After the visit, adult caregivers should take some time to debrief and ask the child what was most interesting, scary, uncomfortable, or even fun, in order to reassure the child and prepare better for the next time. When in-person visits are not possible, other kinds of contact should be encouraged. Children often enjoy making cards and notes that can be used to decorate a hospital room.

When death is imminent, last visits can be meaningful for children old enough to have an understanding of the finality of death. Older children may have the same wishes as adults, to have a few minutes alone with a dying parent, even if comatose, to say a last "I love you" or share an important private moment. If possible, older school-age and teenage children should be asked whether they want to be called to the bedside near the end of life or immediately after the death. For example, does a child want to be brought home from school, or woken in the middle of the night at the time of death, or not? Some children very much want to be included, whereas others may prefer to have healthier memories of their parent or feel afraid and uncomfortable about seeing their parent very ill and dying.

The guiding principle is to provide children with information so that they can make decisions that will help them feel that their needs and wishes are considered during this critical time. Families should, however, remember that there are many opportunities to say good-bye before the death, immediately afterward, and during memorial services and funerals, as well as during private moments of reflection or prayer.

Legacy Leaving

Parents who have come to terms with a diagnosis of a terminal illness often consider specific legacies or communications that they would like to leave for their children. The usual family photos and memorabilia become good foundations for telling stories about a loved one who has departed. Parents may also choose a variety of more intentional communications, such as annotated books, letters, audio recordings, music, or movies specifically for each child, or at particular milestones. There are few data on how surviving children view these communications over time, but they often look for indications—from both the dead parent and surviving adults—about who their parent was as a person, their values and ideals, and what their parent saw in them as their child.

Either before or after the death, children may want to choose special objects to keep themselves. The wider community can also be engaged in legacy leaving, as friends and relatives attending the memorial service can be asked to write down a memory or thought about the parent that can be compiled for the children and shared when they are curious later. A child will have a lifetime to revisit the loss of the parent and may become interested in the parent as they themselves reach different phases in their own life.

Children's Participation in Funerals and Memorial Services

Children of any age may participate in different aspects of funerals and memorial services. Family tradition will dictate whether there is a wake, religious service, interment, or subsequent family gathering afterward, and children may be included for all or part of these events. As with hospital visits, children need to be prepared for what the event will be like, including the setting, who will be there, what will transpire, and what they can and cannot do. It is useful for children to be prepared for a range of feelings expressed by people, from sadness to warmth and humor. For younger children, a familiar adult should care for them throughout and be responsive or escort them out if they cannot sit still or remain quiet.

Older school-age and teenage children can be included in the planning or asked if they want to participate by reading or playing music during the service. Many funeral homes provide the family with privacy for a special children's service or quiet visiting time. Children are sometimes interested in placing a picture, note, or special object in or on top of the casket. Because school-age children may have specific questions about the preparation of the body or cremation, families may want to learn about the process in advance, in order to field questions. Alternatively, families should know whom to ask about these issues during the difficult and chaotic days around the parent's death; funeral directors sometimes have age-appropriate information.

Younger children in particular, who have less understanding of death, may find the interment particularly disturbing if they see their parent lowered into the ground. Indeed, families may consider letting young children forgo the burial and visit the gravesite another time. For families who spread ashes or have services that do not involve a burial site, it may still be important for the family to designate a special place to go to reflect or remember the parent.

Bereavement Interventions

Despite intuitive concern about psychological outcomes for bereaved children and families in which a parent dies, there are few evidence-based programs for families facing this loss. Christ et al. developed a parental guidance intervention for families, to facilitate communication and visits near the end of life (Christ, Raveis, Seigel, Karus, & Christ, 2005). The 88 families were randomized to either parent-guidance or supportive-reflective intervention. Although group comparison outcomes are not clear, the interviews provided rich qualitative data about the roles of preparation, communication, and thematic description of the 157 children's reconstitution after the death.

A Family Bereavement Program (FBP) has been designed for parentally bereaved children ages 8 to 16 years old (Sandler et al., 2003) to address potentially modifiable risk and protective mental health factors. This randomized controlled trial occurred in a heterogeneous, community-based sample of families between 4 and 30 months after the loss; they participated in 12 two-hour group sessions. Four sessions had conjoint activities for parents and children, and the remainder involved separate groups for children, adolescents, and caregivers. Manualized content for caregivers included (1) techniques for improving positive caregiver-child relationship and effective discipline, (2) skills to challenge negative thoughts and increase positive activities, and (3) education to guide children in active problem solving. Child and adolescent groups focused on improving coping efficacy, self-esteem, cognitive reframing, and problem solving. The program provided opportunity for caregiver-child sharing and validating grief-related feelings. The control group received three grief-related books at one-month intervals, along with a syllabus of important issues in adult, child, or adolescent grief. Results indicated that the FBP group had improved parenting, coping, and caregiver mental health and fewer stressful events. At 11-month follow-up, youth with greater psychological difficulties, girls, and parents with the lowest scores on positive parenting had improved family and individual risk and protective factors.

Although not specifically designed for families with young children, the Family Focused Grief Therapy model (Kissane et al., 2006) has been used in families at risk of poor psychosocial outcome, with children as young as 12 years old. The therapy consists of four to eight 90-minute sessions during palliative care and into bereavement, across 9 to 18 months. This family intervention aims to enhance family functioning through exploration of cohesion, communication of thoughts and feelings, and managing conflict. Moderately dysfunctional families, who were characterized as sullen, had the greatest improvement in distress and individual depression scores, highlighting a population of families who may be distressed and yet have capacities to take in the intervention.

Although many families and children are resilient and eventually adapt and resume good function after an ill parent's death, clinicians should be aware of interventions that may be aimed at caregivers, children, or the family unit as a whole. Enhancing the mental health of surviving adult caregivers, as well as improving family communication and problem solving, may be particularly useful to families at highest psychosocial risk.

Conclusion

The untimely death of a parent is one of the most challenging events for families and the clinicians who care for them. Attention to children's needs during this time is clearly an important aspect of clinical care and is also much appreciated by adults in the family. A basic knowledge of child development and the ways that children understand illness and death can provide a template with which to engage families to help their children. When clinicians support honest, child-centered communication and help parents anticipate common situations and questions, families are able to use their own best resources to provide children with thoughtful care. Families with premorbid psychological vulnerabilities may benefit from specific family-based bereavement interventions.

Further Reading

Christ, G. H. (2000). *Healing children's grief: Surviving a parent's death from cancer*. New York: Oxford University Press.

Harpham, W. S. (1997). *When a parent has cancer: A guide to caring for your children*. New York: Harper Collins.

Klass, D., Silverman, P. R., & Nickman, S. L. (Eds.). (1996). *Continuing bonds: New understandings of grief*. Washington, DC: Taylor & Francis.

McCue, K. (1994). *How to help children through a parent's serious illness*. New York: St. Martin's Griffin.

Rauch, P. R., & Muriel, A. C. (2006). *Raising an emotionally healthy child when a parent is sick*. New York: McGraw-Hill.
Worden, J. W. (1996). *Children and grief: When a parent dies*. New York: Guilford Press.

References

Bifulco, A. T., Brown, G. W., & Harris, T. O. (1987). Childhood loss of parent, lack of adequate parental care and adult depression: A replication. *Journal of Affective Disorders, 12*(2), 115–128.
Black, D. (1998). Coping with loss. Bereavement in childhood. *British Medical Journal, 316*(7135), 931–933.
Breier, A., Kelsoe, J. R., Jr., Kirwin, P. D., Beller, S. A., Wolkowitz, O. M., & Pickar, D. (1988). Early parental loss and development of adult psychopathology. *Archives of General Psychiatry, 45*(11), 987–993.
Christ, G. H., & Christ, A. E. (2006). Current approaches to helping children cope with a parent's terminal illness. *CA: A Cancer Journal for Clinicians, 56*(4), 197–212.
Christ, G. H., Raveis, V. H., Seigel, K., Karus, D., & Christ, A. E. (2005). Evaluation of a preventive intervention for bereaved children. *Journal of Social Work in End-of-Life & Palliative Care, 1*(3), 57–81.
Christ, G. H., Siegel, K., Freund, B., Langosch, D., Hendersen, S., Sperber, D., & Weinstein, L. (1993). Impact of parental terminal cancer on latency-age children. *American Journal of Orthopsychiatry, 63*(3), 417–425.
Christ, G. H., Siegel, K., & Sperber, D. (1994). Impact of parental terminal cancer on adolescents. *American Journal of Orthopsychiatry, 64*(4), 604–613.
Dowdney, L. (2000). Childhood bereavement following parental death. *Journal of Child Psychology and Psychiatry, 41*(7), 819–830.
Harris, T., Brown, G. W., & Bifulco, A. (1986). Loss of parent in childhood and adult psychiatric disorder: The role of lack of adequate parental care. *Psychological Medicine, 16*(3), 641–659.
Kaplow, J. B., Saunders, J., Angold, A., & Costello, E. J. (2010). Psychiatric symptoms in bereaved versus nonbereaved youth and young adults: A longitudinal epidemiological study. *Journal of the American Academy of Child and Adolescent Psychiatry, 49*(11), 1145–1154.
Kissane, D. W., Bloch, S., Onghena, P., McKenzie, D. P., Snyder, R. D., & Dowe, D. L. (1996). The Melbourne Family Grief Study, II: Psychosocial morbidity and grief in bereaved families. *American Journal of Psychiatry, 153*(5), 659–666.
Kissane, D. W., McKenzie, M., Bloch, S., Moskowitz, C., McKenzie, D. P., & O'Neill, I. (2006). Family focused grief therapy: A randomized, controlled trial in palliative care and bereavement. *American Journal of Psychiatry, 163*(7), 1208–1218.
Muriel, A. C., Moore, C. W., Baer, L., Park, E. R., Kornblith, A. B., Pirl, W., . . . Rauch, P. K. (2012). Measuring psychosocial distress and parenting concerns among adults with cancer: The Parenting Concerns Questionnaire. *Cancer, 118*(22), 5671–5678.
Nelson, E., Sloper, P., Charlton, A., & While, D. (1994). Children who have a parent with cancer: A pilot study. *Journal of Cancer Education, 9*(1), 30–36.
Nickman, S. L., Silverman, P. R., & Normand, C. (1998). Children's construction of a deceased parent: The surviving parent's contribution. *American Journal of Orthopsychiatry, 68*(1), 126–134.
Nilsson, M. E., Maciejewski, P. K., Zhang, B., Wright, A. A., Trice, E. D., Muriel, A. C., . . . Prigerson, H. G. (2009). Mental health, treatment preferences, advance care planning, location, and quality of death in advanced cancer patients with dependent children. *Cancer, 115*(2), 399–409.
Rosenheim, E., & Reicher, R. (1985). Informing children about a parent's terminal illness. *Journal of Child Psychology and Psychiatry, 26*(6), 995–998.
Saldinger, A., Cain, A., Kalter, N., & Lohnes, K. (1999). Anticipating parental death in families with young children. *American Journal of Orthopsychiatry, 69*(1), 39–48.

Saldinger, A., Cain, A., & Porterfield, K. (2003). Managing traumatic stress in children anticipating parental death. *Psychiatry, 66*(2), 168–181.

Saldinger, A., Porterfield, K., & Cain, A. C. (2004). Meeting the needs of parentally bereaved children: A framework for child-centered parenting. *Psychiatry, 67*(4), 331–352.

Saler, L., & Skolnick, N. (1992). Childhood parental death and depression in adulthood: Roles of surviving parent and family environment. *American Journal of Orthopsychiatry, 62*(4), 504–516.

Sandler, I. N., Ayers, T. S., Wolchik, S. A., Tein, J. Y., Kwok, O. M., Haine, R. A., . . . Griffin, W. A. (2003). The family bereavement program: Efficacy evaluation of a theory-based prevention program for parentally bereaved children and adolescents. *Journal of Consultation and Clinical Psychology, 71*(3), 587–600.

Siegel, K., Karus, D., & Raveis, V. H. (1996). Adjustment of children facing the death of a parent due to cancer. *Journal of the American Academy of Child and Adolescent Psychiatry, 35*(4), 442–450.

Silverman, P. R., Nickman, S., & Worden, J. W. (1992). Detachment revisited: The child's reconstruction of a dead parent. *American Journal of Orthopsychiatry, 62*(4), 494–503.

Thastum, M., Watson, M., Kienbacher, C., Piha, J., Steck, B., Zachariae, R., . . . Romer, G. (2009). Prevalence and predictors of emotional and behavioural functioning of children where a parent has cancer: A multinational study. *Cancer, 115*(17), 4030–4039.

Vida, S., & Grizenko, N. (1989). *DSM-III-R* and the phenomenology of childhood bereavement: A review. *Canadian Journal of Psychiatry, 34*(2), 148–155.

16 Family-Centered Approach to Helping Older Grieving People

J. Shep Jeffreys

Help for grieving elders is based on three concepts operating in harmony: (1) *understanding human grief*, i.e., it is natural and rooted in the primitive reflex for survival; (2) *understanding older adults*, i.e., they have unique needs and realities when bereaved; and (3) awareness of a *family-centered approach*, i.e., the family unit is often the most accessible format for delivering care to grieving older adults.

After reviewing the functions that these play in the delivery of care for the bereaved elderly, I will focus on thoughts, methods, and resources for providing services utilizing a family-centered approach. According to Kissane and Bloch (2002), "This approach involves assessing families, harnessing their strengths and bolstering their capacity to cope adaptively, with the goal of optimizing their supportive role" (p. 1).

Understanding Human Grief

I begin with the first level of understanding—*human grief* as a set of thoughts, feelings, and behaviors in reaction to loss, which is connected to the urge to survive (Parkes, 2002). We are hardwired for fight-flight-freeze responses in times that threaten survival; likewise, we have another survival-loaded set of reactions—the human grief response (Jeffreys, 2011; MacLean, 1973). This is designed to restore the attachments we have made in the service of human continuity into the future and to enable the reclaiming of a functional life. This *biological imperative* is set forth in our genetic heritage. Our gene pools are supposed to allow us to live long enough to protect offspring who will, in turn, have descendants to carry on the mission of survival—a biological version of "Be fruitful and multiply."

Grief is a universal human phenomenon. In a world where television and the Internet bring tragedy from various cultures into the immediate space of billions of others, the anguished faces of loss take on a universal similarity. The skin color may be different, the clothing unusual, the funeral rites unfamiliar—but "the wailing lament of a mother holding a dead child looks and sounds the same everywhere" (Jeffreys, 2011, p. 39).

Some denial and humor are necessary responses to loss. They allow us time to get used to the idea that our loved one is gone forever, the metastatic tumor cannot be controlled, the illness is terminal, the business is bankrupt, the economic disaster has reached into our lives (Jeffreys, 2005), or our prayers were not answered. *It's what humans do.*

As adults mature, they form attachment bonds with other adults to secure their social and psychological survival (MacLean, 1973) and provide offspring who will further the link of continuity. The nature of attachment—secure versus insecure bonds—has a strong shaping effect on relationships and an eventual impact on the nature of grief (Bowlby, 1973, 1979, 1980, 1982; Fraley, 2002). Myths, culture, beliefs, and thoughts from the past "line the walls of our interior system of belief, like shards of broken pottery in an archeological site" (Campbell, 1988/1991, p. xiv). Cave drawings, burial artifacts, and epic writings are filled with heroes' stories of staying alive despite adversity. The almost universal gatherings of kin in rituals and practices aim to support the mourners. The grief response is generated from a basic drive to cope and survive; it is both natural and expected.

Understanding Older Adult Grief

It is an error to assume that advanced age precludes the normal difficulties inherent in facing death.

—T. Rando (1984)

Understanding the needs of grieving elders and the usefulness of a family-centered approach requires awareness of the characteristics of older adults.

More than 2.5 million people die annually in the United States (Hamilton, Martin & Ventura, 2012). The largest proportion of deaths occurs in the over-65 age group. Although older adults comprise 12% of the population, they account for 73% of the deaths. In addition to death or other losses, what else is going on in the older adult's life that affects the nature of bereavement? Who are the co-bereaved and others in their lives who may be available to help?

Studies comparing younger and older people "find more intense grief and more adjustment problems among the younger bereaved" (Hansson & Stroebe, 2007). Most deaths affecting the elderly result from chronic disease or other progressive disorders. About 1.7 million of the annual 2.4 million deaths are due to illness (Jeffreys, 2011). This is especially true of spousal loss. "Contemporary late-life widowhood is best characterized as a process" rather than an event (Carr & Jeffreys, 2011, p. 82). The death of a partner or significant other may represent months or years of caregiving at home, with all the attendant losses and risks. However, when death is sudden, unexpected, and/or violent, bereaved elders are subject to the same levels of distress and post-death trauma reactions as found in younger mourners.

The age of the elderly bereaved can make a difference in how we work with them and their families. Today, the fastest-growing segment of elders is the over-75 age group. With the loss of a spouse, sibling, adult child, or close friend, the grieving elder may not have the years left to devote to rebuilding attachment bonds of comparable importance. Loss of an adult child can also mean that their support and potential for caregiving has vanished.

Factors Affecting the Grief of Older Adults

The older adult has been exposed to ever-increasing losses over time. They may have grieved the death of their parents, many peers, and perhaps siblings and children as well. Each loss creates a permanent modification to the inner world. Each new loss is experienced within a *web of already existing other losses and changes* (Jeffreys, 2011).

Physical Health Factors

As older adults age, health conditions and physical limitations affect their quality of life. Some are biological—a function of wear and tear. Basic body systems, such as cardiac, neurological, digestive, endocrine, muscular-skeletal, and immune, naturally break down. Some limitations result from falls, others from chronic diseases.

It is important that the therapist obtain a good medical history: illnesses, hospitalizations, medications, physical limitations, and the elder's reaction to this aspect of his or her life. The elderly patient's medical concerns may be front and center, requiring many appointments; grief therapy may take a back seat. Who, if anyone, in the family accompanies the elderly relative to appointments? Is it on a schedule? Do others know who is responsible for medical appointments or medication follow-up? If this is a case of spousal loss, was the deceased the caregiver for the bereaved elder?

When working with the elderly, it is very useful to have enough medical knowledge to recognize warning signs that warrant a referral to the physician.

Cognitive Factors

At this time of life, cognitive changes may also affect the performance of familiar tasks and make elderly persons feel inadequate. They may find themselves confused trying to drive to the home of an old friend or trying to fill out a health insurance form. They may experience short-term memory loss, slowed-down reaction time, decreased alertness, and/or decreased ability to select appropriate words. Some cognitive change is reversible if caused by inadequate hydration, drug interactions, or urinary tract infections. For other people, small strokes or the beginning of Alzheimer's disease may be the cause of memory loss. The care provider should not conclude that reduced cognitive ability is permanent before the primary physician has verified the diagnosis.

Social Factors

Many social issues and conditions have an impact on older people's grief reaction.

Loneliness. "Loneliness, the subjective feeling of isolation, not belonging, or lacking companionship, is a common source of distress, suffering, and impaired quality of life in older persons; and is a predictor of functional decline and death" (Perissinotto, Cenzer, & Covinsky, 2012, p. 1). Further, the subjective experience of loneliness is gaining recognition as a separate condition from social isolation and depression. Limited social contact is a reality for some older adults regardless of where they live. Of course, even those in community setups such as assisted living and nursing homes can feel very lonely.

Seniors living independently may be isolated because of lack of transportation, limitations on their physical mobility, or loss of family, friends, and neighbors after a move. Even seniors who live close to their children and grandchildren may feel alone due to family conflict or infrequent visits from the family.

Some senior citizens may experience isolation because so many of their friends have died. Other seniors have fewer opportunities to meet people and make new friends. Also, loss of the role created by caregiving, work, or volunteer involvement can result in social isolation when not replaced. Nevertheless, according to Perissinnotto et al. (2012), "Loneliness may be amenable to psychosocial interventions, and it is possible that it is more treatable than other determinants of functional decline such as age-associated chronic disease" (p. 3).

Disenfranchisement. Older adults are frequently not credited as experiencing the same depth of grief and fearfulness about death as younger people. Younger members of a family may assume that an elder is "used to people dying" because he or she has lived for such a long time. This lack of validation can cause the older adult to withhold his or her grief expression—which, in turn, can increase the risk for physical, mental, and emotional problems.

Social Devaluation. Though many cultures highly value and even revere older people, in other cultures, the term *elderly* conjures up stereotypical images of people who are frail, unproductive, sexless, and unimportant. They may be viewed as unattractive and cognitively impaired, needing medical care or treatment for depression. They may no longer work; they might be deaf or less mobile; they may like to talk about the "old days" and the "way we used to do things when I was growing up." It's not simply that their values may conflict with those of the younger generation; older people's values may be devalued. This has been termed *ageism.*

People of advanced years are an invaluable resource with stories to tell and wisdom to share. Their recollection of deceased family members and friends is lost if not passed on to the next generation. Indeed, many families express regret at not having recorded the legacies of the past.

Bereavement Overload

Bereavement overload, as described by Kastenbaum (1969), results from multiple sequential losses and life transitions in close proximity, such as physical incapacity, financial depletion, illness of loved ones and friends, relocation, and memory failure. The several overload factors listed subsequently can result in depression and withdrawal, heightened anxiety, fatigue, and physical breakdown.

- *Fiscal independence.* Loss of income and purchasing power can create a sense of helplessness and dependence.
- *Work role and status.* When some older people stop working and retire, they may lose not only an income but also a sense of their self-identity and self-worth, status, and social connection.
- *Community roles.* Older people may resign from community leadership positions because of declining health or lack of transportation, or because they move, which also forces them to relinquish the role of neighbor.
- *Mobility.* Older people who stop driving or have trouble walking may become dependent on public transportation, family and friends, or social organizational outreach programs to help them get around.

Spousal Loss

Long-term life partners develop an *identity through being part of a couple*. They develop non-verbal signals and communication, tones, language, mutual ideals, and values. The ending of "the couple" due to physical or social death creates a vacuum that may take much time and hard work to recreate, if ever. The challenge for the surviving spouse is *learning to hold onto the past while connecting to the changed, post-loss world.*

Widowhood is markedly higher in the over-65 age group (Carr & Jeffreys, 2011). Of the approximately 900,000 persons who become widowed annually in the United States, close to three-fourths are 65 or older (Federal Interagency Forum on Aging-Related Statistics, 2010). The opportunity to develop new bonds becomes limited as available numbers of peers shrink, complicated by the fact that eligible males may be in shorter supply because men typically do not live as long as women.

Caregiving

Death of a loved one after a period of caregiving for a lingering illness has brought about not only anticipatory grief, but sometimes fantasies associated with death, funerals, and post-loss life. Sudden, unexpected loss leaves no preparation but sometimes high risk for trauma and reduced post-death adjustment. Furthermore, loss of the positives and benefits of the caregiving role can be mourned along with loss of the loved one (Boerner, Schulz, & Horowitz, 2004).

Understanding Family-Centered Approaches to Helping Grieving Elders

> By family I mean that intimate group of people whom we can count on over time for comfort, care, nuturance, support, sustenance and emotional closeness.
>
> —P. Boss (2004, p. 4)

> The standard of care is the provider of care.
>
> —S. Jeffreys (2012b)

Setting the Scene

Many variables impact grief both within the grieving elder's psyche as well as through his or her external environment. There has been a growing awareness of the importance of practitioners who work in palliative care and bereavement being aware of their own unfinished preoccupations regarding loss and grief, including mental and bodily discomfort (Jeffreys, 2011; Katz and Johnson, 2006; Wallin, 2007; Worden, 2009). The standard of necessary care has been described as being achieved through being an "exquisite witness" (Jeffreys, 2011). Here the practitioner is deeply respectful of the needs and agenda of the bereaved, listening more than talking and observing more than acting (Jeffreys, 2011).

The family has been the basic unit of human existence for more than 60,000 years, from the days of cave clans to the present, serving the critical goal of human survival. A truly accurate depiction of any individual requires the contextual information related to family, community, and other social network realities.

A "family system–centered" approach has the advantage of providing a relational lens that reaches far beyond any individual perspective (Magnavita, 2012). Consideration of family traditions regarding illness, loss, and bereavement; cultural and faith traditions; family history; and stories of loss—all of these collective understandings can be gathered in the family forum, thus providing a level of communication often not available in the past. The family is an interactional system of mutual influence (Worden, 2009). Families can plan, grow in knowledge, and gain skills together. Psycho-educational interventions create a "learning to learn" process, building cohesion for the group (Bateson, 1972). The family plays an important role on the palliative care team: they typically deliver most of the care for a dying patient.

Assessment

Initially, the therapist attends to (1) who shows up, (2) who is missing, (3) who sits next to whom, (4) who speaks up first, (5) whom do members look at when or immediately after they speak, (6) who comforts whom, (7) who does most or all of the comforting, (8) who is or appears to be disengaged, (9) how the others relate to the key bereaved relative, (10) who initiates plans for future, and (11) how the therapist feels about this group and what material from his/her life comes up.

The grief-mediating factors discussed subsequently can be used as a guide for assessing the status of any family. The use of circular questioning not only helps each member to say something but also develops understanding of the varied perspectives that the family carries. Early sessions are a rich opportunity to learn much about the family.

As sessions unfold, the therapist assesses (1) the *communication patterns* of the family group (i.e., Are they open to free expressions of each other? Are they controlling or stifling? Who needs support in getting his or her material out? Do they talk *directly to* or *about* the elder or patient in the room? Do there appear to be forbidden topics?); (2) *family group cohesiveness* in terms of mutual support and mutuality of planning for delegation of responsibilities/care coverage; (3) *areas of conflict and dysfunction* (i.e., Are there existing dyads or triads?); (4) *support resources* the family already has or is planning to involve (i.e., How open is the family system to outside people and services?); (5) *knowledge base* (i.e., How much understanding or information does the family have about medical realities, palliative care, and/or the normative realities of human grief?); and (6) *how the therapist feels* about this group and what material comes up from the therapist's life.

Several factors mediate the nature and functioning of the family. Early on in the clinical process, practitioners working with a family may be mindful of the factors presented subsequently (adapted from Jeffreys, 2011).

Factors Affecting Family Grief

Nature of the Illness or Death. Grief varies with the circumstances under which the loss occurred. Sudden, violent, and unexpected deaths, for example, complicate and intensify grief. Family members who have witnessed violent deaths are more likely to develop

238 J. Shep Jeffreys

post-traumatic reactions. The elderly husband who is unable to waken his wife in the morning and realizes she has died may regret that he could not say good-bye. Lengthy illnesses can drain family members of energy, time, and motivation to engage in other aspects of life. Some mourners may feel some level of relief that their loved one is no longer suffering.

Nature of the Primary Attachments. The quality of the relationship to a sick or deceased relative will affect the nature of grieving. Families with insecure attachments have less interest in cooperative action with each other. Older adult levels of dependency or ambivalence regarding the deceased family member may result in differential levels of grief intensity. In some cases, processing unfinished business with each other or with the deceased is necessary.

Family Values and Belief Systems. These flow from religious, social, and cultural heritages and family traditions that develop over time. Attitudes toward life and death, dealing with rituals, and patterns of communication about grief vary and require great respect from those who help. Family values play a role in any meaning perceived in the experience. Studies have shown that when religious beliefs are strongly held, the level of intensity of grieving is less (Wortman & Park, 2008).

Age of the Person Dying, Deceased, or Bereaved. Grief reactions are often influenced by the age of the person who has died. The death of an older adult is considered an expected death, whereas the death of a child has been called "unthinkable" (Rosen, 1990). However, the loss of an older adult can be just as painful. The older surviving person may have already lost a spouse, siblings, cousins, or friends; their world of contemporaries is shrinking. When the obituaries announce deaths close to the elder's age, mortality issues rise to the forefront of consciousness.

Nature of the Family's Functioning. Families with preexisting conflicts may reflect this in their grief during palliative care and beyond. This can add additional stress to a difficult situation. They may lack connections, fail to support each other, and even continue hostilities. Families may not be available for meetings as a group, and the reasons offered for any absence can provide additional information about the cohesiveness of the system. Family fragments, as opposed to the entire family, can be a very useful part of the system to work with—and more times than not, this is the reality of a family-centered approach. Those members who come in are likely those who will have an active role in developing the support for the bereaved older adult.

Additional Factors Affecting Nature of Grief. How family members grieve will be affected by education level, financial situation, spiritual resources, cultural traditions, and available community support. For example, people who are expected back on the job after a three-day "bereavement leave" are not likely to have had time to sufficiently grieve or make needed arrangements for elders, children, or grandchildren. A family whose financial resources have been drained caring for a terminally ill family member will have additional anxieties to handle on top of their grief. Many hospice programs and hospital pastoral care departments offer a year of bereavement support for families they have served. Some funeral homes have likewise developed "aftercare" support services for families.

Grief Therapy with the Bereaved Family

For families with an older member who has experienced significant loss, goal setting is worthwhile. Worden's key tasks of mourning continue to have relevance for families as a whole (Worden, 2009). Two cases illustrating these goals and interventions follow.

Healing Tasks for the Grieving Family

Worden's (2009) *four tasks of mourning* are readily adapted by family therapists to demonstrate a set of action-oriented behaviors and outcomes that enable families to adapt to and heal in the post-loss world. The practitioner can use these as the basis for assessing the areas of growth needed for a given family group.

Task I: Sharing Acknowledgment of Death or Other Traumatic Loss

Denial versus Acceptance of Reality

The family must ultimately recognize that the medical diagnosis or loss is final and irreversible. Denial may be useful to permit the acceptance of reality in small doses; however, the goal is to have family members share their sense of the loss. Family meetings with staff in palliative care and bereavement services can consider the benefits of traditional rituals including funerals, memorials, prayer services, wakes, sitting shiva, viewings, and interment and cremation rites, highlighting the help they can deliver. Although family members do not have to exactly agree, reasonable accord with planning is helpful.

Facilitating Insights Regarding a Terminal Illness Diagnosis

For a family addressing this task, the care provider can review, clarify, or summarize the patient's current medical information by asking some of the following questions: "What is your understanding of the medical condition?" "What specifically has the doctor or nurse told you?" "Do you need clarification from a medical provider?" "Who do you believe would be most helpful for you to talk to regarding your diagnosis at this point?" "Have you and your family discussed your current advance directives?" Connor gave this prudent guidance: "Patient and families have to be continuously reassessed to discern their readiness to digest more information" (Conner, 2009, p. 59).

Facilitating Reality of the Death

As members of a family may have varied understanding, questions that clarify what has happened prove helpful. Thus, "How did you find out about the death?" "What happened then?" "Who made the funeral arrangements?" "Was there a viewing?" "How was that for you?" "Were you there when (he or she) died?" "Were you able to say good-bye?" "What did he or she look like?"

Endorsing Rituals and Several Other Strategies for Assisting with Reality Testing

Asking questions about the death-associated rituals helps confirm the reality of death. Questions include the following: "What was the funeral like?" "Where was it held?" "Who officiated at the service?" "What can you remember about the eulogies?" "Who gave them?" "Did you say anything at the service?" "At the graveside?" "What was the burial like for you?" When appropriate, consider the following tasks:

- Review the medical examiner's report, death certificate, or newspaper story.
- Review the guest book, condolence cards, or memorabilia items.
- Create a ritual when the funeral was missed; script the details from start to ending.
- Create a guided imagery exercise to recall a loss event, funeral, memorial, or burial.

Identify Changes in Life

To help grieving family members gain a sense of what has changed as a result of the loss, ask these questions in circular style: "What is different in your life now?" "What do you miss the most?" "When is the worst time for you?" "In what way does your body feel different now?" "What are your concerns for the future?" "What are some next steps for you now?"

Closed versus Open Intrafamily Communication

The more easily and openly a family communicates, the more it can engage in necessary sharing. Planning memorials and traditional rituals as well as other joint family events can help move people toward a more open discussion of the reality of loss.

Inactivity versus Activity

Although individuals need private time to mourn, healing is assisted when family members undertake a joint activity. Some useful actions include planning religious services, receiving visitors, sending appreciation cards, creating the obituary, and notifying others in their social network about the illness or death. Families will be particularly sensitive to holidays, birthdays, and anniversaries, which are therefore useful times for rituals, meals, and other commemorations of the loved one, such as by inclusion of candles, blessings, photos, favored foods, toasts, music, and flowers. Again, family and cultural traditions will play an important role in determining how this is accomplished.

Closed versus Open Communication beyond the Family

Connecting with extended family, friends, faith community members, support services, and colleagues can provide families with the opportunities to deliver the painful news and receive support. Ask them, "Whom have you called?"

Task II: Sharing the Pain and Grief

Storytelling

Much of the sharing of pain and grief will take place as the family engages in storytelling with each other and with extended family, friends, and others in the social network (Nadeau, 2001). Grieving people typically need to tell and retell the history, describe characteristics of the loved one, relate medical information and recent history, describe the circumstances of the death, and consider what they will miss and how different life will be. Circular questions prove helpful: What feelings are present now? What is still left over for each of us now regarding the deceased loved one? What do we wish we could still say to her or him?

Making sense of a death and discovering new meanings for the post-loss world are important for reclaiming a functional life. So many times we hear people asking "Why?" "Why did this have to happen?" "Why now?" "Why this family?" People struggle to find answers but can be helped to work these through.

Conspiracy of Silence

In some families, however, there may be a conspiracy of silence, an unstated agreement that "We don't talk about it." Other families simply say, "We are all fine, thank you." The reluctance to share their needs with others may limit the family's support from outside sources. This may be a function of denial and/or cultural or family customs.

Expression of Emotions

Sharing expressions of disappointment, helplessness, relief, guilt, anger, anxiety, panic, or the need for quiet withdrawal are all possible responses to loss—and useful for others in the family to hear and acknowledge. An elderly mourner may feel it inappropriate to show emotions to others and be viewed as not doing much grieving. Guilt and anger are particularly difficult feelings to express to others in the family, but it can be an extraordinary relief for a family member to find out that he or she is not alone in having those feelings. Venting in a family session allows expression of feelings frequently unacceptable to communicate (Conner, 2009; Kubler-Ross, 1978). But again, caution must be taken with those ethnic cultures whose customs restrict open expression of feelings.

Task III: Reorganizing the Family System

Realignments and Reallocations

The realignment of relationships and the reallocation of roles may begin as the family prepares for a funeral and other death-related activities. Who chooses the pallbearers? Should we have an open casket? Such decisions help appropriate individuals adopt new roles. Care providers must raise questions in a family meeting about the future of the family, such as routines, finances, and reorganizing responsibilities. All eyes may turn to the surviving spouse for answers to such questions. If the family is unable or reluctant to discuss their needs for the future, the care provider can assist by having a meeting expressly for planning limited to the immediate future.

Adopting New Family Organization Structures

Grieving families have the opportunity to abandon old family patterns and adopt new, functional structures, especially if the deceased played a dominant role. Whenever there is a significant change, there is the chance to review old traditions and seek *new ways* to, for instance, have recreation and family meals, create and implement a budget, and relate to others outside of the nuclear family.

Replacement Concerns

After the loss of a spouse or life partner, replacement concerns may arise. Social conventions and resistance from the family may dictate the timing of when a grieving elder should decide to resume his or her social life. Immediate family members may exert pressure for the widow or widower to find a new companion or, alternately, to stay unattached as long as possible. The care provider can open up family discussion on specific topics such as relationship concerns. Support groups also can be helpful, as others can share how they approached difficult or awkward situations.

Other Traumatic Losses

In the case of other traumatic loss, such as layoff, financial crisis, divorce, or destruction of home by fire or mugging, elders may be as devastated as if an actual death has occurred. The prospect of living with a severely reduced income, and the loss of a home and all personal belongings, has secondary effects beyond the initial loss event. Elders will voice concerns for survival: "Where will we live?" "How will we pay for food?" "How will I get to doctor appointments?" "When can I see my friends?" "Will I be safe?" Too often, such non-death losses are not viewed as legitimate causes for grief reactions.

Task IV: Creating New Directions, Relationships, and Goals

Moving On in the Face of Loss

This is usually accomplished slowly over time. Families can gradually realize that they can continue to honor the memory of a loved one and stay connected while making changes and adapting to their present-day lives.

A technique called *controlled avoidance* (Jeffreys, 2012a) helps individuals who seek to balance time spent in active grieving with non-grief activity focus. Developing a management system for grief and choosing when to switch the focus affords the bereaved a sense of control over their grief. They recognize that the grieving is an important part of the adaptation process and give it legitimacy—while deciding how much time to allocate and when to engage each phase of focus.

The bereaved may maintain a connection with the lost loved one via a spiritual bond, in a way that neither requires their living presence nor impedes reclaiming a functional post-loss life. By finding ways to honor the deceased's values, priorities, and social causes, the surviving family member can incorporate these special characteristics into his or her own being and carry them into the future.

Rituals comprise a system for staying connected with a deceased loved one. A spiritual connection can be maintained, for instance, by acknowledgement through prayers, blessings, memorials, donations, tree and garden plantings, and other dedications. Likewise, a moment of silence at a holiday meal, graduation, wedding, or baby naming can both celebrate the life of the lost loved one and acknowledge their physical absence.

Creating New Traditions

Sometimes, overidealization of the deceased or past traditions and routines may prevent people from initiating new ideas that more adequately meet the needs of the family as it is now. Many family members will keep certain traditions and routines because Dad or Grandma always did it that way. Some of these family customs may serve to keep the members attached to the deceased loved one, whereas others can be replaced by new and more satisfying ways of doing things.

Treatment Strategies

Among the worthwhile treatment strategies that assist clinically, options include (1) externalization, (2) meaning making, (3) continuing bonds, (4) psycho-education, and (5) normalization.

Externalization

Externalization of the pain and other feelings of grief can take place in the therapeutic setting (Kubler-Ross, 1969, 1978). Many families seek an opportunity to express their pain in a safe place. They may have done little crying in front of each other and are relieved to be able to do so. Therapists can encourage this release and indicate that this is normal for this space and time. Helpful cues include a tissue box within easy reach and a supportive statement such as, "It's what we do here."

Families can learn to tolerate crying and support the person who is expressing his or her grief. Bereaved clients know they can do this safely in sessions and, when possible, with the other members of their family as well.

Meaning Reconstruction as a Goal and Intervention

"The need to make meaning is very common among patients at the end of life," and this can be facilitated by doing a "life review" or oral history involving the family as a group (Conner, 2009, p. 68). As bereaved, we strain to make sense not only of our loss but of our strange new world as well. The value of making new meanings is that death disrupts the assumptions and personal meanings our experiences have created over time. We attempt to (a) make sense of the loss, (b) extract some positive benefit in this experience, and (c) make some modifications in our own identity as a bereaved person (Neimeyer, Baldwin, & Gillies, 2006). Meaning-reconstruction offers great benefit.

In making sense of the loss, we encourage the family to review with each other the circumstances leading up to the death and include as much as possible about the time of dying. Where there is a large gap in the family's information regarding cause of death, a medical provider can be brought in to help. When appropriate, religious and spiritual meanings or support groups can also offer the family some comfort.

Continuing Bonds: Staying Connected to the Loved One Who Has Died

The elderly bereaved typically report an ongoing engagement with the memories and images of the deceased as positive and comforting (Field, 2006; Klass & Goss, 1999). Also helpful are "legacy benefits" (Neimeyer, 2010), as a way for family members to identify with the loved one and internalize those desired traits, values, and beliefs and carry them forward into life.

Psycho-educational Interventions

Lack of control in the world of grief is often associated with a sense of helplessness. Therefore, it is useful to read about the basics of human grief and what to expect from self and others.

Normalizing Grief

For the elderly bereaved, there are many ways to accomplish a sense of "I'm not alone in feeling this way." Normalizing can also be very helpful in educating families about patterns of grief and what to expect. There are, however, times when the ship of grief is blown into stormy waters, leading to complications of grief.

Two Case Examples

Suicide

A couple in their early seventies and their married daughter were seen for help in coping with the suicide of their son. He had ended his life after a long, deteriorating illness. During initial sessions, the family expressed little grief-associated emotional release, as they claimed to be "all cried out" from the years of illness and many hospitalizations. Still, they shared their experience of his illness, their caregiving, and his death. Because they asked if they were "doing this right," much of the family work involved checking whether they were on proper course for their grieving behaviors. Indeed, they were relieved to hear how on target they were. They also reflected on all the dreams for his life that they would miss, such as a family for him and grandchildren for them. They were able to find solace in their daughter's family and extended relatives from their respective families of origin.

The family sought ways to memorialize their son's life and hold onto his values, including kindness and devotion to his parents and sister. A meaningful birthday and anniversary ritual plan proved beneficial for them. They came to appreciate how much closer to each other they now were, even more so for continuing to support one another.

Multiple Loss

An 82-year-old woman was seen with her husband after the death of her adult son from a congenital heart anomaly. She expressed little emotional distress and preferred to talk about a long-lasting estrangement from her own children and grandchildren from her first marriage. Invitations to retell the story of her son's death saw her return to the issue of her "lost" family. Her husband confirmed this as her deepest source of concern and described her considerable anxiety over non-contact with her family. This facilitated expression of her grief, and she recognized her desire to work on the unfinished business of her "lost" family.

Conclusion

Grief can be managed creatively and responsively. Working with elderly bereaved persons within the family setting, engaged with those who know and care about them—who can share family history and reflections of the deceased loved ones—provides a natural setting for post-loss adaptation. In family-focused treatment, we have immediately available resources for emotional support, past recall, planning for the near and distant future, and the development of new traditions and rituals that honor memories and bring solace.

Effective grief care providers will need to have family therapy skills as well as experience working with couples. In addition to a strong understanding of grief and the unique needs of bereaved elders, the provider must also be aware of personal unfinished grief material, which may reduce therapist availability to the family. This attention to personal loss history is critical for the highest level of service. This is why the *standard of care is the provider of care.*

References

Bateson, G. (1972). *Steps to an ecology of mind.* New York: Ballantine.

Boerner, K., Schulz, R., & Horowitz, A. (2004). Positive aspects if caregiving and adaptation to bereavement. *Psychology and Aging, 19,* 668–675.

Boss, P. (2004). Ambiguous loss. In F. Walsh & M. McGodrick (Eds.), *Living beyond loss: Death in the family* (2nd ed., p. 237). New York: Basic Books.

Bowlby, J. (1973). *Attachment and loss: Vol. 2. Separation: Anxiety and anger.* New York: Basic Books.

Bowlby, J. (1979). *The making and breaking of affectional bonds.* London: Tavistock.

Bowlby, J. (1980). *Attachment and loss: Vol. 3. Loss: Sadness and depression.* New York: Basic Books.

Bowlby, J. (1982). *Attachment and loss: Vol. 1. Attachment* (2nd ed.). New York: Basic Books.

Campbell, J. (1988/1991). *The power of myth.* New York: Apostrophe S Productions/Anchor Books.

Carr, D., & Jeffreys, J. (2011). Spousal loss in later life. In R. A. Neimeyer, D. L. Harris, H. R. Winokuer, & G. F. Thornton (Eds.), *Grief and bereavement in contemporary society: Bridging research and practice.* New York: Routledge.

Conner, S. R. (2009). *Hospice and palliative care: The essential guide* (2nd ed.) New York: Routledge.

Federal Interagency Forum on Aging-Related Statistics. (2010). *Older Americans 2010: Key indicators of well-being.* Washington, DC: Government Printing Office.

Field, N. (2006). Continuing bonds in adaptation to bereavement: Introduction. *Death Studies, 30,* 709–714.

Fraley, R. C. (2002). Attachment stability from infant to adulthood. *Personality and Social Psychology Review, 6,* 123–151.

Hamilton, B. E., Martin, J. A., and Ventura, S. J. (2012). National Vital Statistics Reports, vol. 62. no 1. October 11, Hyattsville, MD: National Center for Health Statistics.

Hansson, R. O., & Stroebe, M. S. (2007). *Bereavement in later life.* Washington, DC: American Psychological Association.

Jeffreys, J. S. (2005). *Coping with workplace grief: Dealing with loss, trauma and change*. Boston: Crisp/Thomson/Axzo.

Jeffreys, J. S. (2011). *Helping grieving people – when tears are not enough: A handbook for care providers*. New York: Routledge.

Jeffreys, J. S. (2012a). Controlled avoidance in the management of grief. In R. Neimeyer (Ed.), *Techniques of grief therapy: Creative practices for counseling the bereaved* (pp. 155–157). New York: Routledge.

Jeffreys, J. S. (2012b). *The standard of care is the provider of care*. Retrieved from http://www.Grief-Corner.com

Kastenbaum, R. (1969). Death and bereavement in later life. In A. H. Kutshe (Ed.), *Death and bereavement* (pp. 27–54). Springfield, IL: Thomas.

Katz, R., & Johnson, T. (Eds.). (2006). *When professionals weep: Emotional and countertransference responses in end-of-life care*. New York: Routledge.

Kissane, D., & Bloch, S. (2002). *Family focused grief therapy*. Berkshire, UK: Open University Press.

Klass, D., & Goss, R. (1999). Spiritual bonds to the dead in cross-cultural and historical perspective: Comparative religion and modern grief. *Death Studies, 23*, 547–567.

Kubler-Ross, E. (1969). *On death and dying*. New York: Macmillan.

Kubler-Ross, E. (1978). *To live until we say goodbye*. Englewood Cliffs, NJ: Prentice Hall.

MacLean, P. (1973). *A triune concept of the brain and behavior in evolution*. Toronto, ON: University of Toronto Press.

Magnavita, J. (2012). Advancing clinical science using systems theory as the framework for expanding family psychology with unified psychotherapy. *Couple and Family Therapy in Research and Practice, 1*, 3–13.

Nadeau, J. (2001). Meaning making in family bereavement: A family systems approach. In M. S. Stroebe, R. O. Hansson, W. Stroebe, & H. Shut (Eds.), *Handbook of bereavement research: Consequences, coping and care* (pp. 329–347). Washington, DC: American Psychological Association

Neimeyer, R. (2010). *Advanced training in complicated grief*. 2010 ADEC Convention, Tampa, FL.

Neimeyer, R., Baldwin, S., & Gillies, J. (2006). Continuing bonds and reconstructing meaning: Mitigating complications in bereavement. *Death Studies, 30*, 715–738.

Parkes, C. M. (2002). Foreword. In D. Kissane & S. Bloch (Eds.), *Family focused grief therapy* (p. xiv). Berkshire, UK: Open University Press.

Perissinotto, C. M., Cenzer, I. S., & Covinsky, K. E. (2012). Loneliness in older persons: A predictor of functional decline and death. *Archives of Internal Medicine (Journal of the American Medical Association), 172*(14), 1078–1084.

Rando, T. (1984). *Grief, dying and death*. Champaign, IL: Research Press.

Rosen E. (1990). *Families facing death: A guide for health-care professionals and volunteers*. Lexington, MA: Lexington Books.

Wallin, D. (2007). *Attachment in psychotherapy*. New York: Guilford Press.

Worden, J. W. (2009). *Grief counseling and grief therapy*. New York: Springer.

Wortman, J., & Park, C. (2008). Religion and spirituality in adjustment following bereavement: An integrative review. *Death Studies, 32*, 703–736.

Part IV

Future Directions

The field of family bereavement care needs focused research and dissemination efforts to continue to cultivate its nascent approach. This final section considers family approaches to prevent the development of complicated grief, to respond to the socially disadvantaged in society, and to expand the adoption of such models of bereavement care.

17 Families "At Risk" of Complicated Bereavement

Wendy G. Lichtenthal and Corinne Sweeney

Although the loss of a family member can be profoundly painful, the majority of families find ways over time to heal and reorganize, incorporating the legacy of their lost loved one into their folklore. For some families, however, the adjustment process is hindered by pre-existing dysfunction, challenges with an individual member's reaction, or the absence of adequate family coping skills. The response to the loss can therefore become prolonged and dysfunctional; in short, it can become complicated.

A family systems perspective of loss, which considers the family as the functional unit, focuses on the powerful role that interactional processes play in impacting adjustment to the death of a family member (Walsh & McGoldrick, 2004). The term, *complicated bereavement*, is most commonly used to describe an individual's psychopathological reaction to the loss of a loved one, which can include complications such as prolonged or delayed grief; substance abuse/dependence; or depressive, anxiety, and even psychotic disorders. At the family level, complicated bereavement refers to dysfunction in the family system, which can exist independently of any individual member's psychopathology.

This chapter considers predictors of complicated bereavement reactions in the family following the loss of a loved one. Identification of families at risk for complicated bereavement permits an opportunity for determining when preventive and treatment interventions are warranted and when a family's existing coping skills should be trusted to allow for natural resilience. After reviewing the empirical literature on risk factors, we discuss ways to harness family involvement early on to reduce the potential for dysfunction.

Risk Factors in the Family System

In considering studies of risk factors in grief and bereavement, it is important to note that research on risk factors more generally has been muddied by cross-sectional (as opposed to longitudinal) investigations. It has been further complicated by inexact use of terms such as risk, correlates, and predictors, which are often applied interchangeably. Kraemer, Stice, Kazdin, Offord, & Kupfer (2001) distinguished risk, defined as the probability of an outcome, from a correlate, defined as a measure associated with an outcome. A risk factor precedes the outcome, and a causal risk factor actually changes the outcome when it, itself, changes (Kraemer et al., 2001). Some risk factors, such as demographic variables, are considered fixed markers that cannot be modified (Kraemer et al., 1997, 2001; Sandler et al., 2008). Furthermore, risk factors interact with one another in complex ways; they can be proxies for, overlapping, independent of, mediating, or moderating one another (Kraemer et al., 2001). In the case of identifying families at risk, the way in which risk factors work together becomes even more convoluted. Each family member's individual risk factors, interacting at the intrapersonal level, are also interacting at the interpersonal level.

Precise use of risk-related terms and an understanding of the relationships among risk factors are important because of their implications for intervention development. Attempts to manipulate risk factors that are not causal may result in ineffective treatments (Kraemer et al., 2001; Sandler et al., 2008). For grief interventions, this is a particularly important issue. Several systematic reviews and meta-analyses of grief intervention clinical trials have noted that the interventions are most efficacious when they target symptomatic or high-risk populations and have thus concluded that, rather than developing universal interventions, these groups should be targeted for intervention (Currier, Neimeyer, & Berman, 2008; Jordan & Neimeyer, 2003). Thus, identification of both fixed marker and modifiable risk factors is critical to selecting populations likely to respond to interventions.

Research on risk factors in bereavement suffers, however, from the same malady as the general risk research literature, with numerous cross-sectional studies that claim to have examined risk when they are actually examining correlates of grief reactions (Aranda & Milne, 2000). Recognizing this problem, Burke and Neimeyer (2012) systematically and critically reviewed the literature on risk factors of complicated grief in individuals, focusing on and distinguishing prospective risk factors from variables that may be correlates or consequences of complicated grief. These risk factors will be further considered subsequently.

Resilience and Dysfunction

The extent to which a family is resilient to the disruption caused by the loss of a relative is largely based on its ability to reorganize and integrate the loss (Rando, 1991). In some ways, family adjustment to loss is analogous to individual adjustment. Prolonged and complicated grief in individuals is believed to manifest when they are "stuck" and do not accomplish important grief-related tasks, such as processing the reality of the death (Boelen, 2006; Worden, 2009). Similarly, family complications can develop when these important tasks are not achieved at the systems level.

Walsh and McGoldrick (2004) argued that in order for a family to move toward acceptance of a loss, there are two key adaptational tasks that must be accomplished: (1) acknowledge the reality together and (2) reorganize and move forward. The first task is to share in acknowledging both the reality of the death and the experience of loss, which is aided by open communication about the circumstances of the death (Walsh & McGoldrick, 2004). To do so, family members must tolerate intense and fluctuating emotions that may at times be at odds with one another, particularly in the acute stages of grief (Walsh & McGoldrick, 2004). Mourning rituals such as funerals can facilitate acceptance of the reality of the loss, although it is important to be mindful of cultural differences in the extent to which acknowledgment is outwardly expressed.

Walsh and McGoldrick (2004) noted several challenges that a family may face in accomplishing this first task, thus placing them at risk for grief complications. If one or more family members fail to acknowledge the loss and avoid related discussion, others may become frustrated and even stop speaking to one another. Similar rifts within the family can occur when emotional expression is not tolerated or is blocked because of family or cultural taboos, or when there is "competition" in grieving (Walsh & McGoldrick, 2004). The family member who gives voice to his or her feelings may then be criticized and left feeling greatly unsupported. It may also be that different members of the family end up exclusively expressing one type of emotion, with one person holding all of the anger, for example, whereas another holds all of the sadness. Emotional expression may also be blocked because of circumstances that necessitate the griever to quickly resume "normal" functioning, such as a single widowed parent with young children who does not have the opportunity to sufficiently confront and work through his or her pain.

The other family task deemed necessary by Walsh and McGoldrick (2004) is the reorganization of the family system and reinvestment in other relationships and life pursuits. Family roles need to be reallocated to compensate for the absence of the deceased member. This requires flexibility that continues over time, as changes in the family system beget more changes, more reorganization. Challenges that families face in accomplishing this task may include a "rush" to address feelings related to the disorganization that arises by making immediate changes. This can result in rash decisions that create more problems than they solve (e.g., quickly moving from the home shared with the deceased; Walsh & McGoldrick, 2004). Also problematic is when individuals try to minimize feelings of distress by rigidly keeping things as they were, maintaining old transactional patterns and roles without adapting to new family needs created by the loss. Reinvestment in other relationships and life pursuits can be stymied by feelings of betrayal or concerns about becoming too attached and facing loss again in the future (Walsh & McGoldrick, 2004). When certain family members are ready to reinvest before others, tensions are likely to arise, and ambivalence toward the new relationship can be damaging.

Family-Level Risk Factors

Maladaptive grief in families can manifest in many ways, ranging from avoidance of grief, emotional stifling, guilt and blame, or prolongation of grief. Several factors may make a family more vulnerable to dysfunction. Here, we consider those characteristics and circumstances that heighten risk at both the level of the family and the level of the individual.

Family Functioning Style. Research on family risk factors is fairly limited, with the exception of a body of work conducted by Kissane and colleagues (Kissane, Bloch, Dowe et al., 1996; Kissane, Bloch, Onghena et al., 1996), who pioneered development of an empirically derived typology that describes families based on their style of functioning using a measure of cohesiveness, conflict, and expressiveness. This typology has been used to identify families at the greatest risk for developing grief complications.

Five family types are included in this classification: supportive, conflict-resolving, intermediate, sullen, and hostile families (Kissane, Bloch, Onghena et al., 1996). The former two family types, supportive and conflict-resolving, are generally well-functioning. The latter three family types demonstrate greater dysfunction. Specifically, supportive families report high levels of cohesiveness and at least moderate expressiveness and are generally without conflict. Greater conflict is observed in conflict resolving families, but this is offset by their strong cohesiveness and expressiveness, which results in open communication to help settle disputes adaptively. Supportive and conflict-resolving families adjust better and employ more adaptive family coping strategies than families with dysfunctional styles (Kissane, Bloch, Onghena et al., 1996). Members of conflict-resolving families experience the least intense grief and generally carry low rates of psychosocial morbidity (Kissane & Lichtenthal, 2008). Coping in these families is typically demonstrated through cohesiveness, clear communication, emotional expression, adaptability, and ability to manage conflict (Kissane & Bloch, 1994).

In contrast to these well-functioning family types, sullen, hostile, and intermediate families demonstrate greater risk for developing complications of grief (Kissane, McKenzie, & Bloch, 1997). Intermediate families are characterized by moderate levels of cohesiveness but often experience conflict and distress because of family members' existing psychological morbidity (e.g., depression and anxiety). They are, however, often receptive to interventions and can benefit from professional support. Similarly, sullen families may agree to receive and hopefully benefit from professional intervention. Members of sullen families have generally poorer functioning, with the highest rates of depression and intense grief reactions following a loss. They often have unexpressed anger, as the family system exhibits lower levels of expressiveness as well as cohesiveness and mild to moderate conflict.

The most dysfunctional family type is the hostile family, characterized by a high degree of conflict, low cohesiveness, and limited expressiveness. Hostile families carry the greatest risk for psychosocial morbidity, with significantly higher levels of depression, anxiety, anger, and obsessionality than well-functioning families (Kissane et al., 2003). Approximately 15% of families are either sullen (9%) or hostile (6%), with rates doubling following bereavement (Kissane, Bloch, Dowe et al., 1996; Kissane, Bloch, Onghena et al., 1996). In the palliative care setting, one-third of families are classified as intermediate, but following the patient's death, deterioration in family functioning often results in families moving into the sullen or hostile groups. By 13 months, the majority of these families return to their pre-death state of intermediate functioning (Kissane, Bloch, Dowe et al., 1996; Kissane, Bloch, Onghena et al., 1996).

Individual-Level Risk Factors

As suggested by the family functioning typology, risk for family dysfunction is heightened when individual family members are experiencing psychological problems. There are several ways dysfunction at the individual level may manifest. One of the most well-researched pathological reactions to loss has been prolonged grief disorder (PGD), which is characterized by intense, debilitating grief symptoms that are considered distinct from depression and anxiety and can persist for years if left untreated (Lichtenthal et al., 2004; Prigerson et al., 2009). The majority of research on risk factors and correlates of complicated bereavement outcomes has been conducted among individuals with PGD, also referred to as *complicated grief* (Shear et al., 2011) and *traumatic grief* (Prigerson & Jacobs, 2001) in the grief literature. Thus, much of the subsequent summary focuses on research in individuals exhibiting PGD symptoms.

Specifically, we detail prospective risk factors of PGD, as identified by Burke and Neimeyer (2012) in their review. Risk factors were deemed as *prospective* if they preceded the loss, were related to the death itself, were static at the time of death and through bereavement, or were measured at least two times (with the time 1 variable predicting time 2). Burke and Neimeyer (2012) further classified these variables as *confirmed* risk factors or *potential* risk factors. Confirmed risk factors were those examined in at least three studies or that were statistically significant at least 50% of the time (Burke & Neimeyer, 2012). These factors place individual family members at risk for PGD and thus place the family system at increased risk of developing a complicated bereavement. We first consider the six risk factors identified as "confirmed": (1) low social support, (2) anxious/avoidant/insecure attachment styles, (3) discovering or identifying the body following a violent death, (4) being the spouse or parent of the deceased, (5) high pre-death marital dependence, and (6) high neuroticism.

Low Social Support. The presence of social support is viewed as protective against pathological reactions to loss, and thus, not surprisingly, decreased levels of social support have been associated with more intense and severe grief in several studies (Burke & Neimeyer, 2012; Callahan, 2000; Hibberd, Elwood, & Galovski, 2010; Lobb et al., 2009; Vanderwerker & Prigerson, 2004). Negative social support has detrimental effects as well; individuals perceived as absent, insensitive, or hostile can cause distress and anger in grieving individuals (Wilsey & Shear, 2007). Unsupportive individuals may be part of or outside of the family system, and certainly when negative social support occurs within the family system, there will be a heightened risk for complicated grief reactions.

Anxious/Avoidant/Insecure Attachment Style. Increased risk for complicated grief has been theorized to occur when bereaved individuals fail to integrate an adaptive internalized representation of an attachment figure who has been lost (Shear & Shair, 2005). The likelihood of this increases among individuals with insecure attachment patterns. A number of studies have found that individuals with insecure attachment styles are at elevated risk for PGD (Burke & Neimeyer, 2012; Lobb et al., 2009). This has been observed in caregivers of terminally ill patients (van Doorn, Kasl, Beery, Jacobs, & Prigerson, 1998) and bereaved parents in the Netherlands (Winjgaards-de Meij et al., 2007). In parents whose child died in a pediatric intensive care unit, greater attachment-related anxiety and attachment-related avoidance was associated with higher symptoms of complicated grief (Meert et al., 2010). Insecure attachment patterns may be transmitted across generations. Related preoccupation or avoidant behaviors impact relations among surviving family members and can affect certain reactions to the death of a family member, heightening the risk of grief complications post-loss.

Discovering or Identifying the Body. Seeing the body of the deceased after a violent death such as a suicide was also a consistent and significant predictor of more intense grief reactions (Burke & Neimeyer, 2012). A study of suicide survivors demonstrated that viewing the body at the scene of the death was in fact the strongest predictor of grief symptoms (Callahan, 2000). Families for whom a suicide, accident, or homicide resulted in one or more members seeing the decedent's body firsthand (e.g., in the home) should be considered at heightened risk for PGD.

Being the Spouse or Parent of the Deceased. In general, research has shown that the closer the degree of kinship, the greater the risk of a dysfunctional grief reaction (Burke & Neimeyer, 2012; Lobb et al., 2009). Cleiren's (1993) longitudinal study of individuals bereaved by suicide, accident, or a long-term disease demonstrated specifically that spouses and parents experienced the most morbidity, with worse psychological and physical health outcomes. Heightened risk of problematic grief among those with closer kinship has also been found in specific populations, such as individuals bereaved by suicide (De Groot, De Keijser, & Neeleman, 2006; Mitchell, Kim, Prigerson, & Mortimer-Stephens, 2004). De Groot and colleagues (2006) found not only higher levels of prolonged grief symptoms among first-degree relatives and spouses bereaved by suicide when compared to those who lost family members to natural causes, but also a greater reported need for professional support following their loss. In studies of individuals bereaved by a tsunami, the risk for PGD was highest among those who had lost a child or a partner (Johannesson et al., 2009; Kristensen, Weisæth, & Heir, 2010).

Parents, especially mothers, face a particularly high risk for protracted grief reactions (Burke & Neimeyer, 2012; Davies, 2004). One study with parents whose child died in a pediatric intensive care unit, for example, showed that being the biological mother or female guardian was associated with higher levels of PGD (Meert et al., 2010). Despite studies demonstrating elevated risk for specific kinship relationships, it is important not to place too much emphasis on any one family member in screening families for complicated bereavement; other risk factors should be taken into account.

High Pre-death Marital Dependence. Marital dependence, characterized by excessive reliance on the deceased partner, is an individual-level risk factor in bereaved spouses but clearly has significant family-level implications. A number of studies, including longitudinal investigations, have found that partners who report being dependent on their spouse experience increased grief when that spouse dies (Bonanno et al., 2002; Burke & Neimeyer, 2012; Carr, 2004; Lobb et al., 2009). Bonanno et al. (2002) found that individuals reporting marital dependency pre-loss were more likely to exhibit chronic grief following their spouse's death. A study by Johnson, Zhang, Greer, and Prigerson (2007) further suggests that associations found between perceptions of parental control in childhood and PGD are actually mediated by partner dependency, highlighting the complex contribution that insecure attachment patterns developed early on and security-enhancing relationships may play in the development of protracted grief (van Doorn et al., 1998).

High Neuroticism. An increased risk of PGD has also been linked to higher levels of neuroticism, conceptualized as the tendency to experience negative feelings and emotional instability more easily (Winjgaards-de Meij et al., 2007). Assessing participants longitudinally over six months, van der Houwen and colleagues (2009) found that neuroticism predicted negative mental health outcomes, including grief. In fact, Winjgaards-de Meij et al. (2007) found that neuroticism accounted for even more of the variance in predicting grief than insecure attachment. The presence of a family member exhibiting the anxiety and moodiness that characterize neuroticism will inevitably impact the family system. High emotionality in one member may block others from expressing their grief or may exacerbate, for example, anger, hopelessness, or avoidance by reinforcing maladaptive cognitive responses.

Other Potential Risk Factors to Consider

Burke and Neimeyer (2012) also identified 32 "potential" risk factors that have been examined in prior studies, but for which they noted that the empirical verdict is still out. To assist with our discussion of families at risk of complicated bereavement, we classify these 32 risk factors as either potential family risk factors, which will likely be common to the entire family system (e.g., recency of death), or potential individual risk factors, which will likely be unique to a given individual family member (e.g., pre-existing psychological condition). We recognize that individual risk factors in a given family may be similar (e.g., non-Caucasian, low income, regular church attendance), but when conducting family risk assessments, these should be assessed at the individual level given their potential for variability within a single family.

Potential Family Risk Factors. Based on Burke and Neimeyer's (2012) list, we identify potential family risk factors, which should be common to all bereaved family members, as younger age of the bereaved, violent death, sudden or unexpected death, recency of the death, lack of family cohesion, the deceased's age (both younger and older), good pre-death health of the deceased, and length of illness of the deceased (both too long or too short).

It follows that considering the circumstances of the death is important in assessing families for risk. Sudden and unexpected losses and violent deaths, such as suicide, homicide, and accidents, have been linked to PGD (Burke & Neimeyer, 2012; Mitchell et al., 2004). As mentioned previously, risk is greater still among individuals who discovered or saw the body of the deceased (Burke & Neimeyer, 2012). Stressors unique to these causes of death, such as the inability to bid farewell, may contribute. In fact, feeling unprepared for the death, regardless of the cause, has also been associated with PGD (Barry, Kasl, & Prigerson, 2002; McCarthy et al., 2010). This is important to be mindful of when working with individuals who have lost a loved one following an illness; although they may have had ample time to process that their loved one was dying, they may not have done so. Thus, it is essential to evaluate how prepared each family member was for the death and whether the death was actually perceived as sudden or unexpected. The opportunity to say good-bye is particularly important when there has been unresolved conflict or other types of unfinished business, as perceptions of regret are common among bereaved individuals with chronic grief (Bonanno, Wortman, & Nesse, 2004). Although it is unclear whether individuals with PGD or other pathological reactions to loss are at greater risk of experiencing regret, time to say good-bye affords the opportunity to address unfinished business and can therefore minimize the likelihood of regret.

Although illnesses sometimes allow families time to say good-bye, there are several stressors related to protracted illness that may increase risk of complicated bereavement.

Among parents bereaved by cancer, perceptions that their child's quality of life was poorer at the end-of-life period was associated with higher levels of PGD (McCarthy et al., 2010). Other stressors that may tax a family include the financial costs of supporting a loved one, balancing and delegating caregiving responsibilities between family members, and treatment and life support decision making (Walsh & McGoldrick, 2004).

Potential Individual Risk Factors. We characterize the remaining variables from Burke and Neimeyer's (2012) list as potential individual risk factors, that is, those that should be assessed for each individual family member, including being non-Caucasian, female, younger, less educated, and low income; having prior losses; lack of anticipatory grieving; perception of the death as preventable; searching for meaning; less importance of religion; lack of spiritual beliefs; little time spent talking about the loss; frequent pre-death contact with the deceased; regular church attendance; prior mental health counseling; pre-existing psychological condition; lack of technological connectedness (i.e., e-mail and cell phone); belief in professional counseling; subjectively close relationship with the deceased; problematic relationship with the deceased; deceased's gender opposite of the bereaved's; negative cognitions (about self, life, and the future); and threatening interpretations of one's own grief.

It should be noted that the majority of research conducted on race/ethnicity and PGD has been with African Americans, whom studies have demonstrated have a greater risk of PGD as compared with Whites, even when controlling for education, social support, religious coping, and rates of exposure to sudden death (Goldsmith, Morrison, Vanderwerker, & Prigerson, 2008). Laurie and Neimeyer (2008) additionally found that levels of prolonged grief symptoms were higher in bereaved African American college students, particularly if they spent little time speaking about their grief. There may be other racial and ethnic groups with elevated risk for PGD as well, but research on this topic has been limited.

Other Aspects of Family Functioning to Consider

The ability of families to demonstrate resilience as measured by functional outcomes should not be underestimated. Alam, Barrera, D'Agostino, Nicholas, and Schneiderman (2012) found that following the loss of a child to cancer, the majority of fathers returned to work. Mothers utilized child-focused coping strategies, whereas fathers used more task-focused coping (Alam et al., 2012). Mothers and fathers approached relationships with surviving children disparately, with mothers actively engaging with their children and helping them deal with their own grief, whereas fathers were less involved. Relationships with spouses varied over time, with both patterns of improvement and strain (Alam et al., 2012).

Marital functioning is likely to go through periods of alternating challenges and reconnection after the loss of a child. It is important to keep in mind that despite widespread beliefs that parental divorce following the death of a child is common, research shows that this is not the case (Eilegard & Kreicbergs, 2010; Schwab, 1998). A survey conducted by the Compassionate Friends (2006) found that the divorce rate among bereaved parents is approximately 16%, substantially lower than the national average of 50%. So although there is evidence of marital strain following the loss of a child, divorce is not the norm. In fact, parents often report a strengthening of their relationship in the long run (Schwab, 1998).

The impact of the loss on parents' relationships with surviving children is also variable. Arnold and Gemma (2008) described that parents reported difficulty loving them, feeling anxious and overly protective, or having heightened feelings of love and attachment. Siblings may suffer from poorer self-esteem, sometimes related to idealization of the deceased child (Pettle Michael & Lansdown, 1986). A study examining grief patterns in children aged 4 to 16 years who lost siblings showed that many displayed aggressive behaviors following the loss, perhaps motivated by a desire for parental attention (McCown & Davies, 1995). Gerhardt et al. (2012) found that bereaved siblings, particularly boys, were more vulnerable to social difficulties and were perceived as more sensitive and isolated by their peers.

Evidence Base for Screening Families for Dysfunction in Medical Settings

One of the strongest bodies of evidence on family screening for dysfunction comes from the Melbourne Family Grief Study (Kissane, Bloch, Dowe et al., 1996; Kissane, Bloch, Onghena et al., 1996), which was a three-phase, longitudinal study of family functioning before and after bereavement in 115 families. Using the typology of family functioning described previously, dysfunctional families were distinguished from well-functioning families in this study using the Family Relationship Index (FRI). The FRI is composed of 3 of 10 subscales from the Family Environment Scale (Moos & Moos, 1981): the cohesiveness, conflict, and expressiveness subscales. As detailed earlier in this chapter, supportive and conflict-resolving families were deemed well functioning, whereas intermediate, sullen, and hostile families were considered dysfunctional. Research has demonstrated that the FRI is a reliable screening tool to identify families at risk of morbid bereavement outcome (Edwards & Clarke, 2005; Kissane, Bloch, Dowe et al., 1996; Kissane, Bloch, Onghena et al., 1996; Kissane et al., 2003). Using the FRI routinely in clinical settings has been shown to be feasible and effective in recognition of at-risk families that may benefit from intervention (Kissane & Lichtenthal, 2008).

There have been a few efforts to develop clinical tools to assist in screening individuals that bear mentioning. In 2000, the Centre for Palliative Care in Australia published *Guidelines for the Assessment of Complicated Bereavement Risk in Family Members of People Receiving Palliative Care*, which provided five recommendations for complicated bereavement risk assessment (CBRA) and an accompanying risk factors checklist for families of patients receiving end-of-life, palliative support (Aranda & Milne, 2000). First, all available family members, regardless of the quality of their relationship with the deceased patient, should be involved in the CBRA; it is not meant just for the primary caregiver. Family meetings and the use of genograms can help the medical team to identify which individuals the family considers to be its members (Aranda & Milne, 2000). Second, CBRA requires input from the multidisciplinary team involved in the care of the patient and family. This assures that a wide range of perspectives is included when making risk determinations. Third, CBRA should begin at the point of referral to palliative care services and continue beyond the patient's death. Proactive assessment, as opposed to reactive measures once complicated grief symptoms are observed, is considered a more effective approach (Aranda & Milne, 2000). Conceptualizing the patient's death as one stage in a continuum of bereavement may help clinicians with implementing this guideline. Fourth, CBRA requires structured documentation, review in team meetings, and the use of family assessment. Clear documentation, which can include checklists or risk assessment forms, aids the multidisciplinary team with decision making about managing perceived risk. A specific screening tool was not recommended, but a checklist detailing important pre- and post-death risk factors was provided as an appendix to these guidelines (Aranda & Milne, 2000).

Lastly, CBRA should involve four categories of information: (1) the illness, terminal care, and nature of the death (sudden, traumatic, or stigmatized deaths; lack of forewarning about or anticipation of the death); (2) characteristics of the bereaved (adolescents who lose a parent, younger and elderly spouses, single mothers, parents who lose a child; history of losses; concurrent life stressors; physical and mental illness history; high pre-death distress; poor initial reaction to death; inability to use commonly effective coping strategies; isolation; low levels of internal control beliefs); (3) interpersonal relationships (perceiving others as unsupportive or antagonistic; lack of a confidant; disconnection from sources of support prior to or following death; ambivalent or dependent relationship with the deceased; unusually good and long-term relationships; low levels of cohesion, communication, and conflict resolution); and (4) characteristics of the deceased (child; adolescent; parent of children or adolescents; death due to inherited disorder or sudden or violent). As discussed previously, many of these variables have been linked to poor bereavement outcomes, and some appear to be prospective risk factors.

The Centre for Palliative Care has also more recently published evidence-based *Bereavement Support Standards for Specialist Palliative Care Services* for health care professionals to identify individuals who will benefit the most from intervention services (Hall, Hudson, & Boughey, 2012). Standard 4 focuses on screening and assessment of those at risk of complicated grief throughout the duration of palliative care, commencing as soon as a patient begins receiving palliative care and reassessed immediately following death and again six months later (Hall et al., 2012). During all assessments, individuals should be evaluated for suicidal or self-harming behavior.

Notably, more than a decade after the Centre for Palliative Care's *Guidelines* were published, the *Standards'* authors argued that no standardized measure to screen for complicated bereavement risk has sufficient empirical support to be recommended for systematic use prior to a person's death (Hall et al., 2012). They noted that several tools, such as the Distress Thermometer (Zwahlen, Hagenbuch, Carley, Recklitis, & Buchi, 2008) and the General Health Questionnaire-12 (Goldberg & Williams, 1988), may be utilized as measures of general psychosocial distress and can be used in conjunction with a structured interview for complicated bereavement screening. The authors also commented that the PG-13 may be a useful tool with individuals who are at least six months post-loss (Prigerson & Maciejewski, 2012). A modified version of the PG-13 (excluding the grief duration criterion) administered pre-loss may also have clinical utility because we have found in a study of bereaved caregivers that those reporting higher pre-loss scores on the PG-13 were more likely to meet criteria for PGD approximately six months post-loss (Lichtenthal et al., 2011). A study by Guldin, O'Connor, Sokolowski, Jensen, and Vedsted (2011) suggested that using the Beck Depression Inventory with one additional item ("Even while my relative was dying, I felt a sense of purpose in my life") can be an effective screening tool, with elevated scores at eight weeks post-loss predicting individuals at risk of developing PGD at six months post-loss.

Loss of Meaning and Its Impact on the Whole Family

Inevitably, role shifts must occur when a member of a family dies, which can lead to at least temporary destabilization of the family unit. Well-functioning families find a way to reorganize their roles, taking on the responsibilities of the deceased and re-achieving balance (Rando, 1991). However, even within well-functioning families, role changes bring about role losses; for example, an older child who assumes care of her younger siblings after school but must then sacrifice participation in her beloved school theater production. Because roles, identity, and meaning are inextricably linked, such family shifts can threaten an individual's sense of meaning and purpose.

In addition, family members may also struggle with making meaning of the loss itself. Several studies point to the association between challenges with making meaning of a loss and grief complications, including PGD (Currier, Holland, & Neimeyer, 2006; Keesee, Currier, & Neimeyer, 2008; Lichtenthal, Currier, Neimeyer, & Keesee, 2010). Specifically, difficulty with making sense of a loss (sense making) or with identifying positive consequences related to the loss experience (benefit finding) have been associated with the least favorable grief outcomes (Holland, Currier, & Neimeyer, 2006). Complicating circumstances of the death, such as violent loss, increase the risk of meaning-making challenges (Currier et al., 2006; Lichtenthal, Neimeyer, Currier, Roberts, & Jordan, 2013). Sudden losses for which information about the cause of death is lacking can also lead to challenges with sense making in the family (Walters & Tupin, 1991).

Nadeau (2008) has referred to the process of weaving together individual family members' understanding of how and why the death occurred as *family meaning making*. It is viewed as an interactional process in which co-construction of meanings occur through the development of family narratives (Gudmundsdottir & Chesla, 2006). As it is with grieving individuals, meaning making within families can be an adaptive process. However, when family members develop negative meanings, and particularly when guilt or blame are involved in attributions about why the death occurred, complicated bereavement can develop (Nadeau, 2008). Based on her qualitative research with 33 families, Nadeau (1998, 2008) noted that the presence of negative meanings (e.g., the death was unfair or unjust) can therefore be viewed as a "red flag" or risk factor. Challenges also present when family subsystems create and hold differing meanings, further reinforcing family divisions (Nadeau, 2008).

Just as individuals may struggle to find meaning in their loss, families may similarly assert that meaning simply cannot be found. Nadeau's (1998, 2008) study identified specific factors that may hinder meaning making, including family rules that inhibit discussion of sensitive issues, physical and emotional distance, the absence of family rituals, and protectionism (defined as efforts to protect family members by not speaking about the death). Both the inability to find meaning and the presence of negative meanings can interfere with family adjustment, and thus interventions that facilitate family meaning-making processes are indicated when families have difficulty making sense of their loss.

Harnessing Family Involvement

In palliative care populations, garnering involvement from the entire family while the patient is still alive may reduce the likelihood that families develop maladaptive grief reactions. The Centre for Palliative Care's *Guidelines* described the critical role that family meetings can play, highlighting how this approach may be an especially effective way to gain buy-in from those at greatest risk of difficulties because it avoids pointing the finger at or stigmatizing any one individual family member (Aranda & Milne, 2000). The use of genograms during a family meeting can further elicit discussion about family coping patterns and loss history, and thus it is helpful for clinicians to be able to create and interpret these structured family assessments (Aranda & Milne, 2000).

The potential utility of a family meeting cannot be underscored enough. It provides important information about family coping strengths and weaknesses and family members' respective history of psychological problems. Offering family members the opportunity to express themselves allows professionals to build a working alliance with them, which may be particularly important for those at greatest risk of complicated bereavement outcomes. These individuals can then be linked with resources that can be accessed through bereavement. Our research has shown, in fact, that bereaved caregivers of advanced cancer patients were nearly five times more likely to access bereavement mental health services if they had a discussion with a professional about their emotional concerns while the patient was alive (Lichtenthal et al., 2011).

Once a family is engaged, clinical interventions can address long-standing familial tension, differences in coping styles, division of labor, and mental illness. Attending to such issues may reduce family conflict and prevent the development of complicated bereavement (Lichtenthal & Kissane, 2008). A model of harnessing involvement of more dysfunctional families is the Family Focused Grief Therapy (FFGT) model, developed by Kissane and colleagues (Kissane & Bloch, 2002; Kissane et al., 2006) and described more fully in Chapters 6–9. FFGT is a well-researched family intervention that begins in palliative care during the patient's illness and continues through bereavement and is designed to prevent complicated bereavement outcomes by improving family communication, cohesion, and conflict management (Kissane & Bloch, 2002; Kissane et al., 2006; Kissane & Lichtenthal, 2008; Kissane, Lichtenthal, & Zaider, 2007). Because the intervention targets lower functioning, less cohesive families, engaging individual family members often proves challenging. The use of active strategies such as calling individual family members to personally invite them to sessions, however, may increase family involvement (Kissane & Lichtenthal, 2008).

These "best practices" in working with families during palliative care can be implemented when time and resources permit. However, sudden, unexpected, and/or violent family losses do not commonly allow for such preparatory work. In these instances, particularly given these families' increased risk for complicated bereavement, family meetings through the medical system or community agencies around the time of death are all the more critical.

Conclusion

Mental health professionals often conceptualize complicated bereavement as a negative outcome that affects the bereft *individual*, despite the obvious impact loss has on the family unit. A family systems conceptualization of complicated bereavement considers how a given family can get "stuck" or become derailed from sharing the experience and integrating the loss, reorganizing itself and reinvesting in life, and, more generally speaking, using the types of adaptive coping skills that resilient families exhibit (Walsh & McGoldrick, 2004). In this chapter, we have considered the empirical literature on complicated bereavement risk factors, reviewing those that may characterize the entire family, such as family functioning style (Kissane, Bloch, Dowe et al., 1996; Kissane, Bloch, Onghena et al., 1996), as well as those that may originate in a given family member, but inevitably impact the family system.

Much of the literature on risk of bereavement-related psychopathology has focused on the factors associated with PGD (also referred to as complicated grief in the current literature), and thus our review focuses on factors found to be predictive of this specific bereavement-related syndrome. However, there are several pathological reactions to loss, including depression, post-traumatic stress disorder, and substance abuse, which a given family member may experience. Thus, family assessments should consider transdiagnostic and genetic vulnerabilities as well as the range of outcomes that individual family members may experience.

We have discussed how the risk factor evidence base is complicated by studies that may have intended to examine risk factors but actually found associations reflecting correlates or consequences of PGD (Burke & Neimeyer, 2012; Kraemer et al., 2001). Given this, we have used Burke and Neimeyer's (2012) system for distinguishing prospective risk factors for which there is stronger empirical evidence linking them to PGD from those with a more inconclusive evidence base. Both confirmed and potential risk factors as Burke and Neimeyer (2012) defined them were detailed, as were categories of risk considered important to a CBRA (Aranda & Milne, 2000). We have described the potential use of standardized measures such as the FRI and a checklist that includes possible risk factors in clinical practice (Hall et al., 2012).

Why is the identification of families at risk for complicated bereavement so important? Primarily because recognizing which families are particularly vulnerable to difficulties allows for early intervention and appropriate triaging of resources. Furthermore, studies of risk factors point to how to best intervene with these families. Interventions that target modifiable risk factors may be especially potent. For example, as described previously and further detailed in Chapter 1, FFGT targets families according to the functioning types described previously, with a focus on intermediate, sullen, and hostile families. FFGT has been shown to significantly decrease complications of bereavement, with sullen families showing the most benefit (Kissane et al., 2006). Another family-based intervention that targets risk factors and has demonstrated efficacy is the Family Bereavement Program (FBP), a preventive intervention for bereaved children ages 8 to 16 years and their surviving parents or primary caregivers, described in further detail in Chapter 15. In addition to focusing on modifiable risk factors, FBP also works to enhance protective factors in order to prevent problematic grief in children following the loss of a parent (Sandler et al., 1992, 2008). FBP operates on the theory that multiple risk factors can be addressed simultaneously to reduce overall mental health problems (Sandler et al., 2008).

Risk must first, however, be identified, and thus, regular screening of bereaved families should be the standard of care. However, additional research is needed, not only to develop valid and reliable screening tools, but to also examine how to best target and modify these risk factors in order to prevent or reduce family morbidity after the loss of a loved one.

References

Alam, R., Barrera, M., D'Agostino, N., Nicholas, D., & Schneiderman, G. (2012). Bereavement experiences of mothers and fathers over time after the death of a child due to cancer. *Death Studies, 36*(1), 1–22.

Aranda, S., & Milne, D. (2000). *Guidelines for the assessment of complicated bereavement risk in family members of people receiving palliative care.* Melbourne, Australia: Centre for Palliative Care.

Arnold, J., & Gemma, P. (2008). The continuing process of parental grief. *Death Studies, 32*(7), 658–673.

Barry, L. C., Kasl, S. V., & Prigerson, H. G. (2002). Psychiatric disorders among bereaved persons: The role of perceived circumstances of death and preparedness for death. *American Journal of Geriatric Psychiatry, 10*(4), 447–457.

Boelen, P. A. (2006). Cognitive-behavioral therapy for complicated grief: Theoretical underpinnings and case descriptions. *Journal of Loss & Trauma, 11*(1), 1–30.

Bonanno, G. A., Wortman, C. B., Lehman, D. R., Tweed, R. G., Haring, M., Sonnega, J., . . . Nesse, R. M. (2002). Resilience to loss and chronic grief: A prospective study from preloss to 18-months postloss. *Journal of Personality and Social Psychology, 83*(5), 1150–1164.

Bonanno, G. A., Wortman, C. B., & Nesse, R. M. (2004). Prospective patterns of resilience and maladjustment during widowhood. *Psychology and Aging, 19*(2), 260–271.

Burke, L. A., & Neimeyer, R. A. (2012). Prospective risk factors for complicated grief. In M. Stroebe, H. Schut, & J. van den Bout (Eds.), *Complicated grief: Scientific foundations for health care professionals* (pp. 145–161). New York: Routledge.

Callahan, J. (2000). Predictors and correlates of bereavement in suicide support group participants. *Suicide and Life-Threatening Behavior, 30*(2), 104–124.

Carr, D. S. (2004). African American/Caucasian differences in psychological adjustment to spousal loss among older adults. *Research on Aging, 26,* 591–622.

Cleiren, M. P. H. D. (1993). *Bereavement and adaptation: A comparative study of the aftermath of death.* Washington, DC: Hemisphere.

The Compassionate Friends. (2006). *When a child dies: A survey of bereaved parents.* Retrieved from https://www.compassionatefriends.org/pdf/When_a_Child_Dies-2006_Final.pdf

Currier, J. M., Holland, J. M., & Neimeyer, R. A. (2006). Sense-making, grief, and the experience of violent loss: Toward a mediational model. *Death Studies, 30,* 403–428.

Currier, J. M., Neimeyer, R. A., & Berman, J. S. (2008). The effectiveness of psychotherapeutic interventions for bereaved persons: A comprehensive quantitative review. *Psychological Bulletin, 134*(5), 648–661.

Davies, R. (2004). New understandings of parental grief: Literature review. *Journal of Advanced Nursing, 46*(5), 506–513.

De Groot, M., De Keijser, J., & Neeleman, J. (2006). Grief shortly after suicide and natural death: A comparative study among spouses and first degree relatives. *Suicide and Life-Threatening Behavior, 36*(4), 418–431.

Edwards, B., & Clarke, V. (2005). The validity of the family relationships index as a screening tool for psychological risk in families of cancer patients. *Psycho-Oncology, 14*(7), 546–554.

Eilegard, A., & Kreicbergs, U. C. (2010). Risk of parental dissolution of partnership following the loss of a child to cancer: A population-based long-term follow-up. *Archives of Pediatric Adolescent Medicine, 164*(1), 100–101.

Gerhardt, C. A., Fairclough, D. L., Grossenbacher, J. C., Barrera, M., Gilmer, M. J., Foster, T. L., . . . Vannatta, K. (2012). Peer relationships of bereaved siblings and comparison classmates after a child's death from cancer. *Journal of Pediatric Psychology, 37*(2), 209–219.

Goldberg, D., & Williams, P. (1988). *A user's guide to the General Health Questionnaire.* Slough, UK: NFER-Nelson.

Goldsmith, B., Morrison, R., Vanderwerker, L., & Prigerson, H. (2008). Elevated rates of prolonged grief disorder in African Americans. *Death Studies, 32*(4), 352–365.

Gudmundsdottir, M., & Chesla, C. A. (2006). Building a new world: Habits and practices of healing following the death of a child. *Journal of Family Nursing, 12*(2), 143–164.

Guldin, M., O'Connor, M., Sokolowski, I., Jensen, A., & Vedsted, P. (2011). Identifying bereaved subjects at risk of complicated grief: Predictive value of questionnaire items in a cohort study. *BMC Palliative Care, 10*(9), 1–7.

Hall, C., Hudson, P., & Boughey, A. (2012). *Bereavement support standard for specialist palliative care services.* Melbourne, Australia: Department of Health, State Government of Victoria.

Hibberd, R., Elwood, L. S., & Galovski, T. E. (2010). Risk and protective factors for post-traumatic stress disorder, prolonged grief, and depression in survivors of violent death of a loved one. *Journal of Loss and Trauma, 15,* 426–447.

Holland, J. M., Currier, J. M., & Neimeyer, R. A. (2006). Meaning reconstruction in the first two years of bereavement: The role of sense-making and benefit-finding. *OMEGA—Journal of Death and Dying, 53*(3), 175–191.

Johannesson, K. B., Lundin, T., Hultman, C. M., Lindam, A., Dyster-Aas, J., Arneberg, P., & Michel, P. O. (2009). The effect of traumatic bereavement on tsunami-exposed survivors. *Journal of Traumatic Stress, 22,* 497–504.

Johnson, J. G., Zhang, B., Greer, J. A., & Prigerson, H. G. (2007). Parental control, partner dependency, and complicated grief among widowed adults in the community. *Journal of Nervous and Mental Disease, 195*(1), 26–30.

Jordan, J. R., & Neimeyer, R. A. (2003). Does grief counseling work? *Death Studies, 27*(9), 765–786.

Keesee, N. J., Currier, J. M., & Neimeyer, R. A. (2008). Predictors of grief following the death of one's child: The contribution of finding meaning. *Journal of Clinical Psychology, 64*(10), 1145–1163.

Kissane, D., Lichtenthal, W. G., & Zaider, T. (2007). Family care before and after bereavement. *OMEGA—Journal of Death and Dying, 56*(1), 21–32.

Kissane, D. W., & Bloch, S. (1994). Family grief. *British Journal of Psychiatry, 164*(6), 728–740.

Kissane, D. W., & Bloch, S. (2002). *Family focused grief therapy: A model of family-centered care during palliative care and bereavement.* Buckingham, UK: Open University Press.

Kissane, D. W., Bloch, S., Dowe, D. L., Snyder, R. D., Onghena, P., McKenzie, D. P., & Wallace, C. S. (1996). The Melbourne Family Grief Study, I: Perceptions of family functioning in bereavement. *American Journal of Psychiatry, 153*(5), 650–658.

Kissane, D. W., Bloch, S., Onghena, P., McKenzie, D. P., Snyder, R. D., & Dowe, D. L. (1996). The Melbourne Family Grief Study, II: Psychosocial morbidity and grief in bereaved families. *American Journal of Psychiatry, 153*(5), 659–666.

Kissane, D. W., & Lichtenthal, W. G. (2008). Family focused grief therapy: From palliative care into bereavement. In M. Stroebe, R. Hansson, H. Schut, & W. Stroebe (Eds.), *Handbook of bereavement research and practice: Advances in theory and intervention* (pp. 485–510). Washington, DC: American Psychological Association Press.

Kissane, D. W., McKenzie, D. P., & Bloch, S. (1997). Family coping and bereavement outcome. *Palliative Medicine, 11*(3), 191–201.

Kissane, D. W., McKenzie, M., Bloch, S., Moskowitz, C., McKenzie, D. P., & O'Neill, I. (2006). Family focused grief therapy: A randomized, controlled trial in palliative care and bereavement. *American Journal of Psychiatry, 163*(7), 1208–1218.

Kissane, D. W., McKenzie, M., McKenzie, D. P., Forbes, A., O'Neill, I., & Bloch, S. (2003). Psychosocial morbidity associated with patterns of family functioning in palliative care: Baseline data from the family focused grief therapy controlled trial. *Palliative Medicine, 17*(6), 527–537.

Kraemer, H. C., Kazdin, A. E., Offord, D. R., Kessler, R. C., Jensen, P. S., & Kupfer, D. J. (1997). Coming to terms with the terms of risk. *Archives of General Psychiatry, 54*(4), 337–343.

Kraemer, H. C., Stice, E., Kazdin, A., Offord, D., & Kupfer, D. (2001). How do risk factors work together? Mediators, moderators, and independent, overlapping, and proxy risk factors. *American Journal of Psychiatry, 158*(6), 848–856.

Kristensen, P., Weisæth, L., & Heir, T. (2010). Predictors of complicated grief after a natural disaster: A population study 2 years after the 2004 South East Asian tsunami. *Death Studies, 37,* 134–150.

Laurie, A., & Neimeyer, R. A. (2008). African Americans in bereavement: Grief as a function of ethnicity. *OMEGA—Journal of Death and Dying, 57,* 173–193.

Lichtenthal, W. G., Cruess, D. G., & Prigerson, H. G. (2004). A case for establishing complicated grief as a distinct mental disorder in *DSM-V. Clinical Psychology Review, 24*(6), 637–662.

Lichtenthal, W. G., Currier, J. M., Neimeyer, R. A., & Keesee, N. J. (2010). Sense and significance: A mixed methods examination of meaning-making following the loss of one's child. *Journal of Clinical Psychology, 66*(7), 791–812.

Lichtenthal, W. G., & Kissane, D. (2008). The management of family conflict in palliative care. *Progress in Palliative Care, 16*(1), 1–7.

Lichtenthal, W. G., Neimeyer, R. A., Currier, J. M., Roberts, K., & Jordan, N. (2013). Cause of death and the quest for meaning after the loss of a child. *Death Studies, 37*(4), 311–342.

Lichtenthal, W. G., Nilsson, M., Kissane, D. W., Breitbart, W., Kacel, E., Jones, E. C., & Prigerson, H. G. (2011). Underutilization of mental health services among bereaved caregivers with prolonged grief disorder. *Psychiatric Services, 62*(10), 1225–1229.

Lobb, E. A., Kristjanson, L. J., Aoun, S. M., Monterosso, L., Halkett, G. K. B., & Davies, A. (2009). Predictors of complicated grief: A systematic review of empirical studies. *Death Studies, 34*(8), 673–698.

McCarthy, M., Clarke, N., Lin Ting, C., Conroy, R., Anderson, V., & Heath, J. (2010). Prevalence and predictors of parental grief and depression after the death of a child from cancer. *Journal of Palliative Medicine, 13*(11), 1321–1326.

McCown, D., & Davies, B. (1995). Patterns of grief in young children following the death of a sibling. *Death Studies, 19,* 41–53.

Meert, K. L., Donaldson, A. E., Newth, C. J., Harrison, R., Berger, J., Zimmerman, J., . . . Eunice Kennedy Shriver National Institute of Child Health and Human Development Collaborative Pediatric Critical Care Research Network. (2010). Complicated grief and associated risk factors among parents following a child's death in the pediatric intensive care unit. *Archives of Pediatrics & Adolescent Medicine, 164*(11), 1045–1051.

Mitchell, A., Kim, Y., Prigerson, H. G., & Mortimer-Stephens, M. (2004). Complicated grief in survivors of suicide. *Crisis, 25*(1), 12–18.

Moos, R. H., & Moos, B. (1981). *Family Environment Scale manual.* Stanford, CA: Consulting Psychologists Press.

Nadeau, J. W. (1998). *Families making sense of death.* Thousand Oaks, CA: Sage.

Nadeau, J. W. (2008). Meaning-making in bereaved families: Assessment, intervention, and future research. In J. W. Nadeau (Ed.), *Handbook of bereavement research and practice: Advances in theory and intervention* (pp. 511–530). Washington, DC: American Psychological Association.

Pettle Michael, S. A., & Lansdown, R. G. (1986). Adjustment to the death of a sibling. *Archives of Disease in Childhood, 61,* 278–283.

Prigerson, H., & Maciejewski, P. (2012). *Prolonged grief disorder (PG-13).* Boston: Dana-Farber Cancer Institute Center for Psychooncology & Palliative Care Research.

Prigerson, H. G., Horowitz, M. J., Jacobs, S. C., Parkes, C. M., Aslan, M., Goodkin, K., . . . Maciejewski, P. K. (2009). Prolonged grief disorder: Psychometric validation of criteria proposed for *DSM-V* and *ICD-11*. *PLoS Medicine, 6*(8), e1000121.

Prigerson, H. G., & Jacobs, S. C. (2001). Traumatic grief as a distinct disorder: A rationale, consensus criteria, and a preliminary empirical test. In M. S. Stroebe, R. O. Hansson, W. Stroebe, & H. Schut (Eds.), *Handbook of bereavement research: Consequences, coping, and care* (pp. 613–645). Washington, DC: American Psychological Association.

Rando, T. A. (1991). *How to go on living when someone you love dies.* New York: Bantam Books.

Sandler, I. N., West, S. G., Baca, L., Pillow, D. R., Gersten, J. C., Rogosch, F., . . . Ramirez, R. (1992). Linking empirically based theory and evaluation: The Family Bereavement Program. *American Journal of Community Psychology, 20*(4), 491–521.

Sandler, I. N., Wolchik, S. A., Ayers, T. S., Tein, J., Coxe, S., & Chow, W. (2008). Linking theory and intervention to promote resilience in parentally bereaved children. In M. S. Stroebe, R. O. Hansson, H. Schut, & W. Stroebe (Eds.), *Handbook of bereavement research and practice: Advances in theory and intervention.* Washington, DC: American Psychological Association.

Schwab, R. (1998). A child's death and divorce: Dispelling the myth. *Death Studies, 22*, 445–468.

Shear, K., & Shair, H. (2005). Attachment, loss, and complicated grief. *Developmental Psychobiology, 47*(3), 253–267.

Shear, M. K., Simon, N., Wall, M., Zisook, S., Neimeyer, R., Duan, N., . . . Keshaviah, A. (2011). Complicated grief and related bereavement issues for *DSM-5. Depression and Anxiety, 28*(2), 103–117.

van der Houwen, K., Stroebe, M., Stroebe, W., Schut, H., van den Bout, J., & Wijngaards-De Meij, L. (2009). Risk factors for bereavement outcome: A multivariate approach. *Death Studies, 34*(3), 195–220.

Vanderwerker, L. C., & Prigerson, H. G. (2004). Social support and technological connectedness as protective factors in bereavement. *Journal of Loss and Trauma, 9*(1), 45–57.

van Doorn, C., Kasl, S. V., Beery, L. C., Jacobs, S. C., & Prigerson, H. G. (1998). The influence of marital quality and attachment styles on traumatic grief and depressive symptoms. *Journal of Nervous and Mental Disease, 186*(9), 566–573.

Walsh, F., & McGoldrick, M. (2004). Loss and the family: A systemic perspective. In F. Walsh & M. McGoldrick (Eds.), *Living beyond loss: Death in the family* (pp. 3–26). New York: W. W. Norton.

Walters, D. T., & Tupin, J. P. (1991). Family grief in the emergency department. *Emergency Medicine Clinics of North America, 9*(1), 189–206.

Wilsey, S. A., & Shear, M. K. (2007). Descriptions of social support in treatment narratives of complicated grievers. *Death Studies, 31*(9), 801–819.

Winjgaards-de Meij, L., Stroebe, M., Schut, H., Stroebe, W., van den Bout, J., van der Heijden, P., & Dijkstra, I. (2007). Neuroticism and attachment insecurity as predictors of bereavement outcome. *Journal of Research in Personality, 41*(2),498–505.

Worden, J. W. (2009). *Grief counseling and grief therapy: A handbook for the mental health practitioner* (4th ed.). New York: Springer.

Zwahlen, D., Hagenbuch, N., Carley, M. I., Recklitis, C. J., & Buchi, S. (2008). Screening cancer patients' families with the distress thermometer (DT): A validation study. *Psycho-Oncology, 17*(10), 959–966.

18 The Family with Socioeconomic and Cultural Issues

Sarah Gehlert, Teresa T. Moro, and Lailea Noel

The social environments in which people live, defined as their immediate physical sur-roundings, social relationships, and cultural milieus (Barnett & Casper, 2001), shape their lifelong health. These social environments occur at multiple levels—from the household level to the level of neighborhoods and communities to society as a whole (Warnecke et al., 2008)—and they interact with one another in complex ways to influ-ence health. Strong, supportive families may live in impoverished communities that receive scant resources and attention from society. These communities are often cut off from mainstream society, limiting residents' exposure to health information (Browne, 2011; Fullilove, 2004). Conversely, extremely disengaged families may live within neigh-borhoods and communities that are rich in social and material resources and privy to health information.

Although some individuals' social environments remain constant, over their life course others' change over time. One person may experience rich supports and resources from childhood through to adulthood. Others may either gain or lose supports and resources over the life course.

An increasingly high percentage of the population of the United States (as one global example) lives in adversity throughout their lives, producing marked health disparities across social groups. Disparities in cancer, cardiovascular disease, diabetes, and other chronic diseases have been documented extensively. A startling example is that Asian males in the United States are expected to live approximately 15.4 years more than urban African American males (Murray et al., 2006). These racial and ethnic health disparities are associated with trauma and disease, early death, and an attendant social and financial drain. For this reason, it is reasonable to assume that certain racial and ethnic populations in the United States are exposed to grief earlier in the life cycle than are white Americans.

Evidence is accumulating that adverse events during childhood and adolescence influence psychological functioning, health behaviors, and health outcomes. We know, for instance, that although most cancers are more likely to occur later in life, features of early family relationships increase the risk of their occurrence (Biro & Deardorff, 2012; Ellis, Shirtcliff, Boyce, Deardorff, & Essex, 2011). Events during childhood and adoles-cence may impact lifelong health in at least two ways. First, the social environment can change biology to affect health through a number of pathways. Gehlert and colleagues (2008) concluded that environments with high crime and unsafe housing predisposed African American women to a more aggressive form of breast cancer that occurs earlier in life than the majority of breast cancers. Second, individuals' health behaviors may be shaped by their environments. They may continue to practice health behaviors that they learned early in life. Health behaviors are also influenced by economic conditions and local, state, and federal policies that determine who is eligible to receive health insurance and access to health services.

In this chapter, we address how social environmental factors affect the health and health behaviors of individuals and families, with special attention to family grief behavior. Because social environment is a particularly broad concept, we address the influences of three salient components of social environment—namely, race and ethnicity, socioeconomic status (SES) and employment, and place (in the sense of immigration status). We begin with an overview of how the social environment is known to shape health and then address each of the three components as they affect both health behaviors and health outcomes. In some cases, evidence is available to connect the social environmental component to family grief behavior. When such evidence is not available, however, we draw tentative conclusions based on the evidence that is available. Finally, we make recommendations for clinical practice with vulnerable individuals and families experiencing grief.

An Overview of the Social Environment and Health

Several mechanisms have been proposed to link the social environment to health outcomes and health disparities. A recent review in the *Annual Review of Psychology* (Matthews & Gallo, 2011) posits two pathways from the social environment to disease. In one pathway, lack of psychosocial resources affects biobehavioral pathways to disease when, for example, lack of health insurance limits access to treatment, or the physical or built environment limits social interactions. In a second pathway, the social environment produces stress and adversity, which negatively affects biobehavioral pathways via psychological distress.

Although a widely agreed upon model of the determinants of health disparities has yet to be developed, McGinnis, Williams-Russo, and Knickman (2002) offer a useful organizing framework. In this scheme, which was based on a review of hundreds of empirical articles about early deaths in the United States, approximately 40 percent of early deaths were accounted for by behavioral patterns, 30 percent by genetic predisposition, 15 percent by social circumstances, 10 percent by environmental exposures, and 5 percent by shortfalls in medical care. We have argued elsewhere that social circumstances have received too little attention compared to other determinants (Gehlert & Colditz, 2011).

Public health researchers and other scholars increasingly encourage the consideration of social environment in understanding population health and racial and ethnic health disparities. The social determinants of health most frequently examined are (1) race and ethnic status, and (2) social class or SES and their effects. Each plays a critical role in perpetuating health disparities, and the complex interaction between the two is manifest in the everyday lives of racial and ethnic minority group members and families.

The Center for Interdisciplinary Health Disparities Research (CIHDR)

The CIHDR at the University of Chicago, which was directed by one of the authors of this chapter (S. G.), was funded in 2003 as one of eight Centers for Population Health and Health Disparities in the United States. The CIHDR investigators developed a novel model to identify the relationship of social environment to the persistent disparity in breast cancer mortality between African American and white women, in which African American women, though less likely to develop breast cancer, are 37 percent more likely to die from the disease. The center's four research projects, two of which dealt with women in neighborhoods and two with animal models, each form a link in the chain of causation in a downward, iterative manner from the societal level to the molecular level (Gehlert et al., 2008). That chain, vertically oriented, starts at the top with race-related determinants of health such as policies that foster economic segregation. It then covers issues such as concentrated poverty, neighborhood disruption, and neighborhood crime; then considers isolation, acquired vigilance, and depression; and finally moves to stress-hormone dynamics and cell survival and tumor development.

Social Isolation

Derelict buildings, vacant lots, litter, and excessive traffic interfere with residents' ability to establish and maintain social relationships (Taylor, 2001). The quality and content of the *built environment* of neighborhoods, defined as the buildings, spaces, and products created by people, have a profound effect on health outcomes (see http://www.ncbi.nlm.nih.gov/pubmed/9252316). Neighborhoods with fewer signs of occupation, fewer fences, and higher speed limits are more likely than others to be burglarized (Sampson, Raudenbush, & Earls, 1997). These issues may cause residents to retreat into their homes for safety, thus and increasing social isolation. In addition, residents' attempts to deal with threats may deplete their physical or psychological resources over time.

Evidence from CIHDR animal experiments supports the notion that social isolation affects both social relationships and biology. Two CIHDR projects used rodent models that mimic human breast cancer to identify pathways by which the social environment affects cancer in rodents' mammary glands. The social conditions of Sprague-Dawley rats and SV40 Tag transgenic mice were manipulated at various stages of the life cycle, and biological effects were examined. Hermes et al. (2009) found that normally highly social rats that were socially isolated from the time of weaning became hypervigilant to novel stimuli in their environments and developed larger, more malignant spontaneous mammary gland tumors at an earlier age than their non-isolated peers. Both the mice and rats also developed a heightened stress hormone response to an acute stressor (Hermes et al., 2009; Williams et al., 2009). Investigators discovered that rats that were isolated from reciprocal care and support, particularly in the face of stressors, were more likely to die at an earlier age from mammary tumors (Yee, Cavigelli, Delgado, & McClintock, 2008). This may mirror discrimination and inclusion among humans, which has known health consequences.

People vary in their ability to cope with environmental challenges based on genetic, developmental, and experiential factors, including the long-term effect of early life stressors that may predispose them to overreact physiologically and behaviorally. The work of CIHDR helps us to understand how this might lead to higher breast cancer mortality among African American women. The group of investigators and their community partners found an association between neighborhood variables and stress hormone response of the African American women newly diagnosed with breast cancer in their study (Gehlert, Mininger, & Cipriano-Steffen, 2011).

Race and Ethnicity, Family Functioning, and Health

The degree to which individuals identify themselves as members of a specific racial or ethnic group can impact their response to loss and illness. For example, Salant and Gehlert (2008) found that when African American women were asked about their risk of acquiring cancer, they described collective memories of racial discrimination and victimization. Their interpretation and operationalization of cancer risk was embedded in their collective African American identity.

In the Jackson Heart Study, Sims et al. (2012) found a greater prevalence of hypertension among African American participants who reported higher rates of everyday discrimination and lifetime discrimination than their peers, who reported lower rates of discrimination. In focus group interviews conducted with African American women of childbearing age, Nuru-Jeter et al. (2008) found that women who reported experiences of racism as children said that (1) those memories remained vivid into adulthood, and that (2) they feared that their children would have similar experiences.

Collective racial discrimination and its impact on health have been identified among other racial and ethnic groups. Gee, Spencer, Chen, and Takeuchi (2007) found a significant association between self-reported everyday discrimination and chronic conditions, such as heart disease and respiratory illnesses, among Asian Americans. The researchers posit that physiological stress may be the link between discrimination and chronic health conditions. In addition, Walters et al. (2011) suggest that the experience of historical trauma for Native Americans may have a cumulative effect that undermines the physical, spiritual, and psychological health and well-being of their communities.

A mistrust of the health care system by racial and ethnic minorities has been implicated as a determinant of health disparities in the United States (Masi & Gehlert, 2008). After conducting 49 focus group interviews with more than 445 African American adults, Masi and Gehlert (2008) reported that almost every focus group cited mistrust of the medical establishment and that most participants said that they felt that they were less likely to receive high-quality treatment than their white counterparts. The authors suggest that this mistrust may lead to reluctance to adhere to prescribed treatment.

The social isolation experienced by racial and ethnic minorities living in inner cities is also implicated in the nation's health disparities. Boden-Albala, Litwak, Elkind, Rundek, and Sacco (2005) found that individuals from racial and ethnic minority groups who reported being socially isolated had poorer outcomes after ischemic stroke than their peers who did not report being socially isolated. They attributed this difference to poorer adherence to treatment, along with depression in the absence of social support.

Key Challenges/Therapeutic Strategies

A traditional, clinical approach that follows the Western medical model may prove ineffective (Berg, Meegan, & Deviney, 1998). In assessing racial and ethnic minority members' approach to treatment, it is important to acknowledge the described potential for mistrust of mainstream professionals, as well as cultural and religious beliefs that may discourage a person from seeking mental health assistance. This may entail spending time exploring beliefs and attitudes toward treatment. According to Lum (2005), the clinicians who are most successful in working with racial and ethnic minority groups are those who are willing to recognize cultural differences that impact the therapeutic process.

Evidence-based, culturally competent models of practice are preferable when working with racial and ethnic minority group members. Culturally competent communication involves learning from clients about their history by listening to their stories and working within their boundaries. Other techniques include encouraging clients to discuss family history, focusing on strengths, and engaging them as partners in treatment (Lum, 2005).

These techniques may be essential, because for many individuals, extended family or other kinship networks may have significant control over individual decision making. Thus it is important to consider how social networks (e.g., family, neighborhood or tribe) may contribute to coping with loss and participation in treatment (Berg et al., 1998).

Clinicians also should consider factors that are specific to each racial and ethnic population. For example, in some African American communities the neighborhood may be seen as an extension of the family (Hurd & Zimmerman, 2010). Young people may live near their extended families and maintain close ties with them. In addition, churches historically have been a source of support for members of African American communities.

Many Latinos in the United States practice transnationalism, interacting with the mainstream culture while maintaining strong ties with countries of origin (Lum, 2005). They may practice traditional folk medicine in addition to, or instead of, Western medicine, which can shape their approach to health care. Many Latinos may travel between their country of origin and the United States, and, in some cases, one family member may migrate, leaving a spouse or children in the home country (Drachman & Paulino, 2004). These culturally determined variants of family life impact clearly upon health, illness, death, and bereavement (see Chapter 8 for examples).

Socioeconomic and Employment Status, Family Functioning, and Health

As described previously, impoverished neighborhoods with high rates of crime and fewer safe public spaces may affect both the physical and mental health of their residents. Hudson (2005) outlines ways in which lower SES impacts mental health, such as through increasing victimization, trauma, and social isolation. Over time, repeated exposure to social and other environmental stressors takes its toll on individuals and families (Geronimus, Hicken, Keene, & Bound, 2006). Humans are physiologically equipped to handle episodic stressors, but exposure to continual stressors may increase susceptibility to chronic conditions, such as cancer and heart disease.

Although poverty and unemployment do not always go hand in hand, 12.5 million persons in the United States are unemployed (Bureau of Labor Statistics, U.S. Department of Labor, 2012) and many of these individuals may be of lower SES. Thus, many physical and mental health issues related to poverty also impact families dealing with unemployment. In addition, racial and ethnic minority group members have lower rates of employment than white Americans. Although the global adult unemployment rates for men (7.5 percent) and women (7.4 percent) were similar in 2012, African Americans had the highest rate at 13 percent, Hispanics the second highest at 10.3 percent unemployment, while white Americans have a 7.4 percent unemployment rate. Unemployment occurs for a multitude of reasons, each of which may have profound impact on families. Although some people are voluntarily unemployed, such as parents who choose to stay home with their children, the recent economic climate has ushered in increasingly high rates of involuntary unemployment, a well-recognized form of loss causing grief (Westman, Etzion, & Horovitz, 2004). Unemployment has been linked to several individual-level factors such as poor health, depression (Burgard, Brand, & House, 2007; Price, Choi, & Vinokur, 2002), anxiety (Paul & Moser, 2009; Westman et al., 2004), and grief (Brewington, Nassar-McMillan, Flowers, & Furr, 2004). Involuntary unemployment may create a "chain of adversity" from job loss to poor health, with depression and personal control serving as mediators between the two (Price, Choi, and Vinokur, 2002, pp. 309).

Based on a meta-analysis of literature on emotional health and unemployment, Paul and Moser (2009) concluded that unemployed individuals exhibited more distress than their employed counterparts. Significant differences were found for the following mental health variables: depression, anxiety, psychosomatic symptoms, subjective well-being, and self-esteem. On average, 34 percent of unemployed individuals reported psychological issues, compared to only 16 percent of employed individuals. Several variables were found to moderate the development of psychological problems. Men and women who held blue-collar jobs were more distressed by unemployment than were individuals who previously held white-collar jobs. In addition, people in countries with weaker economic development, unequal income distributions, or limited unemployment protection systems experienced greater distress than people from countries without those features (Paul & Moser, 2009).

Burgard et al. (2007) used data from two large-scale, longitudinal cohorts (Americans' Changing Lives Study and the Wisconsin Longitudinal Study) to explore the impact of involuntary job loss on health. They found that involuntary job loss was associated with poorer self-rated health and higher numbers of depressive symptoms. These effects were even more pronounced in people who had experienced a health-related job loss.

Although the impact of unemployment on the individual is profound, unemployment also has a ripple effect that impacts every family member in unique ways (Strom, 2003). The economic hardship created by unemployment impacts the levels of anxiety (Westman et al., 2004) and well-being (Strom, 2003) of spouses. It also seems to impact divorce rates, although the mechanism through which this occurs is poorly understood (Strom, 2003).

Parental unemployment can affect the entire family (Strom, 2003) and may directly impact health (Clarke et al., 2011; Strom, 2003) and the educational experiences of children (Kalil & Wightman, 2011; Strom, 2003). Clarke and colleagues (2011) utilized data on unmarried single mothers from the 1997–2008 National Health Interview Survey and found that 19 percent of the 21,842 mothers in the pooled study sample were unemployed. Forty percent of those unemployed mothers were African American, 28 percent were white, and 29 percent were Hispanic. Children of uninsured or underinsured single mothers were more likely than children of mothers with health insurance to experience delays in medical care (Clarke et al., 2011).

Parental job loss is also associated with a decrease in children obtaining postsecondary education. This trend is three times greater for middle-class African American than white children, where lack of postsecondary education, in turn, impacts a child's ability to seek and maintain employment (Kalil & Wightman, 2011). African American households also experience longer periods of unemployment than white households (Kalil & Wightman, 2011).

Key Challenges/Therapeutic Strategies

An immediate and profound effect of lower SES and unemployment in countries without a nationalized health care system is a lack of health insurance and mental health coverage. Thus, it may be necessary for clinicians to either offer families a sliding scale fee for services or help them to locate family therapy providers who are equipped to work with uninsured and/or low-income families. In addition, loss of income may also require clinicians to help families locate necessary services such as housing and food banks.

Although grief is a common experience following the death of a loved one, for poor communities this process is complicated by the exigencies of the social and economic conditions in which residents are embedded. Clinicians can help families living in chronic poverty who have histories of multiple losses by acknowledging and openly discussing these cumulative events. Acknowledging these complicated histories of loss may increase the effectiveness of treatment. Family-focused therapeutic interventions are useful because they provide a framework for coping with the impact of poverty and unemployment. For example, when a spouse or partner becomes unemployed, there is often a "crossover" effect in which the stress and anxiety experienced by one partner produces stress and anxiety in the other partner (Westman et al., 2004). It is also important for clinicians to elicit families' feelings of grief and loss and the meaning that they attribute to job loss (Harris & Isenor, 2011). In order to better understand the meaning of job loss, clinicians should gather information about other factors, such as SES before and after job loss, gender, position in the life cycle, dependent family members, and family composition (Strom, 2003).

According to Harris and Isenor (2011), clinicians are often asked both to help individuals search for jobs and aid them in processing their grief and loss. These authors offer several suggestions for working with the unemployed, including contextualizing the loss, making realistic appraisals of skills, recognizing the difficulty of being in limbo, focusing on self-trust, and taking a realistic stance on control. Clinicians working with unemployed individuals also should familiarize themselves with local community unemployment resources and high-quality online resources.

Place (Migration), Family Functioning, and Health

The impact of migration can have profound effects on both mental and physical health of immigrants. Moving to a new country can have a lasting influence on a family's cultural values and family narrative (McGoldrick, Giordano, & Garcia-Preto, 2005). Families must cope with a new set of social norms, expectations, and values that may be vastly different from those of their country of origin (Segal & Mayadas, 2005). Immigrant families have numerous reasons for migrating. In many cases, these families have been exposed to adverse conditions including poverty, difficult living conditions, and limited work opportunities in their countries of origin. Factors that can impact immigrant families include language barriers, legal status, reasons for leaving their country of origin, migration experience, and the reception received in the new country (Pine & Drachman, 2005).

Latin Americans who have immigrated to the United States often experience lower SES, yet a lower mortality rate than their white, non-Latino counterparts during the first generation after immigration (Markides & Eschbach, 2005; Palloni & Arias, 2004). This phenomenon is called the "Hispanic paradox," because lower SES is generally associated with poorer rather than better health (Markides & Eschbach, 2005).

Three general explanations have been offered to explain this paradox (Palloni & Arias, 2004). The first explanation is that the paradox doesn't exist and is seen as a result of data artifacts (e.g., underreporting of Hispanic origin on death certificates, misreporting of age, or how mortality rates are constructed). The second explanation is related to migration effects. Two popular migration hypotheses are called the "healthy-migrant effect" and the "salmon-bias effect" (Palloni & Arias, 2004). According to proponents of the "healthy-migrant effect," the paradox results from healthy people emigrating from their countries of origin. These people are healthier than those who do not emigrate—and healthier than the average individual in the host population. Alternatively, the "salmon-bias effect" emanates from findings that some immigrant groups tend to return to their countries of origin after experiencing unemployment and/or illness (Abraido-Lanza, Dohrenwend, Ng-Mak, & Turner, 1999; Palloni & Arias, 2004). The third explanation is that culture of origin may affect mortality as a result of the dominant health and lifestyle behaviors of the country of origin.

The degree of acculturation has also been linked to health effects in Latino immigrants. Acculturation refers to adopting elements of the dominant culture in which one is immersed, for example, when someone from Latin America assimilates into the mainstream U.S. culture (Lara, Gamboa, Kahramanian, Morales, & Bautista, 2005). In a recent review of the literature, Lara et al. (2005) found that acculturation may have both positive and negative effects on the health of Latino individuals in the United States. What distinguishes one result from the other, however, is not well understood. Some studies suggested that acculturation generates a negative effect because more highly acculturated people develop an increased likelihood of engaging in substance use, poor dietary behaviors, and low birth weight and prematurity. On the other hand, more highly acculturated individuals are more likely to use preventive health care services, have better self-perceived health, have health insurance coverage, and report fewer barriers to health care.

Clearly, undocumented immigrants are at risk of deportation, which can have numerous effects on their entire families, such as separating parents and children or the loss of income (Drachman & Paulino, 2004). In some cases, families may be of mixed status, meaning that some members are legally present in the country while others are not (Pine & Drachman, 2005). Arbona et al. (2010) interviewed 416 undocumented and documented immigrants from Mexico and Central America to find that undocumented immigrants feared deportation and separation from their family, while also carrying more extra-familial stress and less proficiency in English.

Key Challenges/Therapeutic Strategies

Clinicians who work with immigrants may be called upon to address issues such as their reasons for migration, their resources, and the reception they receive in the new country (Pine & Drachman, 2005; Segal & Mayadas, 2005). Immigrants may be seen in a variety of contexts, including community agencies, schools, and mental health services (Drachman & Paulino, 2004). Similar to work with families from racial and ethnic minority group backgrounds, clinicians need to be aware that traditional social work (Segal & Mayadas, 2005) or psychology (Gozdziak, 2004) techniques and clinical approaches may be ineffective with refugees or recent immigrants. The goal of therapy is not to help an individual become more acculturated, but rather to promote retention of positive health behaviors from their culture of origin while mitigating any negative health impact of the host country (Lara et al., 2005). For instance, are factors such as lack of language skills or health insurance impacting care delivery (Lara et al., 2005)?

Several scholars have advocated using the ecological model in working with refugee and immigrant families (Fazel, Reed, Panter-Brick, & Stein, 2012; Goodkind & Foster-Fishman, 2002; Segal & Mayadas, 2005; Williams, 2010). This conceptual framework is congruent with the downward multi-level model of health disparities and focuses on addressing the societal-, community-, and family-level factors that can impact families. Clinicians should involve members of an individual's community of origin when planning community programs and services rather than making assumptions about what they need or want (Goodkind & Foster-Fishman, 2002). Further, clinicians must remember that families with members who are undocumented or of mixed legal status are particularly vulnerable in terms of their ability to seek and access health care and other services (Pine & Drachman, 2005).

The primary therapeutic challenge is to create a culturally sensitive, safe space in which families can describe their experiences. One way in which clinicians can do this is to research the group with which they are working (Drachman & Paulino, 2004; Gozdziak, 2004). This may entail surveying the literature across disciplines, such as anthropology (Gozdziak, 2004), history, and sociology (Drachman & Paulino, 2004), in order to better understand the meaning families attribute to their suffering. Ethnography is another useful framework for understanding mental health practices and exploring the illness narratives of individuals and families because they may interpret their experiences differently from a clinician from a different culture (Gozdziak, 2004). In working effectively with families, clinicians need to gather as much information as possible about their pre- and postmigration experiences, their values, and cultural norms (Fazel, Reed, Panter-Brick, & Stein, 2012; Williams, 2010). For both immigrants and refugees, this includes information on reasons for migrating, resettlement experiences, and perceived reception in the new country (Pine & Drachman, 2005). Increased awareness of the culture or any oppression that they have experienced may help clinicians overcome, or at least understand, patients' and their families' mistrust of authority or fear of divulging personal information (Segal & Mayadas, 2005).

Conclusion

In this chapter, we have provided an overview of SES, employment, and cultural factors that affect how families function and their response to loss. Clearly, a uniform approach to practice does not work with all families. To ensure that services result in desired outcomes, it is important to realize the effect that racial and ethnic minority group and lower SES status, unemployment, and immigration can have on families, their health, and health behavior. We have provided a broad overview. Clinicians can prepare themselves to work with families from specific backgrounds by accessing evidence-based literature on culturally competent practice with certain groups. Clinicians can also inform their practices by spending time in communities and learning from the families themselves.

References

Abraido-Lanza, A. F., Dohrenwend, B. P., Ng-Mak, D. S., & Turner, J. B. (1999). The Latino mortality paradox: A test of the "salmon bias" and healthy migrant hypotheses. *American Journal of Public Health, 89*(10), 1543–1548.

Arbona, C., Olvera, N., Rodriguez, N., Hagan, J., Linares, A., & Wiesner, M. (2010). Acculturative stress among documented and undocumented Latino immigrants in the United States. *Hispanic Journal of Behavioral Sciences, 32*(3), 362–384.

Barnett, E., & Casper, M. (2001). Definition of "social environment." *American Journal of Public Health, 91*(3), 465.

Berg, C. A., Meegan, S. P., & Deviney, F. P. (1998). A social-contextual model of coping with everyday problems across the lifespan. *International Journal of Behavioral Development, 22*(2), 239–261.

Biro, F. M., & Deardorff, J. (2012). Identifying opportunities for cancer prevention during preadolescence and adolescence: Puberty as a window of susceptibility. *Journal of Adolescent Health, 52*(5), S15–20.

Boden-Albala, B., Litwak, E., Elkind, M. S., Rundek, T., & Sacco, R. L. (2005). Social isolation and outcomes post stroke. *Neurology, 64*(11), 1888–1892.

Brewington, J. O., Nassar-McMillan, S., Flowers, C. P., & Furr, S. R. (2004). A preliminary investigation of factors associated with job loss grief. *Career Development Quarterly, 53*(1), 78–83.

Browne, T. (2011). The relationship between social networks and pathways to kidney transplant parity: Experience form black Americans in Chicago. *Social Science & Medicine, 73*(5), 663–667.

Bureau of Labor Statistics, U.S. Department of Labor. (2012). The employment situation—April 2012 (USDL-12–0816). Retrieved from http://www.bls.gov/news.release/pdf/empsit.pdf

Burgard, S. A., Brand, J. E., & House, J. S. (2007). Toward a better estimation of the effect of job loss on health. *Journal of Health and Social Behavior, 48*(4), 369–384.

Clarke, T. C., Arheart, K. L., Muennig, P., Fleming, L. E., Caban-Martinez, A. J., Dietz, N., & Lee, D. J. (2011). Health care access and utilization among children of single working and nonworking mothers in the United States. *International Journal of Health Services: Planning, Administration, Evaluation, 41*(1), 11–26.

Drachman, D., & Paulino, A. (2004). Introduction: Thinking beyond United States' boarder. *Journal of Immigrant & Refugee Services, 22,* 1–9.

Ellis, B. J., Shirtcliff, E. A., Boyce, W. T., Deardorff, J., & Essex, M. J. (2011). Quality of early family relationships and the timing and temp of puberty: Effects depend on biological sensitivity to context. *Development and Psychopathology, 23,* 85–99.

Fazel, M., Reed, R. V., Panter-Brick, C., & Stein, A. (2012). Mental health of displaced and refugee children resettled in high-income countries: Risk and protective factors. *Lancet, 379*(9812), 266–282.

Fullilove, M. (2004). *Root shock: How tearing up city neighborhoods hurts America and what we can do about it.* New York: Random House.

Gee, G. C., Spencer, M. S., Chen, J., & Takeuchi, D. (2007). A nationwide study of discrimination and chronic health conditions among Asian Americans. *American Journal of Public Health, 97,* 1275–1282.

Gehlert, S., & Colditz, G. A. (2011). Cancer disparities: Unmet challenges in the elimination of disparities. *Cancer Epidemiology, Biomarkers & Prevention, 20*(9), 1809–1814.

Gehlert, S., Mininger, C., & Cipriano-Steffen, T. M. (2011). Placing biology in breast cancer disparities research. In L. M. Burton, S. P. Kemp, M. Leung, S. A. Matthews, & D. T. Takeuchi (Eds.), *Communities, neighborhoods, and health: Expanding the boundaries of place* (pp. 57–72). New York: Springer.

Gehlert, S., Sohmer, D., Sacks, T., Mininger, C., McClintock, M., & Olopade, O. (2008). Targeting health disparities: A model linking upstream determinants to downstream interventions. *Health Affairs, 27*(2), 339–349.

Geronimus, A. T., Hicken, M., Keene, D., & Bound, J. (2006). "Weathering" and age patterns of allostatic load scores among blacks and whites in the United States. *American Journal of Public Health, 96*(5), 826–833.

Goodkind, J. R., & Foster-Fishman, P. (2002). Integrating diversity and fostering interdependence: Ecological lessons learned about refugee participation in multiethnic communities. *Journal of Community Psychology, 30*(4), 389–409.

Gozdziak, E. M. (2004). Training refugee mental health providers: Ethnography as a bridge to multicultural practice. *Human Organization, 63*(2), 203–210.

Harris, D. L., & Isenor, J. (2011). Loss of unemployment. In D. L. Harris (Ed.), *Counting our losses: Reflecting on change, loss, and transition in everyday life* (pp. 163–170). New York: Routledge.

Hermes, G. L., Delgado, B., Tretiakova, M., Cavigelli, S. A., Krausz, T., Conzen, S. D., & McClintock, M. K. (2009). Social isolation dysregulates endocrine and behavioral stress while increasing malignant burden of spontaneous mammary tumors. *Proceedings of the National Academy of Sciences of the United States of America, 106*(52), 22393–22398.

Hudson, C. W. (2005). Socioeconomic status and mental illness: Tests of the social causation and selection hypotheses. *American Journal of Orthopsychiatry, 75*(1), 3–18.

Hurd, N., & Zimmerman, M. A. (2010). Natural mentors, mental health, and risk behaviors: A longitudinal analysis of African American adolescents transitioning into adulthood. American *Journal of Community Psychology, 46,* 36–48.

Kalil, A., & Wightman, P. (2011). Parental job loss and children's educational attainment in black and white middle-class families. *Social Science Quarterly, 92*(1), 57–78.

Lara, M., Gamboa, C., Kahramanian, M. I., Morales, L. S., & Bautista, D. E. H. (2005). Acculturation and Latino health in the United States: A review of the literature and its sociopolitical context. *Annual Review of Public Health, 26,* 367–397.

Lum, D. (2005). *Cultural competence, practice stages, and client systems: A case study approach.* Belmont, CA: Thomson Brooks/Cole.

Markides, K. S., & Eschbach, K. (2005). Aging, migration, and mortality: Current status of research on the Hispanic paradox. *Journal of Gerontology: Series B, Psychological Sciences and Social Sciences, 60,* 68–75.

Masi, C. M., & Gehlert, S. (2008). Perceptions of breast cancer treatment among African-American women and men: Implications for interventions. *Journal of General Internal Medicine, 24*(3), 408–414.

Matthews, K. A., & Gallo, L. G. (2011). Psychological perspectives on pathways linking socioeconomic status and physical health. *Annual Review of Psychology, 62,* 501–530.

McGinnis, J. M., Williams-Russo, P., & Knickman, J. R. (2002). The case for more active policy attention to health promotion. *Health Affairs, 21*(2), 78–93.

McGoldrick, M., Giordano, J., & Garcia-Preto, N. (2005). Overview: Ethnicity and family therapy. In M. McGoldrick, J. Giordano, & N. Garcia-Preto (Eds.), *Ethnicity & family therapy* (pp. 1–40). New York: Guilford Press.

Murray, C. J. L., Kulkarni, S. C., Michaud, C., Tomijima, N., Bulzacchelli, M. T., Iandiorio T. J., & Ezzati, M. (2006). Eight Americas: Investigating mortality disparities across races, counties, and race-counties in the United States. *PLoS Medicine, 3*(9), e260.

Nuru-Jeter, A., Dominguez, T. P, Hammond, W. P, Leu, J., Skaff, M., Egerter, S., . . . Braveman, P. (2008). "It's the skin you're in": African-American women talk about their experiences of racism. *Maternal and Child Health Journal, 13*(1), 29–39.

Palloni, A., & Arias, E. (2004). Paradox lost: Explaining the Hispanic adult mortality advantage. *Demography, 41*(3), 385–415.

Paul, K. I., & Moser, K. (2009). Unemployment impairs mental health: Meta-analyses. *Journal of Vocational Behavior, 74*(3), 264–282.

Pine, B. A., & Drachman, D. (2005). Effective child welfare practice with immigrant and refugee children and their families. *Child Welfare, 84*(5), 537–562.

Price, R. H., Choi, J. N., & Vinokur, A. D. (2002). Links in the chain of adversity following job loss: How financial strain and loss of personal control lead to depression, impaired functioning, and poor health. *Journal of Occupational Health Psychology, 7*(4), 302–312.

Salant, T., & Gehlert, S. (2008). Collective memory, candidacy, and victimization: Community epidemiologies of breast cancer risk. *Sociology of Health and Illness, 30*(4), 599–614.

Sampson, R. J., Raudenbush, S. W., & Earls, F. (1997). Neighborhoods and violent crime: A multilevel study of collective efficacy. *Science, 277*(5328), 918–924.

Segal, U. A., & Mayadas, N. S. (2005). Assessment of issues facing immigrant and refugee families. *Child Welfare, 84*(5), 563–583.

Sims, M., Diez-Roux, A. V., Dudley, A., Gebreab, S., Wyatt, S. B., Bruce, M. A., . . . Taylor, H. A. (2012). Perceived discrimination and hypertension among African Americans in the Jackson Heart Study. *American Journal of Public Health, 102*(S2), S258–S265.

Strom, S. (2003). Unemployment and families: A review of research. *Social Service Review, 77*(3), 399–430.

Taylor, R. B. (2001). *Breaking away from broken windows: Baltimore evidence and implications from the nationwide fight against crime, grime, fear and decline.* New York: Westview Press.

Walters, K. L., Mohammed, S. A., Evans-Campbell, T., Beltran, R. E., Chae, D. H., & Duran, B. (2011). Bodies don't just tell stories, they tell histories: Embodiment of historical trauma among American Indians and Alaska Natives. *Du Bois Review, 8,* 179–191.

Warnecke, R. B., Oh, A., Breen, N., Gehlert, S., Paskett, E., Tucker, K. L., . . . Hiatt, R. A. (2008). Approaching health disparities from a population perspective: The NIH Centers for Population Health and Health Disparities. *American Journal of Public Health, 98*(9), 1608–1615.

Westman, M., Etzion, D., & Horovitz, S. (2004). The toll of unemployment does not stop with the unemployed. *Human Relations, 57*(7), 823–844.

Williams, J. B., Pang, D., Delgado, B., Kocherginsky, M., Tretiakova, M., Krausz, T., . . . Conzen, S. D. (2009). A model of gene-environment interaction reveals altered mammary gland gene expression and increased tumor growth following social isolation. *Cancer Prevention Research, 2*(10), 850–861.

Williams, N. (2010). Establishing the boundaries and building bridges. *Journal of Child Health Care, 14*(1), 35–51.

Yee, J. R., Cavigelli, S. A., Delgado, B., & McClintock, M. K. (2008). Reciprocal affiliation among adolescent rats during a mild group stressor predicts mammary tumors and lifespan. *Psychosomatic Medicine, 70,* 1050–1059.

19 Future Development and Dissemination of Models of Family Bereavement Care

David W. Kissane and Talia I. Zaider

In reaching this final chapter, we trust that readers have now become convinced of the value and importance of family-centered approaches in bereavement care. The most available and significant sources of support can be usually found within the social network of the family. To optimize family support and grief sharing, the therapist guides the bereaved down the dual process pathway that oscillates between active grief work for a time and then restoration work that reengages in continued living (Stroebe & Schut, 2001).

Further development and dissemination of this family-centered approach is vital. In this chapter, we explore the research questions that remain to further consolidate and expand upon this model of care. We also present approaches for training and supervising therapists; staffing issues that will ensure an adequate workforce to meet the needs of the bereaved; and our final thoughts about how to integrate family-centered care with other models of bereavement work.

Developmental Issues for Family Grief Therapy

First, let us consider the research agendas that are prominent for family-centered bereavement care: examining issues for adult, child, and adolescent family members; which processes work; and where the limits of therapy apply.

Adult Focus of Family Models to Date

Most research thus far has focused on adult families, preventively screening to identify families that carry some risk of morbid outcome in bereavement (Kissane, Bloch, Dowe et al., 1996; Kissane, Bloch, Onghena et al., 1996; Kissane et al., 2006; Kissane, Zaider, Li, & Del Gaudio, 2013). The beauty of this model is the continuity of care from family support during palliative care, which is sustained into bereavement. The therapist has established trust with the family and met the dying family member and, in later ongoing work, can bring the deceased so readily "back into the therapy room." This approach in palliative medicine offers much that is optimal.

Yet even without access to palliative care, families can be engaged when meeting the therapist for the first time in bereavement, a response that will always be necessary as many deaths occur acutely. When an individual patient is referred for bereavement support, the therapist can invite him or her at the outset to bring along a relative (Kissane &

Hooghe, 2011). Indeed, the more serious the psychiatric disorder in those referred, the more likely their care will benefit if a relative accompanies them.

Further research questions concerning adult family therapy for bereavement care include the following: recognizing "at-risk" families to strengthen preventive care models; predicting the dose of therapy needed; examining the process of therapy to strengthen what works best; and incorporating meaning-centered components into the intervention.

Family Selection

The family-centered model developed in the Melbourne-based, family grief therapy randomized controlled trial (Kissane et al., 2006) and the more detailed "dose of intervention" study conducted in New York have both targeted families at risk or in distress. This approach applies the principle that well-functioning families have the wherewithal to adapt and grieve without detrimental outcomes. Resources are most cost-effectively focused on those in need. Screening with the Family Relationships Index (Moos & Moos, 1981) to determine the nature of family functioning has utility in the palliative care setting, as demonstrated, but it will not always be convenient or available as a starting point.

Identifying those in need can also be accomplished via the well-recognized list of predictors of pathological grief (see Table 19.1). These include risk factors evident in the nature of the dying process, in the strengths and vulnerabilities of the bereaved, in the qualities of the relationship with the deceased, and in the support base and family functioning of the survivors. Whenever any of these risk factors exist, preventive intervention through bereavement counseling is deemed wise to avert the development of greater psychiatric morbidity. Thus, for the widow recently relocated into a new neighborhood, involvement in a bereavement group in the local community would be worthwhile. Just as meritorious are family meetings that expand support to include the extended family members who might live close by. Combinations of individual, group, and family work with the bereaved can optimize the care plan. Bereavement counselors are therefore encouraged to ask themselves in every case, "How might family work assist here?"

Dose of Family Therapy

Many times, a single family meeting opens up channels of communication about matters that may have been perceived too delicate to discuss. Once the conversation has been initiated, the family can sustain this direction of support with worthwhile benefits.

In general, the more difficulties any family has in maintaining quality relationships between its members, the greater the "dose" of family therapy they may need. Another part of this dose consideration is the frequency of meeting. Some psychiatric disorders, like family therapy for anorexia nervosa, may be managed with quite intensive work requiring weekly sessions. In bereavement care, the initial sessions may be weekly and then biweekly. Once progress has led to improved communication, teamwork, and support, sessions may decrease to monthly, then every six weeks, bimonthly, and every three months. This empowers the family to maintain its progress and benefit from having time to work on its issues. For families with greater dysfunction, we have found that 12 to 16 sessions across two years may be needed; for milder dysfunction, 6 to 8 sessions

Table 19.1 Risk Factors in the Bereaved That Identify the Need for Family Bereavement Care

Nature of Risk Factors	Circumstances
1. Experience of the dying process	1a. Untimely death in the life cycle (e.g., death of child)
	1b. Sudden or unexpected (e.g., cardiac or road trauma)
	1c. Traumatic (e.g., natural disaster)
	1d. Stigmatized (e.g., suicide or homicide)
2. Strengths and vulnerabilities of the bereaved	2a. Past psychiatric history (e.g., depression)
	2b. Personality style (e.g., low self-esteem)
	2c. Cumulative experience of losses
3. Quality of relationship with the deceased	3a. Overly dependent (e.g., very close; anxious attachments)
	3b. Ambivalent (e.g., alcohol abuse, infidelity, gambling)
4. Quality of support network	4a. Dysfunctional family (e.g., poor cohesion, reduced communication, or high conflict)
	4b. Isolated (e.g., new migrant, new neighborhood)
	4c. Alienated (e.g., withdrawn from prior support base)

over 12 to 15 months may suffice. Generally, it is wise to extend therapy beyond the first anniversary (Kissane & Zaider, 2011).

Clinical experience over time guides this choice of dose and frequency of family work. There has been almost no research quantifying the evidence base to write guidelines for such work. Here lies a clear agenda for clinically directed research across the next couple of decades.

Process Research to Strengthen What Works Best

Further scholarship is also needed to discern what mediates change within the therapy room. The first Family Focused Grief Therapy Trial showed reduction and prevention of depression in bereavement—yet without global improvement in family functioning among these families (Kissane et al., 2006). It remained unclear whether this lack of change in family functioning was a dose-of-treatment effect, or whether the measures of relational life captured "trait" rather than "state" phenomena. In other words, although some improvement in mutual family support might occur, members retain a memory of their relational life such that, when observed in a self-report questionnaire, they respond with longer-term perceptions of these relationships. In the replication study that we have conducted in New York, Talia Zaider administered measures of family communication after each of four contiguous sessions. This demonstrated statistically significant enhancement in communication as reported by family members, illustrating that family functioning does improve (Zaider & Kissane, 2010). As the therapy sessions progressed, family members perceived that they gradually disclosed more to their family, and that the family as a whole disclosed more in turn. Moreover, families that improved communication in this manner had a significantly deeper sense of life completion for their dying relative (Zaider & Kissane, 2010). This outcome reflects a quality-of-life improvement resulting from the family work.

Families can be asked to identify which sessions were helpful and brought gains to the family, which sessions were neutral in this regard, which ones produced mixed views about any benefit, and which worsened their issues. We found through examination of 205 sessions that 29 percent were immediately perceived by the family to bring about improvement, 38 percent were neutral, 8 percent were controversial, and 25 percent appeared to worsen matters (Zaider & Kissane, 2012). The therapists who brought about improvements were able to (1) engage with the family, (2) become emotionally connected, (3) create a shared sense of purpose, and (4) keep the environment safe. Sessions that made matters temporarily worse or were controversial in this regard had low ratings for the family's sense of safety, even though the therapist engaged with the family and felt emotionally connected to them. Curiously, sessions that the families rated as neutral had the lowest therapist activity overall, and may be sessions in which families engage in a lot of talking and storytelling, while the therapist fails to integrate a deeper understanding of what this conversation means.

More process research of this ilk is needed in the decades ahead to guide our understanding of what works and how best to train therapists to optimize outcomes. Sustaining the family's sense of safety about its work in the therapy room is clearly a vital ingredient. As soon as any misunderstanding arises, the therapist needs to intervene to clarify and protect the well-being of the family as a whole. In conflictual families, the wisdom and art of therapy lie in knowing how much difference of opinion should be exposed, when to intercede with "time out," and when to redirect to constructive approaches or initiate containment of very emotive issues of contention.

Meaning-Centered Focus

As coping theory has matured to recognize meaning-based coping alongside emotion-based and problem-based coping (Folkman, 1997), therapy models have likewise increased their emphasis on meaning making. Relationships are one source of deep meaning in life. Helping families define this meaning, making its presence more explicit and valued, and celebrating the love and generosity found in families appear very worthwhile. Yet when death has intervened, for instance with the loss of a child or spouse, the search for meaning in that life is often delicate and needs to be gently pursued, lest the process appears driven by ideas found to be intellectually true, but not emotionally authentic. Considerable research is needed to better define those components of family therapy that assist in generating meaning and purpose in the life of a family.

Improvement of Pediatric and Adolescent Models

As our work has largely focused on adult families, research is clearly needed to identify which additional dimensions will improve the therapeutic model for younger family members. When should children be invited to draw their family, talk about what their drawing means, and thus integrate art and play into the therapy room? To what degree does it help to move chairs about relative to each other, to invite direct physical comfort of a distressed child, and to have family members talk to each other with puppets? Child psychotherapy uses several techniques that facilitate understanding and improve communication with younger children. It would be delightful to see their more systematic integration into family work in bereavement.

Similarly, for adolescents, tensions can exist between belonging to their family and individuating from it. The natural process of separation-individuation may be interrupted for the adolescent by family needs when a parent is dying and bereavement ensues. Further research could grapple with this balance for the adolescent between inward support for the family and freedom to explore the wider world. The Family Focused Grief Therapy model presented in sections of this book generally works well for families with adolescents. Further fine-tuning may be possible to optimally address the needs of adolescents alongside those of the bereaved parent.

Family Strengths versus Family Dysfunction

Several authors in this book have promoted the clinical wisdom in defining strengths rather than solely evaluating the deficits of a family. Indeed, for many families, exploring these positive pathways, which have worked to improve challenges experienced in earlier phases of family life, leads to constructive outcomes again. When protectiveness blocks more open communication, when life experience has not brought a family in contact with palliative care, and when any dysfunction is mild in nature, a strengths-based approach has great merit.

What, then, are the limits of such a model? Has research adequately defined the indications for one particular model over another?

Within the Family Focused Grief Therapy model, we have been careful to avoid any stance that is critical of the family. We avoid using a term like "problems," preferring to always ask families what are their "concerns" (Kissane & Bloch, 2002). By helping families to define these issues and then search for ways to relate differently, we open up reflection about a pathway for change. One paradox for all systemic therapies is the extent to which the therapist pursues a "change" or "acceptance" agenda. Both strategies can lead to the same beneficial outcome. So much of this is about insight, openness to reflective function, sensitivity to criticism, and readiness to try new approaches. As researchers examine the mediators of improvement in relational life, these subtleties of therapeutic endeavor are intriguing questions for the future.

Engagement

Psychotherapy research has achieved great understanding and refining of processes that optimize establishment of a therapeutic relationship, with the building of a strong alliance. Much of this progress has occurred within the individual therapy model of person-centered care, where empathic engagement fosters this therapeutic alignment. Systemic therapies must also build this alliance between therapist and others, necessitating the therapist's warmth, authentic interest and curiosity, compassionate concern, and willingness to understand and help. Yet when the therapist is faced with multiple family members all at once, the complexity of the task is much greater. Principles of neutrality toward any individual and focus on the family as a whole necessitate differences in approach. Family therapy research has again done much to deepen our understanding of these approaches. But given the central importance of engagement and emotional connection with the family, and the reality that many therapists segue between individual, couple, and family care, more study of these processes is worthwhile. Psychotherapy research has long shown that

10 percent of therapy can do harm (Gurman & Kniskern, 1978, 1991). Our data suggest that this figure may be higher when running family meetings, thus highlighting the imperative of safety and technical competence in pursuit of this clinical work.

Family Refusal and Withdrawal

Many a family declines the invitation to meet as a group. Although the reasons are usually several, the issue of safety and potential for benefit lie very much at the heart of how to handle this issue. For some family members, the solution of distance has already proved helpful as relationships have fractured and too much water has passed under the proverbial bridge. Relatives have tested the value of their relationship and chosen their preferred pathway. There is no place for omnipotence in the mind of the therapist who believes he or she can rescue everyone and work magic! Respect is warranted for established family choices and solutions.

On the other hand, much work is needed in better understanding the early dropouts that occur among families who initially presented willingly to seek help. To enrich our models of care and improve clinical outcomes, we need more thorough descriptions of therapeutic mistakes, more explicit discussion of how clinicians inadvertently get offside or neglect the preservation of safety, push too quickly for change, criticize more than affirm, or fail to offer hope and instill confidence about the direction of work and ensuing benefits. Supervision and training become central here, remain lifelong pursuits through openness to the peer-review process, and become an essential component of disseminating models of family-centered care.

Dissemination Issues for Family Grief Therapy Models of Care

To take the field forward, major efforts are needed in training, curriculum development, supervision of therapists, and deployment of an adequate workforce.

Training

Family support services within hospitals and community agencies are typically designed to meet the informational needs of caregivers, but they do not always address the broad range of family-related concerns that arise in palliative care and bereavement. In most settings, patients and their caregiving family members are assessed and provided support in separate forums (e.g., "caregiver groups" are arranged separately from "patient groups"). What is needed to initiate a wider adoption of whole-family care among both palliative care and bereavement services? An evidence base for the efficacy and value of such a model must sit alongside the development of clinicians' practical abilities to deliver such a program of care. Here we come to an important question: is the clinical psychologist or psychiatrist, the social worker, or the general practitioner trained and equipped to facilitate a family meeting, to define the level of concerns and the nature of family functioning, in order to develop a treatment plan agreeable to all?

The answer lies largely in the degree of family need or level of dysfunction. As with all illness, disability, or impairment, the level of dysfunction determines the need for specialist input. If a family is struggling to adapt to stressors that have temporarily challenged or disrupted its capacity to deal with the predicament, the clinician can empower adaptive choices by facilitating the family's use of its strengths, opening the channels of communication, promoting teamwork, and helping its members to reflect constructively on the best way forward. In these circumstances, the discipline of the clinician is less crucial than the sensible use of generic skills at running a family meeting. The clinical need is too great for anyone to be precious about who should lead such a family meeting.

Generic Skill Development in Running Family Meetings

Critical to the family's need is the development of a broad level of competency in routinely conducting a family meeting by a wide range of disciplines. This can address a current major deficit in care provision. Training this broad group of clinicians would involve a series of workshops that model and foster skill acquisition. This can be developed through role play and practice of skills in joining with families, helping them define their concerns, asking interventive questions, and offering summaries that integrate and promote understanding. Such generic ability in conducting a family meeting ought to be a basic skill in medicine and the allied health disciplines, taught in medical schools, clinical psychology training, and social work courses. Guidelines to support this approach should be made widely available.

Specialist Family Therapy Skill Development

At one extreme of the spectrum, some families present with chronic dysfunction and patterns of relating that have been entrenched across generations, where fractures, separations, and conflict abound and family dissonance has contributed to much psychiatric morbidity. Here referral to a specialist level of practitioner is indicated, and more extensive training in family therapy will equip this clinician with the necessary skill base to understand and respond to the difficulties of these families. Rather than primary-care level, these clinicians would typically staff tertiary-level facilities, ideally in specialty clinics, and would be equipped with years of experience, expertise, and skill development in handling the greater complexity presented by these families. We estimate that fewer than 10 percent of families would warrant referral to such a specialist level of service provision; more than 90 percent of the community needs to be managed at the local level. To accomplish this goal, substantial expansion of skill in the conduct of family meetings is needed.

Competencies

What are the competencies that clinicians should achieve in order to optimize family-level support in palliative care and bereavement? As suggested previously, in any effort to train clinicians of various disciplines, it is important to distinguish between learning to "work with families" (McDaniel, Hepworth, & Doherty, 1992) and learning to deliver intensive family therapy. Doherty and Baird (1986) presented a useful model for this distinction, the so-called Levels of Family Involvement (LFI) model. The LFI model describes different degrees of competence in family-centered care, ranging from minimal emphasis on the family (Level 1), to information provision (Level 2), emotional support (Level 3), helping vulnerable families (Level 4), and highly specialized family therapy (Level 5). Each level features a different set of skills and requires a different knowledge base.

The dominant model of psychosocial support provided to caregivers is best described at Level 3 ("Feelings and Support"). At this level, providers recognize that families are impacted by a member's illness or death. Therefore, in addition to providing information about the patient's condition, providers inquire in general terms about the feelings and needs of family members. The knowledge base required here includes an understanding of family responses to stress, which is used to normalize the family's experiences. Providers at this level offer empathic support, encourage expression of each individual's concerns, and formulate a preliminary assessment of family coping. This skill level is very adequate for resilient, well-functioning families but does not enable providers to respond to highly distressed, non-communicative, or conflict-ridden families.

Optimally, psychosocial providers will have some comfort delivering care at Level 4, which involves closer attention to vulnerable and resourceful relationships within the family. At this level of knowledge, providers appreciate the interconnectedness between family members and can normalize that an adverse event such as a loss affects not only the ill relative or designated caregiver, but also other members and relationships within the family. The care at Level 4 is distinguished from specialist family therapy by the more limited, focused nature of the intervention. The skills required to deliver family-centered support at Level 4 include the following: (1) questioning skills to elicit an understanding of how family dynamics foster or aggravate the caregiving process; (2) using a focused genogram to identify historical influences on the family's response to illness or loss; (3) engaging family members collaboratively, even when members are reluctant, hold differing perspectives, or their communication is restricted; (4) orchestrating a referral for specialist family therapy if needed; and (5) collaborating with the family to generate alternative ways of coping.

Ultimately, any training model needs to encourage not just the uptake of skills but also the adoption of a "family-centered stance," which assumes that we support families most effectively when we (1) focus on their strengths and resources rather than deficits; (2) humanize their response; (3) assist them to counter any sense of helplessness or depletion; and (4) amplify relational strengths (mutual support, communication) that help them metabolize the distress from a loved one's acute illness or loss.

As noted by Berman et al. (2008), sustaining this stance toward families is difficult when the context prioritizes the needs of the individual patient and focuses on intrapersonal, rather than interpersonal risk. They propose a training model whereby providers learn to assess and respond to families in their specific work setting regardless of whether the family has been identified as a "family therapy case" per se. Rait and Glick (2008) describe the "figure-ground" shift needed to bring family issues into the foreground. Butler, Degner, Baile, and Landry (2005) summarize the results of two studies on medical residents who learned to conduct family meetings in medical settings. The residents' challenges included the following: (1) scheduling meetings and enlisting family members' collaboration; (2) managing strong emotions; and (3) facilitating problem-solving when family members had differences in perspectives.

Guidelines published for inpatient oncology providers on aiding caregivers have focused on multidisciplinary family meetings to identify caregivers' needs and prepare them for illness-related transitions (Hudson, Thomas, Quinn, & Aranda, 2009). However, current literature on conducting family meetings is predominantly in end-of-life care; it emphasizes informational needs over assessing and responding to relational concerns or distress in the family as a whole. Furthermore, there is little guidance for clinicians on how to work collaboratively with and support families that present challenges pertaining to cultural differences, language barriers, and/or heightened volatility. There is substantial research on the development and evaluation of training curricula to improve the communication skills of oncology providers (Butler et al., 2005). Existing training programs focus on enhancing providers' interactions with patients themselves, such as breaking bad news and discussing prognosis. But fewer efforts have been directed toward improving interactions with family members who accompany patients—which is identified as an area that needs further investigation (Doherty & Baird, 1986).

Programs that do include some component on improving the quality of family functioning have yielded modest and inconsistent results (Delvaux et al., 2005; Glimelius, Birgegård, Hoffman, Kvale, & Sjödén, 1995). The communication skills practiced may not have been sufficiently tailored to interactions with families. In the more recent Belgium study of communication skills training, skill uptake did not transfer to actual family interactions, nor did it impact relatives' satisfaction with physician interactions (Delvaux et al., 2005). This group concluded that (1) clinicians need more intensive training earlier in their career to develop skills in managing interviews with multiple family members, and (2) consolidation in the practice of newly learned skills is essential beyond the training phase.

Our group delivered a one-session communication skills training module on conducting a family meeting to 40 health care professionals during the 2007–2008 academic years (Gueguen, Bylund, Brown, Levin, & Kissane, 2009). Participants reported a statistically significant increase in confidence: more than 90 percent indicated that the role-play exercises, large-group facilitation, and feedback from peers was useful for developing skills, and that the skills learned were applicable and would help them provide better patient care. This preliminary study suggests that such content is both acceptable and effective in enhancing providers' confidence in delivering family-centered care.

Curriculum

In another ongoing project conducted by our group, an extended training curriculum is being tested, which aims to strengthen skills across various areas of family-centered care (e.g., managing family conflict, families with young children). Table 19.2 illustrates the content of this training curriculum. It has been developed as six didactic and experiential sessions that train hospital social workers, nurse practitioners, and clinical psychologists across a six-month period to run family meetings regularly in the inpatient setting. Consolidation of skills via peer group supervision is an essential feature of this program.

Supervision

All training programs need the opportunity for supervision as generic skills develop. This is a major growth area needed for many sectors of the medical community, requiring those who have trained in family therapy to function in a supervisory role as programs build the skill base of their clinicians across the next couple of decades. Medical colleges, schools of psychology and social work, and training programs for both primary care and specialty medicine disciplines need to develop this generic skill base in

Table 19.2 Curriculum to Develop Skills in Conducting Family Meetings for Psychosocial Clinicians across Medical Centers

Didactic Session	Competencies
1. Becoming an ally to the family: Families in relation to larger systems	(1) Understand the difference between a family-centered, resilience-based approach and a biomedical, individual-based approach to families in the hospital setting. (2) Identify factors that foster/ erode a family's engagement with the medical system. (3) Distinguish and practice interaction styles that promote collaboration and prevent conflict during periods of high stress.
2. Assessing family functioning: Identifying families at risk	(1) Use a family meeting to assess family functioning. (2) Summarize and synthesize adaptive and disruptive relational patterns that may impact and be impacted by patient care. (3) Normalize and provide psychoeducation regarding the relationship between family functioning and the particular illness with which the family is coping.
3. Addressing cultural and historic responses to illness	(1) Sketch a focused genogram that elicits history of illness and prior instances of loss in the family's history; identify important influences on patient care. (2) Inquire about the influence of cultural belief systems and values on the family's response to caregiving.
4. Engaging reluctant families, facilitating communication and teamwork	(1) Engage reluctant or ambivalent family members. (2) Use family interviewing/questioning techniques to facilitate family teamwork around caregiving. (3) Establish realistic support goals when there are long-standing issues.
5. Responding to volatility/conflict in families, transitioning to referral	(1) Elicit and respond to differing perspectives in the family. (2) Manage volatility and affect (e.g., anger, frustration, grief, conflict) while staying neutral. (3) Use family interviewing/questioning techniques to facilitate communication among family members about illness. (4) Transition to appropriate referrals when needed.
6. Working with families with children	(1) Develop strategies for facilitating adaptive levels of engagement for children and adolescents during a parent's hospital stay. (2) Foster meaningful connection with parents and understand developmentally appropriate responses to illness.

conducting family meetings. Supervision is a vital component to consolidate the necessary skills. Attendance at such programs can be required through continued medical education programs until these skills are gradually built.

Across the past two decades of running randomized controlled trials of Family Focused Grief Therapy, we have continuously engaged in peer supervision of family meetings in oncology and palliative care. This has been a rich privilege. Group peer review is a marvelous means of supervision, wherein more experienced family therapists work alongside early career therapists in hypothesizing and considering strategic approaches to helping families, thus better defining their needs. Immersion in these experiences for one to two years is an invaluable experience that should be more broadly available.

Workforce Issues

An obvious corollary to this training is the urgent need for clinical services to employ sufficient numbers of clinicians trained and equipped to lead these programs. Too many psychiatry, psychology, and social work departments are equipped for crisis intervention without having appointed clinicians trained and experienced in family therapy. As a result, these departments fail to offer sufficient supervision and training for early career clinicians and neglect consistent engagement with family-centered care. Their programs are dominated by individual models of care. Family meetings are broadly avoided.

To move beyond rhetoric and truly offer family-centered care within our clinical programs, departmental leaders need to appreciate the import of employing appropriately trained clinicians. So often staff resignations are filled by new entry candidates, with the lowest salary, the simplest recruitment pathway, and the quickest way to deliver clinical output numbers! Such leadership lacks understanding of the true needs of patients and their families, is low on vision, and displays poor clinical wisdom. Our communities need more than this. There is a place for the delivery of comprehensive and well-formulated management plans that recognize the contribution of the family—which is also potentially genetically linked and at some risk of familial disease—and always the social environment of support, comfort, and care provision for the patient, whether with acute, chronic, or life-threatening disease.

Integration of Individual, Group, and Family Approaches in Bereavement Care

The thesis of this book has been that family-centered care is a crucial and essential paradigm of care provision for the medically ill. This is obvious at the beginning of life and throughout pediatric treatment. It is also highly relevant at the end of life and throughout bereavement. We do not, however, advocate that family care replace individual care provision; certainly, there will always be a place for individual and group modes of support for those who are grieving. In this book, we have highlighted the *complementary* role of family therapy in mourning a loss. Though family therapy for bereavement has been a much-neglected approach, we hope to have convinced you that it is a deserving, beneficial, and important component of care. We look forward to future research findings that support the cost-effectiveness of such a care model.

Conclusion

At the beginning of this book, we examined the family of the Norwegian artist Edvard Munch. In tracing his family's history, we identified patterns of coping with loss and illness that illustrated so beautifully and poignantly that grief is a family affair. Much of this book has presented further evidence for models of family-centered care, across many forms of loss, whether traumatic or disenfranchised, at the beginning of life or in old age, and involving mental or physical illness. The argument for the family-centered model is compelling. The therapist's skills used in delivery of such care are now well defined. And the death of a relative brings a predicable set of circumstances where family support is so readily applicable and beneficial. In this final chapter, we have considered the future research agenda, with major attention now needed to promote dissemination of the findings from these past two decades of research. The developmental agenda is still substantial; there remains much work to do. Therapists can proceed with confidence that the benefits that can result are wide-ranging. The time has arrived to foster more family-centered care, including care of the family in bereavement.

References

Berman, E., Heru, A., Grunebaum, H., Rolland, J., Sargent, J., Wamboldt, M., & McDaniel, S. (2008). Family-oriented patient care through the residency training cycle. *Academic Psychiatry, 32*(2), 111–118.

Butler, L., Degner, L., Baile, W., & Landry, M. (2005). Developing communication competency in the context of cancer: A critical interpretive analysis of provider training programs. *Psycho-Oncology, 14*(10), 861–872.

Delvaux, N., Merckaert, I., Marchal, S., Libert, Y., Conradt, S., Boniver, J., & Klastersky, J. (2005). Physicians' communication with a cancer patient and a relative. *Cancer, 103*(11), 2397–2411.

Doherty, W. J., & Baird, M. A. (1986). Developmental levels in family-centered medical care. *Family Medicine, 18*(3), 153–156.

Folkman, S. (1997). Positive psychological states and coping with severe stress. *Social Science & Medicine, 45*(8), 1207–1221.

Glimelius, B., Birgegård, G., Hoffman, K., Kvale, G., & Sjödén, P.-O. (1995). Information to and communication with cancer patients: Improvements and psychosocial correlates in a comprehensive care program for patients and their relatives. *Patient Education and Counseling, 25*(2), 171–182.

Gueguen, J. A., Bylund, C. L., Brown, R. F., Levin, T. T., & Kissane, D. W. (2009). Conducting family meetings in palliative care: Themes, techniques, and preliminary evaluation of a communication skills module. *Palliative and Supportive Care, 7*(2), 171–179.

Gurman, A. S., & Kniskern, D. P. (1978). Deterioration in marital and family therapy: Empirical, clinical and conceptual issues. *Family Process, 17,* 3–20.

Gurman, A. S., & Kniskern, D. P. (Eds.). (1991). *Handbook of family therapy* (2nd ed.). New York: Brunner/Mazel.

Hudson, P., Thomas, T., Quinn, K., & Aranda, S. (2009). Family meetings in palliative care: Are they effective? *Palliative Medicine, 23*(2), 150–157.

Kissane, D., & Hooghe, A. (2011). Family therapy for the bereaved. In R. A. Neimeyer, D. L. Harris, H. R. Winokuer, & G. F. Thornton (Eds.), *Grief and bereavement in contemporary society: Bridging research and practice* (pp. 287–302). New York: Routledge.

Kissane, D. W., & Bloch, S. (2002). *Family focused grief therapy. A model of family-centred care during palliative care and bereavement.* Buckingham, UK: Open University Press.

Kissane, D. W., Bloch, S., Dowe, D. L, Snyder, R. D., Onghena, P., McKenzie, D. P., & Wallace, C. S. (1996). The Melbourne Family Grief Study, I: Perceptions of family functioning in bereavement. *American Journal of Psychiatry, 153,* 650–658.

Kissane, D. W., Bloch, S., McKenzie, M., O'Neill, I., Chan, E., Moskowitz, C., & McKenzie, D. (2006). Family focused grief therapy: A randomized controlled trial in palliative care and bereavement. *American Journal of Psychiatry, 163,* 1208–1218.

Kissane, D. W., Bloch, S., Onghena, P., McKenzie, D. P, Snyder, R. D., & Dowe, D. L. (1996). The Melbourne Family Grief Study II: Psychosocial morbidity and grief in bereaved families. *American Journal of Psychiatry, 153,* 659–666.

Kissane, D. W., Zaider, T., Li, Y., & Del Gaudio, F. (2013). Family therapy for complicated grief. In M. Stroebe, H. Schut, & J. van den Bout (Eds.), *Complicated grief: Scientific foundations for health care professionals* (pp. 248–262). New York: Routledge.

Kissane, D. W., & Zaider, T. I. (2011). Focused family therapy in palliative care and bereavement. In M. Watson & D. Kissane (Eds.), *Handbook of psychotherapy in cancer care* (pp. 185–197). Chichester, West Sussex, UK: Wiley-Blackwell.

McDaniel, S., Hepworth, J., & Doherty, W. (1992). *Medical family therapy: A biopsychosocial approach to families with health problems.* New York: Basic Books.

Moos, R. H., & Moos, B. S. (1981). *Family Environment Scale manual.* Stanford, CA: Consulting Psychologists Press.

Rait, D., & Glick, I. (2008). A model for reintegrating couples and family therapy training in psychiatric residency programs. *Academic Psychiatry, 32*(2), 81–86.

Stroebe, M., & Schut, H. (2001). Model of coping with bereavement: A review. In M. Stroebe, R. Hansson, W. Strobe, & H. Schut (Eds.), *Handbook of bereavement research: Consequences, coping, and care* (pp. 375–403). Washington, DC: American Psychological Association.

Zaider, T. I., & Kissane, D. W. (2010). The association between family relationships and caregivers' end of life experiences. *Psycho-Oncology, 19* (Supplement 2 May, S1816–5), 9.

Zaider, T. I., & Kissane, D. W. (2012). Therapeutic pathways to improved family communication in palliative care. *Asia Pacific Journal of Clinical Oncology, 8*(Supplement S3), 183.

Index

Page numbers in italic format indicate figures and tables.

237–8; psychosocial types of 31–3; sense of control for facing 43–4; stressors related to 255–6; time phases of 33–7; *see also* mental illness
ill parent 220–1, 225–7
immigrants 272–4
incapacitation 33, 38
infant mortality 183, 188
infants and toddlers 222
influencing questions 97, 99, 103
informed consent 70, 75
intergenerational issues: clashes and conflicts and 118, 119; cultural beliefs and 110, 111, 112; past losses and 21
Islam culture 115, 193

Judaic tradition 119

labeling, ethical challenges and 70
Latino families 107–8, 193, 270, 273
legacy leaving 227–8
life pursuits, reinvestment in 26, 83–4, 251
lineal assumptions 96, 97, *98*, 105
loneliness, older adults and 234–5
loss: acknowledgement of 23–4; adaptation to 22–6; assumptive world and 12; coping with 82–5; depression after 11, 171, 174; family life cycle and 8–9; making sense of 243–4, 259; mourning and 11, 25, 250–1; moving on in the face of 242–3; multigenerational legacies of 39; multiple 21; narrative of 79–82; new creativity after 13; responses to 85–7; shared experience of 24–5, 83; stigmatized 19; sudden and unexpected 255; timing of 20–1; *see also* culture and grief; traumatic loss

marital dependence 254
memorial service 24, 227, 228
Memorial Sloan-Kettering Cancer Center 68
mental illness: evolving ideas about 52–5; family care during 59–60; family functioning and 51–2; family therapy for 55–9; parental loss and 221; suicide and 160, 165
migration 272–4
Millennium Development Goal 4 (MDG 4) 187
mourning: after neonatal death 189; continuing bond theory for 142; loss and 11, 25, 250–1; resolution of 13; tasks of 239–43; *see also* culture and grief
multi-family group formats 57
multiple losses 18, 21, 244–5
Munch, Edvard 3–6

National Alliance on Mental Illness (NAMI) 59
Native American culture 193
neonatal death 184, 187–9
neuroticism 254–5
neutrality: defined 95; preserving 100; of therapist 72, 75, 95–6, 119
new traditions, creating 243

older adult grief: family-centered approaches for 236–9; grief therapy for 239–45; human grief and 232–3; understanding 233–6
orienting questions 97, 99, 102

palliative care: family involvement during 260; family meeting and 93, 94; session-by-session account of therapy during 124–33; therapist training and 283–4; *see also* bereavement care
paradoxical thinking 175
parental grief 190–1, 199
parental illness *see* ill parent
parental loss *see* death of a parent
parental suicide 156–62
pathological grief 5, 70, 252, 279
perinatal loss: family grief programs and 191–4; neonatal death 187–9; SIDS 189–91; stillbirths 185–7; types of 183–4
physical heath factors 234
physical illness *see* illness
play therapy 160, 166
post-loss attachment 155
post-traumatic stress disorder (PTSD) 142
pre-death suffering 206
preschoolers 222–3
principlism, features of 64–5
progressive disease 32, 40
prolonged grief disorder (PGD) 252, 253
psychiatric disorders *see* mental illness
psycho-education: for families with mental illness 56–7; interventions 244; for suicide-bereaved families 159–60; for understanding grief 166
psychological family 173

questioning techniques 97–9

race and ethnicity issues 269–70
reflexive questions 97, *98*, 99, 103, 104, 105
refugee families 140, 165, 274
relational bonds 11–12, 154, 163
relational networks 14, 18, 145, 160
relational repair 160–2
religion: belief in 6; family rituals and 9, 24, 82; finding comfort through 205–6; Latino cultural values and 108
rituals *see* family rituals